T0259815

Lecture Notes in Computer Science 11718

More information about this series at http://www.springer.com/series/7408

Xing Fan · Bronis R. de Supinski ·
Oliver Sinnen · Nasser Giacaman (Eds.)

OpenMP:
Conquering the Full
Hardware Spectrum

15th International Workshop on OpenMP, IWOMP 2019
Auckland, New Zealand, September 11–13, 2019
Proceedings

 Springer

Editors
Xing Fan
University of Auckland
Auckland, New Zealand

Bronis R. de Supinski
Lawrence Livermore National Laboratory
Livermore, CA, USA

Oliver Sinnen
University of Auckland
Auckland, New Zealand

Nasser Giacaman
University of Auckland
Auckland, New Zealand

ISSN 0302-9743 ISSN 1611-3349 (electronic)
Lecture Notes in Computer Science
ISBN 978-3-030-28595-1 ISBN 978-3-030-28596-8 (eBook)
https://doi.org/10.1007/978-3-030-28596-8

LNCS Sublibrary: SL2 – Programming and Software Engineering

This Springer imprint is published by the registered company Springer Nature Switzerland AG
The registered company address is: Gewerbestrasse 11, 6330 Cham, Switzerland

Preface

OpenMP is a widely used application programming interface (API) for high-level shared-memory parallel programming in Fortran, C, and C++. Since its introduction in 1997, OpenMP has gained support from most high-performance compiler and hardware vendors. With the recent release of OpenMP specification version 5.0 by the OpenMP Architecture Review Board (ARB) in November 2018, OpenMP added several major new features that enhance portability of its applications and tools, and extend its support for heterogeneous systems and task-based parallelism. Major new features in OpenMP include: context selectors, the metadirectives, and the declare variant construct that use them; the requires directive; memory allocators and support for deep copy of pointer-based data structures; the descriptive loop construct; and first and third-party tools interfaces. OpenMP 5.0 also significantly enhances many existing features, such as by providing implicit declare target semantics and support for task reductions. As its additions (big and small) reflect the requests of the OpenMP user community, OpenMP 5.0 provides multi-language high-level parallelism that is performant, productive, and portable for the entire hardware spectrum from embedded and accelerator devices to multicore shared-memory systems.

OpenMP is important both as a stand-alone parallel programming model and as part of a hybrid programming model for massively parallel, distributed memory systems built from multicore, manycore, and heterogeneous node architectures. As most of the increased parallelism in the exascale systems is expected to be within a node, OpenMP will become even more widely used in these top end systems. Importantly, the features in OpenMP 5.0 support applications on such systems in addition to facilitating portable exploitation of specific system attributes.

The evolution of the specification would be impossible without active research in OpenMP compilers, runtime systems, tools, and environments. The many additions in OpenMP 5.0 reflect the vibrant research community that surrounds it. As we look towards the continued evolution of the language, that research community will continue to have a central role. The papers in this volume demonstrate that while OpenMP 5.0 will significantly enhance user experiences on a wide range of systems, the research community will offer ample potential directions for further improvements.

The community of OpenMP researchers and developers is united under the cOMPunity organization. This organization has held workshops on OpenMP around the world since 1999: the European Workshop on OpenMP (EWOMP), the North American Workshop on OpenMP Applications and Tools (WOMPAT), and the Asian Workshop on OpenMP Experiences and Implementation (WOMPEI) attracted annual audiences from academia and industry. The International Workshop on OpenMP (IWOMP) consolidated these three workshop series into a single annual international event that rotates across Europe, Asia-Pacific, and the Americas. The first IWOMP workshop was organized under the auspices of cOMPunity. Since that workshop, the IWOMP Steering Committee has organized these events and guided development of the series. The first IWOMP meeting was held in 2005, in Eugene, Oregon, USA. Since then, meetings have been held each year, in Reims, France; Beijing, China; West Lafayette, USA; Dresden, Germany; Tsukuba, Japan; Chicago, USA; Rome, Italy; Canberra, Australia; Salvador, Brazil; Aachen, Germany; Nara, Japan; Stony Brook, USA; and Barcelona, Spain. Each workshop has drawn participants from research and industry throughout the world. IWOMP 2019 continues the series with technical papers and tutorials. The IWOMP meetings have been successful in large part due to generous support from numerous sponsors.

The IWOMP website (www.iwomp.org) provides information on the latest event, as well as links to websites from previous years' events. This book contains proceedings of IWOMP 2019. The workshop program included 22 technical papers, 2 keynote talks, and a tutorial on OpenMP. The paper "OMPSan: Static Verification of OpenMP's Data Mapping Constructs," by Prithayan Barua, Jun Shirako, Whitney Tsang, Jeeva Paudel, Wang Chen, and Vivek Sarkar was selected for the Best Paper Award. All technical papers were peer reviewed by at least three different members of the Program Committee.

September 2019

Xing Fan
Bronis R. de Supinski
Oliver Sinnen
Nasser Giacaman

Organization

Program Committee Co-chairs

Bronis R. de Supinski   ·   Lawrence Livermore National Laboratory, USA
Nasser Giacaman   University of Auckland, New Zealand

General Chair

Oliver Sinnen   University of Auckland, New Zealand

Publication Chair

Xing Fan   University of Auckland, New Zealand

Publicity Chair

Kai-Cheung Leung   University of Auckland, New Zealand

Program Committee

Eduard Ayguade	Technical University of Catalunya, Spain
Sergi Bellido	Barcelona Supercomputing Center, Spain
James Beyer	nVidia, USA
Mark Bull	University of Edinburgh, UK
Florina Ciorba	University of Basel, Switzerland
Alex Duran	Intel, Spain
Deepak Eachempati	Cray Inc., USA
Hal Finkel	Argonne National Laboratory, USA
Oscar Hernandez	Oak Ridge National Laboratory, USA
Zhiyi Huang	University of Otago, New Zealand
Chunhua Liao	Lawrence Livermore National Laboratory, USA
Rosa Badia	Barcelona Supercomputing Center, Spain
Larry Meadows	Intel, USA
John Mellor-Crummey	Rice University, USA
Stephen Olivier	Sandia National Laboratories, USA
Joachim Protze	RWTH Aachen University, Germany
Alistair Rendell	Flinders University, Australia
Mitsuhisa Sato	RIKEN Advanced Institute for Computational Science, Japan
Thomas Scogland	Lawrence Livermore National Laboratory, USA
Eric Stotzer	Texas Instruments, USA

Christian Terboven   RWTH Aachen University, Germany
Terry Wilmarth   Intel, USA

IWOMP Steering Committee

Steering Committee Chair

Matthias S. Müller   RWTH Aachen University, Germany

Steering Committee

Dieter an Mey   RWTH Aachen University, Germany
Eduard Ayguadé   BSC, Universitat Politècnica de Catalunya, Spain
Mark Bull   EPCC, University of Edinburgh, UK
Barbara Chapman   Stony Brook University, USA
Bronis R. de Supinski   Lawrence Livermore National Laboratory, USA
Rudolf Eigenmann   Purdue University, USA
William Gropp   University of Illinois, USA
Michael Klemm   Intel, Germany
Kalyan Kumaran   Argonne National Laboratory, USA
Federico Massaioli   CASPUR, Italy
Lawrence Meadows   Intel, USA
Stephen L. Olivier   Sandia National Laboratories, USA
Ruud van der Pas   Oracle, USA
Alistair Rendell   Flinders University, Australia
Mitsuhisa Sato   University of Tsukuba, Japan
Sanjiv Shah   Intel, USA
Josemar Rodrigues   SENAI Unidade CIMATEC, Brazil
  de Souza
Christian Terboven   RWTH Aachen University, Germany
Matthijs van Waveren   KAUST, Saudi Arabia

Contents

Extensions

Tasking

Using OpenMP

Best Paper

OMPSan: Static Verification of OpenMP's Data Mapping Constructs

Prithayan Barua[1(✉)], Jun Shirako[1], Whitney Tsang[2], Jeeva Paudel[2], Wang Chen[2], and Vivek Sarkar[1]

[1] Georgia Institute of Technology, Atlanta, Georgia
prithayan@gatech.edu
[2] IBM Toronto Laboratory, Markham, Canada

Abstract. OpenMP offers directives for offloading computations from CPU hosts to accelerator devices such as GPUs. A key underlying challenge is in efficiently managing the movement of data across the host and the accelerator. User experiences have shown that memory management in OpenMP programs with offloading capabilities is non-trivial and error-prone.

This paper presents **OMPSan** (OpenMP Sanitizer) – a static analysis-based tool that helps developers detect bugs from incorrect usage of the map clause, and also suggests potential fixes for the bugs. We have developed an LLVM based data flow analysis that validates if the def-use information of the array variables are respected by the mapping constructs in the OpenMP program. We evaluate **OmpSan** over some standard benchmarks and also show its effectiveness by detecting commonly reported bugs.

Keywords: OpenMP offloading · OpenMP target data mapping ·
LLVM · Memory management · Static analysis · Verification ·
Debugging

1 Introduction

Open Multi-Processing (OpenMP) is a widely used directive-based parallel programming model that supports offloading computations from hosts to accelerator devices such as GPUs. Notable accelerator-related features in OpenMP include unstructured data mapping, asynchronous execution, and runtime routines for device memory management.

OMP Target Offloading and Data Mapping. OMP offers the `omp target` directive for offloading computations to devices and the `omp target data` directive for mapping data across the host and the corresponding device data environment. On heterogeneous systems, managing the movement of data between the host and the device can be challenging, and is often a major source of performance and correctness bugs. In the OpenMP accelerator model, data movement between device and host is supported either explicitly via the use of a `map` clause

© Springer Nature Switzerland AG 2019
X. Fan et al. (Eds.): IWOMP 2019, LNCS 11718, pp. 3–18, 2019.
https://doi.org/10.1007/978-3-030-28596-8_1

or, implicitly through default data-mapping rules. The optimal, or even correct, specification of map clauses can be non-trivial and error-prone because it requires users to reason about the complex dataflow analysis. To ensure that the map clauses are correct, the OpenMP programmers need to make sure that variables that are defined in one data environments and used in another data environments are mapped accordingly across the different device and host data environments. Given a data map construct, its semantics depends on all the previous usages of the map construct. Therefore, dataflow analysis of map clauses is necessarily context-sensitive since the entire call sequence leading up to a specific map construct can impact its behavior.

1.1 OpenMP 5.0 Map Semantics

Figure 1 shows a schematic illustration of the set of rules used when mapping a host variable to the corresponding list item in the device data environment, as specified in the OpenMP 5.0 standard. The rest of this paper assumes that the accelerator device is a GPU, and that mapping a variable from host to device introduces a host-to-device memory copy, and vice-versa. However, the bugs that we identify reflect errors in the OpenMP code regardless of the target device.

The different map types that OpenMP 5.0 supports are,

- `alloc`: allocate on device, uninitialized
- `to`: map to device before kernel execution, (host-device memory copy)
- `from`: map from device after kernel execution (device-host memory copy)
- `tofrom`: copy in and copy out the variable at the entry and exit of the device environment.

Arrays are implicitly mapped as `tofrom`, while scalars are firstprivate in the target region implicitly, *i.e.,* the value of the scalar on the host is copied to the corresponding item on the device only at the entry to the device environment. As Fig. 1 shows, OpenMP 5.0 specification uses the reference count of a variable, to decide when to introduce a device/host memory copy. The host to device memory copy is introduced only when the reference count is incremented from 0 to 1 and the `to` attribute is present. Then the reference count is incremented every time a new device map environment is created. The reference count is decremented on encountering a `from` or `release` attribute, while exiting the data environment. Finally, when the reference count is decremented to zero from 1, and the `from` attribute is present, the variable is mapped back to the host from the device.

1.2 The Problem

For target offloading, the map clause is used to map variables from a task's data environment to the corresponding variable in the device data environment. Incorrect data map clauses can result in usage of stale data in either host or device data environment, which may result in the following kinds of issues,

- When reading the variable on the device data environment, it does not contain the updated value of its original variable.
- When reading the original variable, it was not updated with the latest value of the corresponding device environment variable.

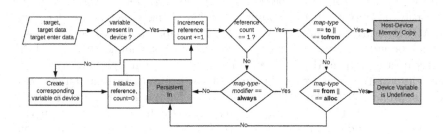

(a) Flowchart for Enter Device Environment

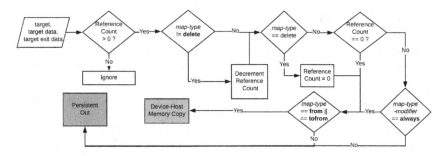

(b) Flowchart for Exit Device Environment

Fig. 1. Flowcharts to show how to interpret the map clause

1.3 Our Solution

We propose a static analysis tool called OMPSan to perform OpenMP code "sanitization". OMPSan is a compile-time tool, which statically verifies the correctness of the data mapping constructs based on a dataflow analysis. The key principle guiding our approach is that: *an OpenMP program is expected to yield the same result when enabling or disabling OpenMP constructs.* Our approach detects errors by comparing the dataflow information (reaching definitions via LLVM's memory SSA representation [10]) between the OpenMP and baseline code. We developed an LLVM-based implementation of our approach and evaluated its effectiveness using several case studies. Our specific contributions include:

- an algorithm to analyze OpenMP runtime library calls inserted by Clang in the LLVM IR, to infer the host/device memory copies. We expect that this algorithm will have applications beyond our OMPSan tool.
- a dataflow analysis to infer Memory def-use relations.
- a static analysis technique to validate if the host/device memory copies respect the original memory def-use relations.
- diagnostic information for users to understand how the map clause affects the host and device data environment.

Even though our algorithm is based on clang OpenMP implementation, it can very easily be applied to other approaches like using directives to delay the OpenMP lowering to a later LLVM pass. The paper is organized as follows. Section 2 provides motivating examples to describe the common issues and difficulties in using OpenMP's *data map* construct. Section 3 provides the background information that we use in our analysis. Section 4 presents an overview of our approach to validate the usage of data mapping constructs. Section 5 presents the LLVM implementation details, and Sect. 6 presents the evaluation and some case studies. Subsection 6.3 also lists some of the limitations of our tool, some of them common to any static analysis.

2 Motivating Examples

To motivate the utility and applicability of OMPSan, we discuss three potential errors in user code arising from improper usage of the data mapping constructs.

2.1 Default Scalar Mapping

Example 1: Consider the snippet of code in Listing 2.1. The `printf` on host, line 8, prints stale value of sum. Note that the definition of sum on line 5 does not reach line 8, since the variable sum is not mapped explicitly using the `map` clause. As such, sum is implicitly `firstprivate`. As Listing 2.2 shows, an explicit `map` clause with the `tofrom` attribute is essential to specify the copy in and copy out of sum from device.

Listing 2.1. Default scalar map

```
1  int A[N], sum=0, i;
2  #pragma omp target
3  #pragma omp teams distribute
       parallel for reduction(+:sum)
       {
4     for(i=0; i<N; i++) {
5        sum += A[i];
6     }
7  }
8  printf("\n%d",sum);
```

Listing 2.2. Explicit map

```
1  int A[N], sum=0;
2  #pragma omp target map(tofrom:sum)
3  #pragma omp teams distribute
       parallel for reduction(+:sum)
       {
4     for( int i=0; i<N; i++) {
5        sum += A[i];
6     }
7  }
8  printf("\n%d",sum);
```

2.2 Reference Count Issues

Example 2: Listing 2.3 shows an example of a reference count issue. The statement in line 12, which executes on the host, does not read the updated value of A from the device. This is again because of the `from` clause on line 5, which increments the reference count to 2 on entry, and back to 1 on exit, hence after line 10, A is not copied out to host. Listing 2.4 shows the usage of `target update` directive to force the copy-out and to read the updated value of A on line 15.

This example shows the difficulty in interpreting an independent map construct. Especially when we are dealing with the global variables and map clauses across different functions, maybe even in different files, it becomes difficult to understand and identify potential incorrect usages of the map construct.

Listing 2.4. Update Clause

Listing 2.3. Reference Count

```
1   #define N 100
2   int A[N], sum=0;
3   #pragma omp target data
4       map(from:A[0:N]) {
5       #pragma omp target
6           map(from:A[0:N]) {
7       for(int i=0; i<N; i++) {
8           A[i]=i;
9       }
10      }
11      for(int i=0; i<N; i++) {
12          sum += A[i];
13      }
14  }
```

```
1
2   #define N 100
3   int A[N], sum=0;
4   #pragma omp target data
5           map(from:A[0:N]) {
6       #pragma omp target
7           map(from:A[0:N]) {
8       for(int i=0; i<N; i++) {
9           A[i]=i;
10      }
11      }
12      #pragma omp target
13          update from(A[0:N])
14      for(int i=0; i<N; i++) {
15          sum += A[iGhosh];
16      }
17  }
```

3   Background

OMPSan assumes certain practical use cases, for example, in Listing 2.3, a user would expect the updated value of A on line 12. Having said that, a skilled ninja programmer may very well expect A to remain stale, because of their knowledge and understanding of the complexities of data mapping rules. Our analysis and error/warning reports from this work are intended primarily for the former case.

3.1   Memory SSA Form

Our analysis is based on the LLVM Memory SSA [10,12], which is an imprecise implementation of Array SSA [7]. The Memory SSA is a virtual IR, that captures the def-use information for array variables. Every definition is identified by a unique name/number, which is then referenced by the corresponding use.

The Memory SSA IR has the following kinds of instructions/nodes,

- $INIT$, a special node to signify uninitialized or live on entry definitions
- $N' = MemoryDef(N)$, N' is an operation which may modify memory, and N identifies the last write that N' clobbers.
- $MemoryUse(N)$, is an operation that uses the memory written by the definition N, and does not modify the memory.
- $MemPhi(N_1, N_2, ...)$, is an operation associated with a basic block, and N_i is one of the may reaching definitions, that could flow into the basic block.

We make the following simplifying assumptions, to keep the analysis tractable

- Given an array variable we can find all the corresponding load and store instructions. So, we cannot handle cases, when pointer analysis fails to disambiguate the memory a pointer refers to.

- A *MemoryDef* node clobbers the array associated with its store instruction. As a result, write to any array location, is considered to update the entire array.
- We analyze only the array variables that are mapped to a target region.

3.2   Scalar Evolution Analysis

LLVM's Scalar Evolution (SCEV) is a very powerful technique that can be used to analyze the change in the value of scalar variables over iterations of a loop. We can use the SCEV analysis to represent the loop induction variables as chain of recurrences. This mathematical representation can then be used to analyze the index expressions of the memory operations.

We implemented an analysis for array sections, that given a load/store, uses the LLVM SCEV analysis, to compute the minimum and maximum values of the corresponding index into the memory access. If the analysis fails, then we default to the maximum array size, which is either a static array, or can be extracted from the LLVM memory *alloc* instructions.

4   Our Approach

In this section, we outline the key steps of our approach with the algorithm and show a concrete example to illustrate the algorithm in action.

4.1   Algorithm

Algorithm 1 shows an overview of our data map analysis algorithm. First, we collect all the array variables used in all the map clauses in the entire module. Then line 5, calls the function ConstructArraySSA, which constructs the Array SSA for each of the mapped Array variables. (In this paper, we use "Array SSA" to refer to our extensions to LLVM's Memory SSA form by leveraging the capabilities of Array SSA form [7].) Then, we call the function, InterpretTargetClauses, which modifies the Array SSA graph, in accordance of the map semantics of the program. Then finally ValidateDataMap checks the reachability on the final graph, to validate the map clauses, and generates a diagnostic report with the warnings and errors.

Example. Let us consider the example in Fig. 2a to illustrate our approach for analysis of data mapping clauses. ConstructArraySSA of Algorithm 1, constructs the memory SSA form for arrays "A" and "C" as shown in Fig. 2b. Then, InterpretTargetClauses, removes the edges between host and device nodes, as shown in Fig. 2c, where the host is colored green and device is blue. Finally, the loop at line 29 of the function InterpretTargetClauses, introduces the host-device/device-host memory copy edges, as shown in Fig. 2d. For example $L1$ is connected to $S2$ with a host-device memory copy for the enter data map pragma

---

Algorithm 1. Overview of Data Mapping Analysis

1: **function** DATAMAPANALYSIS($Module$)
2:     $MappedArrayVars = \phi$
3:     **for** $ArrayVar \in MapClauses$ **do**
4:         $MappedArrayVars = MappedArrayVars \cup ArrayVar$

5:     ConstructArraySSA($Module, MappedArrayVars$)
6:     InterpretTargetClauses($Module, MappedArrayVars$)
7:     ValidateDataMap($MappedArrayVars$)

8: **function** CONSTRUCTARRAYSSA($Module, MappedArrayVars$)
9:     **for** $MemoryAccess \in Module$ **do**
10:         $ArrayVar = $ getArrayVar($MemoryAccess$)
11:         **if** $ArrayVar \in MappedArrayVars$ **then**
12:             **if** $MemoryAccess \in OMP\_targetOffload\_Region$ **then**
13:                 $targetNode = true$ ▷ If Memory Access on device
14:             **else**
15:                 $targetNode = false$ ▷ If Memory Access on host
16:             $Range = $ SCEVGetMinMax($MemoryAccess$)
17:             $underConstruction = $ GetArraySSA($ArrayVar$)
18:   ▷ could be null or incomplete
19:             InsertNodeArraySSA($underConstruction, MemoryAccess, targetNode, Range$)
20:                               ▷ Incrementally construct, by adding this access

21: **function** INTERPRETTARGETCLAUSES($Module, MappedArrayVars$)
22:     **for** $ArrayVar \in MappedArrayVars$ **do**
23:         $ArraySSA = $ GetArraySSA($ArrayVar$)
24:         **for** edge, $(node, Successornode) \in (ArraySSA)$ **do**
25:             $nodeIsTarget = $ isTargetOffload($node$)
26:             $succIsTarget = $ isTargetOffload($Successornode$)
27:             **if** $nodeIsTarget != succIsTarget$ **then**
28:                 RemoveArraySSAEdge($node, Successornode$)

29:     **for** $dataMap \in dataMapClauses$ **do**
30:         $hostNode = $ getHostNode($dataMap$)
31:         $deviceNode = $ getDeviceNode($dataMap$)
32:         $mapType = $ getMapClauseType($dataMap$)
33:                              ▷ alloc/copyIn/copyOut/persistentIn/persistentOut
34:         InsertDataMapEdge($hostNode, deviceNode, mapType$)

35: **function** VALIDATEDATAMAP($MappedArrayVars$)
36:     **for** $ArrayVar \in MappedArrayVars$ **do**
37:         $ArraySSA = $ GetArraySSA($ArrayVar$)
38:         **for** $memUse \in $ getMemoryUseNodes($ArraySSA$) **do**
39:             $useRange = $ getReadRange($memUse$)
40:             $clobberingAccess = $ getClobberingAccess($ArraySSA, memUse$)
41:             **if** isPartiallyReachable($ArraySSA, clobberingAccess, memUse, useRange$) **then**
42:                 Report WARNING
43:             **else if** isNotReachable($ArraySSA, clobberingAccess, memUse$) **then**
44:                 Report ERROR

---

with to: $A[0:50]$ on line 5. Also, we connect the *INIT* node with $L2$, to account for the alloc:$C[0:100]$, which implies an uninitialized reaching definition for this example.

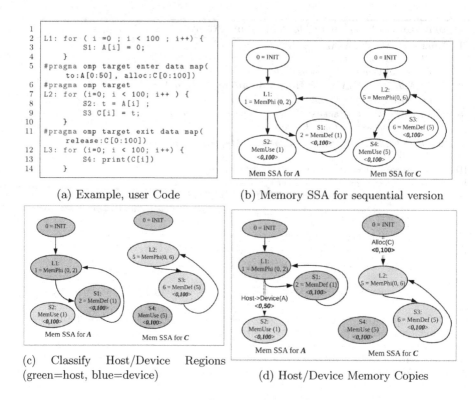

```
1
2   L1: for ( i =0 ; i < 100 ; i++ ) {
3           S1: A[i] = 0;
4       }
5   #pragma omp target enter data map(
        to:A[0:50], alloc:C[0:100])
6   #pragma omp target
7   L2: for (i=0; i < 100; i++ ) {
8           S2: t = A[i] ;
9           S3 C[i] = t;
10      }
11  #pragma omp target exit data map(
        release:C[0:100])
12  L3: for (i=0; i < 100; i++) {
13          S4: print(C[i])
14      }
```

(a) Example, user Code

(b) Memory SSA for sequential version

(c)   Classify   Host/Device   Regions
(green=host, blue=device)

(d) Host/Device Memory Copies

Fig. 2. Example of data map analysis

Lastly, `ValidateDataMap` function, traverses the graph, resulting in the following observations:

- (Error) Node $S4{:}MemUse(5)$ is not reachable from its corresponding definition $L2:5 = MemPhi(0,6)$
- (Warning) Only the partial artial array section $A[0:50]$, is reachable from definition $L1:1 = MemPhi(0,2)$ to $S2:MemUse(1)\langle 0:100\rangle$

Section 6 contains other examples of the errors and warnings discovered by our tool.

5   Implementation

We implemented our framework in LLVM 8.0.0. The OpenMP constructs are lowered to runtime calls in Clang, so in the LLVM IR we only see calls to the OpenMP runtime. There are several limitations of this approach with respect to high level analysis like the one OMPSan is trying to accomplish. For example, the region of code that needs to be offloaded to a device is opaque since it is moved to a separate function. These functions are in turn called from the

OpenMP runtime library. As a result, it is challenging to perform a global data flow analysis for the memory def-use information of the offloaded region. To simplify the analysis, we have to compile with clang twice.

First, we compile the OpenMP program with the flag that enables parsing the OpenMP constructs, and compile it again without the flag, so that Clang ignores the OpenMP constructs and instead generates the baseline LLVM IR for the sequential version. During the OpenMP compilation pass, we execute our analysis pass, which parses the runtime library calls and generates a csv file that records all the user specified "target map" clauses, as explained in Subsect. 5.1.

Next we compile the program by ignoring the OpenMP pragmas, and perform whole program context and flow sensitive data flow analysis on LLVM code generated from the sequential version, to construct the Memory def-use chains, explained in Subsect. 5.2. Then this pass validates if the "target map" information recorded in the csv file, respects all the Memory def-use relations present in the sequential version of the code.

5.1   Interpreting OpenMP Pragmas

Listing 5.1. Example map clause

```
1
2  #pragma omp target
3      map(tofrom:A[0:10])
4      for (i = 0 ; i < 10; i++)
5          A[i] = i;
```

Listing 5.2. Pseudocode for LLVM IR with RTL calls

```
1   void **ArgsBase = {&A}
2   void **Args = {&A}
3   int64_t* ArgsSize = {40}
4   void **ArgsMapType = {
        OMP_TGT_MAPTYPE_TO |
        OMP_TGT_MAPTYPE_FROM }
5   call @__tgt_target
6   (-1, HostAdr, 1, ArgsBase,
7   Args, ArgsSize, ArgsMapType)
```

Listing 5.1 shows a very simple user program, with a target data map clause. Listing 5.2 shows the corresponding LLVM IR in pseudocode, after clang introduces the runtime calls at Line 5. We parse the arguments of this call to interpret the map construct. For example, the 3rd argument to the call at line 6 of Listing 5.2 is 1, that means there is only one item in the map clause. Line 1, that is the value loaded into *ArgsBase* is used to get the memory variable that is being mapped. Line 3, *ArgsSize* gives the end of the corresponding array section, starting from *ArgsBase*. Line 4, *ArgsMapType*, gives the map attribute used by the programmer, that is "tofrom".

We wrote an LLVM pass that analyzes every such Runtime Library (RTL) call, and tracks the value of each of its arguments, as explained above. Once we obtain this information, we use the algorithm in Fig. 1 to interpret the data mapping semantics of each clause. The data mapping semantics can be classified into following categories,

- Copy In: A memory copy is introduced from the host to the corresponding list item in the device environment.
- Copy Out: A memory copy is introduced from the device to the host environment.

- Persistent Out: A device memory variable is not deleted, it is persistent on the device, and available to the subsequent device data environment.
- Persistent In: The memory variable is available on entry to the device data environment, from the last device invocation.

The examples in Subsect. 6.2 illustrate the above classification.

5.2 Baseline Memory Use Def Analysis

LLVM has an analysis called the MemorySSA [10], it is a relatively cheap analysis that provides an SSA based form for memory def-use and use-def chains. LLVM MemorySSA is a virtual IR, which maps `Instructions` to `MemoryAccess`, which is one of three kinds, `MemoryPhi`, `MemoryUse` and `MemoryDef`.

Operands of any `MemoryAccess` are a version of the heap before that operation, and if the access can modify the heap, then it produces a value, which is the new version of the heap after the operation. Figure 3 shows the LLVM Memory SSA for the OpenMP program in Listing 5.3. The comments in the listing denote the LLVM IR and also the corresponding `MemoryAccess`.

Listing 5.3. OpenMP program, for Fig. 3

```
1  int main(){
2      int A[10], B[10];
3      // 2 = MemoryPhi(1,3)
4      for (int i =0 ; i < 10 ; i++) {
5          // %arrayidx = getelementptr %A, 0, %
                idxprom
6          // store %i.0, %arrayidx ,
7          // 3 = MemoryDef(2)
8          A[i] = i;
9      }
10 #pragma omp target enter data map(to:A
            [0:5])
11                    map(alloc:B[0:10])
12 #pragma omp target
13     // 4 = MemoryPhi(2,5)
14     for (int i = 0 ; i < 10; i++) {
15         // %arrayidx7 = getelementptr %A, 0, %
                idxprom6
16         // %2 = load %arrayidx7
17         // MemoryUse(4)
18         int t = A[i];
19         // %arrayidx9 = getelementptr %B, 0, %
                idxprom8
20         // store %2, %arrayidx9
21         // 5 = MemoryDef(4)
22         B[i] = t
23     }
24
25     for (int i = 0 ; i < 10; i++) {
26         //arrayidx19 = getelementptr %B, 0, %
                idxprom18
27         //%3 = load %arrayidx19
28         // MemoryUse(4)
29         printf("%d",B[i]);
30     }
31
32     return 0;
33 }
```

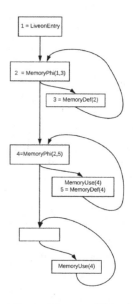

Fig. 3. Memory SSA of Listing 5.3

We have simplified this example, to make it relevant to our context. `LiveonEntry` is a special `MemoryDef` that dominates every `MemoryAccess` within a function, and implies that the memory is either undefined or defined before the function begins. The first node in Fig. 3 is a `LiveonEntry` node. The $3 = MemoryDef(2)$ node, denotes that there is a store instruction which clobbers the heap version 2, and generates heap 3, which represents the line 8 of the source code. Whenever more than one heap versions can reach a basic block, we need a $MemoryPhi$ node, for example, $2 = MemoryPhi(1, 3)$ corresponds to the for loop on line 4. There are two versions of the heap reaching this node, the heap 1, $1 = LiveonEntry$ and the other one from the back edge, heap 3, $3 = MemoryDef(2)$. The next `MemoryAccess`, $4 = MemoryPhi(2, 5)$, corresponds to the for loop at line 14. Again the clobbering accesses that reach it are 2 from the previous for loop and 5, from its loop body. The load of memory A on line 18, corresponds to the $MemoryUse(4)$, that notes that the last instruction that could clobber this read is `MemoryAccess` $4 = MemoryPhi(2, 5)$. Then, $5 = MemoryDef(4)$ clobbers the heap, to generate heap version 5. This corresponds to the write to array B on line 22. This is an important example of how LLVM deliberately trades off precision for speed. It considers the memory variables as disjoint partitions of the heap, but instead of trying to disambiguate aliasing, in this example, both stores/MemoryDefs clobber the same heap partition. Finally, the read of B on line 29, corresponds to $MemoryUse(4)$, with the heap version 4, reaching this load. Since this loop does not update memory, there is no need for a `MemoryPhi` node for this loop, but we have left the node empty in the graph to denote the loop entry basic block.

Now, we can see the difference between the LLVM memory SSA (Fig. 3) and the array def-use chains required for our analysis (Fig. 2). We developed a dataflow analysis to extract the array def-use chains from the LLVM Memory SSA, by disambiguating the array variable that each load/store instruction refers to. So, for any store instruction, for example line 22, Listing 5.3, we can analyze the LLVM IR, and trace the value that the store instruction refers to, which is "B" as per the IR, comment of line 19.

We perform an analysis on the LLVM IR, which tracks the set of memory variables that each LLVM load/store instruction refers to. It is a context-sensitive and flow-sensitive iterative data flow analysis that associates each MemoryDef/MemoryUse with a set of memory variables. The result of this analysis is an array SSA form, for each array variable, to track its def-use chain, similar to the example in Fig. 2.

6   Evaluation and Case Studies

Listing 6.1. DRACC File 23

```
28 int Mult(){
29
30     #pragma omp target map(to:a[0:C],b[0:C])
       map(tofrom:c[0:C]) device(0)
31     {
32         #pragma omp teams
                   distribute parallel for
33         for(int i=0; i<C; i++){
34             for(int j=0; j<C; j++){
35                 c[i]+=b[j+i*C]*a[j];
36             }
37         }
38     }
```

Listing 6.2. DRACC File 30

```
19 int init(){
20     for(int i=0; i<C; i++){
21         for(int j=0; j<C; j++){
22             b[j+i*C]=1;
23         }
24         a[i]=1;
25         c[i]=0;
26     }
-
31 int Mult(){
32
33     #pragma omp target
              map(to:a[0:C],b[0:C*C]) map(from:c[0:
              C*C]) device(0)
34     {
35         #pragma omp teams
                   distribute parallel for
36         for(int i=0; i<C; i++){
37             for(int j=0; j<C; j++){
38                 c[i]+=b[j+i*C]*a[j];
```

For evaluating OMPSan we use the DRACC [1] suite, which is a benchmark for
data race detection on accelerators, and also includes several data mapping errors
also. Table 1 shows some distinct errors found by our tool in the benchmark [1]
and the examples of Sect. 2. We were able to find the 15 known data mapping
errors in the DRACC benchmark.

Listing 6.3. DRACC File 22

```
15 int init(){
16     for(int i=0; i<C; i++){
17         for(int j=0; j<C; j++){
18             b[j+i*C]=1;
19         }
20         a[i]=1;
21         c[i]=0;
22     }
23     return 0;
24 }
25
26
27 int Mult(){
28
29     #pragma omp target map(to:a[0:C]) map(
       tofrom:c[0:C]) map(alloc:b[0:C*C]) device
       (0)
30     {
31         #pragma omp teams
                   distribute parallel for
32         for(int i=0; i<C; i++){
33             for(int j=0; j<C; j++){
34                 c[i]+=b[j+i*C]*a[j];
```

Listing 6.4. DRACC File 26

```
29     #pragma omp target
              enter data map(to:a[0:C],b[0:C*C
              ],c[0:C]) device(0)
30     #pragma omp target device(0)
31     {
32         #pragma omp teams
                   distribute parallel for
33         for(int i=0; i<C; i++){
34             for(int j=0; j<C; j++){
35                 c[i]+=b[j+i*C]*a[j];
36             }
37         }
38     }
39     #pragma omp target exit
              data map(release:c[0:C])
              map(release:a[0:C],b[0:C*C])
              device(0)
40     return 0;
41 }
42
43 int check(){
44     bool test = false;
45     for(int i=0; i<C; i++){
46         if(c[i]!=C){
```

Table 1. Errors found in the DRACC Benchmark and other examples

File Name	Error/Warning
DRACC File 22 Listing 6.3	ERROR Definition of :b on Line:18 is not reachable to Line:34, Missing Clause:to:Line:32
DRACC File 26 Listing 6.4	ERROR Definition of :c on Line:35 is not reachable to Line:46 Missing Clause:from/update:Line:44
DRACC File 30 Listing 6.2	ERROR Definition of :c on Line:25 is not reachable to Line:38 Missing Clause:to:Line:36
DRACC File 23 Listing 6.1	WARNING Line:30 maps partial data of :b smaller than its total size
Example in Listing 2.1	ERROR Definition of :sum on Line:5 is not reachable to Line:6 Missing Clause:from/update:Line:6
Example in Listing 2.3	ERROR Definition of :A on Line:7 is not reachable to Line:9 Missing Clause:from/update:8

6.1 Analysis Time

To get an idea of the runtime overhead of our tool, we also measured the runtime of the analysis. Table 2 shows the time to run OMPSan, on few SPEC ACCEL and NAS parallel benchmarks. Due to the context and flow sensitive data flow analysis implemented in OMPSan, its analysis time can be significant; however the analysis time is less than or equal to the -*O3* compilation time in all cases.

6.2 Diagnostic Information

Another major use case for OMPSan, is to help OpenMP developers understand the data mapping behavior of their source code. For example, Listing 6.5 shows a code fragment from the benchmark "FT" in the "NAS" suite. Our tool can generate the following information diagnostic information on the current version of the data mapping clause.

Table 2. Time to run OMPSan

Benchmark name	-O3 compilation time (s)	OMPSan Runtime (s)
SPEC 504.polbm	17	16
SPEC 503.postencil	3	3
SPEC 552.pep	7	4
SPEC 554.pcg	15	9
NAS FT	32	15
NAS MG	34	31

- $\_tgt\_target\_teams$, from:: "ft.c:311" to "ft.c:331"
- Alloc: $u0\_imag[0 : 8421376], u0\_real[0 : 8421376]$
- Persistent In :: $twiddle[0 : 8421376], u1\_imag[0 : 8421376], u1\_real[0 : 8421376]$
- Persistent Out :: $twiddle[0 : 8421376], u0\_imag[0 : 8421376], u0\_real[0 : 8421376], u1\_imag[0 : 8421376], u1\_real[0 : 8421376]$
- Copy In:: *Null*, Copy Out:: *Null*

Listing 6.5. *evolve* from NAS/ft.c

```
307 static void evolve(int d1, int d2, int d3)
308 {
309   int i, j, k;
311 #pragma omp target map (alloc: u0_real, u0_imag, u1_real, u1_imag, twiddle)
312   {
313 #pragma omp teams distribute
314     for (k = 0; k < d3; k++) {
315 #pragma omp parallel for
316       for (j = 0; j < d2; j++) {
317 #pragma omp simd
318         for (i = 0; i < d1; i++) {
319           u0_real[ ... ] = u0_real[ ... ]*twiddle[ ... ];
321           u0_imag[ ... ] = u0_imag[ ... ]*twiddle[ ... ];
```

6.3 Limitations

Since OMPSan is a static analysis tool, it includes a few limitations.

- Supports statically and dynamically allocated array variables, but cannot handle dynamic data structures like linked lists It can possibly be addressed in future through advanced static analysis techniques (like shape analysis).
- Cannot handle target regions inside recursive functions. It can possibly be addressed in future work by improving our context sensitive analysis.
- Can only handle compile time constant array sections, and constant loop bounds. We can handle runtime expressions, by adding static analysis support to compare the equivalence of two symbolic expressions.
- Cannot handle declare target since it requires analysis across LLVM modules.
- May report false positives for irregular array accesses, like if a small section of the array is updated, our analysis may assume that the entire array was updated. More expensive analysis like symbolic analysis can be used to improve the precision of the static analysis.
- May fail if Clang/LLVM introduces bugs while lowering OpenMP pragmas to the RTL calls in the LLVM IR.
- May report false positives, if the OpenMP program relies on some dynamic reference count mechanism. Runtime debugging approach will be required to handle such cases.

It is interesting to note that, we did not find any false positives for the benchmarks we evaluated on.

7 Related Work and Conclusion

Managing data transfers to and from GPUs has always been an important problem for GPU programming. Several solutions have been proposed to help the programmer in managing the data movement. CGCM [6] was one of the first systems with static analysis to manage CPU-GPU communications. It was followed by [5], a dynamic tool for automatic CPU-GPU data management. The OpenMPC compiler [9] also proposed a static analysis to insert data transfers automatically. [8] proposed a directive based approach for specifying CPU-GPU memory transfers, which included compile-time/runtime methods to verify the correctness of the directives and also identified opportunities for performance optimization. [13] proposed a compiler analysis to detect potential stale accesses and uses a runtime to initiate transfers as necessary, for the X10 compiler. [11] has also worked on automatically inferring the OpenMP mapping clauses using some static analysis. OpenMP has also defined standards, OMPT and OMPD [3,4] which are APIs for performance and debugging tools. Archer [2] is another important work that combines static and dynamic techniques to identify data races in large OpenMP applications.

In this paper, we have developed OMPSan, a static analysis tool to interpret the semantics of the OpenMP map clause, and deduce the data transfers introduced by the clause. Our algorithm tracks the reference count for individual variables to infer the effect of the data mapping clause on the host and device data environment. We have developed a data flow analysis, on top of LLVM memory SSA to capture the def-use information of Array variables. We use LLVM Scalar Evolution, to improve the precision of our analysis by estimating the range of locations accessed by a memory access. This enables the OMPSan to handle array sections also. Then OMPSan computes how the data mapping clauses modify the def-use chains of the baseline program, and use this information to validate if the data mapping in the OpenMP program respects the original def-use chains of the baseline sequential program. Finally OMPSan reports diagnostics, to help the developer debug and understand the usage of `map` clauses of their program. We believe the analysis presented in this paper is very powerful and can be developed further for data mapping optimizations also. We also plan to combine our static analysis with a dynamic debugging tool, that would enhance the performance of the dynamic tool and also address the limitations of the static analysis.

References

1. Aachen University: OpenMP Benchmark. https://github.com/RWTH-HPC/DR ACC
2. Atzeni, S., et al.: Archer: effectively spotting data races in large OpenMP applications. In: 2016 IEEE International Parallel and Distributed Processing Symposium (IPDPS), pp. 53–62, May 2016. https://doi.org/10.1109/IPDPS.2016.68
3. Eichenberger, A., et al.: OMPT and OMPD: OpenMP tools application programming interfaces for performance analysis and debugging. In: International Workshop on OpenMP (IWOMP 2013) (2013)
4. Eichenberger, A.E., et al.: OMPT: an OpenMP tools application programming interface for performance analysis. In: Rendell, A.P., Chapman, B.M., Müller, M.S. (eds.) IWOMP 2013. LNCS, vol. 8122, pp. 171–185. Springer, Heidelberg (2013). https://doi.org/10.1007/978-3-642-40698-0_13
5. Jablin, T.B., Jablin, J.A., Prabhu, P., Liu, F., August, D.I.: Dynamically managed data for CPU-GPU architectures. In: Proceedings of the Tenth International Symposium on Code Generation and Optimization, CGO 2012, pp. 165–174. ACM, New York (2012). https://doi.org/10.1145/2259016.2259038
6. Jablin, T.B., Prabhu, P., Jablin, J.A., Johnson, N.P., Beard, S.R., August, D.I.: Automatic CPU-GPU communication management and optimization. SIGPLAN Not. **46**(6), 142–151 (2011). https://doi.org/10.1145/1993316.1993516
7. Knobe, K., Sarkar, V.: Array SSA form and its use in parallelization. In: Proceedings of the 25th ACM SIGPLAN-SIGACT Symposium on Principles of Programming Languages, POPL 1998, pp. 107–120. ACM, New York (1998). https://doi.org/10.1145/268946.268956
8. Lee, S., Li, D., Vetter, J.S.: Interactive program debugging and optimization for directive-based, efficient GPU computing. In: 2014 IEEE 28th International Parallel and Distributed Processing Symposium, pp. 481–490, May 2014. https://doi.org/10.1109/IPDPS.2014.57

9. Lee, S., Eigenmann, R.: OpenMPC: extended OpenMP programming and tuning for GPUs. In: Proceedings of the 2010 ACM/IEEE International Conference for High Performance Computing, Networking, Storage and Analysis, SC 2010, pp. 1–11. IEEE Computer Society, Washington, DC (2010). https://doi.org/10.1109/SC.2010.36
10. LLVM: LLVM MemorySSA. https://llvm.org/docs/MemorySSA.html
11. Mendonça, G., Guimarães, B., Alves, P., Pereira, M., Araújo, G., Pereira, F.M.Q.: DawnCC: automatic annotation for data parallelism and offloading. ACM Trans. Arch. Code Optim. **14**(2), 13:1–13:25 (2017). https://doi.org/10.1145/3084540
12. Novillo, D.: Memory SSA - a unified approach for sparsely representing memory operations. In: Proceedings of the GCC Developers' Summit (2007)
13. Pai, S., Govindarajan, R., Thazhuthaveetil, M.J.: Fast and efficient automatic memory management for GPUs using compiler-assisted runtime coherence scheme. In: Proceedings of the 21st International Conference on Parallel Architectures and Compilation Techniques, PACT 2012, pp. 33–42. ACM, New York (2012). https://doi.org/10.1145/2370816.2370824

Tools

Score-P and OMPT: Navigating the Perils of Callback-Driven Parallel Runtime Introspection

Christian Feld[1]([✉])[iD], Simon Convent[3], Marc-André Hermanns[1,2][iD],
Joachim Protze[3][iD], Markus Geimer[1][iD], and Bernd Mohr[1][iD]

[1] Jülich Supercomputing Centre, Forschungszentrum Jülich, Jülich, Germany
{c.feld,m.a.hermanns,m.geimer,b.mohr}@fz-juelich.de
[2] JARA-HPC, Jülich, Germany
[3] IT Center, RWTH Aachen University, Aachen, Germany
simon.convent@rwth-aachen.de, protze@itc.rwth-aachen.de

Abstract. Event-based performance analysis aims at modeling the behavior of parallel applications through a series of state transitions during execution. Different approaches to obtain such transition points for OpenMP programs include source-level instrumentation (e.g., OPARI) and callback-driven runtime support (e.g., OMPT).

In this paper, we revisit a previous evaluation and comparison of OPARI and an LLVM OMPT implementation—now updated to the OpenMP 5.0 specification—in the context of Score-P. We describe the challenges faced while trying to use OMPT as a drop-in replacement for the existing instrumentation-based approach and the changes in event order that could not be avoided. Furthermore, we provide details on Score-P measurements using OPARI and OMPT as event sources with the EPCC and SPEC OpenMP benchmark suites.

Keywords: Performance measurement · Performance analysis · OpenMP

1 Introduction

The use of performance analysis tools that measure and analyze the runtime behavior of applications is a crucial part of successful performance engineering. Besides core-level optimizations such as proper vectorization and cache usage, particular attention needs to be paid to efficient code parallelization. In high-performance computing (HPC), OpenMP [26] is commonly used to parallelize computations on the node level to take advantage of the nowadays omnipresent multi-core CPUs. However, before the OpenMP 5.0 specification was released in November 2018, there has been no official interface for tools to capture OpenMP-related information. Nevertheless, performance monitoring tools have been able to obtain OpenMP-related measurement data for quite some time using different approaches.

© Springer Nature Switzerland AG 2019
X. Fan et al. (Eds.): IWOMP 2019, LNCS 11718, pp. 21–35, 2019.
https://doi.org/10.1007/978-3-030-28596-8_2

For example, TAU [30], VampirTrace [14], Scalasca's EPIK [10], ompP [9], and Score-P [15] all leverage the *OpenMP Pragma And Region Instrumentor* OPARI [20]. OPARI is a source-to-source preprocessor that rewrites OpenMP directives found in the source code, inserting POMP API calls [21] for instrumentation. These functions then have to be implemented by the respective tool to gather relevant performance data. Meanwhile, an extended version (OPARI2) is available using an enhanced API.

Another proposal for an OpenMP collector API was published in 2006 by Itzkowitz et al. [12]. However, with its restricted focus on sampling-based tools, this approach did not find widespread adoption. To the authors knowledge, it has only been implemented and used by the Sun/Oracle Developer Studio compiler's OpenMP runtime and the associated performance tools, as well as the OpenUH compiler [16] and TAU [30] as part of an evaluation by Huck et al. [11].

A first draft of the *OpenMP Tools Interface* (OMPT) was published by Eichenberger et al. [6] in 2013. Based on this interface, Lorenz et al. conducted an initial comparison between OPARI2 and OMPT in the context of Score-P [17]. However, early experiences in implementing OMPT support in both OpenMP runtimes and tools led to significant changes of the interface before it was integrated into the OpenMP specification with Technical Report 4 [24]. A slightly updated version is now part of the OpenMP 5.0 specification [26].

In this paper, we present our experiences with this OpenMP 5.0 version of the OMPT interface as implemented in the LLVM OpenMP runtime [3] with the Score-P instrumentation and measurement system. We describe the challenges encountered while trying to reconstruct the event sequences based on a logical execution view expected by Score-P's measurement core as well as the analysis tools building on top of Score-P from the OMPT events generated by the LLVM runtime. Moreover, we highlight major differences between the OMPT-based data collection and our previous OPARI2-based approach. Finally, we show a detailed overhead comparison between both approaches using the EPCC OpenMP benchmark suite [5] and the SPEC OMP2012 benchmarks [22].

2   The OpenMP Tools Interface

In this section, we will briefly introduce the OpenMP Tools Interface (OMPT) and highlight major changes compared to the initial draft [6] used in the study by Lorenz et al. [17]. OMPT is a portable interface enabling tools to gain deeper insight into the execution of an OpenMP program. The design of OMPT accommodates tools based on both sampling and instrumentation. For instrumentation, OMPT defines callbacks for relevant events to be dispatched during execution of a program. A tool can register callback handlers to record information about the execution which includes, for example, the types of threads, tasks, and mutexes, information on the stack frames, and more. Additionally, there are inquiry functions which can be used to extract additional information from within callback handlers, or signal handlers as typically used to implement sampling tools.

Changes to OMPT. In the OpenMP 5.0 specification, tool initialization is now a three-way handshake protocol. This allows the OpenMP runtime to determine early during its initialization whether a tool is present or not. At the same time, a tool can decide against activation for a specific run.

Initially, a tool was able to identify a thread, a parallel team, or a task by an integer ID maintained by the runtime. Tracking OpenMP entities across multiple callback invocations therefore required potentially costly lookups. For most callbacks—a notable exception are the lock and mutex callbacks—the integer ID was replaced by storage for a 64-bit data word that a tool can use to maintain information on behalf of an OpenMP entity, thus enabling more efficient tool implementations.

Moreover, multiple events providing similar information have been folded into a single event callback. While reducing the number of callbacks simplifies the interface, it also reduces the possibilities for a tool to selectively choose a set of interesting events. The initial proposal also contained callbacks indicating that a thread is idling between participation in two consecutive parallel regions; these callbacks have been removed. We will see in Sect. 3, that the *implicit-task-end* event for worker threads can be dispatched late, so that the runtime might effectively report no idle time.

In contrast, callbacks for advanced OpenMP features such as *task cancellation* or *task dependences* have been added. While cancellation information can be relevant for maintaining the OMPT tool data objects, we do not yet see a use case in Score-P for logging these events. On the other hand, task-dependency information can be interesting to perform critical path analysis in tools like Scalasca. Another addition are callbacks for devices including callbacks for the initialization/finalization of devices as well as for data movements between host and devices. However, this part of OMPT is not yet implemented in the OpenMP runtime we are using for our experiments and therefore not considered in our implementation.

To allow a tool to relate events to source code, a pointer argument providing an instruction address was added to various callbacks. For ease of implementation, this pointer is defined as the return address: the next instruction executed after the runtime function implementing an OpenMP construct finished.

Since the order in which the OpenMP runtime and an attached OMPT tool are shut down is not necessarily well-defined, an `ompt_finalize_tool()` function has been introduced. This function can be called by the tool during its finalization and guarantees that any outstanding events that might have been buffered by the runtime get dispatched. If the OpenMP runtime was already finalized, however, all events have been dispatched and this function call results in a no-op.

3   Implementing OMPT Support in Score-P

Score-P—the tool we focus on in this paper—is a highly scalable and easy-to-use instrumentation and measurement infrastructure for profiling, event tracing, and online analysis of HPC applications. It currently supports the analysis tools

Scalasca [10,31], Vampir [14], Periscope [4], and TAU [30], and is open for other tools that are based on the Open Trace Format Version 2 (OTF2) [7] or the CUBE4 [28] profiling format as well as tools that implement a Score-P substrate plugin [29] for event consumption. As outlined before, up until now Score-P uses the source-level instrumentor OPARI2 to rewrite and annotate OpenMP directives to gather OpenMP-specific performance data. To limit the number of required changes in the analysis tools, we aim for generating the same (or at least very similar) event sequences based on a logical execution view from the OMPT events generated by the LLVM runtime. In the following, we describe the various challenges encountered and how we addressed them.

During development and for the experiments in this paper we used an OpenMP runtime implementation based on LLVM/7.0 including a patch which implements `ompt_finalize_tool()` [2]. This implementation roughly represents the interface as defined in Technical Report 6 [25], without callbacks for device-related events. Semantically there is no big difference to the OMPT specification in OpenMP 5.0. The resulting Score-P development version implementing the new OMPT functionality can be downloaded from [8]. Compilation was consistently done using the Intel compiler, version 19.0.3.199 20190206.

Event Sequence Requirements. Score-P stores event data independently per logical execution unit in buffers called *locations*. Events in these locations are required to have monotonically increasing timestamps (*monotonicity requirement*). In addition, as the Score-P event model is based on *regions* that correspond to regions in the source code, most events are paired, either as ENTER/LEAVE or BEGIN/END pairs. These pairs must be properly nested within a location, otherwise the profile measurement or trace analysis fails (*nesting requirement*). Here, special care is taken for events generated from within explicit OpenMP tasks as the nesting requirement might be violated in task scheduling points [18]. For parallel constructs that affect several locations, the happened-before semantics must be reflected in the ordering of timestamps (*HB requirement*). For example, all timestamps belonging to events from within a `parallel` construct must not be larger than the corresponding *parallel-end* timestamp. With OPARI2's instrumentation being entirely inside the parallel region, this requirement is always fulfilled, and thus analysis tools rely on it to calculate performance metrics. To minimize synchronization overhead, the OMPT specification is less strict regarding cross-location happened-before relationships, as detailed below.

`parallel` Construct: Overdue Events. OPARI2 as well as OMPT use the event sequence depicted in Fig. 1 for a `parallel` construct with T_0 as the encountering thread. The events for each thread T_0–T_2 are written to individual Score-P locations, where the encountering thread and the master child thread share one location. With OPARI2 instrumentation, all events of all locations are dispatched before the closing *parallel-end* on the encountering thread. Timestamps taken at dispatch time are guaranteed to meet the fork-join happened-before semantics.

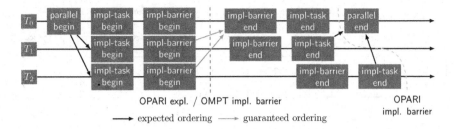

Fig. 1. Event sequence and ordering for a **parallel** construct.

The OMPT specification, however, does not impose the requirement on non-master child threads to dispatch the *implicit-barrier-end* and *implicit-task-end* callbacks earlier than the corresponding *parallel-end* on the encountering thread, only all *implicit-barrier-begin* events are guaranteed to be dispatched before the *implicit-barrier-end*. That is, there might be two *overdue* events per non-master child thread waiting for being dispatched even if the parallel region was already *joined*, as highlighted for thread T_2 in the diagram above. The only guarantee for these *overdue* events is that they are dispatched before any further events on this thread.

As a first consequence, timestamps taken when the overdue events are being dispatched likely violate the HB requirement. The only *implicit-barrier-end* and *implicit-task-end* timestamps guaranteed to conform to the assumed ordering are those on the master thread. To retain the happened-before timestamp order in Score-P, we chose to use these timestamps for all remaining *implicit-barrier-end* and *implicit-task-end* events, thus having identical timestamps per event type for all threads in the team.

parallel Construct: Non-deterministic Scheduling. The next consequence arises from the *combination* of (1) the freedom of the runtime to postpone events, (2) the mapping of OpenMP threads to Score-P locations, and (3) potential non-determinism in mapping of logical OpenMP threads to system threads. Whereas the first item has been described above, the other items need some additional explanation.

Score-P establishes a fixed mapping of OpenMP threads to Score-P locations based on OpenMP nesting characteristics, where the nesting characteristic is determined by the sequence of OpenMP thread numbers from the initial thread to the current one. This mapping is established in *implicit-task-begin* events by assigning a location to thread-local storage. The reasons for a fixed mapping are (1) to provide the user with the *logical* execution view, that is, present events per OpenMP thread number instead of per system thread, and (2) to maximize scalability regarding memory and the number of generated output files. As each distinct nesting characteristic is assigned a single Score-P location, locations are reused in subsequent parallel regions if a nesting characteristic has come to light previously[1]. In contrast, the system thread executing an OpenMP nesting characteristic might change in subsequent parallel regions.

---

[1] In addition, the master thread reuses the encountering thread's location.

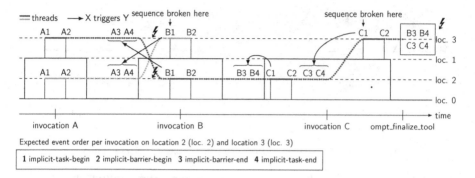

Fig. 2. Three invocations of identical nested parallel regions with two threads in each team. For invocation B the non-master OpenMP threads of the inner regions are invertedly mapped to system threads, for invocation C the non-master threads of both inner regions are mapped to the same blue system thread. A location corresponds to a unique OpenMP ancestry sequence. (Color figure online)

In the advent of *overdue* events combined with a non-deterministic OpenMP thread to system thread mapping we observe two anomalous schedules which tend to break the monotonicity requirement and may lead to data corruption. Figure 2 illustrates these schedule decisions. Assume a parallel region with a team size of two that executes a nested parallel region, also with team size of two, for three subsequent invocations A, B, and C. The two inner parallel regions expose work for four OpenMP threads with different nesting characteristics, thus Score-P will create four locations. The Score-P locations created in invocation A are reused in invocation B and C because of identical nesting characteristics. The first form of the anomaly manifests in a *OpenMP thread to system thread assignment* switch between invocations; while the inner region's non-master implicit task n was served by system thread i in the first invocation, it is served by system thread j in the second one and vice versa for the other inner region, see transition from invocation A to B in the figure. Each two system threads *blue* and *red* carry two *overdue* events A3 and A4 from invocation A to be written to location 3 (blue) and location 2 (red), respectively. Each thread triggers its overdue events before its B1 event of invocation B. In B1 the switch manifests as a location change. As no ordering is enforced by OMPT, thread *red* might write B1 concurrently with thread *blue* writing the overdue events A3 and A4 to location 3 and vice versa for location 2. This race condition potentially violates the monotonicity requirement on either location—the overdue events A3 and A4 need to be written before B1—or worse, leads to corrupted data. Note that there is no race condition in the absence of overdue events.

The second form manifests in invocation C in Fig. 2 being executed by just three of the four threads; the two inner region's non-master implicit tasks get both executed by the same system thread (blue). This time there is no issue on location 2 as all events are delivered in the expected order. The problem arises for location 3 during runtime shutdown. The undelivered events B3 and B4 (red) are dispatched and will violate the monotonicity requirement. If the undelivered C3 and C4 (blue) are dispatched concurrently, data might get corrupted in addition. The runtime implementation we used showed this anomalies only with nested `parallel` constructs.

To address these two anomalies, we need to ensure that any overdue events for a given location are written *before* processing an *implicit-task-begin* event from a subsequent invocation on the same location. Translated to Fig. 2, invocation B and location 3, this means to write A3 and A4 from thread *blue* before B1 from thread *red*. Thus, the first thing to do in B1 is to detect whether there are overdue A3 and A4 events for location 3. To do so, we use location-specific data transferred from invocation A to invocation B, saving a Score-P representation of the latest implicit task data together with synchronization handles. This data is cleared from the location once the overdue events have been processed completely. If the overdue event data is still available when thread *red* dispatches B1, thread *red* takes ownership and processes A3 and A4 first—using the location-specific data provided by thread *blue* in invocation A—while preventing thread *blue* to do the same. If thread *blue* is first, it takes ownership and processes A3 and A4 while blocking thread *red* working on B1 during this time. Applying this synchronization for every *implicit-task-begin* will processes all overdue events except the ones waiting for being dispatched when the program finishes, here C3 and C4 from thread *blue*. These are explicitly triggered by calling `ompt_finalize_tool` during Score-P's shutdown and handled without additional effort. The fine-grained synchronization necessary to orchestrate this mechanism uses atomic updates and two spin-mutexes per location.

Developing this overdue-handling mechanism to maintain the established event sequence for the `parallel` construct was the biggest challenge in implementing support for OMPT in Score-P. Once this was achieved, implementing other OMPT callbacks was straightforward.

4   Differences in Event Sequence and Source Information

To investigate differences emerging from using OMPT callbacks compared to the traditional OPARI2 instrumentation, we ran experiments from the OpenMP 4.5 Examples [8,23].

Worksharing Constructs. Implicit barriers synchronize worksharing constructs, unless a `nowait` clause was given. For OPARI2, these implicit barriers conceptually belong to the construct, that is, the events are nested inside the enclosing construct's ENTER and LEAVE events. In contrast, OMPT dispatches the implicit barrier events after the worksharing's *end* event. The different event order is exemplified with a minimal example using the `worksharing-loop` construct, see Listing 1. This event-sequence change is seen for all worksharing constructs.

```
1  #pragma omp parallel
2  {
3    #pragma omp for
4    for (int i = 0; i<20; i++)
5        work();
6  }
```

```
1     ENTER Region: "!$omp parallel"
2       ENTER Region: "!$omp for"
3  -     ENTER Region: "!$omp barrier"
4  -     LEAVE Region: "!$omp barrier"
5     LEAVE Region: "!$omp for"
6  +  ENTER Region: "!$omp barrier"
7  +  LEAVE Region: "!$omp barrier"
8     ENTER Region: "!$omp barrier"
9     LEAVE Region: "!$omp barrier"
10    LEAVE Region: "!$omp parallel"
```

Listing 1: For the `worksharing-loop` construct, `ENTER` and `LEAVE` events for the implicit barrier are created inside the construct (OPARI2 in red) or outside the construct (OMPT in green).

Barriers. An OMPT implementation might distinguish between *implicit* and *explicit* barriers, but the LLVM runtime we used currently does not. OPARI2, on the other hand, distinguishes between barrier types. Whereas explicit barriers are easily instrumented by OPARI2, implicit ones need special attention. An implicit barrier is transformed to an instrumented explicit barrier, and for worksharing constructs a `nowait` clause is added to the corresponding construct. This way timing information can be obtained and the semantics stay unchanged. However, there are cases where the compiler can safely merge consecutive implicit barriers[2]. By transforming the implicit barrier, OPARI2 prevents the compiler from performing this optimization.

Tasking. OPARI2 takes care that undeferred tasks will not create any events by evaluating the `if` clause. Similar behavior was implemented with OMPT by evaluating the task type. For the remaining tasks, there are some changes regarding the sequence of events written by Score-P. In general, the OMPT specification allows to signal the switch from one task to the next task. However, the current implementation in the LLVM runtime first signals a switch back to the scheduling task before switching to the next task. This additional switch is not observed with OPARI2, which leads to a reduced number of recorded scheduling events. Task switches in OPARI2 are triggered when a task starts running and potentially after scheduling points have been processed [18]. As OPARI2 does not instrument all scheduling point types yet, untied tasks will break the nesting requirement when scheduled in an unsupported type. OMPT provides a robust and complete picture in this regard.

With OPARI2 it is possible to measure the duration of task creation, as the instrumentation provides distinct task-create-begin/end events. OMPT's *task-create* does not provide timing information, nevertheless we mapped it to the task-create-begin/end pair to preserve the existing event sequence.

---

[2] See, for example, `Example_barrier_regions.1.c` from the OpenMP 4.5 Examples [23] where the implicit barrier of the inner parallel region is omitted.

Table 1. Matrix of measurement setups used in the evaluation.

	llvm-ompt-off	llvm-ompt-on	scorep-opari2	scorep-ompt
OMPT Runtime	no	yes	no	yes
Score-P Adapter	—	—	OPARI2	OMPT

Relation to Source Code. To optimize a program after performance analysis, a user needs to relate analysis hotspots to source code. OPARI2, as a source-level translator, has comprehensive knowledge of source locations. Line number and filename of instrumented OpenMP constructs are hard-coded into OPARI2's output files. OMPT's means to relate OpenMP events to their source is to provide a return address (`codeptr_ra`) as a callback argument which is mapped to a Score-P handle dynamically. This address does not point to the corresponding OpenMP construct, but to the application code being executed once the OpenMP region related to the event is completed. Usually the instruction before this address resolves to the corresponding *filename:lineno* source location[3].

Other Differences Between OMPT and OPARI. In addition, we want to mention differences regarding the following constructs just briefly:

Named criticals. While OPARI2 provides the optional name of a `critcal` construct, OMPT distinguishes the underlying locks by a numeric `wait_id`.
Atomic construct. The LLVM runtime only dispatches callbacks for *atomic-events* if the compiler is not able to emit a native atomic instruction. OPARI2 is able to instrument all `atomic` constructs, but due to the large relative overhead involved, it allows for deactivating this feature.
Section construct. The LLVM runtime currently does not provide events regarding the `section` construct (within the `sections` construct) although the specification defines the corresponding `ompt_callback_dispatch`.
omp_test_lock and omp_test_nest_lock. The LLVM runtime does not yet distinguish between *locks* and *test locks* and their nested counterparts.

5   Evaluation

We used the EPCC OpenMP micro-benchmark suite [5] and the SPEC OMP2012 benchmarks version 1.0 [22] to evaluate the measurement dilation introduced by the Score-P measurement adapters using OPARI2 and OMPT. The platform for our evaluation is the cluster partition of the JURECA supercomputer [13] operated by the Jülich Supercomputing Centre of Forschungszentrum Jülich in Germany. All measurements were taken on the same JURECA node, which consists of two Intel Xeon E5-2680 Haswell CPUs (2.5 GHz, 12 cores each) and 128 GB

---

[3] To convert addresses into file names and line numbers, we rely on the *Binary File Descriptor library* (BFD) [1] and debug symbols in the binary.

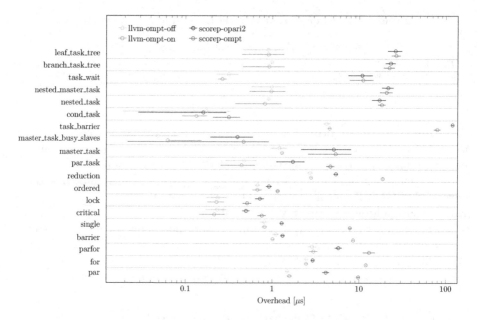

Fig. 3. Overhead reported by the EPCC OpenMP Benchmark Suite for individual OpenMP constructs in the four different measurement setups with 12 threads on a single socket of a JURECA Cluster Module [13] node.

RAM. For easier evaluation and reproducibility, we used the Jülich Benchmarking Environment (JUBE) [19] in version 2.2.2 to configure and run the measurements [8]. The Score-P measurements were done in profiling-only mode.

In our evaluation, we explore four different measurement setups as shown in Table 1. As OPARI2 (scorep-opari2) does not need OMPT runtime support, we disabled it in the LLVM runtime and provide a baseline measurement for this setup (llvm-ompt-off). For the OMPT adapter (scorep-ompt), we used a separate installation of the same LLVM runtime version with OMPT support enabled and also provide a separate baseline measurement (llvm-ompt-on). Data for baseline measurements are indicated by desaturated colors, whereas vivid colors indicate measurements with Score-P attached. Blue indicates OMPT to be disabled in the measurement, whereas orange indicates OMPT to be enabled.

EPCCbench. The EPCC OpenMP micro-benchmark suite was developed to identify overheads created by individual OpenMP constructs. We use it here to compare the overhead that Score-P adds to the OpenMP measurement of individual constructs for each adapter—OPARI2 and OMPT—by comparing the overhead reported by the benchmark with and without Score-P attached.

Figure 3 shows the measurements on a single node of the JURECA cluster with 12 threads bound to a single socket[4]. For these measurements, we inten-

---

[4] We used `OMP_PROC_BIND=close` and `OMP_PLACES={0}:12` for all measurements.

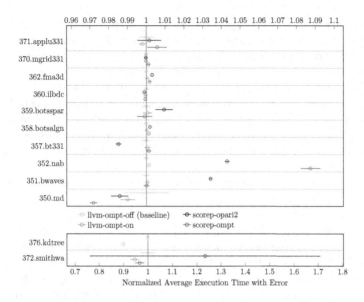

Fig. 4. Normalized execution time of the configured SPEC OMP2012 benchmark applications for the four different measurement setups using the *ref* input size with 12 threads on a single socket of a JURECA Cluster Module [13] node.

tionally did not occupy both sockets of the JURECA node to eliminate potential NUMA effects in the measurements caused by inter-socket memory accesses. We ran the benchmark with 150 outer repetitions, a test time of $5000\,\mu s$, and the delay time set to $15\,\mu s$. The EPCC benchmark uses the configured outer repetitions to provide an average overhead and uncertainty bounds for it as shown in the figure.

We notice that measurement setups llvm-ompt-off and llvm-ompt-on show very similar performance, i.e., OMPT overhead is minimal if no tool is attached.

While most of the task constructs are equally costly with OPARI2 and OMPT, we see a higher overhead with the Score-P OMPT adapter for kernels involving worksharing and barrier constructs. Analysis revealed that the additional overhead is caused inside Score-P by mapping `codeptr_ra` callback arguments to Score-P-handles concurrently[5]. We are confident to be able to improve this mapping in a future implementation. However, there will always be more overhead involved compared to OPARI2, as in this case all required information is statically available after source-to-source translation.

SPEC OMP2012. To evaluate the influence that users may expect of the two different Score-P adapters on measurements of real-world applications, we measured the runtime of 12 benchmarks of the SPEC OMP 2012 benchmark suite. We used the `runspec` command to build the respective benchmark applications,

---

[5] The `addr2line` lookup is done only once per address and is negligible.

but used JUBE to run the experiments. To enable time measurements even without the presence of a performance tool, we introduced coarse-grained time measurement and output around the outer iteration, excluding initialization and I/O where possible, to minimize external influences on the measurement.

Figure 4 shows measurements using the *ref* input size. As absolute execution time with this input size spreads significantly across the different benchmarks, we normalized the data. The average time of each application in measurement setup llvm-ompt-off acts as the baseline for the other measurement setups reported for that application. Therefore all of these measurements are displayed as 1, crossed by the vertical baseline indicator. For each data point, the average of 5 runs is reported, error bars indicating the standard deviation. The measurements show that for most of the SPEC applications, the runtime dilation due to the Score-P measurements is within an acceptable range independent of the adapter used. 352.nab generates a large number of worksharing and barrier events which are—due to the contended `codeptr_ra` lookup—likely to cause the additional overhead seen with the OMPT adapter [27]. More than 99% of 357.applu331's events are flush events. For these, we also do a `codeptr_ra` lookup, but apparently with less contention. 351.bwaves with its numerous, subsequent `parallel do` constructs revealed a smaller number of parallel and barrier events in the OMPT case, which might be due to the compiler's ability to fuse subsequent loops. A more in-depth investigation is needed, though. The measurements for 376.kdtree aborted for both the OPARI2 and the OMPT adapter, as memory requirements for the excessive number of explicit tasks could not be fulfilled by Score-P. The reason for the large standard deviation of the OPARI2 measurement of 372.smithwa could not yet be determined and is still under investigation.

6   Conclusion

With the availability of an official OpenMP Tools Interface, instrumentation-based performance tools need to consider to replace the common source-level OPARI2 approach, mainly to reduce the maintenance burden in the long run. In this paper, we presented the challenges implementing an OMPT tool based on the LLVM runtime as a drop-in replacement for OPARI2 in the context of Score-P and described the unavoidable changes in the order of OpenMP events. OMPT provides a *runtime* execution view, but as Score-P-based analysis tools historically rely upon a *logical* execution view, our first implementation tried to retain the latter. This choice presented a challenge handling the `parallel` construct, whereas implementing other OMPT callbacks was straightforward and provided sufficient measurement data to serve as a replacement.

From the EPCC micro-benchmarks, we saw that OMPT overhead is minimal if no tool is attached, recording task events is costly with both OPARI2 and OMPT, and our OMPT tool consistently generates higher overhead for work-sharing and barrier constructs. The latter is caused by contended mapping of `codeptr_ra` callback arguments to Score-P-handles within Score-P and will be addressed in the future. However, this overhead does not propagate in great severity to real-world applications from SPEC OMP2012 but manifests in programs with a high number of `codeptr_ra` lookups.

Once additional OpenMP runtimes with OMPT support are available from compiler vendors, we are eager to verify whether they also provide sufficient data to our tool to replace the source-level OPARI2 approach. In addition, we will investigate how analysis tools consuming the Score-P measurement data have to be adapted to deal with the remaining differences in event order.

Acknowledgements. The authors gratefully acknowledge the computing time granted through JARA-HPC on the supercomputer JURECA [13] at Forschungszentrum Jülich. Part of this work was performed under the POP2 project and has received funding from the European Union's Horizon 2020 research and innovation programme under grant agreement 824080.

References

1. GNU Binutils. https://sourceware.org/binutils/
2. LLVM runtime with experimental changes for OMPT. https://github.com/OpenMPToolsInterface/LLVM-openmp/commits/tool_finalization_tr7, branch tool_finalization_tr7, commit dcf2962eb6d92d82e74bd374f27e6ef836a5e2b3
3. Support for the OpenMP language in LLVM. http://openmp.llvm.org
4. Benedict, S., Petkov, V., Gerndt, M.: Periscope: an online-based distributed performance analysis tool. In: Müller, M.S., Resch, M.M., Schulz, A., Nagel, W.E. (eds.) Tools for High Performance Computing 2009, pp. 1–16. Springer, Heidelberg (2010). https://doi.org/10.1007/978-3-642-11261-4_1
5. Bull, J.M., Reid, F., McDonnell, N.: A microbenchmark suite for OpenMP tasks. In: Chapman, B.M., Massaioli, F., Müller, M.S., Rorro, M. (eds.) IWOMP 2012. LNCS, vol. 7312, pp. 271–274. Springer, Heidelberg (2012). https://doi.org/10.1007/978-3-642-30961-8_24
6. Eichenberger, A.E., et al.: OMPT: an OpenMP tools application programming interface for performance analysis. In: Rendell, A.P., Chapman, B.M., Müller, M.S. (eds.) IWOMP 2013. LNCS, vol. 8122, pp. 171–185. Springer, Heidelberg (2013). https://doi.org/10.1007/978-3-642-40698-0_13
7. Eschweiler, D., Wagner, M., Geimer, M., Knüpfer, A., Nagel, W.E., Wolf, F.: Open trace format 2 - the next generation of scalable trace formats and support libraries. In: Proceedings of the Internatioanl Conference on Parallel Computing (ParCo), Ghent, Belgium, 30 August–2 September 2011. Advances in Parallel Computing, vol. 22, pp. 481–490. IOS Press (2012). https://doi.org/10.3233/978-1-61499-041-3-481
8. Feld, C., Convent, S., Hermanns, M.A., Protze, J., Geimer, M.: [Reproducibility] Score-P and OMPT: navigating the perils of callback-driven parallel runtime introspection, June 2019. https://doi.org/10.5281/zenodo.3251871
9. Fürlinger, K., Gerndt, M.: ompP: A profiling tool for OpenMP. In: Mueller, M.S., Chapman, B.M., de Supinski, B.R., Malony, A.D., Voss, M. (eds.) IWOMP -2005. LNCS, vol. 4315, pp. 15–23. Springer, Heidelberg (2008). https://doi.org/10.1007/978-3-540-68555-5_2
10. Geimer, M., Wolf, F., Wylie, B.J.N., Ábrahám, E., Becker, D., Mohr, B.: The Scalasca performance toolset architecture. Concurr. Comput. Pract. Exp. **22**(6), 702–719 (2010). https://doi.org/10.1002/cpe.1556

11. Huck, K.A., Malony, A.D., Shende, S., Jacobsen, D.W.: Integrated measurement for cross-platform OpenMP performance analysis. In: DeRose, L., de Supinski, B.R., Olivier, S.L., Chapman, B.M., Müller, M.S. (eds.) IWOMP 2014. LNCS, vol. 8766, pp. 146–160. Springer, Cham (2014). https://doi.org/10.1007/978-3-319-11454-5_11
12. Itzkowitz, M., Mazurov, O., Copty, N., Lin, Y.: An OpenMP runtime API for profiling. White paper (2002). http://www.compunity.org/futures/omp-api.html
13. Jülich Supercomputing Centre: JURECA: modular supercomputer at Jülich super-computing centre. J. Large-Scale Res. Facil. **4**(A132) (2018). https://doi.org/10.17815/jlsrf-4-121-1
14. Knüpfer, A., et al.: The Vampir performance analysis tool-set. In: Resch, M., Keller, R., Himmler, V., Krammer, B., Schulz, A. (eds.) Tools for High Performance Computing, pp. 139–155. Springer, Heidelberg (2008). https://doi.org/10.1007/978-3-540-68564-7_9
15. Knüpfer, A., et al.: Score-P: a joint performance measurement run-time infrastructure for Periscope, Scalasca, TAU, and Vampir. In: Brunst, H., Müller, M., Nagel, W., Resch, M. (eds.) Tools for High Performance Computing 2011, pp. 79–91. Springer, Heidelberg (2012). https://doi.org/10.1007/978-3-642-31476-6_7
16. Liao, C., Hernandez, O., Chapman, B., Chen, W., Zheng, W.: OpenUH: an optimizing, portable OpenMP compiler. Concurr. Comput. Pract. Exp. **19**(18), 2317–2332 (2007)
17. Lorenz, D., Dietrich, R., Tschüter, R., Wolf, F.: A Comparison between OPARI2 and the OpenMP tools interface in the context of Score-P. In: DeRose, L., de Supinski, B.R., Olivier, S.L., Chapman, B.M., Müller, M.S. (eds.) IWOMP 2014. LNCS, vol. 8766, pp. 161–172. Springer, Cham (2014). https://doi.org/10.1007/978-3-319-11454-5_12
18. Lorenz, D., Mohr, B., Rössel, C., Schmidl, D., Wolf, F.: How to reconcile event-based performance analysis with tasking in OpenMP. In: Sato, M., Hanawa, T., Müller, M.S., Chapman, B.M., de Supinski, B.R. (eds.) IWOMP 2010. LNCS, vol. 6132, pp. 109–121. Springer, Heidelberg (2010). https://doi.org/10.1007/978-3-642-13217-9_9
19. Lührs, S., Rohe, D., Schnurpfeil, A., Thust, K., Frings, W.: Flexible and generic workflow management. In: Parallel Computing: On the Road to Exascale. Advances in Parallel Computing, vol. 27, pp. 431–438. International Conference on Parallel Computing 2015, Edinburgh, UK, 1–4 September 2015. IOS Press, Amsterdam, September 2016. https://doi.org/10.3233/978-1-61499-621-7-431. https://www.fz-juelich.de/jsc/jube/
20. Mohr, B., Malony, A., Shende, S., Wolf, F.: Design and prototype of a performance tool interface for OpenMP. J. Supercomput. **23**, 105–128 (2002). https://doi.org/10.1023/A:1015741304337
21. Mohr, B., et al.: A performance monitoring interface for OpenMP. In: Proceedings of the 4th European Workshop on OpenMP (EWOMP 2002), Rome, Italy, September 2002
22. Müller, M., et al.: SPEC OMP2012 an application benchmark suite for parallel systems using OpenMP. In: Proceedings of the 8th International Conference on OpenMP in a Heterogeneous World, pp. 223–236, June 2012. https://doi.org/10.1007/978-3-642-30961-8_17
23. OpenMP Architecture Review Board: OpenMP Application Programming Interface - Examples - Version 4.5.0. http://www.openmp.org/wp-content/uploads/openmp-examples-4.5.0.pdf

24. OpenMP Architecture Review Board: TR4: OpenMP Version 5.0 Preview 1. Specification, November 2016. http://www.openmp.org/wp-content/uploads/openmp-tr4.pdf
25. OpenMP Architecture Review Board: TR6: OpenMP Version 5.0 Preview 2. Specification, November 2017. http://www.openmp.org/wp-content/uploads/openmp-TR6.pdf
26. OpenMP Architecture Review Board: OpenMP Application Program Interface Version 5.0. Specification, November 2018. https://www.openmp.org/wp-content/uploads/OpenMP-API-Specification-5.0.pdf
27. Protze, J., Hahnfeld, J., Ahn, D.H., Schulz, M., Müller, M.S.: OpenMP tools interface: synchronization information for data race detection. In: de Supinski, B.R., Olivier, S.L., Terboven, C., Chapman, B.M., Müller, M.S. (eds.) IWOMP 2017. LNCS, vol. 10468, pp. 249–265. Springer, Cham (2017). https://doi.org/10.1007/978-3-319-65578-9_17
28. Saviankou, P., Knobloch, M., Visser, A., Mohr, B.: Cube v4: from performance report explorer to performance analysis tool. Procedia Comput. Sci. **51**, 1343–1352 (2015). https://doi.org/10.1016/j.procs.2015.05.320
29. Schöne, R., Tschüter, R., Ilsche, T., Schuchart, J., Hackenberg, D., Nagel, W.E.: Extending the functionality of Score-P through plugins: interfaces and use cases. In: Niethammer, C., Gracia, J., Hilbrich, T., Knüpfer, A., Resch, M.M., Nagel, W.E. (eds.) Tools for High Performance Computing 2016, pp. 59–82. Springer, Cham (2017). https://doi.org/10.1007/978-3-319-56702-0_4
30. Shende, S.S., Malony, A.D.: The Tau parallel performance system. Int. J. High Perform. Comput. Appl. **20**(2), 287–311 (2006). https://doi.org/10.1177/1094342006064482
31. Zhukov, I., Feld, C., Geimer, M., Knobloch, M., Mohr, B., Saviankou, P.: Scalasca v2: back to the future. In: Niethammer, C., Gracia, J., Knüpfer, A., Resch, M., Nagel, W. (eds.) Tools for High Performance Computing, pp. 1–24. Springer, Cham (2015). https://doi.org/10.1007/978-3-319-16012-2_1

SCALOMP: Analyzing the Scalability of OpenMP Applications

Anton Daumen[1,2](✉), Patrick Carribault[1], François Trahay[2],
and Gaël Thomas[2]

[1] CEA, DAM, DIF, 91297 Arpajon, France
{anton.daumen.ocre,patrick.carribault}@cea.fr
[2] Télécom SudParis, Institut Polytechnique de Paris, Évry, France
{francois.trahay,gael.thomas}@telecom-sudparis.eu

Abstract. Achieving good scalability from parallel codes is becoming increasingly difficult due to the hardware becoming more and more complex. Performance tools help developers but their use is sometimes complicated and very iterative. In this paper we propose a simple methodology for assessing the scalability and for detecting performance problems in an OpenMP application. This methodology is implemented in a performance analysis tool named SCALOMP that relies on the capabilities of OMPT for analyzing OpenMP applications. SCALOMP reports the code regions with scalability issues and suggests optimization strategies for those issues. The evaluation shows that SCALOMP incurs low overhead and that its suggestions lead to significant performance improvement of several OpenMP applications.

Keywords: Performance tool · Scalability · OMPT

1 Introduction

The lifespan of simulation codes is several times longer than the lifespan of supercomputers. Thus, a single code will be used on multiple very different architectures, making the portability and the optimization of codes difficult. Furthermore computer architectures are more and more complex as their design has to become more intricate in order for performance to continue increasing. In their chase for better performance, developers rely on performance analysis tools to understand and analyze their code.

Many performance tools provide a wide range of features, metrics, and analysis. However the more features a performance tool has, the more complex it is to use. The developer has to learn how to use the tools in order to start efficiently using them for code analysis. Furthermore a lot of tools use an incremental methodology for analyzing codes, the tool first reports the global behavior of the code and the developer then focuses his analysis on important regions. The developer then tries to detect the issues in said regions by using other features of the tool and analyzing the source code directly, forming hypothesis and using

X. Fan et al. (Eds.): IWOMP 2019, LNCS 11718, pp. 36–49, 2019.
https://doi.org/10.1007/978-3-030-28596-8_3

the tool to verify them and quantify the importance of a performance problem before trying to fix it in the code.

In this paper we propose a simple methodology for analyzing the performance of a parallel application with a focus on the scalability of OpenMP applications. This approach is implemented in ScaLOMP, that reports directly to the user the parallel regions where time is lost due to scalability issues and to automatically deduce the sources of these losses in order for the developer to directly know where time was lost and why. The whole process needs to be as closely related to the source code as possible in order for the developer to immediately understand where an issue resides. When possible, ScaLOMP provide hints on how an issue may be solved.

The remainder of this paper is organized as follows: in Sect. 2 we present state-of-the-art tools that illustrate the typical methodology of performance tools. We detail our methodology in Sect. 3, and we describe ScaLOMP internals in Sect. 4. We evaluate our approach in Sect. 5, and in Sect. 6 we conclude this paper.

2   Related Work

The performance tool landscape is filled with a significant number of tools that provide a very broad variety of features.

A lot of effort has been spent on tools that help the developper better visualize the behavior of an application [8,15]. These tools allow developper to precisely examine the application execution, but the analysis has to be done manually.

Automatic analysis relieve the developper from the analysis. Several works have focused on detecting the root causes of scalability issues in parallel applications. Most of these works are focused on MPI; For example, performance models can help finding weak scaling issues [6]. A backward replay of an execution trace can be used for identifying the root cause of wait-states in MPI applications [5].

Other work focuses on detecting and reporting problems in multi-threaded applications. For instance, imbalance issues in OpenMP parallel regions and worksharing constructs can affect the scalability of an application [18]. Running micro-benchmarks and building a compositional model can predict the performance of OpenMP applications on a given machine [16]. However, this approach is limited to memory-bound applications and only works on OpenMP applications using the *static* scheduler. In order to detect false-sharing, a recent work uses the OMPT API to instrument OpenMP constructs, and collects hardware counters at a fine granularity [9]. The collected data then train a classifier which can then spot false sharing in applications. Automated performance modeling can be used to examine the scalability of OpenMP runtime constructs [12], or to analyze the memory access patterns of OpenMP applications [4].

While all of these approaches are functional and allow a developper to identify issues, verifying every possible problem using different tools is time consuming. Moreover each approach has its own requirements and limitations which can make using these tools together difficult, and does not match our view on how the performance analysis of an application should work.

Some tools do integrate multiple analysis successfully. Intel VTune [17] provides an OpenMP *time gain* analysis that estimates the potential gain that could be obtained if various performance problems (lock contention, imbalance, scheduling overhead, etc.) were fixed. However Vtune *time gain* is lacking a scalability analysis, which means that if a performance issue is not detected, a code region may be wrongfully considered as having no issue. Finally, VTune uses profiling to measure the time spent in OpenMP constructs. While this limits the instrumentation overhead, it also affects the measurements precisions and lacks some insight that tracing may give.

3   Performance Analysis of OpenMP Applications

As described in Sect. 2, even with modern performance tools, most of the analysis remains the work of the developer and is done manually. Our work focuses on alleviating this burden as much as possible from the developper hands. This section presents our approach for assessing the scalability of a multithreaded application and how a performance analysis tool can provide developers with optimisation hints. We implement this approach in SCALOMP, whose implementation details are described in Sect. 4.

3.1   Methodology

There are multiple sources of performance problems in OpenMP applications, such as load imbalance, or lock contention. Once the problem is identified, the developper may improve the performance of the application in several ways. Some issues require code changes, while changing the execution settings may fix some other problems. In this section, we describe a methodology for detecting performance problems in OpenMP applications, and providing optimization suggestions to the developper.

As an input, the developer provides a compiled version of the application, along with the command line that runs it. The application is instrumented and runs while varying the number of threads in order to measure the scalability of each parallel region and to detect performance problems. As a result, SCALOMP computes the parallel efficiency of each parallel region (defined by the speedup multiplied by the initial number of threads divided by the current number of threads), and estimates the potential time gain for each parallel region. The output is the list of parallel regions sorted according to the potential time gain, and for each region, a set of optimization hints and their respective potential time gain.

Using this approach, a developer can focus on optimizing the most promising parallel regions of his application. Moreover, the optimization hints indicate how the performance could be improved.

3.2   Scalability Analysis on Parallel Regions

The performance analysis of an application starts with a scalability analysis which aims at identifying the OpenMP parallel regions that may be worth optimizing. SCALOMP does this by running the application multiple times while automatically varying the number of threads across a range given as input. For each run, SCALOMP measures the duration of each parallel region. As a result, SCALOMP computes the parallel efficiency of all the regions and estimates the time lost in each by comparing their efficiency to the expected behaviour of a perfectly scalable region [7].

Thus, SCALOMP identifies the parallel regions where most time is lost and never underestimate a parallel region's impact due to not detecting its issues or wrongly quantifying their effects. These parallel regions are good candidates for optimizations: the poor scalability of a region means that some performance issues affects its parallel efficiency; and the significant amount of time lost means there is good hope of gaining back time by improving the region's performance.

3.3   Quantifying the Impact of Performance Problems

A poor parallel efficiency in an OpenMP parallel region may be caused by several types of problems. In this section, we describe some of these problems and how a performance analysis tool can estimate their impact on performance. As a result, it is possible to quantify the potential time gain for each problem in each parallel region.

Barriers. One of the main synchronization mechanisms in OpenMP is the barrier that allows threads to wait for each other. This synchronization may be explicit (when using the `omp barrier` directive), or implicit (e.g., at the end of a parallel for loop). While barriers allow developers to ensure the correctness of parallel programs, they introduce synchronization points that may degrade the parallel efficiency.

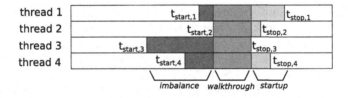

Fig. 1. Illustration of threads passing through an OpenMP barrier

As illustrated in Fig. 1, when a set of threads pass through an OpenMP barrier, three phases can be distinguished:

– the *imbalance phase* starts when the first thread enter the barrier, and ends when the last thread reaches the barrier. If a thread arrives late to a barrier, it delays the other threads. This means that the ideal case is when all the threads reach the barrier simultaneously. Hence the time lost by imbalance is the difference between the average time a thread took to reach the barrier from the last point of synchronization, and the maximum time. A long *imbalance phase* may be caused by an uneven work distribution between the threads, or by some delay that applies to a thread (such as a late MPI communication). If the imbalance is significant, SCALOMP suggests to improve the work distribution, for example by using a `schedule dynamic` clause in a parallel loop.
– the *walkthrough phase* starts when all the threads have reached the barrier and ends when the first thread leaves the barrier. We consider this phase to be the incompressible time spent resolving the barrier. This is an optimistic estimation since part of the barrier is resolved every time a thread arrives. If the walkthrough phase takes a significant part of the overall execution time, SCALOMP suggests to either reduce the number of OpenMP barriers, or to improve the barrier algorithm (for instance, by choosing a more performant OpenMP runtime)
– the *startup phase* starts when the first thread leaves the barrier and ends when the last thread leaves the barrier. The time lost from threads not leaving at the same time is paid at the next point of synchronization. For example if there is no imbalance in the work of threads between two barriers, some tools could detect differences in arrival times and report it as imbalance when the real culprit is the previous barrier delay when releasing threads. SCALOMP detects those delays and shifts the blame to the previous barrier runtime instead.

Locks. Locking is another major synchronization mechanism in OpenMP that may significantly impact the performance. As depicted in Fig. 2, the time spent acquiring a lock can be separated in two phases:

– the *waiting* phase happens when a thread tries to acquire a lock that is currently held by another thread. This phase corresponds to the contention that applies to the lock. To reduce the waiting phase, SCALOMP suggests to either change the application to reduce the number of concurrent access to this lock, or to use another locking mechanism that is less affected by contention (for instance MCS or AHMCS [10]).
– the *acquisition* phase happens when the lock is available. This phase corresponds to the incompressible time required for running the locking algorithm. A significant part of the whole execution spent in the acquisition phase means that the thread often acquires locks without contention. In that case, SCALOMP suggests to either reduce the number of calls to locking primitives, or to use another synchronization mechanism (such as the `atomic` directive or a locking mechanism that works better with no contention).

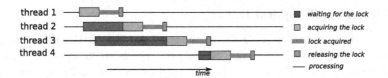

Fig. 2. Illustration of threads acquiring a lock

In order to estimate how much time is due to the contention, and to the lock algorithm, SCALOMP measures the time spent acquiring the lock and assumes that the fastest measured acquisition was contention free. This gives an estimate of the constant time required for executing the locking algorithm, and the remaining time is attributed to the contention on the lock.

4   Implementation

In order to compute the metrics described in Sect. 3, we implemented SCALOMP. In this section, we detail how SCALOMP instruments an OpenMP application, and how it measures the duration of OpenMP constructs without altering the application behavior.

4.1   Instrumenting an OpenMP Application with OMPT

As OpenMP relies on both compiler directives and a runtime API, instrumentation can be tedious. One solution consists in building a set of wrappers that intercept the calls to the OpenMP runtime API. However, this method is specific to one OpenMP implementation and it cannot grasp the whole OpenMP semantics. Opari [14] performs a source-to-source transformation on the application and inserts POMP calls in the source code. This makes this approach more portable, but it requires to recompile the application.

SCALOMP uses the OpenMP Tools interface (OMPT) that was introduced in the OpenMP 5.0 standard [11]. OMPT makes the OpenMP runtime collaborate with performance analysis tools: the tools register callbacks for OpenMP events, and the OpenMP runtime then triggers the callbacks when the corresponding events happen. With this approach, SCALOMP can collect performance data from any OpenMP application without recompiling it.

4.2   Identifying OpenMP Parallel Regions

An application may consist of tens of OpenMP parallel regions, some of them being invoked multiple times. Thus, SCALOMP needs to identify a parallel region in order to aggregate the performance data from multiple calls to it. When the application starts an OpenMP parallel region, the OMPT interface invokes SCALOMP through a callback and provides a pointer to the OpenMP call in the application binary. The first time SCALOMP encounter an unknown callsite, it uses *libbfd* to retrieve the line of code associated with this address.

4.3   Measuring Temporal Data

As described in Sect. 3, SCALOMP analysis of the OpenMP barriers requires to collect several OpenMP events: SCALOMP needs to know when a thread starts a region's work, enters at a barrier, exits a barrier and ends the region. The lock analysis also requires to collect information when a thread starts and stops acquiring a lock. For each of these events, SCALOMP records a timestamp using the TSC counter. These timestamps are then used for measuring various durations in the thread processing. The TSC counter allows SCALOMP to record timestamps at a low cost, but these timestamps cannot be compared accross threads running on different sockets. Thus, SCALOMP also records a system-wide timestamp using `clock_gettime` at the beginning of each region execution in order to compare different threads timestamps.

4.4   Mitigating Instrumentation Overhead with Adaptive Sampling

While recording a timestamp using the TSC counter is lightweight, this overhead may significantly alter the application's performance if timestamps are recorded too often. In order to reduce this overhead, SCALOMP uses a sampling mechanism. Since the OMPT interface allows to dynamically activate or de-activate callbacks, SCALOMP only collects performance data on certain executions of a parallel region. The idea is that while two executions of a region may not be exactly the same, their behaviour is essentially similar.

Depending on the parallel region, the sampling frequency should be selected carefully: if a parallel region is only repeated a few times, all its executions should be captured, whereas a region that runs many times should only be captured from time to time. Thus, SCALOMP uses an adaptive sampling where the first executions are all measured, and then as the region is repeated, SCALOMP de-activates the callbacks for some executions. The more a region is repeated, the more often SCALOMP de-activates the OMPT callbacks.

As a result, the rare regions are all captured, while frequent regions are sparsely captured, and the overhead of SCALOMP on the application execution remains low.

5   Experiments and Results

In this Section, we evaluate SCALOMP implementation and assess how the performance analysis can help the developper improve a parallel application. First, we evaluate the overhead of SCALOMP on 16 applications. Then, we evaluate how SCALOMP detects load imbalance problems, and lock contention issues.

For our evaluation, we use a machine equipped with two Intel Xeon Haswell E5-2698 v3 processors with 16 cores each (32 cores in total), and 128 GB of RAM. The machine runs Linux version 3.10, and the applications were compiled with Intel Compiler version 17.0.6. For OpenMP we use the open-source OpenMP runtime from Intel now maintained in LLVM. When compiling applications, we use the -O3 optimization level.

We evaluate SCALOMP using several OpenMP applications:

- **Mandelbrot** is an application that computes the Mandelbrot set;
- **HydroMM** is an hydrodynamics mini-application;
- **Lulesh 2.0** is a mini-application that performs an hydrodynamics simulation [13];
- **BT, CG, DC, EP, FT, IS, LU, MG, UA** are kernels from the OpenMP NAS Parallel Benchmarks version 3.3.1 [3];
- **miniFE** is a Finite Element mini-application [2];
- **Snap** is a particle transport mini-application [2];
- **AMG** is a parallel algebraic multigrid solver for linear systems [1];
- **Pennant** is a mini-application for hydrodynamics [1].

5.1 Overhead of SCALOMP

To evaluate the overhead of SCALOMP, we run the 16 applications described in Sect. 5 with and without SCALOMP. For each application, the problem size is chosen so that the reference time (i.e. the execution time when running without SCALOMP) is between 10 and 100 s with a few exception to see how scale affects the overhead. Each measurement is repeated 5 times and we report the average execution time. Table 1 reports the execution time when running the application without SCALOMP, and the overhead when running with SCALOMP.

Table 1. Overhead induced by the tool

Application	Mandelbrot	HydroMM	Lulesh2.0	BT.B	CG.C	DC.A	EP.D	FT.C	IS.D
Reference time	11.34 s	13.63 s	82.02 s	10.35 s	12.23 s	16.21 s	52.67 s	11.67 s	27.09 s
Overhead	2.24%	6.18%	12.34%	0.00%	0.03%	−0.27%	3.55%	−0.55%	−0.01%
Application	LU.C	LU.D	MG.D	UA.B	UA.D	miniFE	Snap	AMG	Pennant
Reference time	36.53 s	1352.66 s	88.06 s	12.61 s	1161.65 s	18.49 s	80.24 s	94 s	41.32 s
Overhead	−0.17%	0.14%	0.12%	13.78%	4.04%	2.24%	−0.64%	−1.03%	2.33%

The results show that SCALOMP has little impact on the performance of most applications. The overhead is higher for Lulesh (12.34%) because this application performs many small parallel regions; The observed overhead goes down to −4.31% if the size is increased to 120 (from 80) and the number of iteration lowered to 350 (from 1000) so that the time stay similar. UA.B also suffers from a significant overhead (13.78%) due to the heavy number of lock operations (8.1M locks per second per thread on average). When running UA with a larger problem size (class D), the application take locks less often and the SCALOMP's overhead is reduced to 4.04%. We conclude that SCALOMP does not significantly alter the application execution except in some extreme cases.

5.2 Detecting Imbalance Issues

SCALOMP reports that several of the applications evaluated in Sect. 5.1 suffer from load imbalance. In this section, we focus on two of these applications.

Mandelbrot. When running the **mandelbrot** application with 32 threads, SCALOMP reports that the parallel efficiency is only 42%. SCALOMP reports that the load imbalance between the threads in one parallel region is responsible for all of the lost time. It suggests to improve the load balancing for this parallel region, as it predicts a perfect load balance may save 5.37 s.

Based on this suggestion, we analyze the source code of this application. The incriminated parallel region computes the divergence of a set of complex numbers in the Mandelbrot set. The computation cost for each complex number depends on how fast it diverges. The default OpenMP scheduling policy assigns many numbers that diverge quickly to some threads while some other threads have to process many numbers that diverge slowly. As a result, some threads finish their loop iterations earlier than the other threads, leading to a load imbalance and a poor parallel efficiency. As suggested by SCALOMP, we change the scheduling policy for this parallel region to `dynamic`, and we observe that the application's execution time is reduced to 6.16 s. This means we gained 5.20 s which is close to the 5.37 predicted. When analyzing the parallel region with *dynamic* SCALOMP find the load balance to be 99.9% perfect.

HydroMM. When running HydroMM with 32 threads, SCALOMP reports that the parallel efficiency is only 51%, and reports that the load imbalance in one parallel region is responsible for 87% of the total lost time. SCALOMP suggests to improve the load balancing of this parallel region, it also predicts the performance of the application if this parallel region was perfectly load balanced.

Based on SCALOMP suggestion, we analyze the source code of HydroMM, and change the OpenMP scheduling policy to `dynamic` in order to improve the load balancing between the threads. Figure 3 reports the speedup measured for HydroMM when using the default scheduling policy (`static`) and when using the `dynamic` scheduling policy. It also reports the speedup predicted by SCALOMP. We observe that changing the scheduling policy significantly improves the application's performance. The results also show that up to 16 threads, the speedup obtained when applying SCALOMP suggestion is close to the predicted speedup.

For 32 threads, the predicted speedup is significantly overestimated. This may be due to memory effects being ignored by SCALOMP: up to 16 threads, all the threads execute on one socket of the machine, while when running 32 threads, the two sockets are used.

5.3   Detecting Locking Issues

In this section, we assess how SCALOMP detects locking issues using two applications. First, we evaluate how SCALOMP differentiates contended locks and non-contended locks using a micro-benchmark. Then, we present a case study on the UA kernel from the NAS Parallel Benchmarks. For both applications, we compare the optimization suggestions provided by SCALOMP with those obtained with Intel VTune [17].

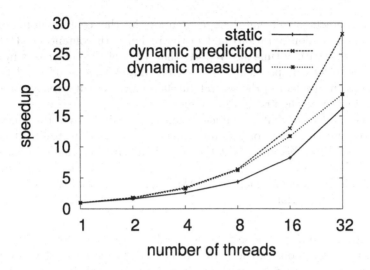

Fig. 3. Speedup obtained when running **HydroMM**

Micro-benchmark. We implemented an OpenMP application that consists in two parallel regions. In these parallel regions, each thread acquires an OpenMP lock, releases it, and busy waits for some time. In the first parallel region, each thread accesses a different lock which does not suffer from contention. In the second parallel region, all the threads access the same lock which suffers from contention. We choose the busy wait time so that the time spent acquiring lock is similar for both parallel region.

Table 2. Lock Micro-benchmark

		Without contention	With contention
	Total duration (s)	14.14	14.34
	Lock duration (s)	4.63 (32%)	4.35 (29.6%)
VTune	Overhead	2.61%	10.19%
	Lock contention	2.64 s (18.19%)	5.5 s (34.81%)
	Other problems	0.67 s (4.6%)	0.02 s (0.1%)
ScaLOMP	Overhead	4.00%	1.04%
	Lock duration	3.93 s (26.97%)	5.24 s (36.45%)
	- Lock algorithm	3.40 s (23.14%)	0.03 s (0.23%)
	- Lock contention	0.56 s (3.83%)	5.21 s (36.22%)

We run this micro-benchmark and analyze it with VTune and ScaLOMP. The results of this experiment are reported in Table 2. The time spent acquiring locks and the total duration of the two regions are similar.

VTune detects significant lock contention in the contention-free region (18.19% of the region duration) and in the region with contention (34.81% of the region duration). VTune also reports that 4.6% of the time spent in region 1 is lost due to "Other" problems. We conclude that VTune is able to detect the lock contention problem in the second parallel region, but it wrongfully detects a lock contention in the first parallel region.

SCALOMP detects that a significant time is spent in locks in the contention-free region, and that most of it is due to the lock algorithm itself. SCALOMP indicates that the problem is that the threads acquire too many locks. In the second parallel region, SCALOMP detects that most of the locking time is due to contention. We conclude that SCALOMP rightly identifies the lock problems in the two parallel regions.

Case Study: UA. In this section, we analyze UA and apply optimizations based on the suggestions provided by SCALOMP. Since one of these optimizations gives an incorrect result with the Intel Compilers, we use the GNU Compilers version 7.3.0 in this section.

When running UA.B, SCALOMP measures a parallel efficiency of 56% with 32 threads. One parallel region is responsible for most of the time loss because of several problems: 10% of the total execution time is lost due to load imbalance; and 19.4% of the total execution time is spent acquiring locks in this parallel region.

SCALOMP also points that 2 704 354 500 locks are acquired during the 8.68 s execution of this parallel region, meaning that on average, each thread acquires a lock every 102 ns. Due to a high number of region execution (more than 2000), SCALOMP automatically uses the sampling mechanism described in Sect. 4.4 and records the duration of only 16% of the all locks acquisition. As a result, the overhead induced by SCALOMP remains low, but SCALOMP still captures a significant amount of performance data.

SCALOMP reports that most of the time spent acquiring locks is due to the lockings algorithm, and contention on locks is low in this application. An analysis of UA source code shows that there are 334 600 differents locks, which limits the probability of a thread acquiring a lock that is already taken by another thread. Moreover, most of the locks are used for protecting simple instructions such as x = x + y.

Based on this analysis, we create two additional implementations of the application:

- **UA-Hint** uses the lock hint mechanism from OpenMP 5.0 and specifies that the locks are uncontended. This allows the OpenMP runtime to select the lock implementation that performs the best when there is no contention;
- **UA-Atomic** replaces the critical sections protected by locks with OpenMP atomic operations when possible.

We compare the performance of these two implementation with the UA-Default implementation. Figure 4 reports the speedup of the implementations as

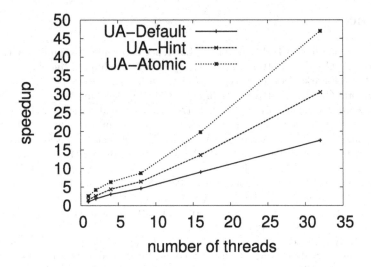

Fig. 4. Speedup obtained when running **UA**

compared to the execution time obtained when running UA-Default with one thread. As suggested by ScaLOMP, UA-Hint performs better than UA-Default in all cases (including in sequential) because the locking algorithm achieves better performance when the lock is uncontended. UA-Atomic outperforms UA-Default (by 267 on 32 threads) and UA-Hint (by 154 on 32 threads) for all the tested number of threads. This is due to the single atomic instruction that replaces a call to a locking function and the critical section.

We conclude that ScaLOMP suggests optimizations that may significantly improve the performance of an OpenMP application that suffers from locking problems.

6   Conclusion

Performance analysis of an application involves a lot of work from the developper. In this paper we presented a methodology that focuses on the scalability of an application in order to help the developer improve its performance. We implemented this approach in ScaLOMP that relies on the OMPT API to instrument OpenMP applications. The evaluation show that ScaLOMP collect performance data from applications with a low overhead. The experiments also show that ScaLOMP analysis successfully detect load imbalance problems, and locking problems in several applications. The optimization hints provided by ScaLOMP help the developer significantly improve the application's performance.

References

1. Coral-2 benchmarks. Technical report, Lawrence Livermore National Lab. (LLNL), Livermore, CA, USA. https://asc.llnl.gov/coral-2-benchmarks/index.php
2. Coral benchmarks. Technical report, Lawrence Livermore National Lab. (LLNL), Livermore, CA, USA. https://asc.llnl.gov/CORAL-benchmarks/
3. NAS parallel benchmarks applications (NPB). Technical report, NASA Advanced Supercomputing Division. https://www.nas.nasa.gov/publications/npb.html
4. Barthou, D., Rubial, A.C., Jalby, W., Koliai, S., Valensi, C.: Performance tuning of x86 OpenMP codes with MAQAO. In: Müller, M., Resch, M., Schulz, A., Nagel, W. (eds.) TTools for High Performance Computing 2009, pp. 95–113. Springer, Heidelberg (2010). https://doi.org/10.1007/978-3-642-11261-4_7
5. Bohme, D., Geimer, M., Wolf, F., Arnold, L.: Identifying the root causes of wait states in large-scale parallel applications. In: 2010 39th International Conference on Parallel Processing, pp. 90–100 (2010)
6. Calotoiu, A., Hoefler, T., Poke, M., Wolf, F.: Using automated performance modeling to find scalability bugs in complex codes. In: Proceedings of the International Conference on High Performance Computing, Networking, Storage and Analysis, p. 45 (2013)
7. Coarfa, C., Mellor-Crummey, J.M., Froyd, N., Dotsenko, Y.: Scalability analysis of SPMD codes using expectations. In: Proceedings of the 21th Annual International Conference on Supercomputing, ICS 2007, Seattle, Washington, USA, 17–21 June 2007, pp. 13–22 (2007)
8. Coulomb, K., Degomme, A., Faverge, M., Trahay, F.: An open-source tool-chain for performance analysis. Tools High Perform. Comput. **2011**, 37–48 (2012)
9. Ghane, M., Malik, A.M., Chapman, B., Qawasmeh, A.: False sharing detection in OpenMP applications using OMPT API. In: International Workshop on OpenMP, pp. 102–114 (2015)
10. Guerraoui, R., Guiroux, H., Lachaize, R., Quéma, V., Trigonakis, V.: Lock-unlock: is that all? A pragmatic analysis of locking in software systems. ACM Trans. Comput. Syst. (TOCS) **36**(1), 1 (2019)
11. Huck, K.A., Malony, A.D., Shende, S., Jacobsen, D.W.: Integrated measurement for cross-platform OpenMP performance analysis. In: DeRose, L., de Supinski, B.R., Olivier, S.L., Chapman, B.M., Müller, M.S. (eds.) IWOMP 2014. LNCS, vol. 8766, pp. 146–160. Springer, Cham (2014). https://doi.org/10.1007/978-3-319-11454-5_11
12. Iwainsky, C., et al.: How many threads will be too many? On the scalability of OpenMP implementations. In: Träff, J.L., Hunold, S., Versaci, F. (eds.) Euro-Par 2015. LNCS, vol. 9233, pp. 451–463. Springer, Heidelberg (2015). https://doi.org/10.1007/978-3-662-48096-0_35
13. Karlin, I., Keasler, J., Neely, J.: LULESH 2.0 updates and changes. Technical report, Lawrence Livermore National Lab. (LLNL), Livermore, CA, USA (2013)
14. Knüpfer, A., et al.: Score-P: a joint performance measurement run-time infrastructure for periscope, Scalasca, Tau, and Vampir. In: Brunst, H., Müller, M., Nagel, W., Resch, M. (eds.) Tools for High Performance Computing 2011, pp. 79–91. Springer, Heidelberg (2012). https://doi.org/10.1007/978-3-642-31476-6_7
15. Müller, M.S., et al.: Developing scalable applications with Vampir, Vampirserver and Vampirtrace. In: Parallel Computing (PARCO), vol. 15, pp. 637–644 (2007)

16. Putigny, B., Goglin, B., Barthou, D.: A benchmark-based performance model for memory-bound HPC applications. In: 2014 International Conference on High Performance Computing & Simulation (HPCS), pp. 943–950 (2014)
17. Reinders, J.: VTune performance analyzer essentials (2005)
18. Woodyard, M.: An experimental model to analyze OpenMP applications for system utilization. In: Chapman, B.M., Gropp, W.D., Kumaran, K., Müller, M.S. (eds.) IWOMP 2011. LNCS, vol. 6665, pp. 22–36. Springer, Heidelberg (2011). https://doi.org/10.1007/978-3-642-21487-5_3

A Framework for Enabling OpenMP Autotuning

Vinu Sreenivasan[1], Rajath Javali[1], Mary Hall[1(✉)], Prasanna Balaprakash[2],
Thomas R. W. Scogland[3], and Bronis R. de Supinski[3]

[1] University of Utah, Salt Lake City, UT 84103, USA
mhall@cs.utah.edu
[2] Argonne National Laboratory, Argonne, IL 60439, USA
[3] Lawrence Livermore National Laboratory, Livermore, CA 94550, USA

Abstract. This paper describes a lightweight framework that enables autotuning of OpenMP pragmas to ease performance tuning of OpenMP codes across platforms. This paper describes a prototype of the framework and demonstrates its use in identifying best-performing parallel loop schedules and number of threads for five codes from the PolyBench benchmark suite. This process is facilitated by a tool for taking a compact search-space description of pragmas to apply to the loop nest and chooses the best solution using model-based search. This tool offers the potential to achieve performance portability of OpenMP across platforms without burdening the programmer with exploring this search space manually. Performance results show that the tool identifies different selections for schedule and thread count applied to parallel loops across benchmarks, data set sizes and architectures. Performance gain over the baseline with default settings of up to 1.17×, but slowdowns of 0.5× show the importance of preserving default settings. More importantly, this experiment sets the stage for more elaborate experiments to map new OpenMP features such as GPU offloading and the new `loop` pragma.

Keywords: Autotuning · Loop scheduling · Performance portability

1 Introduction

OpenMP is an API which is used to explicitly direct thread-level, shared memory parallelism. By design, OpenMP programmers express parallelism with only modest changes to a sequential code through the addition of pragmas that are used by the compiler to map the code to a parallel platform. As all widely-used

This research was supported in part by the Exascale Computing Project (17-SC-20-SC), a joint project of the U.S. Department of Energy's Office of Science and National Nuclear Security Administration, and by the U.S. Department of Energy, Office of Science, Office of Advanced Scientific Computing Research, Scientific Discovery through Advanced Computing (SciDAC) program under the RAPIDS Subcontract Award Number 4000159989.

X. Fan et al. (Eds.): IWOMP 2019, LNCS 11718, pp. 50–60, 2019.
https://doi.org/10.1007/978-3-030-28596-8_4

compilers understand OpenMP pragmas and can generate parallel code, such an approach allows for a single source code that is *portable* across systems.

Achieving high parallel efficiency with OpenMP usually requires *prescriptive* pragmas that explicitly define the program behavior, specifying, for example, parallel schedules and number of threads to use. As pragmas become increasingly prescriptive, the advantage of cross-architecture portability decreases. Descriptive directives pass information about code semantics to the compiler to allow it to optimize without specifying how it might choose to do that. By leaving degrees of freedom in the mapping of OpenMP code, an application code can more readily adapt to different data sets and architectures.

We achieve this goal through the use of autotuning. Autotuning relies on empirical measurement to explore alternative implementations of a computation, and has been used in the HPC community to achieve performance portability across hardware platforms. In this work, we develop a tool we call a *pragma autotuner*, as the alternative implementations it evaluates involve alternative OpenMP pragmas. To manage the large search spaces that arise even with the limited experiment in this paper, our approach incorporates the Search using Random Forests (SuRF) framework, which creates a statistical model of the search space and constrains the time required for empirical measurement [8].

For this paper, we apply the pragma autotuner to the problem of scheduling parallel loops, designated as `#pragma omp parallel for` and equivalent. Even for such a limited experiment, the search space consists of how many threads to use, whether to use static or dynamic scheduling of loop iterations, and the chunk size which selects the granularity of the scheduling. For architectures with large numbers of cores, this search space can be quite large. Moreover, we envision such a tool will be much more necessary as recent features of OpenMP gain wider use, including GPU offload and the prescriptive `loop` construct which leaves the compiler significant freedom in mapping the code.

Related Work and Contribution. Autotuning on high-performance computing has been demonstrated as an important strategy for achieving performance portability across different architectures, starting with BLAS libraries PhiPAC [3] and ATLAS [11], early autotuning compilers [4] and generalizations to other scientific computing motifs [12]. A survey of autotuning for HPC can be found here [2]. The concept of autotuning OpenMP code is well-established and the most prevalent of these employ tuning to go beyond loop schedules, to look at parallel tasks, function inlining, and tuning for energy [5–7,10]. Most closely related to our paper, the work of Liao et al. performed autotuning of OpenMP loop schedules on SMG2000, examining a larger search space and achieving a speedup of more than 5× on 6 threads due to autotuning. However, prior work on autotuning OpenMP requires the use of specialized libraries or specific compilers, and would require more extensive adaptation as new OpenMP constructs are added. In contrast, this paper contributes a general framework that can be used to explore user-directed search spaces of any pragmas, even beyond OpenMP. The centerpiece of this work, a *pragma autotuner*, works with the C preprocessor to update the pragmas at marked locations in the code. In future work, such an approach could be fully automated using rewrite rules.

2   Search Space for Loop Scheduling

We illustrate the approach with a simple example, the main computation from the `atax` benchmark from PolyBench [9]. This computation has two parallel loops, one for initialization of the output vector, and the other nested loop to compute the result A*Ax.

```
#pragma omp parallel
{
  #pragma omp for
  for (i = 0; i < _PB_NY; i++)
    y[i] = 0;
  #pragma omp for private(j)
  for (i = 0; i < _PB_NX; i++) {
    tmp[i] = 0;
    for (j = 0; j < _PB_NY; j++)
      tmp[i] = tmp[i] + A[i][j] * x[j];
    for (j = 0; j < _PB_NY; j++)
      y[j] = y[j] + A[i][j] * tmp[i];
  }
}
```

The scheduling of the parallel loops uses default settings for the following three parameters:

- Number of threads to use
- Static vs. dynamic scheduling of loop iterations to threads
- Chunk size, which is the scheduling unit

Figure 1 shows the input to our framework that permits tuning based on these parameters for a 4-core desktop platform with a maximum of 8 threads. We use the Search using Random Forests framework to navigate the search space that arises from this specification.

3   Pragma Autotuner System Design

Figure 2 depicts the organization of the pragma autotuner, used to optimize OpenMP. It needs a configuration file which has the search space definition; for example, the loop scheduling parameters in Fig. 1(b). The original loop scheduling pragmas are replaced with the mapped pragmas. For each replacement pragma in the search space, a separate output OpenMP code file is generated.

```
#pragma omp parallel num_threads(#P2)
{
  #pragma omp for schedule(#P0, #P1)
  for (i = 0; i < _PB_NY; i++)
   y[i] = 0;
  #pragma omp for private (j) schedule(#P0, #P1)
  for (i = 0; i < _PB_NX; i++) {
    tmp[i] = 0;
    for (j = 0; j < _PB_NY; j++)
      tmp[i] = tmp[i] + A[i][j] * x[j];
    for (j = 0; j < _PB_NY; j++)
      y[j] = y[j] + A[i][j] * tmp[i];
  }
}
```

(a) Code with markers for autotuner.

```
problem.spec_dim(p_id=0, p_space=["static", "dynamic"], default="static")
problem.spec_dim(p_id=1, p_space=[1, 8, 16], default=1) # chunksize
problem.spec_dim(p_id=2, p_space=[1, 2, 4, 8], default=4) # threads
```

(b) Excerpt of parameter specification for **atax** example.

Fig. 1. Modified code to permit pragma autotuning (top) and search space specification (bottom).

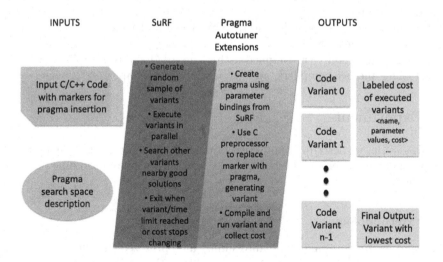

Fig. 2. System design of current pragma autotuner.

The tool also takes in a parameter list which maps different replacement policies to loops marked in the code.

One requirement for code modification of the autotuner is that it requires manual tagging of the beginning of a loop, which is used by the tool to parse the code and generate multiple code files with all combinations of pragmas. The C preprocessor then replaces this mark with the selection of pragmas identified through autotuning search. Then all the output files are executed to record the execution times of the modified loop. Based on the times a suggestion is made by the autotuner software regarding which pragma performs well.

The autotuner has a configuration file through which we can specify the path of the benchmark we want to run. The benchmark source file should have proper markers placed at the corresponding positions where we want to optimize the loops. Later, in the problem definition, we need to define the possible options for those markers using pragmas. We need to pass this problem definition with parameters, their possible values and default values to SuRF, which will return individual points in the search space to examine next.

The parser method in the autotuner then replaces the markers in the source file with the corresponding values received from the search tool and generates a new source file that will be saved in a temporary location in the experiment directory. Later, the generated source files are compiled and run with the options from the configuration file. Once the run has been completed, the execution time will be passed to SuRF as a cost measurement. Based on the execution time, SuRF will return the best combination suitable for the benchmark to run efficiently. To limit the overhead associated with autotuning, the system limits the time of the search, in the case of this paper to 10,000 s.

Sometimes we need an empty string for a parameter to indicate that the default values or no parallelization should be used. Therefore the autotuner supports the empty string parameter value. Whenever the value "None" has been returned from the search tool, the parser will replace it as an empty string in the final code generation.

The generated source is compiled with standard OpenMP compilers; we have tested clang and gcc compilers, and gcc is used in this paper.

4   Experiment

In this section, we describe a simple experiment to demonstrate the capability of the pragma autotuner and its ease of use. We revisit the loop scheduling problem from Sect. 2.

4.1   Methodology

Our goal is to determine via autotuning an optimized schedule (static or dynamic), a chunksize (1, 8 or 16 to coincide with a fully dynamic schedule or a cache line), and number of threads (1, 2, 4 or 8). We execute this experiment on a desktop platform, an Intel CORE i7-4770 with 4 Cores and 8 threads due to hyperthreading. We apply the system to five benchmarks from PolyBench shown in Table 1. This subset of benchmarks were chosen as representative of 1D, 2D and 3D loop nests, and all have OpenMP parallel for loops without reductions. We used two inputs to test adaptability, Default and Large. For each input, Table 1 provides the settings for Schedule, Chunk and Threads identified by the framework.

We have recently ported the system to a local cluster and are performing multi-node experiments where the evaluations can execute in parallel across nodes. This cluster has dual-socket, 28-core Intel Xeon Broadwell nodes. For this experiment, we show results for just `atax` and, use only the Large dataset, and set the default to 4 threads.

Table 1. PolyBench benchmarks used in this experiment.

Name	Selection (default)			Selection (large)		
	Sched	Chunk	Threads	Sched	Chunk	Threads
atax	dyn	8	4	stat	16	8
3 mm	stat	1	4	stat	1	8
convolution-2d	stat	16	4	stat	16	8
covariance	dyn	8	4	stat	1	8
correlation	dyn	8	4	stat	1	8

4.2   Performance Results

Figure 3(a) shows the results of the desktop system experiments, speedup over baseline for the five benchmarks and each of the two input data sets. We observe modest speedups for all benchmarks other than `convolution-2d`. The most significant speedups of 1.17× are for the long-running `correlation` benchmark. We believe the slowdown for `convolution-2d` is likely because we are not including the default chunksize in our search space.

Figure 3(b) shows speedups on the cluster system for just the large dataset and benchmark `atax`. As compared to a baseline using 4 threads, a speedup of over 3× is achieved, although as a result of 28 threads.

5   Future Work: From Descriptive to Prescriptive OpenMP

The above simple experiment shows modest performance gains, but we anticipate the true productivity advantage of the pragma autotuner will be to derive pragmas for more complex codes targeting the architectural diversity of current and future systems. This paper describes a work-in-progress as to applications

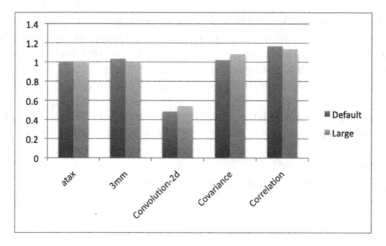

(a) Desktop system performance results.

Name	Selection (large)			Speedup
	Sched	Chunk	Threads	
atax	static	8	28	3.09×

(b) Cluster system initial performance results.

Fig. 3. Performance improvements over default Baseline schedule.

of the pragma autotuner. In this section, we detail an experiment we are design-ing to explore a search space for the `#pragma omp loop` that was introduced in OpenMP 5. This construct indicates to the OpenMP compiler that the loop's iterations are independent but leaves it to the discretion of the compiler writer to generate the most appropriate code. In an ongoing experiment, we wish to replace the descriptive `loop` pragma with prescriptive OpenMP pragmas that express how to optimize the loops. For example, we consider the following alter-natives:

- A parallel for loop, with the scheduling parameters from the previous section.
- For multi-dimensional loops, we might augment the parallel for loop with a `collapse` clause to assign multiple loop dimensions to a single thread dimen-sion.
- If our target architecture supports efficient `simd` execution, we might want to use the `pragma omp simd` directive.
- If our target architecture supports GPU offload, we might want to map coarse-grain loops to the GPU using the `pragma omp target` directive.

5.1   Case Study: 27-Point Stencil

Since `loop` is a new feature of OpenMP that is not even supported yet by the compilers used in our experiment, there do not currently exist benchmarks that use this construct. However, we note that a similar descriptive construct in OpenACC is the `#pragma acc independent` pragma. We found an example use of this pragma in the 27 point stencil code from the EPCC OpenACC Benchmark Suite [1]. Figure 4 shows the input code (once converted to use `loop`), and the autotuning search space used for the desktop system in the previous section. The same approach can be used to derive the best mapping of the code.

This more complex experiment has a number of challenges. We plan to explore how to compactly describe the search space, but the example in Fig. 4 illustrates the bulleted items in the above list absent the GPU offload since there is no GPU on our target desktop system.

5.2 Handling Errors

As search spaces become more complex, as in the previous example, SuRF may generate invalid pragma combinations, such as the following example. Here, the middle loop has a `collapse` clause, which has the effect of making the j and k loops into a single 1D loop. After `collapse` is applied, there is therefore no longer a k loop to execute using the `simd` construct. The OpenMP compiler will throw an error when it encounters this kind of combination.

```
for (iter = 0; iter < ITERATIONS; iter++) {
  #pragma omp parallel for
  for (i = 1; i < n+1; i++) {
    #pragma omp for collapse(2)
    for (j = 1; j < n+1; j++) {
      #pragma omp simd
      for (k = 1; k < n+1; k++) {
          <27pt stencil calculation goes here>
}}}}
```

For erroneous configurations, the tool must minimally check the exit code from the compiler and report to SuRF an execution time of `MAX_DBL` so that such configurations are avoided by the search. Ideally, we prefer to build configuration rules into the system to detect errors before generating the code and attempting the compilation. This encoding of OpenMP domain knowledge will increase the complexity of the tool implementation, but reduce the tuning time, and is the subject of future work.

5.3 Automation for Unmodified OpenMP Code

Because OpenMP has a fixed and limited collection of pragmas, we believe it is possible to derive a collection of standard rewrite rules for generating search spaces for pragmas that could automatically be explored for unmodified OpenMP codes. In this way, the user of the tool need not add the markers for the C preprocessor, but rather the tool parses the pragmas in the code to identify rewrite rules that may apply. If possible, this would greatly expand the users for OpenMP autotuning, and is an important area of future work.

```
for (iter = 0; iter < ITERATIONS; iter++) {
  // P0
  #pragma omp loop
  for (i = 1; i < n+1; i++) {
    // P1
    #pragma omp loop
    for (j = 1; j < n+1; j++) {
      // P2
      #pragma omp loop
      for (k = 1; k < n+1; k++) {
      a1[i*sz*sz+j*sz+k] = (
          a0[i*sz*sz+(j-1)*sz+k] + a0[i*sz*sz+(j+1)*sz+k] +
          a0[(i-1)*sz*sz+j*sz+k] + a0[(i+1)*sz*sz+j*sz+k] +
          a0[(i-1)*sz*sz+(j-1)*sz+k] + a0[(i-1)*sz*sz+(j+1)*sz+k] +
          a0[(i+1)*sz*sz+(j-1)*sz+k] + a0[(i+1)*sz*sz+(j+1)*sz+k] +
          a0[i*sz*sz+(j-1)*sz+(k-1)] + a0[i*sz*sz+(j+1)*sz+(k-1)] +
          a0[(i-1)*sz*sz+j*sz+(k-1)] + a0[(i+1)*sz*sz+j*sz+(k-1)] +
          a0[(i-1)*sz*sz+(j-1)*sz+(k-1)] +
          a0[(i-1)*sz*sz+(j+1)*sz+(k-1)] +
          a0[(i+1)*sz*sz+(j-1)*sz+(k-1)] +
          a0[(i+1)*sz*sz+(j+1)*sz+(k-1)] +
          a0[i*sz*sz+(j-1)*sz+(k+1)] + a0[i*sz*sz+(j+1)*sz+(k+1)] +
          a0[(i-1)*sz*sz+j*sz+(k+1)] + a0[(i+1)*sz*sz+j*sz+(k+1)] +
          a0[(i-1)*sz*sz+(j-1)*sz+(k+1)] +
          a0[(i-1)*sz*sz+(j+1)*sz+(k+1)] +
          a0[(i+1)*sz*sz+(j-1)*sz+(k+1)] +
          a0[(i+1)*sz*sz+(j+1)*sz+(k+1)] +
          a0[i*sz*sz+j*sz+(k-1)] + a0[i*sz*sz+j*sz+(k+1)]) * fac;
}}}}
```

(a) 27 point stencil input code.

```
problem.spec_dim(p_id=0, p_space=["None",
        "#pragma omp for schedule(#P3, #P4) nthreads(#P5)",
        "#pragma omp for schedule(#P3, #P4) collapse(#P6) nthreads(#P5)",
        ], default="#pragma omp for schedule(#P3, #P4) nthreads(#P5)")
problem.spec_dim(p_id=1, p_space=["None",
        "#pragma omp for schedule(#P3, #P4) nthreads(#P5)",
        "#pragma omp for schedule(#P3, #P4) collapse(#P6) nthreads(#P5)",
        ], default="#pragma omp for schedule(#P3, #P4) nthreads(#P5)")
problem.spec_dim(p_id=2, p_space=["None",
        "#pragma omp for schedule(#P3, #P4) nthreads(#P5)",
        "#pragma omp simd",
        ], default="#pragma omp simd")
problem.spec_dim(p_id=3, p_space=["static", "dynamic"], default="static")
problem.spec_dim(p_id=4, p_space=[1, 8, 16], default=1)
problem.spec_dim(p_id=5, p_space=[1, 2, 4, 8], default=1)
problem.spec_dim(p_id=6, p_space=[2,3], default=1)
```

(b) Customized search space for this code.

Fig. 4. 27-point stencil code input (top), and associated search space (bottom).

6   Conclusion

This paper has described a pragma autotuner that we have developed to ease the performance portability of OpenMP applications and reduce the programmer's burden of tuning their code as they migrate to the increasingly diverse hardware platforms, and support complex codes. We showed modest gains could be achieved using this system for loop scheduling parameters, and discussed how it could be extended to derive mappings for the new `#pragma omp loop` construct. As OpenMP's capabilities continue to expand to support a diversity of architectures, we believe autotuning will play an increasingly important role in achieving performance portability of current and future OpenMP codes.

References

1. EPCC OpenACC benchmark suite. http://www.epcc.ed.ac.uk/research/compu ting/performance-characterisation-and-benchmarking/epcc-openacc-benchmark-suite
2. Balaprakash, P., et al.: Autotuning in high-performance computing applications. Proc. IEEE **106**(11), 2068–2083 (2018). https://doi.org/10.1109/JPROC.2018. 2841200
3. Bilmes, J., Asanovic, K., Chin, C.W., Demmel, J.: Optimizing matrix multiply using PHiPAC: a portable, high-performance, ANSI C coding methodology. In: ACM International Conference on Supercomputing 25th Anniversary Volume, pp. 253–260. ACM, New York (2014). http://doi.acm.org/10.1145/2591635.2667174
4. Chen, C., Chame, J., Hall, M.: Combining models and guided empirical search to optimize for multiple levels of the memory hierarchy. In: International Symposium on Code Generation and Optimization, pp. 111–122, March 2005. https://doi.org/ 10.1109/CGO.2005.10
5. Katarzynski, J., Cytowski, M.: Towards autotuning of OpenMP applications on multicore architectures. CoRR abs/1401.4063 (2014). http://arxiv.org/abs/1401. 4063
6. Liao, C., Quinlan, D.J., Vuduc, R., Panas, T.: Effective source-to-source outlining to support whole program empirical optimization. In: Gao, G.R., Pollock, L.L., Cavazos, J., Li, X. (eds.) LCPC 2009. LNCS, vol. 5898, pp. 308–322. Springer, Heidelberg (2010). https://doi.org/10.1007/978-3-642-13374-9_21
7. Mustafa, D., Aurangzeb, A., Eigenmann, R.: Performance analysis and tuning of automatically parallelized OpenMP applications. In: Chapman, B.M., Gropp, W.D., Kumaran, K., Müller, M.S. (eds.) IWOMP 2011. LNCS, vol. 6665, pp. 151–164. Springer, Heidelberg (2011). https://doi.org/10.1007/978-3-642-21487-5_12
8. Nelson, T., et al.: Generating efficient tensor contractions for GPUs. In: 2015 44th International Conference on Parallel Processing, pp. 969–978, September 2015. https://doi.org/10.1109/ICPP.2015.106
9. Pouchet, L.N., Yuki, T.: Polybench/c 4.2. http://sourceforge.net/projects/ polybench/
10. Silvano, C., et al.: Autotuning and adaptivity in energy efficient HPC systems: the ANTAREX toolbox. In: Proceedings of the 15th ACM International Conference on Computing Frontiers, CF 2018, pp. 270–275. ACM, New York (2018). https:// doi.org/10.1145/3203217.3205338

11. Whaley, R.C., Dongarra, J.J.: Automatically tuned linear algebra software. In: Proceedings of the 1998 ACM/IEEE Conference on Supercomputing, SC 1998, pp. 1–27. IEEE Computer Society, Washington, DC (1998). http://dl.acm.org/citation.cfm?id=509058.509096
12. Williams, S.: Auto-tuning performance on multicore computers. Ph.D. thesis, University of California, Berkeley (2008)

Accelerators

HetroOMP: OpenMP for Hybrid Load Balancing Across Heterogeneous Processors

Vivek Kumar[1]([✉]), Abhiprayah Tiwari[1], and Gaurav Mitra[2]

[1] IIIT-Delhi, New Delhi, India
vivekk@iiitd.ac.in
[2] Texas Instruments, Houston, USA

Abstract. The OpenMP accelerator model enables an efficient method of offloading computation from host CPU cores to accelerator devices. However, it leaves it up to the programmer to try and utilize CPU cores while offloading computation to an accelerator. In this paper, we propose *HetroOMP*, an extension of the OpenMP accelerator model that supports a new clause `hetro` which enables computation to execute simultaneously across both host and accelerator devices using standard tasking and work-sharing pragmas.

To illustrate our proposal for a hybrid execution model, we implemented a proof-of-concept work-stealing HetroOMP runtime for the heterogeneous TI Keystone-II MPSoC. This MPSoC has host ARM CPU cores alongside accelerator Digital Signal Processor (DSP) cores. We present the design and implementation of the HetroOMP runtime and use several well-known benchmarks to demonstrate that HetroOMP achieves a geometric mean speedup of 3.6× compared to merely using the OpenMP accelerator model.

Keywords: OpenMP accelerator model ·
Heterogeneous architectures · Hybrid work-stealing

1 Introduction

Modern processor design relies heavily on heterogeneity to deliver high performance and energy-efficiency. As a result, contemporary High Performance Computing (HPC) systems are widely composed of accelerator devices alongside multi-core CPU processors. Popular accelerator devices include Graphics Processing Units [21] (GPU) and Field Programmable Gate Arrays [25] (FPGA), while more unconventional accelerators include Digital Signal Processors [17] (DSP). Such accelerators can be targeted using popular programming models such as Nvidia's CUDA [20] and Khronos OpenCL [19]. However, understanding how to use CUDA and OpenCL efficiently is non-trivial. The OpenMP 4.0 [2] accelerator model was introduced to address this issue. It provides a high-level, portable and compiler directive-based interface which aims to have a

© Springer Nature Switzerland AG 2019
X. Fan et al. (Eds.): IWOMP 2019, LNCS 11718, pp. 63–77, 2019.
https://doi.org/10.1007/978-3-030-28596-8_5

much smaller learning curve compared to both CUDA and OpenCL. The accelerator model is host-centric where the programmer designates regions of code to be offloaded from the host to an accelerator device while orchestrating a map/copy of input and output data for that region as required. The OpenMP compiler then generates accelerator specific low-level code and API calls into an OpenMP runtime environment which manages input data transfers between host and accelerator, launches compute kernels on the accelerator and transfers results back from the accelerator to the host. Although this approach enables high programmer productivity, a major limitation is that it does not target both host and accelerator devices simultaneously. While offloading code to an accelerator, the onus is on the programmer to manually partition the workload and run a computation on the host CPU cores.

Several factors affect the efficiency of manual partitioning: (i) the host and accelerator devices might have very different performance characteristics; (ii) there may be high communication latency between host and accelerator affecting partition granularity; and (iii) there may be several layers of parallelism in a compute kernel. These factors make manual partitioning an NP-hard problem. In most cases host CPU cores remain idle or busy-wait for accelerator cores to finish computation, thereby wasting CPU cycles and reducing energy-efficiency. OpenMP does not provide default support to best utilize both host and accelerator resources on a system. In this paper we target this limitation of the OpenMP accelerator model by focusing on two research questions:

RQ1: Without affecting programmer productivity, is it possible to extend the OpenMP accelerator model to identify computation suitable for hybrid execution over both host and accelerator device?

RQ2: Is it possible to design and implement a high-performance OpenMP runtime that could *dynamically* load balance computation across heterogeneous processing elements?

To address RQ1, we propose HetroOMP, an extension of the OpenMP accelerator model with a new clause "hetro". It enables execution of OpenMP task and parallel for loops simultaneously across both host and accelerator devices using compiler source-to-source translation. The critical focus on energy-efficiency has led the HPC community to consider low-power heterogeneous ARM SoC based embedded systems with various accelerators (GPU, DSP) on-chip as possible alternatives to conventional HPC systems. To address RQ2 we use such an embedded system, the Texas Instruments Keystone II [24] *Hawking* (K2H) Multi-Processor System-on-chip (MPSoC) which houses a quad-core ARM CPU and eight-core DSP accelerator on-chip.

We present the design of a novel, lightweight work-stealing [6] runtime implemented on K2H which enables high-performance load-balancing across both ARM and DSP cores. Several OpenMP tasking and **parallel for** benchmarks are used to compare the performance of the HetroOMP runtime to the default OpenMP device and host-only executions using the TI OpenMP runtime. We show that HetroOMP is highly competitive and can outperform default OpenMP. In summary, this paper makes the following contributions:

- HetroOMP, an extension to OpenMP accelerator model, which enables hybrid parallelism across host and accelerator device.
- A lightweight runtime implementation of HetroOMP that uses work-stealing for dynamic load-balancing across heterogeneous processing elements.
- Evaluation of HetroOMP on TI Keystone-II MPSoC by using several well-known tasking and **parallel for** benchmarks.

2   Related Work

OpenACC [26] is a directive-based programming model for Nvidia GPUs. OmpSs [10] extended the OpenMP task directives to the StarSs [22] programming model supporting kernel offloads for GPUs and FPGAs [10]. Chapman et al. [7] and Mitra et al. [18] presented implementations of OpenMP accelerator model for TI Keystone-II MPSoC. Mitra et al. further improved the OpenMP implementation for TI Keystone-II MPSoC [4] by presenting a framework that automatically addressed the parallelization of code annotated with OpenMP 4.0 directives. However, none of these implementations support dynamic load balancing across both host and accelerators.

There have been prior studies on hybrid execution across host and device. Luk et al. [16] presented a heterogeneous programming model that automatically partitioned loop level parallelism across host and GPU for hybrid execution. Barik et al. [5] presented another such hybrid programming model for CPU-GPU platforms. A common limitation in both these studies is that a prior training run of an application is mandatory to discover the optimal work partition ratio. Ozen et al. proposed extensions to OpenMP accelerator model to support hybrid execution across CPU and GPU. As GPUs are mostly suited for data-parallelism, their proposed extensions were tailored for work-sharing pragmas. Linderman et al. proposed a map-reduce based programming model for automatic distribution of computations across heterogeneous cores and evaluated it over a CPU-GPU based processor [15]. CnC-HC programming model [23] provided a work-stealing based dynamic load balancing across CPUs, GPUs and FPGAs. Kumar et al. [13] presented HC-K2H programming model for TI Keystone-II MPSoC that used a hybrid work-stealing runtime for dynamic load balancing across ARM and DSP cores (Sect. 3.2).

3   Background

3.1   TI Keystone-II MPSoC

Recent work [17] has considered the TI ARM/DSP K2H SoC for HPC workloads. It has 4 ARM Cortex-A15 cores running at up to 1.4 GHz and 8 TI C66x floating-point DSP cores running at up to 1.2 GHz. The ARM cores have 32 KB of L1 cache each and 4 MB of shared L2 cache while DSP cores can have 32 KB of L1 cache and 1 MB of L2 cache each. The ARM cores have hardware managed cache coherence, while the DSP cores do not. Additionally, there is no cache coherence between ARM and DSP cores. Both ARM and DSP cores share the same memory bus to off-chip DDR memory but have separate address spaces. The Multicore Shared Memory Controller in K2H provides 6 MB of shared scratchpad memory (SRAM) between ARM and DSP cores. The Multicore Navigator provides hardware queues (henceforth mentioned as *HardwareQueue*) that can be used to communicate and dispatch tasks between ARM and DSP cores. There are two queue managers with 8192 queues each and 64 descriptor memory regions per queue manager.

3.2   Hybrid Work-Stealing Methodology

We address RQ2 (Sect. 1) by implementing a hybrid work-stealing runtime. It shares characteristics with HC-K2H [13] which supported an async–finish [8] based parallel programming model. An async–finish program is represented as "finish{ async S1; S2 } S3;". Here, the async clause creates a task S1 that could run in parallel to task S2. Statement finish starts a finish scope and ensures both tasks S1 and S2 are completed before starting the execution of S3. HC-K2H supports the forasync loop-level parallelism construct which recursively divides a for loop's iterations into two halves with each recursion step being an async.

HC-K2H used a hybrid work-stealing runtime for dynamic load balancing of async tasks across ARM and DSP cores. Work-stealing is a very efficient strategy for distributing work in a parallel system and is implemented as shown in Fig. 1. It consists of a pool of threads, where each thread (*worker*) maintains a data structure (*deque*) to *push* the local set of *tasks* (from the *tail* end). When a worker becomes idle, it attempts to *pop* a task from the tail of its deque. If it fails to pop, then it becomes a *thief* and searches for a *victim* in the thread pool from which to *steal* a task (from the *head* end).

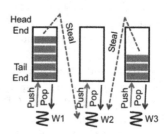

Fig. 1. Work-stealing implementation

This double ended software deque (henceforth mentioned as *CilkDeque*) was introduced by the Cilk language [11]. HC-K2H used a similar CilkDeque based work-stealing implementation for ARM cores (ARM_WS). As DSP cores do not support CilkDeque which could be accessed directly by any other DSP or ARM cores, HC-K2H used a separate work-stealing runtime for DSP cores (DSP_WS) that used HardwareQueue instead of CilkDeque. A HardwareQueue differs significantly from a CilkDeque as it is not double-ended and can be used only in two modes, either as a Last-In-First-Out (LIFO) queue or as a First-In-First-Out (FIFO) queue. DSP_WS uses the LIFO implementation of HardwareQueue where all three operations push, pop and steal happen only from the tail end. Whenever ARM or DSP workers go idle in HC-K2H, they first attempted an *intra-arch* steal before attempting an *inter-arch* steal. ARM workers can directly perform inter-arch steals from DSP worker's HardwareQueue. As DSP workers cannot

```
1 int *A /*size=N*/, *B /*size=N*/, *C /*size=N*/, N;
2 int cache_line = omp_cache_granularity();
3 int MIN_CHUNK = cache_line/sizeof(int);
4 main() {
5   int i;
6   #pragma omp target map(tofrom:C[0:N]) \
7       map(to:A[0:N], B[0:N], N)
8   #pragma omp parallel for firstprivate(A, B, C) \
9           private(i) schedule(hetro, MIN_CHUNK)
10  for(i=0; i<N; i++) {
11      C[i] = A[i] + B[i];
12  }
13 }
```

(a) Parallel vector addition in HetroOMP by using work-sharing pragma

```
1  int* A /*size=N*/, N;
2  int cache_line = omp_cache_granularity();
3  int MIN_CHUNK = cache_line/sizeof(int);
4  void msort(int left, int right) {
5    if(right-left > MIN_CHUNK) {
6      int mid = left+(right-left)/2;
7      #pragma omp task untied \
8          firstprivate(left, mid) hetro(A:N)
9      msort(left, mid);
10     msort(mid+1, right);
11     #pragma omp taskwait
12     merge(left, mid, right);
13   } else {
14     sequentialSort(left, right);
15   }
16 }
17 main() {
18   #pragma omp target map(to:N) \
19       map(tofrom:A[0:N])
20   #pragma omp parallel \
21       firstprivate(A,N) hetro
22   #pragma omp single
23   msort(0, N-1);
24 }
```

(b) Parallel recursive MergeSort in HetroOMP by using tasking pragma

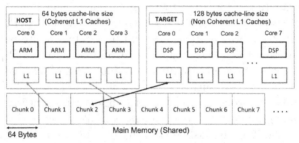

(c) Example of false sharing happening across ARM and DSP cores during a hybrid execution. ARM cache line size is 64 bytes whereas for DSP it is 128 bytes. Cache write back from DSP can overwrite the results calculated by ARM unless ARM also operates on 128 bytes cache line granularity.

Fig. 2. HetroOMP programming model. Underlined code in Figs. 2(a) and (b) are HetroOMP specific code in standard OpenMP.

access ARM's CilkDeque, a shared HardwareQueue was used by ARM workers to offer tasks to DSP workers for inter-arch stealing.

4   HetroOMP Programming Model

HetroOMP addresses RQ1 (Sect. 1) by extending the OpenMP accelerator model with a new clause, hetro, which can be used to perform hybrid execution of computation kernels with work-sharing and tasking pragmas. Figure 2 shows usage of the hetro clause in two different OpenMP programs, a parallel for based vector addition in Fig. 2(a), and task-based parallel divide-and-conquer implementation of MergeSort in Fig. 2(b). HetroOMP specific code in both these examples has been underlined. Removing the HetroOMP code will leave a valid OpenMP 4.0 program that simply offloads computation to the accelerator. Clause hetro could be used in three different ways: (a) as a clause to pragma omp parallel

indicating the scope of hybrid execution, (b) as a parameter to `schedule` clause
in `pragma omp for`, with an optional chunk size showing hybrid execution of
loop iterations, and (c) as a clause to `pragma omp task` along with the name
and count of all writable type shared variables in this task, e.g., "`Var1:Count1,
Var2:Count2, ..., VarN:CountN`" (detailed explanation in Sect. 6.2).

False sharing is a well-known performance bottleneck in shared memory
parallel programs. However, it can also affect the correctness of a HetroOMP
program. This could happen due to differences in cache line sizes and cache
coherency protocols across host and accelerator. To understand this, consider
Fig. 2(c) that represents the execution of a HetroOMP program shown in
Fig. 2(a) with a chunk size of 16 instead of MIN_CHUNK. The total number of
chunks (tasks) generated would be N/16 with each chunk 64 bytes in size. ARM
cores (host) on K2H are cache coherent with L1 cache line size of 64 bytes,
whereas DSP cores (device) are not cache coherent and have L1 cache line size
of 128 bytes. Cache coherent ARM cores compute Chunk1 and Chunk3 with
results automatically written back to the main memory. Chunk2 is calculated
later by a DSP core, and explicit write-back of L1 cache is performed for the
result to appear on main memory. However, this 128 byte write-back could possibly corrupt the result of either Chunk1 or Chunk3. HetroOMP programmers
can resolve this either by using chunk size in multiples of 32 (128 bytes) or by
padding the result C vector such that each chunk is of size 128 bytes (or it's
multiple). HetroOMP provides a new API `omp_get_min_ganularity` to calculate the cache line granularity. Programmers can follow conventional task cutoff
techniques for controlling the task granularity of compute-bound programs that
does not depend on MIN_CHUNK (e.g., `Fib` in Sect. 7).

5 Design of HetroOMP Runtime

5.1 Limitations of HardwareQueue

Recall from Sect. 3.2, HC-K2H uses HardwareQueue for implementing DSP_WS
where all three operations, push, pop and steal happen at the tail end (LIFO).
In spite of design simplicity, such a HardwareQueue based work-stealing runtime
suffers from two subtle issues unlike the CilkDeque: (a) load imbalance among
DSP cores leading to frequent steals, and (b) cache write-back and invalidation
operation (henceforth mentioned as *CacheWBInv*) at *every* end finish scope.

CilkDeque is designed to support push and pop operations from the tail end
(LIFO) and stealing operations from the head end (FIFO). LIFO accesses by vic-
tims improves locality whereas FIFO accesses by thieves reduce load imbalance
(frequent steals). In regular divide-and-conquer applications, older tasks (available on the head) are more computationally intensive than the recently created
tasks (available on tail). Hence, stealing from FIFO end will execute a more significant chunk of computation than from LIFO end. However, HardwareQueue
based DSP_WS in HC-K2H lacked this benefit as both victim and thief workers
operated from the same side, thereby leading to frequent steals.

The other limitation of HardwareQueue based DSP_WS is mandatory CacheW-BInv at every end finish scope. Recall, HardwareQueue is directly accessible to all ARM and DSP cores. Due to this some of the async tasks generated within a finish scope can execute at cache coherent ARM cores while some of them could execute at cache incoherent DSP cores. As task owner (DSP) itself is cache incoherent, they cannot discover that an async task was stolen unless they perform explicit CacheWBInv at every end finish scope. This is a costly operation that won't affect the performance of flat finish based kernels (e.g., parallel for) but can significantly hamper the performance of task parallelism based applications containing nested finish scopes.

5.2 Private Deque Based DSP_WS

HetroOMP has been designed considering two main factors (a) CacheWBInv is not required at every end finish scope but it should be done only when a steal happens between two cache-incoherent processors under a finish scope, and (b) DSP_WS can reap the benefits of work-stealing only if it also allows steal operations from its head end (FIFO) and push/pop from its tail end (LIFO). These two factors are accounted in HetroOMP by using a *private deque* [3] (henceforth mentioned as *PvtDeque*) based implementation of DSP_WS instead of HardwareQueue. Acar et. al. originally introduced PvtDeque but in the context of reducing the overheads associated with memory fence operations in CilkDeque. PvtDeque differs from CilkDeque only in terms of steal operation as it doesn't allow a thief to steal a task directly. The thief has to make an entry in the *communication cell* hosted by a victim which keeps checking this communication cell during its push and pop operations. If they notice a waiting thief, they steal a task (on the thief's behalf) from the head end (FIFO) of its PvtDeque and then transfer it to the thief. For implementing a PvtDeque for each DSP core in HetroOMP, we reconfigured the default 1 MB L2 cache available to each DSP such that 512 KB remained as L2 cache and the rest as un-cached SRAM containing the PvtDeque.

6   Implementation of HetroOMP Runtime

6.1   Source-to-Source Translation of a HetroOMP Program

We extended the OpenMP-to-X [12] framework, such that it can perform source-to-source translation of HetroOMP code into a C program with calls to the HetroOMP runtime. OpenMP-to-X uses Clang LibTooling [1] and was designed to perform source-to-source translation of an OpenMP program into a HClib [14] program. Figure 3 shows the result of this source-to-source translation for the program shown in Fig. 2(b). The underlined code in Fig. 3 demonstrates the modifications to default HC-K2H program to support the HetroOMP runtime API calls. Translation of HetroOMP to C code begins from the main method. Pragma target map (Fig. 2(b), Line 18) gets replaced with an API call for variable initialization at DSP (Fig. 3, Line 43). The tofrom and to clauses are ignored as

```
 1  int* A /*size=N*/, N;                         24   /*end current finish scope*/
 2  int cache_line = DSP_CACHE_LINE; //128 bytes  25     while(finish->pendingAsyncs>0) {
 3  int MIN_CHUNK = cache_line/sizeof(int);       26       if(tasks_on_my_deque()>0) {
 4  void msort(int left, int right) {             27         help_incoherentCore_steal();
 5   if(right-left > MIN_CHUNK) {                  28         pop_and_execute();
 6    int mid = left+(right-left)/2;               29       }
 7    /*start new nested finish scope*/            30       else steal_and_execute();
 8    finish=allocate();                           31     }
 9    setup_current_finish(finish);                32     if(finish->incoherentCoreSteals) {
10    finish->writable_vars(A, sizeof(int)*N);     33       cacheWbInv(finish->get_writable_vars());
11    finish->incoherentCoreSteals=false;          34     }
12    /*launch task*/                              35     setup_current_finish(finish->parent);
13    task=create_task(msort, left, mid);          36     /*continue seqential execution*/
14    if(ARM) {                                    37     merge(left, mid, right);
15      push_CilkDeque(task);                      38   } else {
16    }                                            39     sequentialSort(left, right);
17    if(DSP) {                                    40   }
18      push_PrivateL2Deque(task);                 41  }
19      help_incoherentCore_steal();               42  main() {
20    }                                            43    initialize_at_DSP_device(A, N);
21    ATOMIC(finish->pendingAsyncs++);             44    hybrid_execution(true);
22    /*this will create nested async-finish*/     45    msort(0, N-1);
23    msort(mid+1, right);                         46  }
```

Fig. 3. Source-to-source translation of HetroOMP program shown in Fig. 2(b). All underlined code are the changes in HC-K2H runtime code to support HetroOMP.

data does not need to be copied between host and accelerator device as shared DDR memory between ARM and DSP is being utilized. Clause `hetro` on pragma `parallel` (Fig. 2(b), Line 12) indicates hybrid execution across host and accelerator (Fig. 3, Line 44). Without the `hetro` clause DSP-only offload will occur. The translation of code in Fig. 2(a) happens in a similar fashion. The only difference being, the pragma `parallel for` will be converted to a `forasync` API with chunk size `MIN_CHUNK` to avoid false sharing.

In this prototype implementation of the HetroOMP translator, a naive approach toward source code translation for pragma `task` and pragma `taskwait` is adopted. The pragma `task` is replaced with an `async` creation (Fig. 3, Lines 13–21) and pragma `taskwait` is replaced with an end finish scope (Fig. 3, Lines 25–35). In order to decide when to generate the start finish scope, a boolean flag is used. It is set to true at pragma `parallel` (Fig. 2(b), Line 20). After this when the translator encounters a pragma `task` (Fig. 2(b), Line 7), it will first generate a start finish scope (Fig. 3, Lines 8–11) followed by an `async` creation. The boolean flag is then set to false. Any further pragma `task` will then be translated to an `async` only. This flag is reset to true again at pragma `taskwait` (Fig. 2(b), Line 11).

6.2 HetroOMP Code Flow

In Fig. 3, the call to recursive `msort` method first creates a `finish` object at Line 8. This `finish` object then stores the pointer to its parent `finish` (Line 9), and the list of writable type shared variables under this `finish` scope (Line 10). These writable type shared variables are the ones indicated by the user in the `hetro` clause to pragma `omp task` (Fig. 2(b), Line 8).

HetroOMP has a boolean counter `incoherentCoreSeals` at each finish (Fig. 3, Line 11) for tracking when CacheWBInv is required at the end finish scope. ARM cores in HetroOMP directly push a task to CilkDeque (Line 15). HC-K2H did it differently as in that case ARM cores pushed few tasks to shared HardwareQueue in advance for DSPs to steal. Delaying it until an actual steal request from DSP helps HetroOMP understand the finish scope from where a task went to a cache incoherent core. A DSP core in HetroOMP first pushes a task to the tail of its PvtDeque (Line 18) and then executes the method help_incoherentCore_steal to transfer a task to any waiting thief (Line 19). At the end finish scope both ARM and DSP cores find and execute tasks until there are no more pending under this finish scope (Line 25). If tasks are available on local deque then while inspecting, both ARM and DSP workers in HetroOMP first execute the method help_incoherentCore_steal (Line 27) for transferring a task to any waiting thief followed by popping a task for self-execution (Line 28). Each DSP in HetroOMP has a dedicated HardwareQueue based communication cell where a thief (ARM/DSP) can indicate its steal request. Another Hardware-Queue is shared between ARM and DSP where an ARM core can push a task for DSPs to steal. For transferring a task to a waiting thief (at an incoherent core), a DSP can steal a task from the head of its PvtDeque and then move it to waiting thief (ARM/DSP), whereas an ARM worker steals a task from the head of its CilkDeque and pushes it to shared HardwareQueue (for DSP). As a thief receives a task from the head end of either of the deques, the number of steals can be reduced between cache incoherent workers. Whenever a core transfers a task via help_incoherentCore_steal, it will first perform a CacheWBInv followed by updating the counter incoherentCoreSeals in the current finish as true. For stealing, each core first attempts an intra-arch steal followed by an inter-arch steal upon failing (Line 30). Once out of the spin loop but before ending current finish scope, both ARM and DSP will do a CacheWBInv for all writable type shared variables (Line 33) based on the status of incoherentCoreSeals (Line 32). This technique avoids costly cache flushes in HetroOMP at every end finish scope.

7 Experimental Methodology

Across all experimental evaluations two broad categories of OpenMP benchmarks were used: (a) recursive divide-and-conquer applications that used nested task and taskwait pragmas, and (b) applications using parallel for loop pragmas. Each of these benchmarks is described in Table 1. We have chosen only those benchmarks where it was straightforward to remove false sharing between ARM and DSP either by loop tiling, by padding of shared data structures, or by altering task granularity. Padding was only applied as last strategy.

Five different versions of each benchmark were used: (a) OpenMP ARM-only implementation that runs only on ARM cores, (b) OpenMP DSP-only implementation that runs only on DSP cores, (c) HetroOMP version that uses the hetro clause but supports all 3 configurations (ARM-only, DSP-only, and Hybrid), (d) HC-K2H version that also supports all 3 configurations similar to HetroOMP, and (e) Sequential ARM implementation that executes on ARM and is obtained

Table 1. Benchmarks used for the evaluation of HetroOMP

Name	Description	Common settings	Source	OpenMP category
Fib	Calculate Nth Fibonacci number	N = 40. Task cutoff at N = 20	HC-K2H [13]	Tasking
Matmul	Multiplication of two matrices	Size = 1024 × 1024. Task cutoff at 6xMIN_CHUNK	Cilk [11]	Tasking
Knapsack	Solves 0–1 knapsack problem using branch and bound technique	N = 500 and capacity = 20000. Task cutoff at depth = 10	Cilk	Tasking
MergeSort	Merge sort algorithm	Array size = 4096 × 4096. Task cutoff at 4xMIN_CHUNK	Authors	Tasking
Heat	Heat diffusion using Jacobi type iterations	nx = 8192, ny = 2048 and nt = 10. Task cutoff at MIN_CHUNK	Cilk	Tasking
BFS	Breadth first search algorithm	Input as graph4M.txt. Chunks = 512 (first parallel for) and Chunks = 4192 (second parallel for)	Rodinia [9]	Parallel for
Hotspot	Iterative thermal simulation	grid_rows = grid_cols = 4096, sim_time = 10, temp_file = temp_4096, power_file = power_4096. Chunks = 1	Rodinia	Parallel for
Srad	Diffusion method based on partial differential equations	rows = cols = 4096, y1 = x1 = 0, y2 = x2 = 127, lambda = 0.5, iterations = 2. Chunks = 1	Rodinia	Parallel for
LUD	Decomposes a matrix as the product of a lower triangular matrix and an upper triangular matrix	Matrix dimension = 4096 and block size = 64. Chunks = 1	Rodinia	Parallel for
B+Tree	Similar to binary search tree but each node can have up to n − 1 keys instead of just two	file = mil.txt and command = command2.txt. Chunks = 32	Rodinia	Parallel for

by removing all OpenMP pragmas. For all three configurations (ARM-only, DSP-only, and Hybrid) the measurements are reported using all available cores under that configuration, i.e., ARM-only uses all 4 ARM cores, DSP-only uses all 8 DSP cores, and Hybrid uses all 12 cores (4 ARMs and 8 DSPs). Task cutoff in tasking type and total chunks in parallel for type benchmarks were chosen such that they achieved the best performance in each of the four parallel versions. A `static` schedule was used in both OpenMP multicore and accelerator model variants of each benchmark as it delivered the best performance. Each of the five implementations was executed ten times and we report the mean of the execution time, along with a 95% confidence interval. To generate ARM binaries, the ARM Linaro gcc compiler version 4.7.3 was used with these flags: `-O3 -mcpu=cortex-a15 -mfpu=vfpv4 -mfloat-abi=hard -fopenmp`. To generate DSP binaries with OpenMP, the TI CLACC OpenMP Accelerator Model Compiler version 1.2.0 was used with these flags: `--hc=''-O3 -fopenmp -marm -mfloat-abi=hard'' --tc=''-O3''`. To generate DSP binaries for HC-K2H and HetroOMP the TI C66x compiler *cl6x* version 8.0.3 was used with flags: `abi=eabi -mv6600 -op3 -ma multithread -O3`.

8 Experimental Evaluation

8.1 Total Number of Steals in PvtDeque v/s HardwareQueue

In Sect. 5 we described our choice of PvtDeque based implementation for DSP_WS in HetroOMP. It is basically for reducing load imbalance between DSP workers by supporting FIFO steal operations. In this section the benefit of this approach is illustrated. For each benchmark, we calculated the total number of steals during DSP-only execution across both HC-K2H and HetroOMP runtimes. The ratio between the result obtained for

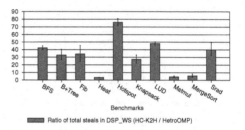

Fig. 4. Total number of `DSP-only` steals in HC-K2H normalized to HetroOMP

HC-K2H and that of HetroOMP is then measured. Results of this experiment are shown in Fig. 4. We can observe that the total number of steals among DSP workers in HC-K2H is 76× (`Hotspot`) to 4.5× (`MergeSort`) of that in HetroOMP. The reason for this wide variation is task granularity as there are always lesser number of steals for coarse granular tasks than fine granular tasks. Both HetroOMP and HC-K2H execute a `parallel for` loop in a recursive divide-and-conquer fashion. Hence, for both tasking and `parallel for` type benchmarks, FIFO steals based PvtDeque displace a significant chunk of computation unlike the LIFO steal based HardwareQueue implementation inside HC-K2H.

8.2 Performance Analysis

In this section, we describe the performance of HetroOMP on K2H. For this study, all three versions of each benchmark (HetroOMP, HC-K2H, and OpenMP) were executed, first by using all four ARM cores only (`ARM-only`), and then by using all eight DSP cores only (`DSP-only`). Apart from this, hybrid execution

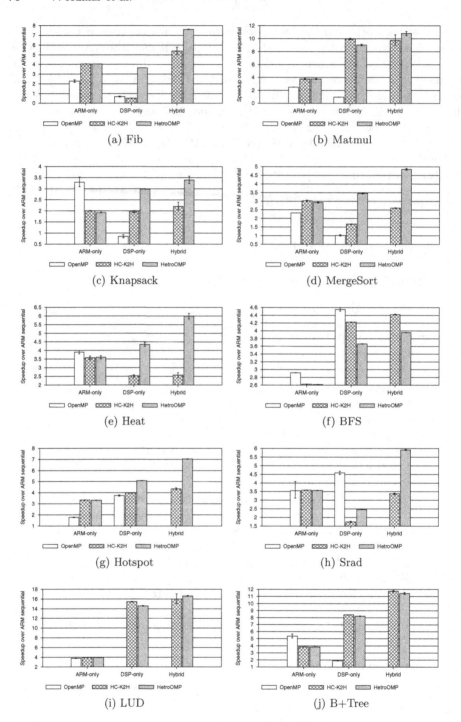

Fig. 5. Speedup over sequential execution at ARM. Benchmarks in (a)–(e) are of tasking type whereas those in (f)–(j) are `parallel for` type.

of HetroOMP and HC-K2H implementations was also performed across all four ARM and eight DSP cores (`Hybrid`). The speedup was then calculated for each execution (`ARM-only`, `DSP-only`, and `Hybrid`) over Sequential execution on ARM core. Results of this experiment are shown in Fig. 5. OpenMP's `DSP-only` execution of `Heat` and `LUD` did not complete due to which the results of these experiments are missing in Figs. 5(e) and (i).

Tasks Based Benchmarks: Figures. 5(a)–(e) show the experimental results for tasking benchmarks. These benchmarks recursively spawn and synchronize on asynchronous tasks similar to `MergeSort` implementation shown in Fig. 2(b). We can observe that due to the reduced number of steals in `DSP_WS` and due to the reduced number of CacheWBInv operations, HetroOMP outperformed HC-K2H for both `DSP-only` and `Hybrid` executions. `Matmul` is an outlier as its performance with both these runtimes are in the same ballpark. This is due to high steal ratio in `Matmul`, unlike all other benchmarks. It was found to be around 65% for `DSP-only` and `Hybrid` execution in both these runtimes. `ARM_WS` implementation is similar across HetroOMP and HC-K2H resulting in identical performance. `Hybrid` execution of HetroOMP always outperformed `ARM-only` and `DSP-only` based OpenMP executions (except `Knapsack`).

Parallel for Type Benchmarks: Figures 5(f)–(j) show the experimental results for `parallel for` benchmarks. `ARM-only` execution is again identical across both HetroOMP and HC-K2H (explained above). For `DSP-only` and `Hybrid` executions, HetroOMP performance relative to HC-K2H was in the range $0.86\times$–$1.7\times$ (higher is better). In spite of the benefits of FIFO steals, PvtDeque also has a limitation that it performs slightly weak for coarse granular tasks. It is because the victim is not able to quickly respond to a steal request while executing coarse granular tasks compared to fine granular tasks. Also, due to an implicit barrier at the end of `pragma omp for`, these benchmarks are of flat `finish` type, i.e., a single level of task synchronization. Optimizations for reducing CacheWBInv in HetroOMP are suitable only for nested `finish` type benchmarks and hence are not enabled during the execution of flat `finish` benchmarks. Here too `Hybrid` execution of HetroOMP always outperformed `ARM-only` and `DSP-only` based OpenMP executions. `BFS` is an outlier as even with bigger chunk sizes (see Table 1), both HC-K2H and HetroOMP incurred tasking overheads due to the largest number of tasks (around 120 K while the average number across five benchmarks was 53K). Unlike HC-K2H and HetroOMP, OpenMP executions used `static` schedule where tasks are statically assigned to the threads. Overall, HetroOMP and HC-K2H obtained a geometric mean speedup of $3.6\times$ and $2.6\times$ respectively over `DSP-only` OpenMP execution.

9 Conclusion and Future Work

In this paper, we studied the limitations of the OpenMP accelerator model by using a heterogeneous MPSoC. We demonstrated that for achieving optimal performance, it is essential to utilize the computing power of all the processing elements instead of solely using the accelerator. We proposed extensions to the standard OpenMP accelerator model to enable simultaneous execution across both host and accelerator devices. We presented and evaluated a novel hybrid work-stealing runtime for OpenMP that efficiently executed computation across all processing elements of a heterogeneous SoC and outperformed standard OpenMP accelerator model. As a future work, we aim to extend HetroOMP with energy efficient execution capabilities.

Acknowledgments. We are grateful to the anonymous reviewers for their suggestions on improving the presentation of the paper, and to Eric Stotzer from Texas Instruments for shipping a brand new TI Keystone-II MPSoC to IIIT Delhi.

References

1. Clang LibTooling, April 2019. https://clang.llvm.org/docs/LibTooling.html
2. OpenMP API, version 4.5, March 2018. http://www.openmp.org/wp-content/uploads/openmp-4.5.pdf
3. Acar, U.A., Chargueraud, A., Rainey, M.: Scheduling parallel programs by work stealing with private deques. In: PPoPP, pp. 219–228 (2013). https://doi.org/10.1145/2442516.2442538
4. Aguilar, M.A., Leupers, R., Ascheid, G., Murillo, L.G.: Automatic parallelization and accelerator offloading for embedded applications on heterogeneous MPSoCs. In: DAC, pp. 49:1–49:6 (2016). https://doi.org/10.1145/2897937.2897991
5. Barik, R., Farooqui, N., Lewis, B.T., Hu, C., Shpeisman, T.: A black-box approach to energy-aware scheduling on integrated CPU-GPU systems. In: CGO, pp. 70–81 (2016). https://doi.org/10.1145/2854038.2854052
6. Blumofe, R.D., Leiserson, C.E.: Scheduling multithreaded computations by work stealing. J. ACM **46** (1999). https://doi.org/10.1145/324133.324234
7. Chapman, B., Huang, L., Biscondi, E., Stotzer, E., Shrivastava, A., Gatherer, A.: Implementing OpenMP on a high performance embedded multicore MPSoC. In: IPDPS, pp. 1–8 (2009). https://doi.org/10.1109/IPDPS.2009.5161107
8. Charles, P., Grothoff, C., Saraswat, V., et al.: X10: an object-oriented approach to non-uniform cluster computing. In: OOPSLA, pp. 519–538 (2005). https://doi.org/10.1145/1094811.1094852
9. Che, S., Boyer, M., Meng, J., Tarjan, D., Sheaffer, J.W., Lee, S.H., Skadron, K.: Rodinia: a benchmark suite for heterogeneous computing. In: IISWC, pp. 44–54 (2009). https://doi.org/10.1109/IISWC.2009.5306797
10. Duran, A., Ayguadé, E., Badia, R.M., Labarta, J., Martinell, L., Martorell, X., Planas, J.: OmpSs: a proposal for programming heterogeneous multi-core architectures. Parallel Process. Lett. **21**(02), 173–193 (2011). https://doi.org/10.1142/S0129626411000151
11. Frigo, M., Leiserson, C.E., Randall, K.H.: The implementation of the Cilk-5 multithreaded language. In: PLDI, pp. 212–223 (1998)
12. Grossman, M., Shirako, J., Sarkar, V.: OpenMP as a high-level specification language for parallelism. In: IWOMP, pp. 141–155 (2016). https://doi.org/10.1007/978-3-319-45550-1_11

13. Kumar, V., Sbîrlea, A., Jayaraj, A., Budimlić, Z., Majeti, D., Sarkar, V.: Heterogeneous work-stealing across CPU and DSP cores. In: HPEC, pp. 1–6 (2015). https://doi.org/10.1109/HPEC.2015.7322452
14. Kumar, V., Zheng, Y., Cavé, V., Budimlić, Z., Sarkar, V.: HabaneroUPC++: a compiler-free PGAS library. In: PGAS 2014 (2014). https://doi.org/10.1145/2676870.2676879
15. Linderman, M.D., Collins, J.D., Wang, H., Meng, T.H.: Merge: a programming model for heterogeneous multi-core systems. In: Proceedings of the 13th International Conference on Architectural Support for Programming Languages and Operating Systems, pp. 287–296. ASPLOS (2008). https://doi.org/10.1145/1346281.1346318
16. Luk, C.K., Hong, S., Kim, H.: Qilin: exploiting parallelism on heterogeneous multiprocessors with adaptive mapping. In: MICRO, pp. 45–55 (2009). https://doi.org/10.1145/1669112.1669121
17. Mitra, G., Bohmann, J., Lintault, I., Rendell, A.P.: Development and application of a hybrid programming environment on an ARM/DSP system for high performance computing. In: IPDPS, pp. 286–295 (2018). https://doi.org/10.1109/IPDPS.2018.00038
18. Mitra, G., Stotzer, E., Jayaraj, A., Rendell, A.P.: Implementation and optimization of the OpenMP accelerator model for the TI Keystone II architecture. In: Using and Improving OpenMP for Devices, Tasks, and More, pp. 202–214 (2014). https://doi.org/10.1007/978-3-319-11454-5_15
19. Munshi, A.: The OpenCL specification. In: IEEE Hot Chips, pp. 1–314 (2009)
20. Compute Unified Device Architecture Programming Guide, April 2019
21. ORNL: Summit supercomputer. https://www.olcf.ornl.gov/summit/. Accessed April 2019
22. Planas, J., Badia, R.M., Ayguadé, E., Labarta, J.: Hierarchical task-based programming with StarSs. IJHPCA **23**(3), 284–299 (2009). https://doi.org/10.1177/1094342009106195
23. Sbîrlea, A., Zou, Y., Budimlíc, Z., Cong, J., Sarkar, V.: Mapping a data-flow programming model onto heterogeneous platforms. LCTES **47**, 61–70 (2012). https://doi.org/10.1145/2248418.2248428
24. Texas Instruments: C66AK2H multicore DSP+ARM Keystone II System-On-Chip. Texas Instruments Literature: SPRS866
25. Paderborn University: Noctua supercomputer. https://pc2.uni-paderborn.de/about-pc2/announcements/news-events/article/news/supercomputer-noctua-inaugurated/. Accessed April 2019
26. Wienke, S., Springer, P., Terboven, C., an Mey, D.: OpenACC first experiences with real-world applications, pp. 859–870. EuroPar (2012). https://doi.org/10.1007/978-3-642-32820-6_85

Concepts for OpenMP Target Offload Resilience

Christian Engelmann[1(✉)], Geoffroy R. Vallée[2], and Swaroop Pophale[1]

[1] Oak Ridge National Laboratory, P.O. Box 2008, Oak Ridge, TN 37831, USA
{engelmannc,pophaless}@ornl.gov
[2] Sylabs, Inc., 1191 Solano Ave, Unit 6634, Albany, CA 94706, USA
geoffroy@sylabs.io

Abstract. Recent reliability issues with one of the fastest supercomputers in the world, Titan at Oak Ridge National Laboratory (ORNL), demonstrated the need for resilience in large-scale heterogeneous computing. OpenMP currently does not address error and failure behavior. This paper takes a first step toward resilience for heterogeneous systems by providing the concepts for resilient OpenMP offload to devices. Using real-world error and failure observations, the paper describes the concepts and terminology for resilient OpenMP target offload, including error and failure classes and resilience strategies. It details the experienced general-purpose computing graphics processing unit (GPGPU) errors and failures in Titan. It further proposes improvements in OpenMP, including a preliminary prototype design, to support resilient offload to devices for efficient handling of errors and failures in heterogeneous high-performance computing (HPC) systems.

Keywords: Supercomputing · Resilience · OpenMP

1 Introduction

Resilience, i.e., obtaining a correct solution in a timely and efficient manner, is a key challenge in extreme-scale HPC. Heterogeneity, i.e., using multiple, and

Research sponsored by the Laboratory Directed Research and Development Program of Oak Ridge National Laboratory, managed by UT-Battelle, LLC, for the U.S. Department of Energy. This manuscript has been authored by UT-Battelle, LLC under Contract No. DE-AC05-00OR22725 with the U.S. Department of Energy. The United States Government retains and the publisher, by accepting the article for publication, acknowledges that the United States Government retains a non-exclusive, paid-up, irrevocable, world-wide license to publish or reproduce the published form of this manuscript, or allow others to do so, for United States Government purposes. The Department of Energy will provide public access to these results of federally sponsored research in accordance with the DOE Public Access Plan (http://energy.gov/downloads/doe-public-access-plan).

X. Fan et al. (Eds.): IWOMP 2019, LNCS 11718, pp. 78–93, 2019.
https://doi.org/10.1007/978-3-030-28596-8_6

potentially configurable, types of processors, accelerators and memory/storage in a single platform, adds significant complexity to the HPC hardware/software ecosystem. The diverse set of compute and memory components in today's and future HPC systems require novel resilience solutions.

There is only preliminary work in resilience for heterogeneous HPC systems, such as checkpoint/restart for GPGPUs using OpenCL with VOCL-FT [16]. There is also fine-grain transaction-based application-level checkpoint/restart with the Fault Tolerance Interface (FTI) [2]. Rolex [12] is an initial set of C/C++ language extensions for fine-grain resilience, which specify how data variables and code block execution may be repaired during program execution.

In contrast, the Titan supercomputer at ORNL experienced severe GPGPU reliability issues over its life time (2012–2019). In late 2016, 12 out of Titan's 18,688 GPGPUs failed per day [21]. Approximately 11,000 GPGPUs were replaced in the 2017–2019 time frame due to failures or high failure probability. The only mitigation available was application-level checkpoint/restart, which was never designed to efficiently handle such high failure rates. Titan's successor, the Summit supercomputer at ORNL [20], has 27,648 GPGPUs. While it is the expectation that Titan's severe reliability issues were a rather unique experience, hope is not a strategy. There is an urgent need for fine-grain and low-overhead resilience capabilities at the parallel programming model that permit specifying what types of errors and failures should be handled and how.

Efficient software-based solutions to fill gaps in detection, masking, recovery, and avoidance of errors and failures require coordination. Based on the underlying execution model and intrinsic resilience features of the hardware, the various components in a heterogeneous system can be organized into protection domains. Employed resilience solutions can handle errors and failures in specific components and granularities where it is most appropriate to do so and in coordination with the rest of the system, which prevents errors from propagating and failures from cascading beyond these protection domains.

This paper describes concepts for resilience in OpenMP based on real-world observations from the largest heterogeneous HPC system in the world. It focuses on offload to devices as a first step toward resilience in OpenMP. The paper describes the used concepts and terminology, including general fault, error and failure classes. It derives error and failure scopes and classes for OpenMP target offload and maps them to the experienced GPGPU errors and failures in Titan. Using these concepts, this paper proposes improvements to enable resilience for OpenMP offload to devices and details a preliminary prototype design based on the concept of quality of service (QoS).

2   System Model

This section describes the involved concepts and terminology for OpenMP target offload. It continues with a short overview of general fault, error and failure classes and common terms that will be used in this context. It further defines the error and failure scopes and classes for OpenMP target offload.

2.1 OpenMP Target Offload

An *OpenMP thread* offloads the code and data of a *target region* in the form of a *target task* from the *host device* (*parent device*) to a *target device* using a *target construct*. The *target device* can be specified by a *device number*, otherwise the *default device number* is used. The *target task* may be *undeferred*, *i.e.*, the *OpenMP thread* waits for the completion of the *target task*, or *deferred*, *i.e.*, the *OpenMP thread* does not wait for the completion of the *target task*. *Target task* input and output data is *mapped* to and from the *host device* to the *target device*. Space for *target task* runtime data may be allocated on the *target device*.

The work presented in this paper primarily focuses on an *OpenMP thread* running on a conventional processor core and offloading a *target region* as a *target task* to a GPGPU. It does not focus on an *OpenMP thread* executing an *OpenMP task* on the *host device*, as the shared memory aspects are significantly more complex and require different error and failure models. This work is, however, applicable to a great extend to offloading a *target region* as a *target task* to other types of *target devices* that OpenMP may support.

The system model assumes that *target task* input data is transferred or made accessible to the *target device* before the *target task* starts, *target task* runtime data is allocated before it starts, and *target task* output data is transferred to or made accessible to the *host device* after it ends. Only the *target task* modifies its input, output, and runtime data during its execution, *i.e.*, the data is not shared with the *host device*. The *target task* is typically a parallel execution on the GPGPU and the data may be shared between threads on the GPGPU, i.e., *target task* data may be shared within the *target device* during its execution.

2.2 Faults, Errors and Failures

Error and failure behavior in OpenMP is currently undefined. Consequently, implementations are left to handle them (or not) in a non-uniform way. In general, a *fault* is an underlying flaw/defect in a *system* that has potential to cause problems. A fault can be *dormant* and can have no effect. When *activated* during system operation, a fault leads to an *error* and an illegal *system state*. A *failure* occurs if an *error* reaches the service interface of a *system*, resulting in behavior that is inconsistent with the system's specification. Prior work [11,19] identified the following general fault, error and failure classes and common terms:

– {*benign,dormant,active*} {*permanent,transient,intermittent*} {*hard,soft*} *fault*
  • *Benign:* An inactive fault that does not activate.
  • *Dormant:* An inactive fault that potentially becomes active at some point.
  • *Active:* A fault that causes an error at the moment it becomes active.
  • *Permanent:* The presence of the fault is continuous in time.
  • *Transient:* The presence of the fault is temporary.
  • *Intermittent:* The presence of the fault is temporary and recurring.
  • *Hard:* A fault that is systematically reproducible.
  • *Soft:* A fault that is not systematically reproducible.

- The following common terms map to these fault classes:
  * *Latent fault:* Any type of *dormant fault.*
  * *Solid fault:* Any type of *hard fault.*
  * *Elusive fault:* Any type of *soft fault.*
- *{undetected,detected} {unmasked,masked} {hard,soft} error*
  - *Undetected:* An error whose presence is not indicated.
  - *Detected:* An error whose presence is indicated by a message or a signal.
  - *Masked:* An error whose impact is compensated so that the system specification is satisfied despite the incorrect state; its propagation is limited.
  - *Unmasked:* An error that has not been compensated and has the potential to propagate.
  - *Hard:* An error caused by a permanent fault.
  - *Soft:* An error caused by a transient or intermittent fault.
  - The following common terms map to these error classes:
    * *Latent error* or *silent error:* Any type of *undetected error.*
    * *Silent data corruption (SDC):* An *undetected unmasked hard* or *soft error.*
- *{undetected,detected} {permanent,transient,intermittent} {complete,partial, Byzantine} failure*
  - *Undetected:* A failure whose occurrence is not indicated.
  - *Detected:* A failure whose occurrence is indicated by a message or a signal.
  - *Permanent:* The presence of the failure is continuous in time.
  - *Transient:* The presence of the failure is temporary.
  - *Intermittent:* The failure is temporary but recurring in time.
  - *Complete:* A failure that causes service outage of the system.
  - *Partial:* A failure causing a degraded service within the functional specification.
  - *Byzantine:* A failure causing an arbitrary deviation from the functional specification.
  - The following common terms map to these failure classes:
    * *Fail-stop:* An *undetected* or *detected failure* that completely halts system operation, which often causes an irretrievable loss of state.
    * *Fail-safe:* A mode of system operation that mitigates the consequences of a system failure.

While a *fault* is the cause of an *error*, its manifestation as a *state change* is considered an *error*, and the transition to an incorrect service is observed as a *failure* (see Fig. 1). A *fault-error-failure chain* is a directed acyclic graph (DAG) with *faults*, *errors* and *failures* represented by its vertices. In a system composed of multiple components, *errors* may be transformed into other *errors* and *propagate* through the system generating further *errors*, which may eventually result in a *failure*. A *failure cascade* occurs when the failure of a component A causes an error and subsequently a failure in component B interfaced with A.

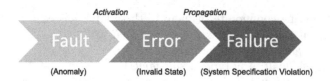

Fig. 1. Relationship between fault, error and failure

2.3 OpenMP Target Offload Error and Failure Scopes and Classes

In terms of hardware errors and failures, OpenMP offloading has a *host device* and *target device* scope. In terms of software errors and failures, *OpenMP thread* and *target task* scopes exist. The *host device* and *OpenMP thread* scopes are not considered in this work due to the complex shared memory aspects it involves. Only *target device* and *target task* errors and failures are considered. The following error and failure classes are defined:

- {*undetected, detected*} {*unmasked, masked*} {*hard, soft*} *target device error*
- {*undetected, detected*} {*unmasked, masked*} {*hard, soft*} *target task error*
- {*undetected, detected*} {*permanent, transient, intermittent*} {*complete, partial, Byzantine*} *target device failure*
- {*undetected, detected*} {*permanent, transient, intermittent*} {*complete, partial, Byzantine*} *target task failure*

A total of 16 error classes for *target devices* and *target tasks* are defined based on the general error classes. Undetected masked errors are rather irrelevant, as the masking makes them undetectable by any error detector. Detected masked errors are less relevant, as the masking already limits error propagation. A resilience strategy may still do something about a detected masked error though, such as to avoid it in the future. Undetected errors may become detectable through a resilience strategy. Undetected errors that do not become detectable are problematic, as no resilience strategy is able to deal with them.

A total of 36 failure classes for *target devices* and *target tasks* are defined based on the general error failure classes. Undetected failures may become detectable through a resilience strategy. Undetected failures that do not become detectable are problematic, as no resilience strategy is able to deal with them.

3   Observed Errors and Failures

This section provides an overview of the observed and inferred errors and failures in the Titan supercomputer at ORNL that are relevant for OpenMP target offload with GPGPUs. It maps these errors and failures the previously defined OpenMP offloading error and failure classes.

3.1 GPGPU Errors and Failures in Titan

The Titan supercomputer deployed at ORNL in November 2012 as the fastest in the world will be decommissioned in 2019, still being the 9th fastest. It is a hybrid-architecture Cray XK7 with a theoretical peak performance of 27 PFlops and a LINPACK performance of 17.95 PFlops. Each of Titan's 18,688 compute nodes consists of an NVIDIA K20X Kepler GPGPU and a 16-core AMD Opteron processor. A significant amount of work has been published about the observed and inferred errors and failures in Titan [9,13–15,21]. The following Titan GPGPU (*target device/task*) errors can be mapped to the previously defined OpenMP offloading error classes (see Table 1 for a summary):

- *Target device error correcting code (ECC) double-bit error:* A *detected unmasked soft error* in *target device* memory. This error is detected and signaled by the *target device*. It typically transitions to a *target task abort*.
- *Target device SDC:* An *undetected unmasked soft error* in *target device* memory or logic. It is not signaled and can propagate to a *target task SDC*, a *target task abort*, or a *target task delay*, including an indefinite delay (hang).
- *Target task SDC:* An *undetected unmasked soft error* in *target task* data. It is not signaled and can transition to a *target task abort* or a *target task delay*, including an indefinite delay. It may propagate to incorrect *target task* output.

These Titan GPGPU (*target device/task*) failures can be mapped to the previously defined OpenMP offloading failure classes (see Table 2 for a summary):

- *Target device Peripheral Component Interconnect (PCI) bus width degrade:* A *detected transient, intermittent or permanent partial failure* of the PCI connection between the *host device* and the *target device*. It is typically caused by a PCI hardware failure. This failure results in degraded transfer performance for *target task* input and output data. It can cascade to a *target task delay*.
- *Target device PCI bus disconnect:* A *detected permanent complete failure* of the PCI connection between the *host device* and the *target device* or a *detected permanent complete failure* of the *target device*. It is typically caused by a PCI hardware or GPGPU failure. This failure can cascade to a *target task abort*.
- *Target device dynamic page retirement (DPR):* A *detected transient complete failure* of the *target device* memory. It is typically caused by the GPGPU when preventing or repairing a *detected permanent partial failure* of the *target device* memory. This failure can cascade to a *target task abort*.
- *Target device SXM power off:* A *detected permanent complete failure* of the *target device*. It is typically caused by a voltage fault. This failure can cascade to a *target task abort*.
- *Target task abort:* A *detected permanent complete failure* of a *target task*. It is typically caused by a *target task error* or a *target device error* or *failure*.
- *Target task delay:* A *detected permanent partial failure* of a *target task*. It is typically caused by *target task SDC* or a *target device PCI width degrade*.

Table 1. Mapping of Titan GPGPU errors to the OpenMP offloading error classes

Error	Error class
Target device ECC double-bit error	Detected unmasked soft target device error
Target device SDC	Undetected unmasked soft target device error
Target task SDC	Undetected unmasked soft target task error

Table 2. Mapping of Titan GPGPU failures to the OpenMP offloading failure classes

Failure	Failure class
Target device PCI width degrade	Detected transient partial target device failure
	Detected intermittent partial target device failure
	Detected permanent partial target device failure
Target device PCI disconnect	Detected permanent complete target device failure
Target device DPR	Detected transient complete target device failure
Target device SXM power off	Detected permanent complete target device failure
Target task abort	Detected permanent complete target task failure
Target task delay	Detected permanent partial target task failure

4   Resilience for OpenMP Target Offload

Errors may propagate or transition to failures and failures may cascade in other parts of the system, such as the *host device* and *OpenMP threads*, depending on employed resilience strategies. Since OpenMP currently does not employ resilience strategies, a *target task abort failure* will cascade to an *OpenMP thread abort failure* and a *target task delay failure* will cascade to an *OpenMP thread delay failure*. Additionally, any *complete target device failure* will cascade to an *OpenMP thread abort failure*. *Target task SDC* may propagate to a *OpenMP thread SDC*, which then may transition to an *OpenMP thread delay* or *abort failure* or propagate to incorrect *OpenMP thread* output. This section discusses the individual needs for changes in the OpenMP standard and implementations to employ a reasonable set of resilience strategies for OpenMP offload to devices.

4.1   Error and Failure Detection and Notification

Errors and failures need to be detected and employed resilience strategies need to be notified in order to be able to deal with them.

Errors and failures detected by the *target device* are reported to the OpenMP runtime after attempted *target task* execution. Employed resilience strategies may transparently handle them. However, some resilience strategies need application feedback to decide on the course of action, such as to asses if an error or failure is acceptable. A reporting and feedback capability for device-detected errors and failures is needed in OpenMP. This could be implemented using function callbacks and an OpenMP language feature for defining resilience policies using the previously defined OpenMP offloading error and failure classes. Since detailed error and failure information could be helpful to make decisions, such as to assess the severity of a *target device ECC double-bit error*, OpenMP support for *target device* error reporting to the application is needed.

Errors and failures may also be detected by the application, such as by checking the correctness of *target task* output. A notification capability for application-detected errors and failures is needed in OpenMP to enable the use of resilience strategies by the application. This could be implemented using an OpenMP language feature for raising error notifications to the OpenMP runtime.

4.2 Fail-Fast and Graceful Shutdown

The *fail-fast* resilience strategy is designed to detect and report errors and failures as soon as possible. It also stops normal operation if there is no other resilience strategy in place to handle a specific error or failure. At the very least, the default error and failure behavior of OpenMP in general should be defined as *fail-fast*. This permits resilience strategies that are in place outside of OpenMP to efficiently handle errors and failures. A primary example is application-level checkpoint/restart, where any computation an application continues after an unrecoverable error or failure is wasted time.

For OpenMP target offload, *fail-fast* means that the *host device* detects and reports errors and failures as soon as possible. It also means that the OpenMP runtime aborts *target tasks* impacted by the error or failure as soon as possible. For performance failures, such as the *target device PCI width degrade* that can cascade to a *target task delay*, this means aborting a *target task*. The resilience strategy of graceful degradation, which would risk/accept a *target task delay* is described in the following subsection. The *fail-fast* strategy can also be employed in conjunction with application-level error or failure detection, such as through an application-level correctness check of the *target task* output and a corresponding abort upon error detection.

Graceful shutdown avoids error propagation and failure cascades beyond the component that is being shutdown. An uncontrolled stop of normal operation, such as a crash, can result in errors or failures in other system components. Operating system (OS) features usually prevent such effects by triggering cleanup procedures, such as after a crash. However, the OS may not have control over everything an OpenMP application is involved in, such as when an OS bypass is employed for networking/storage or a workflow software framework is used. Another example is the clean execution of an Message Passing Interface (MPI) abort after an OpenMP abort due to a *target task failure*. *Error handlers* can perform application-level cleanup during a *graceful shutdown*, but they would need to be triggered by the OpenMP runtime upon a *fail-fast* abort.

4.3 Graceful Degradation

Graceful degradation continues operation after an error or failure at the cost of performance or correctness that is deemed acceptable. In case of a performance failure, such as the *target device PCI width degrade* that can cascade to a *target task delay*, this means not aborting a *target task* and accepting the possible performance degradation, but reporting the failure to the application/user.

In case of a resource outage, such as the *target device PCI disconnect* that can cascade to a *target task abort*, this means continuing operation with less resources while employing a resilience strategy for aborted tasks. For example, an aborted task may be re-executed on a different *target device* using a rollback recovery strategy (described in the following subsection) while the failed *target device* is removed from OpenMP's pool of *target devices*. This requires OpenMP support for shrinking the number of *target devices* after a failure.

In case of a detected error, *graceful degradation* means to continue operation despite the error and to accept a possible error propagation. The application may need to make a decision if an error is acceptable.

4.4 Rollback Recovery

The *rollback recovery* resilience strategy transparently re-executes an erroneous or failed *target task* using the original *target task* input. The re-execution may be performed on the same *target device*, assuming that it is available and has not been removed from OpenMP's pool of *target devices* due to *graceful degradation*. If it has been removed, the re-execution is performed on a different *target device*. Successive *target task errors* or *failures* may result in corresponding successive re-executions. The number of successive rollbacks should be restricted to avoid endless rollbacks. On systems where the *target task* input is not copied to the *target device* but used in-place, the input may be backed up before offloading to assure its integrity, i.e., to protect it from being corrupted.

An OpenMP language extension is needed to specify the *rollback recovery* resilience strategy and its parameters, such as the maximum number of rollbacks, for each *target task*. The OpenMP runtime relies on *target device error* and *failure* detection and on application error detection notification to initiate rollbacks.

4.5 Redundancy

Redundancy in space executes *target tasks* at the same time on different *target devices*, while redundancy in time executes them sequentially on the same *target device*. A mix between both executes them on multiple *target devices*, where at least one *target device* is being reused. Common levels of redundancy are two and three, where two redundant *target tasks* detect a *target task error* and detect and mask a *target task failure*. Three redundant *target tasks* detect and mask a *target task error* and two *target task failures*. Error detection uses *target task* output comparison, while error masking uses the output of the majority. Failure detection and masking uses the output of the fastest surviving *target task*.

An OpenMP language extension is needed to specify the *redundancy* resilience strategy and its parameters, such as redundancy level (2 or 3) and resource usage (space, time or both). The OpenMP runtime relies on *target device error* and *failure* detection and on application error detection notification. It also relies on *target task* output comparison (e.g., bit-wise comparison or error bounds).

5   Preliminary Prototype

We detail in this section some aspects of the design and implementation of our solution for OpenMP target offload resilience. Both are driven by software engineering concerns, best-practices in extreme scale computing and available standards and libraries.

5.1   Design Details

Because our work is in the context of complex software components (a compiler), a standard (OpenMP) and a set of new concepts (QoS), one of our main challenges from a design and software engineering point-of-view is the separation of concerns. It is for example beneficial to have a clear separate implementation of the QoS and OpenMP support, and enable a fine-grain interaction of the resulting libraries. By doing so, it becomes easier to define, implement, modify and maintain each component, as well as explicitly and precisely define how these components interact. We believe this is especially critical when using complex production-level software such as a main-stream compiler (Low Level Virtual Machine (LLVM)). Another level of complexity comes from the asynchronous aspect of the problem we are trying to solve: the QoS runtime needs to asynchronously interact with the OpenMP runtime to enable system monitoring, fault detection and potentially recovery.

Our design centers on a novel concept for QoS and corresponding OpenMP language and runtime extensions. The QoS language extensions allow application developers to specify their resilience strategy without focusing on the implementation details. The QoS runtime extensions create a corresponding contract that maps application resilience requirements to the underlying hardware and software capabilities.

A QoS contract is defined as a set of QoS parameters that reflect the users' resilience requirements by identifying the requested resilience strategies. We propose a QoS language that provides all the required semantics to manipulate QoS parameters which can be applied to both application's data and tasks. These parameters are handled via generic "get/set" interfaces, and can be expressed as: (1) key/value pairs; (2) bounded values; and (3) ranges of values. The interface uses the block concept, similarly to OpenMP, to define the scope in which parameters are valid and the QoS contract with the runtime system. To simplify the definition of new QoS contracts, predefined QoS classes offer coherent sets of parameter that achieve popular resilience strategies. By using these classes, users only need to specify a few, if any, parameters, and let the system manage QoS policies that are already available. The following example uses QoS key/value pairs for specifying triple redundancy for a *target task*:

```
#pragma omp qoskv resilience (TASK_REDUNDANCY, BOOL, TRUE)
#pragma omp qoskv resilience (TASK_REDUNDANCY_FACTOR, INT, 3)
{
  #pragma omp target ...
  ...
}
```

An implementation of OpenMP is extended to offer an event-based QoS-aware runtime for resilience with a QoS Scheduler and QoS Negotiation Schemes at its core (see Fig. 2). The QoS Negotiation Schemes drive the method to enforce the QoS requirements, specifying the type of contract that the application and the system establish. Two types of schemes are proposed: (1) *best effort*, for which the system will match the requirements without strong guarantees, i.e., breaches of QoS contracts are possible, reported, but do not stop the execution of the application; (2) *guaranteed*, for which the system will match the requirements with strong guarantees, i.e., the application will stop in the event of a breach.

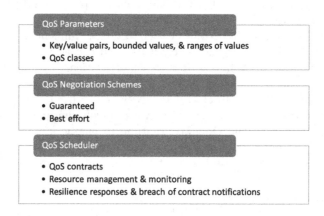

Fig. 2. Core components of a QoS-aware parallel programming model runtime

The QoS Scheduler instantiates QoS parameters and resilience strategies, deploying a QoS contract that relies on system services (e.g., for monitoring of task offloading and error/failure detection), as well as resource allocators (e.g., for deploying a task on a specific GPGPU). The QoS scheduler ensures that everything complies with the QoS contract. If a discrepancy is observed, a breach of contract will be raised (software exception). This generates an event that activates the configured responses, such as resilience actions. Application developers are able to specify a function (handler) that would be automatically called by the QoS scheduler upon a breach of a QoS contract. This enables a programmatic way to handle breaches of QoS contracts when custom actions are required, without imposing complex modifications of the application's code. Figure 3 presents an overview of the core components that are involved for the specification, implementation and control of QoS contract.

Our design requires coordination between the QoS and OpenMP runtimes. Such an inter-runtime coordination requires the following capabilities: (i) *notifications*, e.g., in order to guarantee progress, a runtime should be able to raise an event to generically notify another runtime/library for coordination purposes (e.g., resource management); and (ii) a *key/value store* shared by runtimes/libraries, for example to store and load QoS parameters. Fortunately, the PMIx [4] standard supports these features and existing libraries can easily be extended to be PMIx compliant by using the PMIx reference implementation.

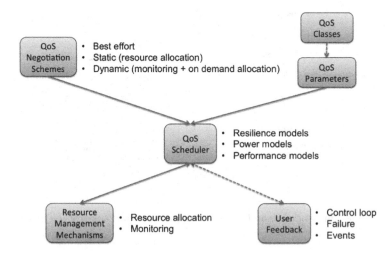

Fig. 3. Schematic overview of the QoS solution

5.2   Implementation Details

As previously stated, our QoS library, ORQOS, developed to provide the QoS runtime capabilities, is based on PMIx. We also extended the OpenMP runtime to be PMIx-compliant, which ultimately enables inter-library communication and coordination. Practically, our prototype is therefore composed of our QoS library, ORQOS, and an extension of OpenMP based on the LLVM 7.0.0 release. Specifically, the QoS directives and clauses for OpenMP were added to clang and LLVM. As a result, the QoS library is fairly easy to maintain because of its limited size and can potentially be reused in a different context. For example, we are considering reusing it with other programming languages, such as MPI. Similarly, the LLVM extensions remain fairly limited and easy to maintain.

Figure 4 shows the workflow for compiling OpenMP code with QoS extensions. When the OpenMP code is compiled, it is transformed into an intermediate code with the QoS directives converted into calls to ORQOS. These calls perform two tasks: (i) initialize PMIx to permit data exchange between libraries through its key/value store; and (ii) store QoS key/value pairs to make them accessible to other runtimes. After generating the intermediate code, LLVM creates the binary with all the required library dependencies, including PMIx and ORQOS. At runtime, a PMIx server that is hosting the key/value store is implicitly created when the ORQOS and OpenMP runtimes connect to it. This enables inter-runtime coordination through PMIx key/value pairs and PMIx events. Monitoring and enforcement of QoS contracts is implemented only in the ORQOS runtime, limiting the need for further modifying other components.

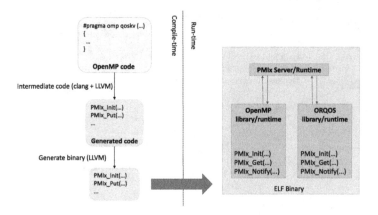

Fig. 4. Compile-time workflow and run-time interactions of the prototype using LLVM.

6   Related Work

The current state of practice for HPC resilience is global application-level checkpoint/restart. It is a single-layer approach that burdens the user with employing a strategy at extreme coarse granularity, i.e., the job level. Part of the current state of practice for HPC resilience are also hardware solutions at extreme fine granularity, such as ECC for memories, redundant power supplies, and management systems for monitoring and control.

The current state of research is more advanced and includes fault-tolerant MPI, fault-aware MPI, redundant MPI, proactive fault tolerance, containment domains, and resilient algorithms. MPI solutions provide resilience at process granularity. Fault-tolerant MPI [3] and fault-aware MPI [10] require global reconfiguration and either local or global recovery. Redundant MPI [8] has significant overheads. Containment domains [5], or sometimes referred to as recovery blocks, use finer-grain checkpoint/restart strategies, such as at the sequential execution block level (e.g., task) or the parallel execution block level (e.g., parallel loop, iteration or application phase). There is also fine-grain transaction-based application-level checkpoint/restart with the FTI [2] essentially implements containment domains at the parallel execution block level. Resilient algorithms [1,6,7,18] utilize data redundancy, computational redundancy, or self stabilization. Individual solutions tend to be algorithm specific.

Resilience Oriented Language Extensions (Rolex) [12] offers C/C++ data type qualifiers for resilience and C/C++ pragma directives for fault tolerant execution blocks. While developed independently from OpenMP, Rolex does offer OpenMP-like resilient programming. It does not offer support for heterogeneous systems. Rolex is also not transparent, as it requires the application programmer to specify resilience strategies in detail. Another OpenMP pragma-based resilience scheme explored in DIvergent NOde cloning (DINO) [17] focuses on data protection by immediately performing correctness check after the last use of a variable based on a vulnerability factor metric. This scheme is limited to soft errors in memory.

There is only preliminary work in resilience for heterogeneous systems. VOCL-FT [16] offers checkpoint/restart for computation offloaded to GPGPUs using OpenCL. VOCL-FT transparently intercepts the communication between the originating process and the local or remote GPGPU to automatically recover from ECC errors experienced on the GPGPU during computation.

7   Conclusion

This paper is motivated by experiences with GPGPU errors and failures from the largest heterogeneous HPC system in the world. It offers concepts for resilience using target offload as a first step toward resilience in OpenMP. It describes the underlying concepts and terminology and the observed errors and failures. It derives error and failure classes for OpenMP target offload from the observations using the underlying concepts and terminology. This paper proposes a number of improvements to enable OpenMP target offload resilience, including a preliminary prototype design and some implementation aspects using a novel concept for QoS.

Future work includes improving the prototype to demonstrate the proposed improvements on a large-scale heterogeneous HPC system with a scientific application. Its evaluation will use appropriate metrics, such as, ease of use, performance, and resilience. The ease of use evaluation identifies how much effort in terms of additional lines of code and implementation time is required to use the QoS capabilities. The performance evaluation compares an unmodified OpenMP with the developed prototype under error- and failure-free conditions. The resilience evaluation performs error and failure injection experiments and measures the time to correct solution under various error and failure conditions with different QoS contracts. Additional future work will focus on the OpenMP language extensions for QoS, specifically on clearly defining QoS parameters and classes. Other future work could also focus on the reuse of our QoS library in the context of other HPC programming languages. For instance, it would be interesting to investigate whether the concept of QoS could be used in the context of MPI to specify resilience, performance and energy consumption requirements in a portable manner. In this context, users could use QoS contracts to specify requirements at both the application and job level but let the runtime find the best compromise to satisfy all or most of the expressed requirements. If possible this would enable a new set of capabilities without drastically increase the size and complexity of standards such as OpenMP and MPI.

References

1. Ashraf, R., Hukerikar, S., Engelmann, C.: Pattern-based modeling of multiresilience solutions for high-performance computing. In: Proceedings of the 9th ACM/SPEC International Conference on Performance Engineering (ICPE) 2018, pp. 80–87, April 2018. https://doi.org/10.1145/3184407.3184421, http://icpe2018. spec.org
2. Bautista-Gomez, L., Tsuboi, S., Komatitsch, D., Cappello, F., Maruyama, N., Matsuoka, S.: FTI: high performance fault tolerance interface for hybrid systems. In: International Conference on High Performance Computing, Networking, Storage and Analysis (SC11), pp. 1–12, November 2011. https://doi.org/10.1145/2063384. 2063427
3. Bland, W., Bouteiller, A., Herault, T., Bosilca, G., Dongarra, J.: Post-failure recovery of MPI communication capability: design and rationale. Int. J. High Perform. Comput. Appl. **27**(3), 244–254 (2013). https://doi.org/10.1177/1094342013488238
4. Castain, R.H., Solt, D., Hursey, J., Bouteiller, A.: PMIx: process management for exascale environments. In: European MPI Users' Group Meeting (EuroMPI 2017), pp. 14:1–14:10, September 2017. https://doi.org/10.1145/3127024.3127027
5. Chung, J., et al.: Containment domains: a scalable, efficient, and flexible resilience scheme for exascale systems. In: Proceedings of the International Conference on High Performance Computing, Networking, Storage and Analysis (SC 2012), pp. 58:1–58:11. IEEE Computer Society Press, November 2012. https://doi.org/10. 1109/SC.2012.36
6. Davies, T., Chen, Z.: Correcting soft errors online in LU factorization. In: Proceedings of the 22nd International Symposium on High-performance Parallel and Distributed Computing (HPDC 2013), pp. 167–178 (2013). https://doi.org/10.1145/ 2493123.2462920
7. Elliott, J., Hoemmen, M., Mueller, F.: Evaluating the impact of SDC on the GMRES iterative solver. In: 28th International Parallel and Distributed Processing Symposium (IPDPS 2014), pp. 1193–1202, May 2014. https://doi.org/10.1109/ IPDPS.2014.123
8. Fiala, D., Mueller, F., Engelmann, C., Ferreira, K., Brightwell, R., Riesen, R.: Detection and correction of silent data corruption for large-scale high-performance computing. In: Proceedings of the 25th IEEE/ACM International Conference on High Performance Computing, Networking, Storage and Analysis (SC 2012), pp. 78:1–78:12, November 2012. https://doi.org/10.1109/SC.2012.49, http://sc12. supercomputing.org

9. Gupta, S., Patel, T., Engelmann, C., Tiwari, D.: Failures in large scale systems: long-term measurement, analysis, and implications. In: International Conference on High Performance Computing, Networking, Storage and Analysis (SC 2017), pp. 44:1–44:12, November 2017. https://doi.org/10.1145/3126908.3126937

10. Hassani, A., Skjellum, A., Brightwell, R.: Design and evaluation of FA-MPI, a transactional resilience scheme for non-blocking MPI. In: 2014 44th Annual IEEE/IFIP International Conference on Dependable Systems and Networks, pp. 750–755, June 2014. https://doi.org/10.1109/DSN.2014.78

11. Hukerikar, S., Engelmann, C.: Resilience design patterns: a structured approach to resilience at extreme scale (version 1.2). Technical report ORNL/TM-2017/745, Oak Ridge National Laboratory, August 2017. https://doi.org/10.2172/1436045

12. Hukerikar, S., Lucas, R.F.: Rolex: resilience-oriented language extensions for extreme-scale systems. J. Supercomput. 1–33 (2016). https://doi.org/10.1007/s11227-016-1752-5

13. Meneses, E., Ni, X., Jones, T., Maxwell, D.: Analyzing the interplay of failures and workload on a leadership-class supercomputer. In: Cray User Group Meeting (CUG 2014), March 2014. https://cug.org/proceedings/cug2015_proceedings/includes/files/pap169.pdf

14. Nie, B., Xue, J., Gupta, S., Engelmann, C., Smirni, E., Tiwari, D.: Characterizing temperature, power, and soft-error behaviors in data center systems: Insights, challenges, and opportunities. In: International Symposium on the Modeling, Analysis, and Simulation of Computer and Telecommunication Systems (MASCOTS 2017), pp. 22–31, September 2017. https://doi.org/10.1109/MASCOTS.2017.12

15. Nie, B., et al.: Machine learning models for GPU error prediction in a large scale HPC system. In: International Conference on Dependable Systems and Networks (DSN 2018), pp. 95–106, June 2018. https://doi.org/10.1109/DSN.2018.00022

16. Pena, A.J., Bland, W., Balaji, P.: VOCL-FT: introducing techniques for efficient soft error coprocessor recovery. In: Proceedings of the International Conference on High Performance Computing, Networking, Storage and Analysis (SC 2015), pp. 1–12, November 2015. https://doi.org/10.1145/2807591.2807640

17. Rezaei, A., Mueller, F., Hargrove, P., Roman, E.: DINO: divergent node cloning for sustained redundancy in HPC. J. Parallel Distrib. Comput. 109, 350–362 (2017). https://doi.org/10.1016/j.jpdc.2017.06.010

18. Sao, P., Vuduc, R.: Self-stabilizing iterative solvers. In: Proceedings of the Workshop on Latest Advances in Scalable Algorithms for Large-Scale Systems (ScalA 2013), pp. 4:1–4:8, November 2013. https://doi.org/10.1145/2530268.2530272

19. Snir, M., et al.: Addressing failures in exascale computing. Int. J. High Perform. Comput. Appl. (IJHPCA) 28(2), 127–171 (2014). https://doi.org/10.1177/1094342014522573, http://hpc.sagepub.com

20. Vazhkudai, S., et al.: The design, deployment, and evaluation of the CORAL pre-exascale systems. In: Proceedings of the International Conference on High Performance Computing, Networking, Storage and Analysis (SC 2018), pp. 52:1–52:12, November 2018. https://doi.org/10.1109/SC.2018.00055

21. Zimmer, C., Maxwell, D., McNally, S., Atchley, S., Vazhkudai, S.S.: GPU age-aware scheduling to improve the reliability of leadership jobs on Titan. In: Proceedings of the International Conference on High Performance Computing, Networking, Storage and Analysis (SC 2018), pp. 7:1–7:11, November 2018. https://doi.org/10.1109/SC.2018.00010

OpenMP on FPGAs—A Survey

Florian Mayer[1]([✉]), Marius Knaust[2], and Michael Philippsen[1]

[1] Programming Systems Group,
Friedrich-Alexander University Erlangen-Nürnberg (FAU), Erlangen, Germany
{florian.andrefranc.mayer,michael.philippsen}@fau.de
[2] Zuse Institute Berlin, Berlin, Germany
knaust@zib.de

Abstract. Due to the ubiquity of OpenMP and the rise of FPGA-based accelerators in the HPC world, several research groups have attempted to bring the two together by building OpenMP-to-FPGA compilers. This paper is a survey of the current state of the art (with a focus on the OpenMP `target` pragma). It first introduces and explains a design space for the compilers. Design space dimensions include how FPGA infrastructure is generated, how work is distributed, and where/how target outlining is done. A table concisely condenses the available information on the surveyed projects which are also summarized and compared. The paper concludes with possible future research directions.

1 Introduction

OpenMP was originally intended to standardize the parallel programming of CPU-based SMP and NUMA systems. Prior to OpenMP 4.0, CPU-based systems were the only ones supported. Later, OpenMP 4.0 introduced the `target` pragma and allowed HPC programmers to exploit a cluster's heterogeneity by marking highly parallel regions of an algorithm to be offloaded to a more suited device (e.g. GPUs, FPGAs, etc.). Figure 1 illustrates the new situation and the typical approach to outline code for GPU and FPGA targets in the front-end of the compiler. Note that Fig. 1 simplifies. At least for GPUs there exists a compiler whose back-end builds code for both the host and the target. The thin dashed arrows show the traditional compilation pipeline prior to 4.0. In bold are the new challenges for the OpenMP implementer, as they now have to target both FPGAs and GPUs. Figure 1 also sketches the internals of an FPGA: Acc_1 through Acc_n denote hardware units doing actual calculations. The other blocks represent the infrastructure needed in order to run these hardware units on the FPGA. As almost

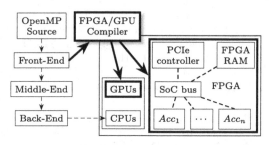

Fig. 1. OpenMP compilation.

X. Fan et al. (Eds.): IWOMP 2019, LNCS 11718, pp. 94–108, 2019.
https://doi.org/10.1007/978-3-030-28596-8_7

everything in the FPGA can be configured arbitrarily, one of many possible configurations is shown. To make use of the accelerators, OpenMP compilers need to solve novel problems: How to transfer data from the CPU to GPUs/FPGAs and back? What kinds of handshaking to use? What hardware blocks to chose to make up the FPGA configuration? What FPGA-internal bus system to use? Over the years, several researchers answered some of those questions in various ways.

Here we survey these papers and cover the current state of the art. Section 2 sketches the design space of OpenMP-to-FPGA compilers. Section 3 discusses the published research using that design space.

2 Design Space

When mapping OpenMP code to FPGA-based accelerators, a tool chain has a variety of different design decisions to choose from. This section covers feasible approaches and identifies the dimensions that the next section uses to categorize published systems. Of course, categories are not always black-and-white.

In this paper the term *architecture* refers to all components a system is built from, how those components behave, and how they interact with each other. An FPGA (or FPGA chip) usually consists of both a reconfigurable part and a fixed ASIC part (for instance ARM cores, RAMs, etc.). This paper uses the term FPGA *fabric* (or just fabric) to denote the reconfigurable part. A fabric can emulate arbitrary hardware. Its *configuration* (the *bitstream*) encodes this hardware. Without the configuration there are not even connections to the static ASIC parts of the FPGA. Any real-world configuration thus must consists of two parts: First functional entities, also known as kernel IPs (Intellectual Property) that perform desired calculations from the regions inside the OpenMP program, and second, the infrastructure for getting data to/from those functional blocks, also known as Low-Level Platform (LLP). This part of the configuration enables internal and external communication.

2.1 Low-Level Platform

While kernel IPs are application specific, in general and in this paper, the LLP is composed from pre-built IPs that implement bus communication, memory management, etc. These static LLP IPs sometimes can be configured (e.g., a bus IP could be configured to host more than 4 bus masters). Conceptually the compiler could generate application-specific LLP IPs from the ground up to best fit the served kernel IPs, but we do not know of any such attempt.

There are 4 classes of LLP:

Generic-Static: Fixed and pre-built ahead of time for *all* OpenMP programs. Such LLPs typically include a memory controller for FPGA memory, a communication controller (PCIe), an on-chip bus system (AXI), and sometimes a softcore CPU that manages the overall system. Because the bus system is fixed for all OpenMP programs, this type of LLP is limited to a constant number of accelerator blocks.

Specialized-Static: Specific for *one* OpenMP program and built at compile time. The compiler uses some static code analyses to compose LLPs of this type according to the needs of the OpenMP program at hand. For example, for a throughput-heavy OpenMP program the compiler would pick a different bus system than for compute-bound code. Similarly, an AXI streaming bus is not added to the fabric if the code cannot make use of it. Such tailoring saves fabric space that can be used for additional or larger kernel IPs. The LLP is static as it does not change after it has been configured to run on the FPGA.

Generic-Dynamic and *Specialized-Dynamic:* pre-built for *all*/specialized for *one* OpenMP program/s, but adapting based on runtime measurements. LLPs of these two *dynamic* classes adapt themselves depending on the current runtime requirements of the OpenMP program. They require a partially reconfigurable FPGA [38]. The LLP could for instance use different bus systems in different phases of the execution. After a throughput-heavy initialization, another bus system can be used, freeing space for additional computational kernels. To the best of our knowledge there is not yet an OpenMP-to-FPGA compiler that employs a dynamic LLP, neither a *generic* one (that fits all OpenMP programs) nor a *specialized* one that reconfigures itself from a tailored set of LLP-IPs.

2.2 Distribution of Work

OpenMP 4.0 allows computations to be distributed over all available computing devices. For the distribution decision, the compiler first assigns code blocks to the devices statically and decides how many copies of the code block to instantiate. We survey approaches that also decide statically where to execute the code blocks. A runtime system could optionally schedule them dynamically.

C^x	*CPU with instruction set x*
G^x	*GPU with instruction set x*
F_{hc}	*FPGA with a hardcore CPU*
F_{sc}	*FPGA with a softcore CPU*
F_{hw}	*FPGA with custom hardware*
$F_{hw,sc}$	*FPGA with custom hardware and a softcore CPU*

Fig. 2. Abbreviations for devices.

Dynamic scheduling is outside the focus of this paper as it is – if at all on FPGAs – used for `task` scheduling only [7]. Figure 2 lists some of the abbreviations used in this paper. While conceptually it is possible to let the programmer specify the static distribution explicitly or to use some sophisticated optimization routine to find a best-performing distribution at compile time, existing OpenMP-to-FPGA compilers make a rather simplistic choice and fall into either of the following two categories: CF_{hw}: Plain code, including the main thread, executes on the CPU, while for `target` pragma annotated code, FPGA hardware is synthesized that performs the calculation. This is called the *host-centric* approach. Note, that whenever possible the hardware synthesis tool makes use of available ASIC blocks on the FPGA (like DSPs).

$F_{hw,sc}$: In the *fpga-centric* approach, both the plain code (including the main thread) and the pragma code execute on the FPGA; the sequential code runs on a softcore CPU on the fabric. Again, the hardware synthesis tool makes use of ASIC blocks for both the softcore and the custom hardware.

There are other design choices. For example to use multiple FPGAs, to employ an ASIC hardware CPU if it is available, to also offload code to a GPU, etc. To the best of our knowledge these choices have not yet been explored.

2.3   Outlining

To the best of our knowledge, all OpenMP 4.0 compilers that support target offloading to FPGAs so far implement this as follows: They replace the marked code with function calls (that may be bundled into a stub). Some of the functions handle the communication of data between the host and the accelerator. One function initiates the execution of the payload code on the accelerator that implements the marked code block. To construct this payload, the compiler *outlines* the marked code block into a separate function that is then fed into an accelerator-specific tool chain. This can be a compiler for a GPU or a high-level synthesis tool (HLS) in the case of an FPGA as shown in Fig. 3. Some GPU compilers spit out GPU code in their back-ends. But as it still has to be explored if this is a better choice for FPGA code, we focus on the front-end outlining options in this survey. It is common practice to outline each `target` region individually. The design choice is whether to execute the outlining on the level of the abstract syntax tree (AST) or to do it on the immediate representation (IR) of the code.

As in general, the host and the accelerator do not share memory, data needs to be shipped to the accelerator (and back) so that the kernel IP can access it. Hence, the compiler and the runtime system must solve three problems. First, *identify the values that need to be passed to the outlined code*. Used techniques range from naively copying all the data in the scope to relying on compiler analyses or programmer specifications (data `map` clause) to limit the amount of moved data and to thus gain performance. Second, *create a parameter list for the payload function (fed into the accelerator tool chain)*. Used techniques range from naively creating one parameter for each value, to bundling values in structs or arrays. For FPGAs, fewer parameters result in fewer bus ports in the generated FPGA hardware which saves valuable resources on the fabric that then can be used for the functional entities. Despite the importance, most papers do not reveal how they generate parameter lists. Third, *generate API calls to transfer values to the accelerator*. Value transfer routines can be asynchronous (non-blocking) or synchronous (blocking). What works best depends on the accelerator hardware. Both techniques are used to transfer data to/from computing devices. For FPGAs, their ASIC devices constrain what transfer method works best for any given application. While conceptually it is possible to tailor the transfer routines to fit the LLP (and vice versa), to the best of our knowledge there is not yet an OpenMP-to-FPGA compiler that exploits this option.

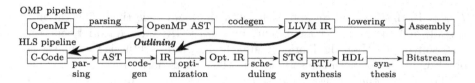

Fig. 3. Front-end outlining options in an OpenMP-to-FPGA compiler.

Ability to Compose Streams: It is state-of-the-art to outline each code block individually. This implies that modified data is shipped back from the accelerator to the host CPU even if the next outlined code block uses the same data. In this case, regardless of the type of accelerator, transfer cost can be saved. On FPGAs, this optimization idea may have an even larger impact than on GPUs as two subsequent `target` regions could use a streaming design to exploit pipeline-style parallelism for better performance. To the best of our knowledge this has not yet been explored.

2.4　Supported Pragmas

When distributing/mapping a code block to the FPGA, compilers may or may not be able to exploit OpenMP pragmas. For the discussion, we distinguish between OpenMP pragmas that are defined in the standard and HLS-specific ones defined by tool vendors. OpenMP-to-FPGA projects that use HLS-tools often *pass through* the latter to the HLS tool chain when they outline the code according to Fig. 3.

As the surveyed projects are still prototypes, they ignore most of the regular OpenMP pragmas. Tables 1 and 2 hold a positive list of those pragmas that they support, in the sense that a pragma somehow affects the code they build during outlining and that they feed into the HLS tool chain. As mentioned before, data shipment between host and FPGA matters. Hence, Tables 1 and 2 also cover whether a system supports the `map` clauses of the `target` pragma.

2.5　Optimization Techniques

OpenMP compilers also differ w.r.t. the (few) optimization technique they apply along their pipelines. This is outside the scope of this survey.

2.6　High-Level Synthesis

As shown in Fig. 3, the OpenMP-to-FPGA tool chain uses a High-level synthesis (HLS) tool to transform C/C++ code into FPGA hardware. The design spaces comprises three different types of HLS: *Data path* based (DP), *finite state machine* based (FSM), and *hybrid* HLS [31]. A DP-based HLS produces the best hardware for C/C++ code that is highly data parallel. It does not work well for code that has many branches in it [16]. FSM-based HLS tools can translate most programs (with the exception of programs that use recursion, malloc, or function pointers). Unfortunately, FSMs in hardware in general suffer from a higher latency than DP designs. Hybrid HLS tools are most commonly used because they (try to) combine the advantages of the two pure types: Vivado HLS [40], Intel OpenCL SDK for FPGA [18], or Intel Quartus Prime (previously Altera Quartus) [20] are well known hybrid commercial tools. LegUp [9] is a alternative from the research community. There also is a commercial fork available [25]. CoDeveloper [17] is a special HLS that only accepts the Impulse-C language. It does not fit into any of the above categories.

Which type of HLS to use for each target region is a design space decision. All surveyed projects treat *every* region the same way and use the same hardware synthesis for it, even though (at least conceptually) the decision can be made on a per-region basis as the amount of parallelism varies among them.

3   Survey

Tables 1 and 2 illustrate which design space decisions existing approaches took. The columns are ordered with the latest system first. As most authors have not named their systems, we use the name of the first author instead. We did not find more recent papers than the cited ones. There are references to code archives if systems are available for download. However, unfortunately none of the systems ran out-of-the box for us. The rows of the table are grouped according to the design space discussion in Sect. 2. Some areas of the table give more details on the design space aspects. In the HLS section the table lists which tools have been used. The *Misc.* rows mention which compiler frameworks and libraries have been used to build the system (e.g., Clang [24], LLVM [28,36], Mercurium [2], GCC [35], Nanos++ [3], or libomptarget [42]), for which FPGA boards they can be used, how the structure of the target systems looks, and whether the system offers a complete workflow that does not require any intermediate manual work along the tool chain. Simplified block diagrams sketch the target structure. Here M stands for memory, B for bus interconnect, C for CPU, G for GPU, A for application specific kernel IP, S for synchronization core, D for hardware debugger, and T for timer. Lines represent physical connections and parts in cyan live on the fabric. The superscripts give additional information on a component (e.g., C^{xeon} for a Xeon CPU). The subscripts show instance counts or memory sizes (e.g., C_4 for a 4-core CPU, A_n for n application specific kernel IPs, M_{2gb} for a memory block with 2 gigabytes of storage).

Table 1. Project overview (2019–2014)

	Knaust	Bosch	Ceissler	Sommer	Podobas
Year	2019	2018	2018	2017	2014–2016
Papers	[21]	[7]	[12]	[34]	[30,31]
Code	✗	[5]	[11]	✗	✗
LLP	generic-static	specialized-static	generic-static	specialized-static	specialized-static
Work distrib.	*host-centric* CF_{hw}	*host-centric* CGF_{hw}	*host-centric* CF_{hw}	*host-centric* CF_{hw}	*fpga-centric* $F_{hw,sc}$
OpenMP	target (with map)	target (with map), task, taskwait	parallel, parallel for, target (with map), target data, declare target	target (with map)	parallel, task, single, taskwait
HLS	✔	✔	✗	✔	✗
Level HLS	IR	AST	n.a.	AST	AST
HLS	Hybrid: Intel OpenCL	Hybrid: Vivado HLS	n.a.	Hybrid: Vivado HLS	Configurable from FSM- to DP-based
Streaming	✗	✔	✗	✗	✗
Compiler Toolkit	Clang, LLVM	Mercurium, Nanos++	Clang, LLVM, libomptarget	Clang, LLVM, libomptarget, TPC [22,23]	Custom C89 Compiler
Target system(s)	Intel Board with Arria 10 GX	Xilinx Board with Zynq Ultrascale+	Amazon AWS F1, Intel HARP2	Xilinx VC709 Board	Altera ED5 Board with Stratix V
Target Structure	$C_4^{\text{w2125,xeon}}$ — B^{pci} – M^{ddr} — B^{avalon} — A_n	$C_4^{\text{arm,A52}}$ $C_2^{\text{arm,R5}}$ — B^{axi4} – $G^{\text{arm,Mali}}$ — A_n M_{4gb}^{ddr4}	M^{ddr} – $C^{\text{xeon,e5}}$ — B^{pci} B^{qpi} — FiFo — A	$C_4^{\text{intel,i7-6700}}$ — B^{pcie} M_{16gb}^{ddr4} — B^{axi} — A_n M_{4gb}^{sdram}	C^{niosII} D — B^{avalon} T — A_n M
Complete workflow	✔	✔	✗	✔	✔

(Row groups labelled at left: Pragmas, Outlining, Misc.)

3.1 Projects

Below we describe the essence of the systems and their main contributions. Readers may skip the lines in fine print that detail the corresponding cells of the table. In bold is the name of the addressed cell of Tables 1 and 2. Most papers evaluate their compilers. Where appropriate, we summarize the evaluation results with respect to the benchmarks used, the method of comparison, and the main evaluation results obtained.

Knaust's host-centric prototype uses Clang to outline omp target regions at the level of the LLVM IR and feeds them into Intel's OpenCL HLS to generate a hardware kernel for the FPGA. This approach relies on an undocumented IR interface of the HLS. For the communication between host and FPGA, Knaust uses Intel's OpenCL API. It is unique how this work exploits a state-of-the-art commercial HLS with low transformation efforts.

Table 2. Project overview (2014–2006)

	Filgueras	Choi	Cilardo	Cabrera	Leow
Year	2014	2013	2013	2009	2006
Papers	[15]	[13]	[14]	[8]	[26]
Code	[4]	[10]	✗	✗	✗
LLP	specialized-static	generic-static	specialized-static	generic-static	n.a.
Work distrib.	*fpga-centric*, (*host-centric*) $F_{hw,hc}$, (CF_{hw})	*fpga-centric* $F_{hw,sc}$	*fpga-centric* $F_{hw,sc}$	*host-centric* CF_{hw}	*fpga-centric* F_{hw}
OpenMP	parallel, target (with map), task, taskwait	parallel for (with reduction), parallel, master, critical, atomic	Complete OpenMP 3.1	target (with map), task, block	threadprivate, barrier, for, parallel, parallel for, master, critical, atomic, single, section, for section, ordered, flush
HLS	✔	✗	?	✗	✗
Level	AST	IR	AST	n.a.	n.a.
HLS	Hybrid: Vivado HLS	Hybrid: LegUp	Impulse CoDeveloper	n.a.	FSM-based
Streaming	✗	✗	✗	✗	✗
Compiler Toolkit	Mercurium, Nanos++	LLVM-GCC	Custom OpenMP, Xilinx EDK	Mercurium, GCC, SGI RASClib	C-Breeze [27]
Target system(s)	Xilinx Board with Zynq-7000	Altera Board with Stratix IV	Boards supported by Xilinx EDK	SGI RASC 2.2 Board with 2 Virtex 4	Celoxica RC100 Board with Spartan II
Target Structure	M | $B^{amba} - B^{axi}$ | | | A_n | $C_2^{arm\ A9} - B^{axi}$	C^{mips} | B^{avalon} | A_n	$C_c^{\mu Blaze}$ | S | / $B^{axi} - T$ | \\ M_k^{rom} | A_n M_m^{ram}	$C_{128}^{itanium}$ | B / \\ $A_k A_n$	M_2^{ssram} | A
Complete workflow	✔	✔	✔	✗	✔

LLP: The internals of the LLP cannot be classified exactly because Intel's SDK is proprietary. However, the *Floorplan Optimization Guide* of the SDK mentions that the LLP is loaded only once and that partial reconfiguration is used to hot-swap kernel IP bitstreams at runtime [19]. **Pragmas:** Knaust passes the `unroll` pragma to the underlying HLS. From the `map` clauses of the `target` pragma, only *array sections* are unsupported.

Evaluation: Two Sobel filters (unoptimized and optimized for FPGAs) run on a $4096 \cdot 2160 \cdot 8$ bit matrix. The CPU-only version is compiled without `-fopenmp`. The pure optimized kernel for the FPGA is 4× as fast as one CPU core, but this can hardly amortize the cost of transfer and initialization.

OmpSs@FPGA by *Bosch* et al. improves and generalizes the work by Filgueras et al. Memory on the accelerator is used for data sharing (streaming). This is the only system in the surveyed set that not only outlines code to the FPGA but also addresses the GPU. Moreover, the `tasks` are *dynamically* scheduled onto the devices.

LLP: The authors do not describe the structure of the LLP in detail. However, in contrast to Filgueras et al. there are hints that it falls into the specialized-static class.

Evaluation: On three benchmarks (matrix multiplication, n-body, Cholesky decomposition) the authors compare the baseline runtime (measured on a $C_4^{ARM-A52}$ with 4 GB of shared memory) with their FPGA versions. For the Cholesky decomposition, the performance drops by about 2×. For n-body, the FPGA version is 15× faster. The matrix multiplication on the FPGA achieves 6× the GFLOP/s.

Ceissler et al. propose HardCloud, a host-centric extension for OpenMP 4.X. There is no outlining of code blocks. Instead, HardCloud makes pre-synthesized functional units for FPGAs easier to use in existing OpenMP code.

LLP: While the authors do not describe the internals of their LLP, the first figure in [12] suggests it to be generic-static. **Complete Workflow:** Users need to manually design hardware and synthesize it to a kernel IP as there is no outlining. HardCloud automates the data transfer and device control.

Evaluation: The authors claim to have achieved speed-ups on the HARP 2 platform between 1.1× and 135×. However there is no further information about the context or the benchmark codes.

Sommer et al. use Clang to extract `omp target` regions from the source program (at AST-level) and feed them into the Vivado HLS that then generates kernel IPs. Calls to their Thread Pool Composer (TPC) API (now called TaPaSCo) injected into the program implement the host-to-FPGA communication. The strength of the prototype is that it fully supports `omp target` (including its `map` clause). This project is the first that integrated libomptarget.

LLP: TPC assembles a specialized-static LLP from the following set: the kernel IPs, configuration files describing the IPs, and an architecture configuration file describing for example what bus system to use (only AXI in their work).

Evaluation: For 6 benchmarks from the Adept benchmark suite [1], the authors compare the runtime of -O3-optimized i7 CPU code (4 cores) to their FPGA-only version (with HLS pragmas). The CPU outperforms the FPGA version by 3× to 3.5× (without the HLS pragmas: 6× to 9×).

In the system by *Podobas* et al. the compiler extracts `task`-annotated functions and synthesizes a specialized system on a chip (SoC) for them. It rewrites the main program to use these units and compiles it to run on a softcore CPU that is also placed on the FPGA. While their first system builds isolated FPGA hardware per `task`, the authors later fuse `task` kernel IPs for resource sharing. To do so they use Gecode [32] to solve constraint programs in which the constraints express what to share.

LLP: Altera Quartus builds the specialized-static LLP. It connects the kernel IPs and assigns an own address space on a shared Avalon bus to each of them. It also connects auxiliary blocks and the softcore to that bus. **Pragmas:** The behaviour of the pragmas `parallel` and `single` slightly differ from the OpenMP specification. If both pragmas are written consecutively in the source code, the system replaces them by a function call that initializes the LLP. The behaviour of just one pragma is left open. **HLS:** The authors use the custom hardware synthesis tool fpBLYSK. Depending on the command line flags, their HLS can generate purely FSM-based designs that execute one instruction per state, or it can combine several instructions into each FSM state, giving the design a DP taste.

Evaluation: The authors study three basic benchmarks (π, Mandelbrot, and prime numbers). For the first two compute-bound benchmarks, the FPGA version outperforms both CPU-only versions (57-core Intel Xeon PHI and 48-core AMD Opteron 6172) by a factor of 2 to 3. However, for the memory-bound third benchmark, the CPU versions are about 100 times faster.

Filgueras et al. add support for the Xilinx Zynq FPGA [41] to the OmpSs framework [6] that provides `task` offloading to any kind of supported accelerator. Although their prototype exclusively uses the FPGA's ASIC CPUs for the sequential portion of the source code (fpga-centric, $F_{hw,hc}$). The authors claim any work distribution to be possible (e.g., CF_{hw}). The system is the first that combines this flexibility with the task based paradigm (including task dependencies).

LLP: The authors do not describe in detail how the compiler builds the LLP. **Pragmas:** The `task` pragma is extended so that it can be used to annotate functions and to specify dependencies between tasks (clauses `in`, `out`, or `inout`). **Compiler Toolkit:** A custom pass implemented in the Mercurium framework outlines and injects calls for data shipment. The Nanos++ OpenMP runtime provides task parallelism and dependency-based task scheduling.

Evaluation: On four numeric benchmarks (two matrix multiplications with different matrix sizes, complex covariance, and Cholesky decomposition) the FPGA version achieves speed-ups between $6\times$ to $30\times$ compared to a single ARM A9 core.

The system by *Choi* et al. is fpga-centric. Its main objective is to exploit the information on parallelism that the programmers provide in (six supported) pragmas, to generate better, more parallel hardware. The compiler synthesizes one kernel IP per thread in the source program (for example a code block annotated with `parallel num_threads(4)` specifies 4 hardware threads). The support for the `reduction` clause of `parallel` or `parallel for` is unique, although the authors do not elaborate on how they achieve reduction on variables in hardware.

Pragmas: The system is limited to OpenMP constructs for which the compiler can statically determine the number of threads to use. Nested parallelism is possible, although limited to two levels. **HLS:** The extended LegUp generates parallel hardware for `parallel` and `parallel for` and utilizes the other pragmas (`atomic`, etc.) to synchronize between the threads. For `atomic` and `critical`, a hardware mutex core is synthesized.

Evaluation: With the best compiler configuration for the FPGA versions, 7 benchmarks (Black-Scholes option pricing, simulated light propagation, Mandelbrot, line of sight, integer set division, hash algorithms, double-precision floating point sine function) show a geomean speed-up of 7.6× and a geomean area-delay product of 63% compared to generated sequential hardware.

Cilardo et al. think of OpenMP as a system-level design language (e.g., for heterogeneous targets like the Xilinx Zynq) and present a compiler that uniquely supports the complete OpenMP 3.1 specification. They map the whole OpenMP program to the FPGA (where they use softcore processors to run threads with many branches). Note, that the authors even map nested parallelism (i.e., nested omp work sharing constructs) to hardware (by exploiting the tree-like structure to minimize path lengths for common control signals).

LLP: The Xilinx Embedded Development Kit (EDK) [39] was used to build the LLP, but the authors only reveal that they use the MicroBlaze [37] softcore for the sequential parts. **Pragmas:** As their custom front-end only supports OpenMP-parsing, it is unlikely that HLS pragmas are passed through.

Evaluation: When comparing their sieve of Eratosthenes to the results from Leow et al. the authors see twice the speed-up. Furthermore, a runtime overhead inspection of the implemented OpenMP directives (`private`, `firstprivate`, `dynamic`, `static`, and `critical`) shows significantly less overhead than the SMP versions on an Intel i7 (6×, 1.2×, 3.1×, 10.5×, and 2.64×, respectively).

Cabrera et al. extend OpenMP 3.0 with new semantics for `task` and `target` to ease the offloading to pre-synthesized functional units, i.e., hand-built kernel IPs. There is no outlining of code blocks. Their main contribution is that they provide support for SGI's RASC platform [33] and a multi-threaded runtime library layer with a bitstream cache that enables parallel computation on both the host and the FPGA even while the bitstream is being uploaded.

LLP: The target system is embedded into an SGI Altix 4700 server and a proprietary generic-static LLP provided by SGI is used. **Pragmas:** The work introduces the pragma block that helps to guide loop restructuring and data partitioning of arrays. **HLS:** Xilinx ISE 9.1 (now part of the Vivado Design Suite) is used to generate bitstreams. **Compiler Toolkit:** Offloading is implemented as a plugin for the Mercurium compiler. The host-side code compiles with GCC 4.1.2 and links against a custom runtime library.

Evaluation: The paper only shows runtimes of a matrix multiplication (32^2, 64^2, and 128^2) without any comparisons with CPU codes.

Leow et al. view OpenMP programs as a hardware description language that programmers use to explicitly control the parallelism of the resulting hardware. In contrast to other systems, the result is a *single* hardware entity (F_{hw}) without any outlining and work distribution at all.

HLS, Compiler Toolkit: The translation is integrated into the C-Breeze compiler framework as a custom high-level synthesis pass. It can generate both Handel-C [29] and VHDL code, but different restrictions apply. For example, the VHDL back-end cannot deal with global variables in the input program.

Evaluation: For the first two of the benchmarks (matrix multiplication, sieve of Eratosthenes, Mandelbrot), the FPGA versions achieves speed-ups of 25× and 7× over a symmetrical SMP (UltraSPARC III with 8GiB). For Mandelbrot, the FPGA version is slower than the SMP, even though all SMP codes were compiled with -O0.

3.2 Discussion

The surveyed projects are prototypes focusing only on a small subset of OpenMP pragmas and require users with compiler- and/or FPGA-expertise. Almost half of the tools still require manual outlining and invoking of HLS tools, and for only three systems the source code is available.

About half the systems are *host-centric*. The general idea is to achieve performance and efficiency by standing on the shoulders of giants. Research falls into two groups. Systems in one group (Ceissler and Cabrera) assume pre-synthesized, highly optimized and efficient kernel IPs that need to be interconnected. The underlying hope is that the generated glue hardware is not that crucial for performance. Because of the pre-built kernels those systems are tied tightly to specific FPGA platforms, e.g., Intel HARP2, Amazon AWSF1, or SGI RASC.

The other group outlines code blocks and feeds them into an HLS tool chain for building the kernel IP. The hope is that vendors invest enough money and man power into these tools so that they synthesize efficient FPGA hardware. As shown in Fig. 3, outlining can either be done on the level of ASTs or at the IR-level. The latter approach (taken by Knaust) not only suffers from not being future-proof as current HLS tools only provide undocumented IR-level interfaces. The other disadvantage is that it is complicated to pass HLS pragmas to the HLS tool. The problem is that such pragmas need to be transformed into unofficial IR annotations that are even more likely to change or to become unavailable in the future. AST-based outlining does not have these disadvantages because passing HLS pragmas is easy as ASTs can be trivially converted to C code and because using the HLS on AST-level can be expected to work for the foreseeable future. The main problem of using an HLS from a certain vendor is that only this vendor's FPGAs can be used.

The *fpga-centric* approaches understand a whole OpenMP program as a high-level description of the FPGA hardware that has to be built, i.e., the FPGA is no longer used as an accelerator but it is the only device. This group of researchers usually builds specific compilers that focus on optimizing transformations for pragmas that are directly relevant for the hardware synthesis. Depending on the size and the importance of the sequential code blocks, systems either use a softcore processor on the fabric for it, or they include the sequential code into the kernel IP. On the one hand, FPGAs programmed with compilers that use the pragma information are claimed to perform better because the programmer can specify application-specific parallelism. The main drawback, on the other hand, is that host CPUs (optimized for memory-intensive sequential workloads) stay unused. The general problem of the fpga-centric approaches is that in general they only work for a specific FPGA and/or tool chain.

4   Conclusion and Future Work

The basic technical issues of host-centric target offloading with a CF_{hw} work distribution have been covered extensively, both with outlining on the AST- or IR-level. Similarly, the fpga-centric compilers that treat OpenMP as some sort of hardware/system-level description languages use basic mapping regimes to assemble FPGA bitstreams for targets and to distribute the work in various ways.

The field is in a proof-of-concept state. We think that what is needed now is a focus on performance and efficiency. There is not yet a benchmark to quantitatively compare systems. Little work has been done so far on optimization. For example, self-adapting, dynamic LLPs may be the better infrastructure and may free FPGA resources for functional entities/kernel IPs. Instead of treating each `omp target` region in isolation, it may be promising to explore how to automatically connect kernel IPs in a streaming fashion (as human FPGA engineers usually do). Currently, FPGA-expertise is required to achieve better performance than leaving the FPGA unused. This burden needs to be taken from the OpenMP programmer, i.e., they should no longer need to be experts in HLS pragmas and in the tools of FPGA vendors.

From our perspective, the key to all of this is a better code analysis that not only spans across all the OpenMP pragmas used in a given code, but that also spans from IR-level to low-level HLS transformations. We feel that at least there should be a (to be designed) interface between the various tools along the tool chain to convey optimization-related analysis data.

Acknowledgments. The authors acknowledge the financial support by the Federal Ministry of Education and Research of Germany in the framework of ORKA-HPC (project numbers 01IH17003C and 01IH17003D).

References

1. Adept: Adept Benchmark Suite. http://www.adept-project.eu/benchmarks.html
2. Barcelona Supercomputing Center: Mercurium C/C++/Fortran source-to-source compiler. https://www.bsc.es/research-and-development/software-and-apps/software-list/mercurium-ccfortran-source-source-compiler
3. Barcelona Supercomputing Center: Nanos++. https://pm.bsc.es/nanox
4. Barcelona Supercomputing Center: OmpSs@FPGA. https://pm.bsc.es/ompss-at-fpga
5. Barcelona Supercomputing Center: Repository of the Mercurium C/C++/Fortran source-to-source compiler. https://www.github.com/bsc-pm/mcxx
6. Barcelona Supercomputing Center: The OmpSs Programming Model. https://pm.bsc.es/ompss
7. Bosch, J., et al.: Application acceleration on FPGAs with OmpSs@FPGA. In: Proceedings of the International Conference on Field-Programmable Technology (FPT 2018), Naha, Japan, December 2018

8. Cabrera, D., Martorell, X., Gaydadjiev, G., Ayguade, E., Jiménez-González, D.: OpenMP extensions for FPGA accelerators. In: Proceedings of the International Conference on Systems, Architectures, Modeling and Simulation (SAMOS 2009), Samos, Greece, pp. 17–24, July 2009
9. Canis, A., et al.: LegUp: high-level synthesis for FPGA-based processor/accelerator systems. In: Proceedings of the International Symposium on Field Programmable Gate Arrays (FPGA 2011), Monterey, CA, pp. 33–36, February 2011
10. Canis, A., Choi, J., Chen, Y.T., Hsiao, H.: LegUp High-Level Synthesis. http://legup.eecg.utoronto.ca/
11. Ceissler, C.: HardCloud Github Wiki. https://github.com/omphardcloud/hardcloud/wiki
12. Ceissler, C., Nepomuceno, R., Pereira, M.M., Araujo, G.: Automatic offloading of cluster accelerators. In: Proceedings of the International Symposium on Field-Programmable Custom Computing Machines (FCCM 2018), Boulder, CO, p. 224, April 2018
13. Choi, J., Brown, S., Anderson, J.: From software threads to parallel hardware in high-level synthesis for FPGAs. In: Proceedings of the International Conference on Field-Programmable Technology (FPT 2013), Kyoto, Japan, pp. 270–277, January 2013
14. Cilardo, A., Gallo, L., Mazzeo, A., Mazzocca, N.: Efficient and scalable OpenMP-based system-level design. In: Proceedings of Design, Automation and Test in Europe (DATE 2013), Grenoble, France, pp. 988–991, March 2013
15. Filgueras, A., et al.: OmpSs@Zynq all-programmable SoC ecosystem. In: International Symposium on Field-Programmable Gate Arrays (FPGA 2014), Monterey, CA, pp. 137–146, February 2014
16. Halstead, R.J., Najjar, W.A.: Compiled multithreaded data paths on FPGAs for dynamic workloads. In: Proceedings of the International Conference on Compilers, Architecture and Synthesis for Embedded Systems (CASES 2013), Montreal, QC, pp. 21–30, September 2013
17. Impulse Accelerated Technologies: Impulse CoDeveloper. http://web.archive.org/web/20180827120514/impulseaccelerated.com/tools.html
18. Intel Corporation: Intel FPGA SDK for OpenCL. https://www.intel.de/content/www/de/de/software/programmable/sdk-for-opencl/overview.html
19. Intel Corporation: Intel FPGA SDK for OpenCL Board Support Package Floorplan Optimization Guide. https://www.intel.com/content/dam/www/programmable/us/en/pdfs/literature/an/an824.pdf
20. Intel Corporation: Intel Quartus Prime. https://www.intel.de/content/www/de/de/software/programmable/quartus-prime/overview.html
21. Knaust, M., Mayer, F., Steinke, T.: OpenMP to FPGA offloading prototype using OpenCL SDK. In: Proceedings of the International Workshop High-Level Parallel Programming Models and Supportive Environment (HIPS 2019), Rio de Janeiro, Brazil, p. to appear, May 2019
22. Korinth, J., Chevallerie, D.d.l., Koch, A.: An open-source tool flow for the composition of reconfigurable hardware thread pool architectures. In: Proceedings of the International Symposium on Field-Programmable Custom Computing Machines (FCCM 2015), Vancouver, BC, pp. 195–198, May 2015
23. Korinth, J., Hofmann, J., Heinz, C., Koch, A.: The TaPaSCo open-source toolflow for the automated composition of task-based parallel reconfigurable computing systems. In: Proceedings of the International Symposium on Applied Reconfigurable Computing, (ARC 2019), Darmstadt, Germany, pp. 214–229, April 2019

24. Lattner, C., The Clang Team: Clang: a C language family frontend for LLVM. https://clang.llvm.org/
25. LegUp Computing: LegUp. http://www.legupcomputing.com/
26. Leow, Y., Ng, C., Wong, W.: Generating hardware from OpenMP programs. In: Proceedings of the International Conference on Field Programmable Technology (FPT 2006), Bangkok, Thailand, pp. 73–80, December 2006
27. Lin, C., Guyer, S., Jimenez, D.: The C-Breeze Compiler Infrastructure. https://www.cs.utexas.edu/users/c-breeze/
28. LLVM Team: llvm-gcc - LLVM C front-end. https://releases.llvm.org/2.9/docs/CommandGuide/html/llvmgcc.html
29. Mentor: Handel-C. https://www.mentor.com/products/fpga/handel-c/
30. Podobas, A.: Accelerating parallel computations with OpenMP-driven system-on-chip generation for FPGAs. In: Proceedings of the International Symposium on Embedded Multicore/Manycore SoCs (MCSoC 2014), Aizu-Wakamatsu, Japan, pp. 149–156, September 2014
31. Podobas, A., Brorsson, M.: Empowering OpenMP with automatically generated hardware. In: Proceedings of the International Conference on Systems, Architectures, Modeling and Simulation (SAMOS 2016), Agios Konstantinos, Greece, pp. 245–252, January 2016
32. Schulte, C., Lagerkvist, M., Tack, G.: Gecode. https://www.gecode.org
33. Silicon Graphics: Reconfigurable Application-Specific Computing User's Guide, March 2006. https://irix7.com/techpubs/007-4718-004.pdf
34. Sommer, L., Korinth, J., Koch, A.: OpenMP device offloading to FPGA accelerators. In: Proceedings of the International Conference on Application-specific Systems, Architectures and Processors (ASAP 2017), Seattle, WA, pp. 201–205, July 2017
35. The GCC Team: GCC, the GNU Compiler Collection. https://gcc.gnu.org/
36. The LLVM Team: The LLVM Compiler Infrastructure. https://llvm.org/
37. Xilinx: MicroBlaze Soft Processor Core. https://www.xilinx.com/products/design-tools/microblaze.html
38. Xilinx: Partial Reconfiguration in the Vivado Design Suite. https://www.xilinx.com/products/design-tools/vivado/implementation/partial-reconfiguration.html
39. Xilinx: Platform Studio and the Embedded Development Kit (EDK). https://www.xilinx.com/products/design-tools/platform.html
40. Xilinx: Vivado Design Suite. https://www.xilinx.com/products/design-tools/vivado.html#documentation
41. Xilinx: Zynq-7000 SoC Data Sheet. https://www.xilinx.com/support/documentation/data_sheets/ds190-Zynq-7000-Overview.pdf
42. Yviquel, H., Hahnfeld, J.: libomptarget - OpenMP offloading runtime libraries for Clang. https://github.com/clang-omp/libomptarget

OpenMP Dynamic Device Offloading
in Heterogeneous Platforms

Ángel Álvarez$^{(\boxtimes)}$ ⓘ, Íñigo Ugarte$^{(\boxtimes)}$ ⓘ, Víctor Fernández$^{(\boxtimes)}$ ⓘ,
and Pablo Sánchez$^{(\boxtimes)}$

Microelectronics Engineering Group, University of Cantabria, Santander, Spain
{alvarez,ugarte,victor,sanchez}@teisa.unican.es

Abstract. Heterogeneous architectures which integrate general purpose CPUs with specialized accelerators such as GPUs and FPGAs are becoming very popular since they achieve greater performance/energy trade-offs than CPU-only architectures. To support this trend, the OpenMP standard has introduced a set of offloading constructs that enable to execute code fragments in accelerator devices. The current offloading model heavily depends on the compiler supporting each target device, with many architectures still unsupported by the most popular compilers (e.g. GCC and Clang). In this article, we introduce a new methodology for offloading OpenMP annotated code to accelerator devices. In our proposal, the software compilation and/or hardware synthesis processes to program the accelerator are independent from the host OpenMP compiler. As a consequence, multiple device architectures can be easily supported through their specific compiler/design tools. Also, the designer is able to manually optimize the original offloaded code or provide an alternative input to the design flow (e.g. VHDL/Verilog or third party IP cores for FPGA), thus leading to an effective speed-up of the application. In order to enable the proposed methodology, a powerful runtime infrastructure that dynamically loads and manages the available device-specific implementations has been developed.

Keywords: OpenMP · Offloading · GPU · FPGA

1 Introduction

Heterogeneous computing architectures which combine general purpose CPUs and dedicated accelerators such as GPUs and FPGAs have become extensively used both in large processing centers and on embedded systems. These platforms outperform homogeneous multi-core CPU systems in terms of computing capabilities and especially energy efficiency (operations per watt) [1]. In order to facilitate the design for hardware accelerators, programming models such as OpenCL [2] and CUDA [3] have emerged and powerful hardware synthesis tools

This work has been funded by EU and Spanish MICINN through project ECSEL2017-1-737451 and Spanish MICINN through project TEC2017-86722-C4-3-R.

X. Fan et al. (Eds.): IWOMP 2019, LNCS 11718, pp. 109–122, 2019.
https://doi.org/10.1007/978-3-030-28596-8_8

have been introduced by the industry to enable the use of high-level languages such as C, C++ and OpenCL to generate FPGA-based accelerators.

The performance of a code executing on a CPU (*host device*), can be improved by *offloading* a code fragment (*target region* or *kernel*) to a hardware accelerator (*target device*), like a GPU or FPGA. Since its origin, OpenMP has proven to be an efficient and widely used model for programming shared-memory symmetric multiprocessor (SMP) architectures. In recent versions, the standard [4] has introduced a set of extensions to support code offloading to accelerators. This model relies on the compiler to support the generation of the executable code for the accelerator device. The implementation of the OpenMP offloading features in GCC [5] and Clang [6] is still under development, with many architectures still unsupported.

This paper introduces a new offloading methodology which allows both large compatibility with different device architectures and flexibility in the design of the computation kernels. In our approach, the SW compilation/HW synthesis and (optionally) design flows for the accelerator device are independent from the OpenMP compiler. In order to support the above, a flexible and interoperable runtime infrastructure has been developed, which fully integrates with the standard OpenMP runtime.

The rest of this paper is organized as follows. In Sect. 2, the proposed offloading methodology is introduced. Section 3 describes the implemented runtime infrastructure, which we evaluate over some heterogeneous architectures in Sect. 4. Section 5 provides related work. Finally, Sect. 6 concludes the paper and discusses future work.

2   Methodology

2.1   Motivation

As explained in the previous section, one drawback of the current offloading process in OpenMP is the fact that target devices must be supported by the OpenMP compiler. Also, this scheme leaves the designer with very little or no flexibility to modify the design in some scenarios such as offloading to hardware accelerators, in which specific optimizations as well as code/algorithm modifications are required to generate efficient implementations.

This work focuses on the development of a new OpenMP offloading methodology. The key idea of our approach is to dissociate the OpenMP compiler from device specific compilation/synthesis processes and provide an efficient mechanism to integrate device implementations with the host executable during runtime. In order to make it possible, a runtime infrastructure which integrates with the OpenMP runtime is developed.

The elementary requirements that the proposed infrastructure has to meet are summarized as follows:

1. Allowing the development of new device implementations after compilation of the host code. Runtime mechanisms are defined for dynamic loading of the new device-specific implementations.

2. Enabling the runtime infrastructure to identify, during execution time, all the available implementations as well as computing resources required to execute them.
3. Enabling the runtime infrastructure to provide dynamic task allocation during execution time. The designer will be able to use runtime library routines to set the target device.
4. Allowing device-specific implementations to optionally include performance metadata, like memory requirements, execution time or power consumption. Similarly, identified computing resources may include information such as memory size and clock frequency. This could be used to guide device selection at runtime. In order to use this information, new OpenMP runtime functions should be defined.

Let offloading to FPGA serve as an example of application. A proof-of-concept implementation of OpenMP offloading to FPGA which integrates with the LLVM offloading infrastructure has already been presented in [7]. It uses Vivado HLS to generate the hardware from the C/C++ original code. Despite the fact that the designer can add synthesis directives (pragmas) in the original code to be used by the high-level synthesis tool, the code cannot be modified with the aim of optimizing the generated hardware. In practice, it is well known by hardware designers that a deep knowledge of the synthesis tool and wisely modifying the input code (along with the use of directives) are key points to get an efficient hardware design.

Our approach is based on generating a host binary which integrates device-specific implementations during runtime and breaking apart the device code compilation flow. Then, the original code of the OpenMP target regions can be used as an input to the HLS tool though the designer is able to get into the design flow and generate an optimized code as well. Moreover, hardware description languages such as VHDL or Verilog or even external IP cores can be used depending on the designer preferences. The integration of these implementations is supported by the proposed runtime infrastructure. In addition, high flexibility in terms of supported devices is provided since designers use device-specific compilers or synthesis tools no matter whether they are supported by the current OpenMP compilers.

2.2 Target Platforms and Supported Devices/Accelerators

With the increasing importance of heterogeneous platforms which integrate CPUs, GPUs and FPGA-based hardware accelerators, supporting as many targets as possible is at the core of our methodology. From OpenMP API 4.0 (released in 2013) some directives to instruct the compiler and runtime to offload a region of code to a device are available to the programmer [4,8]. However, support for the target devices must be included into the compiler infrastructure in order to allow device offloading. In practice, offloading support in the most commonly used compilers is still immature [5,6]. In our approach, by making the device-specific design flow independent from the OpenMP compiler, it is possible to offload a code region to almost any target provided that device compilers or synthesis tools are available to the designer. We will focus on proving the compatibility of the proposed methodology with: (i) GPUs, which can be programmed through OpenCL or propietary languages such as CUDA, and (ii) FPGA devices, through high-level synthesis or hardware description languages.

2.3   Offloading Design Flow

Consider a computation node with a host device (CPU) connected to one or multiple accelerators. The starting point in the OpenMP accelerator model flow is a source file with standard OpenMP code, in which the region of code (known as *target region*) to be offloaded to an accelerator (known as *target device*) is specified by the `target` directive.

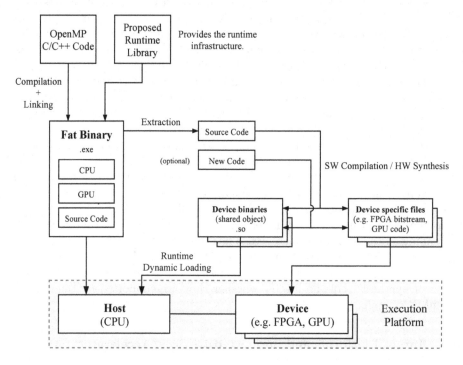

Fig. 1. Design flow for the proposed OpenMP dynamic device offloading methodology.

In our proposal (summarized in Fig. 1), the original input source file has to be compiled and linked with a library which provides a runtime infrastructure to allow the use of the new dynamic offloading methodology. This infrastructure integrates with the standard OpenMP runtime and will be detailed in Sect. 3.

When a compiler supports offloading to a certain architecture, a binary for each target is commonly inserted into the host fat binary file. In order to support any potential target device, the source code corresponding to the target region has to be included in the fat binary as well. Then, this code is extracted to be used as the input of a separate compilation/synthesis flow. Automation of these steps and integration of the proposed methodology into an existing OpenMP open-source compiler are out of the scope of this paper.

The compilation/synthesis of the target code for the accelerator device are dissociated from the OpenMP compilation process in the presented methodology. On the one hand, the original source code of the target region can be directly used to program the accelerator (e.g. as the input to a high-level synthesis tool to generate an RTL design for FPGA). Also, the OpenMP code may be converted to an OpenCL kernel to be executed on a GPU/FPGA [12]. On the other hand, the designer has the possibility of modifying the code to achieve an effective speed-up of the application in a particular device or even taking a different approach, such as VHDL or Verilog in the case of FPGA or CUDA for a GPU from NVIDIA. This flexibility is one of the biggest advantages of the proposed methodology. Compilation/synthesis for the accelerator are carried out prior to the program execution. Compilation at runtime, also known as just-in-time (JIT) compilation, would not be feasible in terms of performance (e.g. FPGA bitstream generation is too time-consuming) and flexibility (the designer must be able to provide new code). New device implementations can be generated and new accelerators can be supported without recompiling the host code.

In order to run the target region in the accelerator device, the necessary executable code for the host is generated in the form of a shared object (i.e. a dynamic library). The tasks performed by these shared objects include managing the device status, the data transfer and the execution on the device. They are not inserted into the fat binary—instead, they are designed to integrate with the original host binary during runtime. Also, some device specific files can be produced in the design process, such as a bitstream to configure an FPGA device. Different implementations to accelerate the target region in multiple devices may be available. A single shared object can contain different implementations, or individual shared objects corresponding to each accelerator can be used (e.g. lib_GPU.so, lib_FPGA.so, etc). During execution time, the runtime infrastructure is able to identify all the available devices and implementations.

3   Proposed Runtime Infrastructure

In this section, the features and implementation details of the proposed runtime infrastructure are presented. First, we illustrate how it can be used from a programmer's point of view. Then, internal implementation details are given.

3.1 Programmer's Perspective

The runtime library provides the programmer with a set of routines to select and check the accelerator device during execution time. Their functionality could be added to their OpenMP counterparts (see Table 1). It is fully interoperable with the OpenMP runtime and all functions are designed to have a C binding, so that it supports C and C++. An example of the use of the runtime library to offload a code region from a programmer's perspective is shown in Listing 1. In the code, two concurrent OpenMP host threads are created, with identifiers '0' and '1'. In thread 0, some code in function1 will be executed on the CPU. In thread 1, some compute-intensive code is marked for offloading with the omp target directive. This code will be moved to the accelerator with device number '2', which is assumed to be an FPGA in the execution platform. In the example, the map clause has been used to explicitly indicate the variables to be copied to and from the device data environment.

Table 1. OpenMP runtime library routines modified to enable the new methodology.

Function	Description
void omp_set_default_device(int device_num)	Selects the default target device
int omp_get_default_device(void)	Returns the default target device
int omp_get_num_devices(void)	Returns the number of target devices

3.2 Implementation Details

As a result of the proposed design flow, two kinds of files are used at execution time:

The host binary (required), which includes the original code and an implementation corresponding to every target region marked for offloading for, at least, the CPU. Implementations for other devices may be included into the executable as well when supported by the OpenMP compiler.

Shared objects (optionally), which include implementations for one or multiple additional target devices, corresponding to one or various of the target regions marked for offloading.

During the host program execution, the runtime infrastructure is initialized the first time that a runtime routine or target region is executed. The available shared objects containing device implementations are loaded and some runtime lists are built: (i) a list of devices, (ii) a list of target-region functions and (iii) a list of implementations for each function. This data structures are shown in Fig. 2 and explained below.

Listing 1. Device offloading example with the proposed infrastructure.

```
1    #define GPU  1
2    #define FPGA 2
3
4    void host_code(char *image_in, char *image_out, int width, int height)
5    {
6        UC_set_default_device(FPGA);
7        omp_set_num_threads(2);
8
9        #pragma omp parallel
10       {
11           int id = omp_get_thread_num();
12           // ----Thread #0----
13           if(id == 0){
14               function1();
15           }
16           // ----Thread #1----
17           if(id == 1){
18               #pragma omp target map(to: image_in[0:width*height], width,
                         height) map(from: image_out[0:width*height])
19               {
20                   int x, y;
21                   for(y=0; y<height; y++){
22                       for(x=0; x<width; x++){
23                           // Some computation
24                           image_out[y*width + x] = image_in[y*width + x] * 0.5;
25                       }
26                   }
27               }
28           }
29       }
30   }
```

Devices. The accelerators devices supported by the host compiler and the ones defined in loaded shared objects are added to the global list of devices. Device 0 corresponds to the CPU and is always present. Every element in the list of devices contains metadata (such as name, type, status...) and pointers to device-specific management functions, which are detailed in Subsect. 3.3. Also, performance characteristics can be included (number of cores, memory size...). The above may be useful to add new functionality to the OpenMP runtime in the future, such as guiding the device selection process during execution.

Functions. For each target region marked for offloading with the **target** directive in the code, a *target-region function* is extracted and added to the global list of functions. Every element in the list contains information related to the arguments of the function (number, type and direction) and points to a list of implementations targeting one or more target devices (al least, the default CPU version is available).

Implementations. The available implementations for each *target-region function* are added to the list of implementations. Every element in the list contains data (such as the target device), pointers to implementation-specific management functions (explained in Subsect. 3.3) and a pointer to the executable code. Overall, the information handled by the proposed runtime method is organized

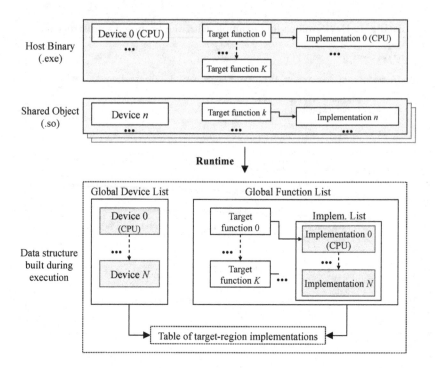

Fig. 2. Overview of data structures built by the runtime infrastructure.

in a *table of target-region implementations*, as represented in Table 2. In this version of the runtime, each device is associated with only one implementation and vice versa (i.e. for target region 0—first row in the table—Impl.(0,0) corresponds to Device 0, Impl.(0,1) to Device 1...). When the device required for offloading of a target region does not have an implementation available, the default implementation (Implementation 0) is launched on the CPU. The *table of target-region implementations* allows to integrate our proposal with the current OpenMP offloading methodology since it uses a similar approach.

Table 2. Table of target-region implementations handled by the runtime.

	Device 0	Device 1	...	Device N
Function 0	Impl. (0,0)	Impl. (0,1)	...	Impl. (0,N)
Function 1	Impl. (1,0)	Impl. (1,1)	...	Impl. (1,N)
⋮	⋮	⋮	⋮	⋮
Function K	Impl. (K,0)	Impl. (K,1)	...	Impl. (K,N)

3.3   Management of Devices and Implementations

For every device and implementation, a set of functions are provided to manage and configure the accelerator and the execution during runtime. These functions are summarized in Table 3. The runtime infrastructure internally employs these functions, although the tasks they perform are specific for each device/implementation. Owing to that reason, they are defined in the shared objects containing device implementations (default versions are in the host binary as well).

Table 3. Internal runtime routines to manage devices and implementations.

	Function	Description
Device	`open_device()`	Checks if the device is in the execution platform. If present, initializes the device. Allocates memory in the host to store device data
	`close_device()`	Releases the device. Deletes device data stored in the host memory
	`lock_device()`	Disables access to the device from other host thread
	`unlock_device()`	Enables access to the device from other host thread
Implementation	`init_implementation()`	Initializes the implementation (e.g. allocates memory in the device)
	`close_implementation()`	Clears the implementation (e.g. deallocates memory in the device)

Figure 3 shows the execution flow when a code region is offloaded to a device, in order to illustrate how the runtime infrastructure makes use of the above functions. As an example, consider offloading to a GPU through OpenCL. The implementation and management functions have been loaded from a shared object. When the runtime is initialized, all the available devices are recognized and opened. Only the devices included in the global device list can be recognized. In this case, opening the device means initializing the OpenCL variables related to the device, such as the *context* and the *queue*, as well as allocating memory in the host to store these new information. When the host requires the execution of the target region, the required implementation is initialized, which in this example builds the OpenCL kernel and creates the buffers to store the transferred data in the GPU memory. Before and after the execution, lock and unlock routines set the device as busy/idle to control access to the device from other host threads while it is being used. If the host thread terminates, the implementation and devices are closed, deleting the stored information and releasing the allocated memory from the host and the device. Otherwise, the implementation is not closed by the runtime, since it is frequent that the target region needs to be executed repeatedly (e.g. when processing a sequence of video frames). In this case, a 'soft' initialization is performed in successive executions. For example, there might be no need to rebuild the kernel or reallocate memory buffers—in the 'soft' initialization, this is checked to decide whether they can be reused from previous executions.

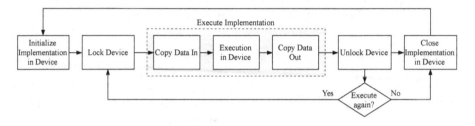

Fig. 3. Execution flow for device offloading performed by the runtime infrastructure.

3.4   Host Code Transformation

Previously, the implemented runtime support has been discussed. Allowing the execution of different device implementations requires some host side support. As a consequence, the host code needs to be preprocessed and transformed during compilation in order to enable the connection to multiple device implementations. Listing 2 shows how the code in Listing 1 is modified by replacing the target region by a call to a wrapper function which eventually manages the execution of any device implementation.

In Listing 3, the simplified implementation for the wrapper is shown. The arguments passed to the wrapper derive from the explicit mapping of variables defined by the programmer. When a target region is executed for the first time, an initialization is performed by building a list of the associated device implementations (which corresponds to a row in Table 2). This is carried out in code line 17, with `target1_struct` being an element with information about the *target-region function* as described in Sect. 3.2, and `implementation_struct_array` being an array of pointers to elements with information about each implementation as described in Sect. 3.2. An array of pointers to every implementation itself is then built (code line 19). The particular code for each device is external to the host code, since it is embedded in a shared object file. All shared objects available at the moment of execution are dynamically loaded at startup. The number of devices and implementations is unknown at the moment of compilation of the fat binary. The above allows to support new devices or optimize existing implementations without recompiling the host code. When the initialization for a target region has already been completed, the currently selected device is obtained and used to select the implementation to be launched (code lines 24-25).

Listing 2. Transformed host code, in which target regions marked in the original code are replaced by a wrapper function.

```
1  #define GPU  1
2  #define FPGA 2
3
4  void host_code(char *image_in, char *image_out, int width, int height)
5  {
6      UC_set_default_device(FPGA);
7      omp_set_num_threads(2);
8
9      #pragma omp parallel
10     {
11         int id = omp_get_thread_num();
12         // ----Thread #0----
13         if(id == 0){
14             function1();
15         }
16         // ----Thread #1----
17         if(id == 1){
18             wrapper1(image_in, image_out, width, height);
19         }
20     }
21 }
```

Listing 3. Code generated at the moment of compilation to connect the transformed host code to different device implementations (simplified).

```
1  // Create function pointer type
2  typedef int (*ptr_function)(char*, char*, int, int);
3  // Declare array of pointers to implementations
4  static ptr_function *implementations = NULL;
5
6  static int num = 0, initialized = 0;
7
8  // Wrapper to connect host code to different implementations
9  int wrapper1(char* image_in char* image_out, int width, int height)
10 {
11     ptr_function fn;
12     // Initialize list of implementations for current target region
13     if(initialized == 0) {
14         num = UC_get_num_devices();
15         implementations = (ptr_function *) calloc(num, sizeof(ptr_function));
16
17         (void) UC_Init_Impl( &target1_struct, &implementation_struct_array);
18         for(int i=0; i<num; i++){
19             implementations[i] = implementation_struct_array[i]->function;
20         }
21         initialized = 1;
22     }
23     // Select and launch implementation
24     fn = implementations[UC_get_default_device()];
25     return fn(image_in, image_out, width, height);
26 }
```

4   Experimental Evaluation

In this section, a proof-of-concept of the proposed methodology is presented. The runtime infrastructure has been evaluated using two heterogeneous architectures: a Zynq UltraScale+ MPSoC (CPU-FPGA) and a PC (CPU-GPU).

The serial video processing system represented in Fig. 4 is used as a test case. First, an RGB frame is taken from a camera. The image is converted to grayscale and a sobel filter is applied, which is an edge detection algorithm. The output image is shown on screen.

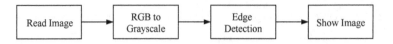

Fig. 4. Block diagram of the video processing sequence used as a test case.

The system is parallelized using OpenMP with four host threads concurrently executing the four tasks in which the system is divided. Therefore, a pipeline is established with four images being processed at the same time. In order to evaluate the proposed methodology, the edge detection function is marked for offloading with a `target` directive. In order to program the GPU attached to the PC, an OpenCL kernel has been generated. For execution on the Zynq MPSoC device, Xilinx SDSoC has been used to produce the driver functions for the host (dynamically loaded by the runtime) and the files to program the Zynq device (a hardware accelerator for the FPGA logic has been generated from the original target code with Vivado High-Level Synthesis). The host application code along with the developed runtime structure has been compiled with GCC for both x86 and ARM architectures.

Tables 4 and 5 summarize the execution time of the previously described example over two heterogeneous platforms: (i) a Xilinx ZCU102 board featuring a Zynq UltraScale+ MPSoC with 1.20 GHz 4 cores ARM Cortex-A53 CPU integrated with FPGA programmable logic and (ii), a laptop PC with 2.30 GHz 4 cores Intel Core i7-3610QM CPU and a NVIDIA GT630M GPU, both running Linux. In the experiments, the input images are 640 × 480 and obtained from the filesystem to avoid being limited by the camera framerate. The results are averaged over 100 executions.

Table 4. Performance on Xilinx ZCU102 - Zynq MPSoC ARM Cortex-A53 + FPGA.

Mode	Frames per second
Serial (CPU)	9.2
Parallel + Offloading (CPU)	16.9
Parallel + Offloading (FPGA)	39.5

Table 5. Performance on PC - Intel Core i7-3610QM CPU + NVIDIA GT630M GPU.

Mode	Frames per second
Serial (CPU)	79.2
Parallel + Offloading (CPU)	147.3
Parallel + Offloading (GPU)	295.3

5   Related Work

Several previous researches have studied and implemented code offloading from OpenMP annotated programs to accelerator devices. Liao *et al.* [8] first reviewed the *OpenMP Accelerator Model* when support for heterogeneous computation was introduced in the OpenMP API 4.0 back in 2013. They presented an initial implementation built upon an OpenMP compiler based on ROSE [9], with support for GPUs from NVIDIA by generating CUDA code.

More recently, some authors have worked to include OpenMP offloading support into the LLVM compiler infrastructure. To cite some of them, Bertolli *et al.* [10] focused on delivering efficient OpenMP offloading support for Open-Power systems and describe an implementation targeting NVIDIA GPUs. Their approach automatically translates the target region code to PTX language and eventually to low-level native GPU assembly, called SASS. Different optimization strategies were integrated into Clang with the aim of maximizing performance when compared to CUDA-based implementations. The CUDA device driver is used to map data to/from the GPU. In [11], Antao *et al.* generalize the previous approach to handle compilation for multiple host and device types and describe their initial work to completely support code generation for OpenMP device offloading constructs in LLVM/Clang. Pereira *et al.* [12] developed an open-source compiler framework based on LLVM/Clang which automatically converts OpenMP annotated code regions to OpenCL/SPIR kernels, while providing a set of optimizations such as tiling and vectorization. Lastly, a proof-of-concept implementation of OpenMP offloading to FPGA devices which also integrates with the LLVM infrastructure was presented by Sommer *et al.* [7]. In their work, Vivado HLS is used for generating the hardware from the C/C++ target regions. Compared to previous work, our proposal describes an alternative offloading methodology in which the device-specific compilation is no longer attached to the OpenMP host compiler, thus requiring little compiler support and integration effort.

6   Conclusions and Future Work

This paper introduces a new OpenMP device offloading methodology. In our proposal, the device-specific software compilation and/or hardware synthesis processes are dissociated from the OpenMP host compiler. The advantages of this approach include: (i) support for multiple devices (i.e. different architecture GPUs, FPGAs...), while the standard offloading method heavily depends on the compiler supporting each architecture; (ii) large design flexibility (in terms of languages, design tools...) is provided to program the accelerator devices, being specially demanded by hardware designers to generate efficient FPGA implementations (iii) little compiler support and integration effort is required. To allow the application of the proposed methodology, we have presented a flexible runtime infrastructure that dynamically loads and manages the available device-specific implementations. Our future work includes integrating the presented runtime into an open-source compiler infrastructure and exploring the use of performance data to guide the selection of an available accelerator device during execution time.

References

1. Horowitz, M.: Computing's energy problem (and what we can do about it). In: 2014 IEEE International Solid-State Circuits Conference Digest of Technical Papers (ISSCC) (2014)
2. Khronos Group: OpenCL: the open standard for parallel programming of heterogeneous systems (2010). https://www.khronos.org/opencl/
3. NVIDIA: CUDA – Compute Unified Device Architecture. https://developer.nvidia.com/cuda-zone
4. Open MP API Specification: Version 5.0 November 2018. https://www.openmp.org/specifications/
5. Offloading support in GCC. https://gcc.gnu.org/wiki/Offloading
6. Clang 9 documentation: OpenMP support. https://clang.llvm.org/docs/OpenMPSupport.html
7. Sommer, L., Korinth, J., Koch, A.: OpenMP device offloading to FPGA accelerators. In: 2017 IEEE 28th International Conference on Application-specific Systems, Architectures and Processors (ASAP), Seattle, WA, pp. 201–205 (2017)
8. Liao, C., Yan, Y., de Supinski, B.R., Quinlan, D.J., Chapman, B.: Early experiences with the OpenMP accelerator model. In: Rendell, A.P., Chapman, B.M., Müller, M.S. (eds.) IWOMP 2013. LNCS, vol. 8122, pp. 84–98. Springer, Heidelberg (2013). https://doi.org/10.1007/978-3-642-40698-0_7
9. Liao, C., Quinlan, D.J., Panas, T., de Supinski, B.R.: A ROSE-based OpenMP 3.0 research compiler supporting multiple runtime libraries. In: 6th International Workshop on OpenMP (IWOMP), Tsukuba, Japan, 14–16 June 2010
10. Bertolli, C., et al.: Integrating GPU support for OpenMP offloading directives into Clang. In: LLVM-HPC2015, Austin, Texas, USA, 15–20 November 2015
11. Antao, S.F., et al.: Offloading support for OpenMP in Clang and LLVM. In: LLVM-HPC2016, Salt Lake City, Utah, USA, 13–18 November 2016
12. Pereira, M.M., Sousa, R.C.F., Araujo, G.: Compiling and optimizing OpenMP 4.X programs to OpenCL and SPIR. In: de Supinski, B.R., Olivier, S.L., Terboven, C., Chapman, B.M., Müller, M.S. (eds.) IWOMP 2017. LNCS, vol. 10468, pp. 48–61. Springer, Cham (2017). https://doi.org/10.1007/978-3-319-65578-9_4

Compilation

Design and Use of Loop-Transformation Pragmas

Michael Kruse[(✉)] and Hal Finkel[(✉)]

Argonne Leadership Computing Facility, Argonne National Laboratory,
Lemont, IL 60439, USA
{mkruse,hfinkel}@anl.gov

Abstract. Adding a pragma directive into the source code is undoubtedly easier than rewriting it, for instance for loop unrolling. Moreover, if the application is maintained for multiple platforms, their difference in performance characteristics may require different code transformations. Code transformation directives allow replacing the directives depending on the platform, i.e. separation of code semantics and its performance optimization.

In this paper, we explore the design space (syntax and semantics) of adding such directive into a future OpenMP specification. Using a prototype implementation in Clang, we demonstrate the usefulness of such directives on a few benchmarks.

Keywords: OpenMP · Pragma · C/C++ · Clang · Polly

1 Introduction

In scientific computing, but also in most other kinds of applications, the majority of execution time is spent in loops. Consequently, when it comes to improving an application's performance, optimizing the hot loops and their bodies is the most obvious strategy.

While code should be written in a way that is the easiest to understand, it will likely not the variant the will execute the fastest. Platform details such as cache hierarchies, data temporal/spatial locality, prefetching, NUMA, SIMD, SIMT, occupancy, branch prediction, parallelism, work-groups, etc. will have a profound impact on application performance such that restructuring the loop is necessary. Since an application rarely runs on just a single platform, one may end up in multiple versions of the same code: One that is written without considering hardware details, and (at least) one for each supported platform, possibly even using different programming models.

OpenMP is intended to be a programming model for many architectures, and ideally would allow to share the same code all of them. It is comparatively low-effort to replace an OpenMP directive, for instance, using the C/C++ preprocessor and OpenMP 5.0 introduced direct support for this via the `metadirective`.

X. Fan et al. (Eds.): IWOMP 2019, LNCS 11718, pp. 125–139, 2019.
https://doi.org/10.1007/978-3-030-28596-8_9

Currently, this can only change the parallelization, offloading and vectorization decisions, but not the structure of the code itself.

In our last year's contribution [5], we proposed additional directives in OpenMP for transforming loops, e.g. loop fusion/fission, interchange, unrolling etc. In this paper, we discuss choices of syntactic and semantics elements (Sect. 2) for such an addition, give and update on our prototype implementation (Sect. 3), and demonstrate how loop transformation can be used in applications and the performance improvements (Sect. 4).

2   Specification Design Considerations

In this section we explore some of the decisions to make for including loop transformation directives into a potential newer OpenMP standard. By its nature, this cannot be an exhaustive discussion, but a subjective selection of the most important features that came up in discussion with members of the OpenMP language committee members and others.

The first decision to make is whether to include such directive at all. Since the "MP" in OpenMP stands for "MultiProcessing", obviously the original targets of OpenMP were (symmetric) multi-core and -socket platforms and still today, most implementation are based on the pthreads API. Multiprocessing obviously does not include sequential loop transformations, but this is not per se a reason to exclude such transformations from OpenMP.

For one, there is a need of supporting functionality: The `collapse` clause has been added in OpenMP 3.0, although it is not directly related to multiprocessing. OpenACC [7] also supports a tile-clause. The `simd` construct has been added in OpenMP 4.0, which is exploits instruction-level parallelism, which also not included in the term multiprocessing.

Second, the scope of OpenMP has extended relative to its original goal. With target offloading also introduced in OpenMP 4.0, it also supports accelerators such as GPGPUs and FPGAs.

There are alternatives to not include code transformations into OpenMP:

- Continue with the current practice of compiler-specific extensions. Without standardization, this means these will be incompatible to each other.
- Include into a future version the host languages' specifications (C/C++/ Fortran). This would compel OpenMP to add clarifications how its directives interact with the host language's directives. However, it is questionable whether e.g. the C++ standard committee will add specifications of pragma-directives. Even if all host languages add transformation directives, their semantics are unlikely to match, complicating OpenMP compatibility clarifications.
- Create a separate language specification using C/C++/Fortran with OpenMP as its host language. This new language would probably diverge from OpenMP over time as they might add features incompatible to each other. Comparisons can be drawn from OpenACC, which started as an initiative to add accelerator offloading to OpenMP.

For the directives themselves, we distinguish three aspects: Syntax, semantics and the available code transformations. The syntax describes which token streams are accepted by the compiler and the semantics define their meaning. Once these base rules have been defined, it should be straightforward to add transformations consistent with these rules.

2.1 Syntax

In our first proposal [5], we suggested the following syntax

`#pragma omp [loop(<loopname(s)>)] <transformation> <clauses...>`

i.e. every transformation is a top-level directive. The `loop`-clause before the directive could be used to refer to a loop that is not on the following line or the result of another transformation on the next line. Since then, the OpenMP 5.0 standard was announced which includes a `loop`-directive. Even though a disambiguation is possible using the parenthesis following the clause, but not the directive, overloading the keyword might be ambiguous. Hence, we explore alternatives in this section.

Loop Directive. OpenMP 5.0 introduced the loop construct with the goal to give the compiler more freedom on optimization decisions. The first OpenMP specification was designed with symmetric multiprocessing in mind, but in the era of heterogeneous computing sensible defaults vary widely.

The idea of the loop-directive was to become the new default worksharing construct, since in most cases, or at least before performance-optimizing an application, the programmer does not care about how the body is executed in parallel, as long as the default choice is reasonable. In future OpenMP revisions, the loop-construct would gain features of the prescriptive worksharing-construct and preferred when adding new features. This maxim also applies to transformation-directives.

Clauses or (Sub-)Constructs. A transformation could be either expressed as a construct (as in [5]), or as a clause. Constructs usually indicate to the compiler to do something, whereas clauses pass options to the construct's doing. Therefore, a clause requires a construct to be added to.

Currently, OpenMP already uses both syntactic elements for what we might consider loop transformations. For instance, `#pragma omp simd` can be seen as a loop transformation that does vectorization. On the other side, the collapse clause (valid for multiple constructs such as loop, simd, etc.) is a transformation that occurs before the construct's effect.

When using the loop-construct, the transformation could either be clauses like the collapse-clause, or sub-constructs of the loop clause, similarly as every OpenMP construct is follows after an "omp" token. However, this would be a new syntactic element in OpenMP, since e.g. `#pragma omp for simd` is a combined construct, each of them can be used independently.

The order of any OpenMP 5.0 clauses is irrelevant, but transformations carried out in different orders generally result in different loop nests. This contradiction can be solved by either make such clauses order-dependent, require the compiler to ignore the order and instead apply an heuristic to determine the best order, or disallow multiple transformations on a single pragma.

If using the (sub-)construct as the primary syntax, clauses can still be allowed as syntactic sugar where it makes sense and does not cause ambiguity. Combined constructs could be allowed as well.

Loop Chains. Bertolacci et. al. [1] proposed a loopchain-construct with a schedule-clause. The loopchain encloses a loop nest to transform with the schedule clause that defines the transformations to apply on the loop nest, as illustrated in the example below (simplified from the paper).

```
#pragma omplc loopchain schedule(tile(10, parallel, serial))
{
  for (int i = lb ; i <= ub ; i += 1)
    A[i] = (B[i-1] + B[i] + B[i+1]);
  for (int i = lb ; i <= ub ; i += 1)
    A[i] = A[i] * (1.0 / 3.0);
}
```

Since the schedule applies the loop nest as a whole, the schedule must also specify an operation on parts that are not transformed. In the excerpt, the non-transformed part is indicated by the `serial` operator. If the loop chain is large with many transformations, the schedule clause can quickly become convoluted.

Referring to Other Loops. Some transformations such as tiling and loop fusion consume more than one loop on the next line and replace them with potentially more than one generated loop, which may be consumed by a follow-up transformation. For instance, the result of tiling two nested loops are four loops, we might want the parallelize the outermost, unroll-and-jam one of the middle loops and vectorize the innermost loop. Therefore, a syntax is needed to refer to loops that are not directly following the transformation directive.

This can either be done by assigning names to loops and referring to them, or with a path selector from the loop that is annotated. Loop names/identifiers have been described in [5], but also used by IBM xlc [4] and XLang [2].

Path selectors have been for node selection in trees, such as XPath [9] on XML. In some sense, the collapse clause, taking the number of perfectly nested loops as an argument, is such an selector. With more complex cases, such as "the third loop inside the following loop nest of two loops", maintainability becomes a problem: Adding or removing a loop before between the selector and the selected loop requires updating the selector.

2.2 Semantics

Prescriptive vs. Descriptive. Code transformations are inherently prescriptive: When used, the programmer is already working on performance optimization and cares about the executions order. The loop-construct is designed to be descriptive and, by default, applies the semantics of order(concurrent), which allows the compiler to reorder the loop as it fits. Then changing the order using a loop transformation directive has no meaning: As the order(concurrent) clause allows an arbitrary permutation/thread-distribution, applying a user-defined permutation will have an undetermined result. It is also a worksharing-construct, meaning that it is meant to be executed in a parallel context. Non-worksharing, simple transformed loops would just run redundantly on every thread in the context.

One solution is to introduce new clauses that disable the default descriptive and worksharing behavior, such as order(sequential) and noworksharing. To avoid this boilerplate to be repeated with every loop construct, they might be implicit when a loop transformation is defined.

2.3 Level of Prescriptiveness

To avoid differences in performance when using different compilers, the specification should define the replacement code of a transformation. However, for code that is not performance-sensitive (such as edge cases, fallback code and pro- and epilogue), the compiler might retain some freedom. Taking the tile-construct as an example, the following decisions are not necessarily performance-relevant:

- Fallback code for rare cases where the transformation would be invalid, such as address range aliasing of two arrays that would cause a change in semantics.
- Where and how to execute partial tiles at the logical iteration space border: like a full tile but with additional border conditions or separately after/before all full tiles have been executed.
- If the iteration counter of the first iteration is not zero, divide tiles using the logical or physical iteration space?
- Assuming only the code inside a tile is performance-relevant, the outer iteration order over tiles does not need to be defined.
- If the specification allows tiling of non-perfectly nested loops, there is not obvious way to archive this.

A sensible approach could be to leave these decisions to the compiler, but consider adding clauses that fix this behavior.

OpenMP 5.0 already allows non-perfectly nested loops with the collapse-clause and only requires code between the loops to be executed at most as many times as it would be executed if moved inside the innermost loop, but at least as many times as in the original loops nest. Executing code more often than in the original code might be an unexpected side-effect of tiling. In the interest of user-friendless, the specification could disallow non-perfectly loop nests, but add a nestify transformation to make this behavior explicit in the code.

Transformation Order. The order in which multiple transformations are applied on the same loop can be either defined the programmer, the specification, or by the compiler. When defined by the programmer, the order is derived from the syntax. Otherwise, any order in the source is ignored and either the OpenMP specification has to specify the rule in which order transformations are applied, or it is implementation-defined such that the compiler can apply heuristics to determine the best ordering.

It might be straight-forward with transformations that consume one loop and replace it with another, but not all orderings are valid with other transformations. For instance, loop interchange requires at least two loops and cannot be applied if the previous transformation only returns a single loop. If the order is user-defined, the compiler can emit an error. Otherwise, either the OpenMP has to define which order to use, or the compiler developers.

However, performance optimization engineers will unlikely want to leave such decision up to the compiler or specification. This is because when using transformations, they will try to get a specific result that is optimal on the target platform and without transformation constructs, would write an alternative code path. A compiler "improving" its heuristic in later versions would also not helpful since it would regress the once-archived performance.

Compatibility with Legacy Directives. Several existing constructs and clauses in OpenMP can be interpreted as a loop transformation:

- The `for`, `loop` and `distribute`-constructs divide loop iterations between threads or teams.
- The `sections`-constructs distributes code regions between threads.
- The `simd` construct vectorizes a loop such that multiple input loop iterations are processed by one iteration of a generated loop, similarly to (partial) unrolling.

With this interpretation, applying other transformations to occur before and after the construct should be possible and make a syntax for new transformations that resemble existing transformations preferable.

Furthermore, existing combined constructs can be redefined as a sequence of transformations, instead of a textual definition. For instance,

```
#pragma omp for simd schedule(static) simdlen(4)
for (int i = 0; i < n; i+=1)
```

could be *defined* as

```
#pragma omp simd simdlen(4)
#pragma omp for schedule(static)
for (int i = 0; i < n; i+=1)
```

Note that this is different from

```
#pragma omp for schedule(static)
#pragma omp simd simdlen(4)
for (int i = 0; i < n; i+=1)
```

Table 1. Safety modes for transformation directives. Green is for safe transformations, red may have changed the code's semantics as does orange but only in corner cases.

	Heuristic	Default	Fallback	Force
always valid	original*or* transformed	transformed	transformed	transformed
valid with rtc	original*or* rtc	transformed	rtc	warning
invalid	original	transformed	warning	warning
impossible	original	warning	warning	warning

which might be more efficient if the number of iterations is not a multiple of the vector width. Using this transformation extension, it is possible to choose between the variants.

Semantic Safety. Generally, the OpenMP specification requires compilers to apply its directives without regard to whether it is semantically valid to do, i.e. the user guarantees that it is. This ensures that otherwise conservative compilers still honor the OpenMP directive, but defers the responsibility to the programmer.

In some scenarios the user might want the compiler to do a validity check. For instance, the programmer might be unsure themselves or the transformation is added by an autotuner trying out different loop transformations without understanding the code. For these cases, the directives may support options to instruct the compiler to verify semantic validity.

Table 1 shows how safety modes handle different situations for applying a code transformation. "Always valid" refers to code to which the transformation can be applied without changing its semantics. In the case of unrolling this is any loop since unrolling cannot change the code's effect (except execution time). "Valid with rtc" refers to code that can be transformed under conditions that can be checked dynamically. For instance, a transformation may require that two memory regions are not overlapping (alias), which can be checked at runtime if the compiler can deduce which addresses are accessed. "Invalid" means that the compiler cannot determine a reasonable runtime condition, i.e. must assume that the transformation will change the code's semantics. "Impossible" is code that the compiler can structurally impossible to transform, such as reversing a while-loop.

Note that these categories may depend on compiler capabilities; e.g. a compiler may have deduced the number of iterations of a while-loop. For the sake of a standardization, OpenMP should define minimum requirements for compilers to support with everything beyond being a quality-of-implementation.

Without OpenMP, the compiler would heuristically determine whether a transformation is profitable or not. Hence, it might apply it or not (indicated by "original" in Table 1), but if it does, it has to ensure that the semantics do not change.

The default behavior of OpenMP directives[1] is to always apply even if it the code's semantics changes. It does not add a runtime check, meaning that the program result can also change in the "Valid with rtc" case. The compiler should emit a warning to the user if the transformation could not be applied at all.

With `fallback` semantics, the compiler must not emit semantically invalid code, but is allowed to generate fallback code in case a runtime condition fails. Still, it should warn if the transformation directive had no effect. In contrast to the heuristic approach, the compiler skips the profitability check and trusts the directive that the transformation is profitable.

Due to the possible fallback, it is still possible that the non-transformed code is executed without compiler warning and surprise the performance engineer. Instead `force` semantics can be used, which guarantees that either the transformed code is executed, or the compiler emits a warning. An additional `required` clause could change the warning to an hard error.

Another idea is a `hint` clause, which informs the compiler that the transformation is valid (i.e. skips the validity check), but still considers the profitability, possibly with a bump in favor of applying the transformation instead of the compiler's usual conservativeness.

2.4   Transformations

In addition to the general syntax and semantics, the available transformations have to be defined, including when they are applicable and what the result is. A convenient approach is to think of transformations as replacements: Remove the code it applies to and insert the result instead. Any follow-up transformation can apply on the transformed code as if the replacement was written in the source code. This should happen internally in the compiler, not textually.

In the remainder of the chapter, we try to define a selected set of transformations.

Loop Peeling. Some loop transformations work best when the loop is a multiple of a constant, such as (partial) unrolling, vectorization and tiling. If this is not a case, some iterations have to be extracted out of the main loop, which by itself is also a transformation. Unlike to relying on the implicit peeling, explicitly using a peeling transformation allows more options and naming the resulting prologue- and epilogue-loop to be referenced in follow-up transformations.

We can either the first k iterations into an prologue before the loop or the last k iterations into an epilogue after the loop. Peeling the first iterations is always possible, but for peeling the last iterations the number of iterations must be known in advance, which is the case of canonical loops as defined by OpenMP.

---

[1] Our previous paper [5] suggested to use safe semantics as the default, in conflict to the normal OpenMP behavior.

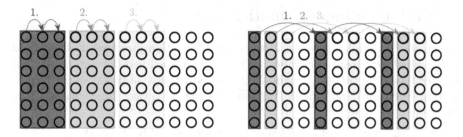

Fig. 1. (a) Strip-mining, (b) Stripe-mining

The number of iterations to peel can either be specified directly as the number k or indirectly as a goal to archive. A goal can be:

1. Make remaining main loop have a multiple of a constant number of iterations; useful for the aforementioned transformations.
2. Make the first access to an array aligned; useful for vectorized loads/stores and accesses that are faster when the compiler knows they are aligned.

Peeling might be necessary spanning multiple loops in a loop nests, since transformations like tiling and unroll-and-jam also apply on multiple nested loops.

Collapse. This combines multiple nested loops into a single logical loop that can be referred to by other transformations. It should not change the execution order of the inner body. OpenMP added a clause with similar semantics in version 3.0 and even assigns logical iteration numbers to loop body executions. A collapse loop-transformation would allow using this functionality independently of other constructs.

Strip- and Stripe-Mining. Strip-mining can be seen as one-dimensional tiling. In contrast to tiling in general, the execution order is not changed, i.e. like unrolling never changes the program's result. Unlike unrolling, it increases the control-flow complexity and therefore is only intended to be used in combination with other transformations. For instance, partial unrolling can be implemented by strip-mining followed by a full unroll of the inner loop. The name is inspired by the term from open-pit mining: The pit is deepened by one strip at a time, as visualized in Fig. 1a.

In contrast, stripe-mining does change the execution order: Each inner loop processes a constant number of iterations that are equidistantly distributed over the iteration space. As shown in Fig. 1b, each form a set of stripes, lending to the transformation's name.

3 Prototype Implementation

We created an implementation of some transformation directives in Clang and Polly, which we already described in [6]. Because such transformations are not part of OpenMP yet, use a hybrid of Clang's native syntax for loop transformation extensions and OpenMP construct/clauses syntax. The general syntax is:

> #pragma clang loop(<loopname>) <transforamtion> <clauses...>

Our code is available on Github[2] Currently, it should be considered as prototype quality and is not intended for use in production. For instance, it may crash on syntax errors instead of diagnostic output.

In addition to the transformations mentioned in [6], we implemented unrolling, unroll-and-jam, thread-parallelization and peeling for tiled loops. The parallelization transformation, in contrast to OpenMP's worksharing constructs, can be combined with other transformations. It should become unnecessary once the interaction between OpenMP's parallelization constructs and loop transformations have been specified. We unfortunately did not implement loop distributions such that it had to be replicated manually for the evaluation.

4 Evaluation

In this section, we explore how transformation directives can be useful to improve the performance of a selection of kernels. Please keep in mind that we do not intend to discover new techniques how to improve these kernels over typically hand-optimized kernels in specialized libraries or in literature. Instead, we want to illustrate how these directives help exploring common optimization techniques. This is most relevant if no hand-optimized library for the kernel in question is available for a platform.

Unless mentioned otherwise, the execution time was measured on an Intel Core i7 7700HQ (Kaby Lake architecture), 2.8 Ghz with Turbo Boost off and compiled using the -ffast-math switch. When using parallelism, we use all 8 hardware threads (4 physical cores).

4.1 heat-3d

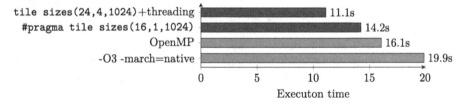

_____

The benchmark "heat-3d" from Polybench [8] is 3-dimensional 10-point stencil. We are using a volume of 800^3 and 10 time-steps. Typical for repeated stencil codes, it alternatingly switches input- and output arrays. Its 3rd dimension makes it more difficult for the hardware prefetcher.

The baseline can be improved only slightly using OpenMP parallelism (*#pragma omp parallel for collapse(2)* and *#pragma omp simd* for the innermost loop). Tiling improves the performance even more on just a single thread, but can further improved with threading.

The tile sizes were determined using trial-and-error, a task which could also be done by an autotuner. More advanced time-tiling techniques such as diamond-overlap and tiling and could also result in an improvement.

4.2 syr2k

Polybench's "syr2k" is a rank-2k matrix-matrix update; we are benchmarking matrices of size 4000^2 and $2000 * 5200$. We run this benchmark on a 2-socket Intel Xeon Gold 6152 CPU (22 cores each, 88 threads in total) with an NVidia Tesla V100-SXM2 GPU.

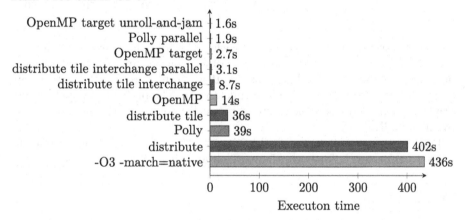

We use the default DATASET_EXTRALARGE for Polybench's "syr2k". In contrast to the stencils, we can gain very high speed-ups.

While loop distribution does not gain a lot by itself, tiling (by $256 \times 96 \times 16$) improves the performance by a factor more than 11, followed by a speed-up of another 4x with a loop interchange. With parallelization on all 44 cores (88 threads), the execution time has improved by a factor of 140 over the original loop.

Interestingly, while single-threaded performance of the Polly-optimized version (using a tile size of 32 in all dimensions and not interchange) is worse, with parallelization it is even better with a speed-up factor of 330. Evidently, the shared memory bandwidth of the shared caches changes the bottleneck, such that the tile size optimized for single-thread performance is worse. Replication of Polly's optimized loop nest using pragmas replicates the same performance. We might be able to further improve the performance by searching for a tile size that minimized the traffic higher-level caches. Using `#pragma omp parallel for` alone utilizing 88 OpenMP threads yields an improvement of the factor 31.

The performance characteristics changes when offloading to the GPU. With a straightforward `#pragma omp target teams distribute collapse(2)` of the outer loops and `#pragma omp parallel for reduction` of the inner loops, the kernel computes in 2.7 s, which is slower than the best CPU performance. Only with an additional unroll-and-jam did we beat the two CPUs. Tiling did not show any improvement.

4.3   covariance

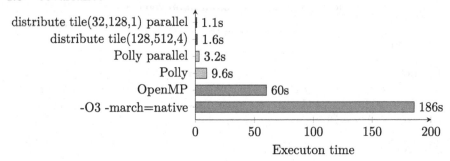

The main issue with the covariance benchmarks from Polybench is that the fastest iterator moves the outer data array dimensions leading to strided accesses which cause most of cache lines unused. If we just transpose the data array (manually), execution time already shrinks to 15 s. The problem can be lessened with tiling. Unlike the non-tiled version, parallelism improves the execution time only marginally.

Polly's sub-optimal choice of a tile size of 32 for each dimensions also leads to lower performance, for both, the parallel- and single-threaded cases.

4.4   dgemm

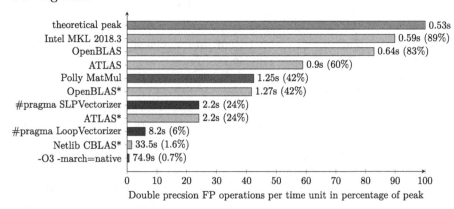

In [5], we already optimized Polybench's "gemm" kernel, but because of lack of support by LLVM's loop vectorizer, we could only vectorize the innermost loop.

This is sub-optimal because this means that the register dependency is also carried by the innermost loop, restricting the CPU's ability to reorder instructions.

```
#pragma clang loop(i1) pack array(B) \
    isl_redirect("{ [c,j,k]    -> [B[x,y] -> PackedB[floord(y,8) mod 256,x mod 256,y mod 8]] }")
#pragma clang loop(j2) pack array(A) \
    isl_redirect("{ [c,j,k,l] -> [A[x,y] -> PackedA[floord(x,4) mod 16 ,y mod 256,x mod 4]] }")
#pragma clang loop(i2) unrollingandjam factor(4)
#pragma clang loop(j2) unrollingandjam factor(8)
#pragma clang loop(i1,j1,k1,i2,j2) interchange permutation(j1,k1,i1,j2,i2)
#pragma clang loop(i,j,k) tile sizes(64,2048,256) \
                          floor_ids(i1,j1,k1) tile_ids(i2,j2,k2) peel(rectangular)
    for (int i = 0; i < M; i += 1)
        for (int j = 0; j < N; j += 1)
            for (int k = 0; k < K; k += 1)
                C[i][j] += A[i][k] * B[k][j];
```

Fig. 2. Replication of Polly's matrix-multiplication optimization using directives; Libraries marked with (*) were precompiled from the Ubuntu software repository, hence not optimized for the evaluation system

To avoid this problem, Polly's matrix-multiplication optimization [3] unroll-and-jams non-inner loops and relies on LLVM's SLP vectorizer to combine the unrolled iterations into vector instructions. We replicate this behavior in Fig. 2. The isl_redirect-clause ensures that the packed arrays' data layout follow the changed access pattern. For production implementations of the array packing, this should be derived automatically by the compiler.

Unfortunately, the performance is even worse than with the innermost-loop vectorization because, unlike with Polly's output, the SLP vectorizer does vectorize the jammed loops. We are working on identifying and fixing the issue in the prototype version.

4.5 456.hmmer

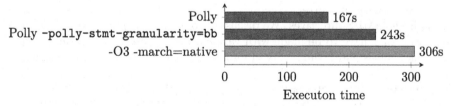

The most performance-critical code of "456.hmmer" from SPEC CPU 2006 is shown in Fig. 3. Even though it is just one loop, it does 3 logical computations, of which 2 have no loop-carried dependencies. Separating the sequential computation allows the parallelization and/or vectorization of the two other parts.

The vectorization speed-up (of the entire 456.hmmer run on an Intel Xeon E5-2667 v3 (Haswell architecture) running at 3.20 GHz) is shown in the graph. Earlier versions of Polly only separated one of the computations (using the -polly-stmt-granularity=bb option). However, the current version separates all 3 computations using its automatic optimizer. The same would be possible using a loop distribute directive.

```
for (k = 1; k <= M; k++) {
  mc[k] = mpp[k-1]   + tpmm[k-1];
  if ((sc = ip[k-1]  + tpim[k-1]) > mc[k]) mc[k] = sc;
  if ((sc = dpp[k-1] + tpdm[k-1]) > mc[k]) mc[k] = sc;
  if ((sc = xmb  + bp[k])         > mc[k]) mc[k] = sc;
  mc[k] += ms[k];
  if (mc[k] < -INFTY) mc[k] = -INFTY;
  dc[k] = dc[k-1] + tpdd[k-1];
  if ((sc = mc[k-1] + tpmd[k-1]) > dc[k]) dc[k] = sc;
  if (dc[k] < -INFTY) dc[k] = -INFTY;
  if (k < M) {
    ic[k] = mpp[k] + tpmi[k];
    if ((sc = ip[k] + tpii[k]) > ic[k]) ic[k] = sc;
    ic[k] += is[k];
    if (ic[k] < -INFTY) ic[k] = -INFTY;
  }
}
```

Compute mc[k] (*vectorizable*)

Compute dc[k] (**not** vectorizable)

Compute ic[k] (*vectorizable*)

Fig. 3. 456.hmmer hotspot code

5 Conclusion

Loop – and more generally, code – -transformation directives can be a useful tool to improve a hot code's performance without going too low-level. Completely automatic optimizers such as Polly rely on heuristics which are necessarily approximation they do not know the code's dynamic properties (such as number of loop iterations) and have an incomplete performance model of the target machine. They are also conservative, i.e. rather do nothing than to regress performance.

Transformation directives take the burden of profitability analysis off the compile and to the programmer who either knows which transformations are beneficial or can try out multiple approaches, possibly assisted by an autotuner.

We seek to add such transformation directives into a future OpenMP specification, to replace the current compiler-specific pragmas and ensure composability with OpenMP's directives. We discussed some design choices for syntax and semantics that have to be made with various (dis-)advantages in terms of compatibility, consistency, complexity of implementation and ease of understanding.

Acknowledgments. This research was supported by the Exascale Computing Project (17-SC-20-SC), a collaborative effort of two U.S. Department of Energy organizations (Office of Science and the National Nuclear Security Administration) responsible for the planning and preparation of a capable exascale ecosystem, including software, applications, hardware, advanced system engineering, and early testbed platforms, in support of the nation's exascale computing imperative.

This research used resources of the Argonne Leadership Computing Facility, which is a DOE Office of Science User Facility supported under Contract DE-AC02-06CH11357.

References

1. Bertolacci, I., Strout, M.M., de Supinski, B.R., Scogland, T.R.W., Davis, E.C., Olschanowsky, C.: Extending OpenMP to Facilitate loop optimization. In: de Supinski, B.R., Valero-Lara, P., Martorell, X., Mateo Bellido, S., Labarta, J. (eds.) IWOMP 2018. LNCS, vol. 11128, pp. 53–65. Springer, Cham (2018). https://doi.org/10.1007/978-3-319-98521-3_4
2. Donadio, S., et al.: A language for the compact representation of multiple program versions. In: Ayguadé, E., Baumgartner, G., Ramanujam, J., Sadayappan, P. (eds.) LCPC 2005. LNCS, vol. 4339, pp. 136–151. Springer, Heidelberg (2006). https://doi.org/10.1007/978-3-540-69330-7_10
3. Gareev, R., Grosser, T., Kruse, M.: High-performance generalized tensor operations: a compiler-oriented approach. ACM Trans. Archit. Code Optim. **15**(3), 34:1–34:27 (2018). https://doi.org/10.1145/3235029
4. IBM: Product documentation for XL C/C++ for AIX, V13.1.3 (2015)
5. Kruse, M., Finkel, H.: A proposal for loop-transformation pragmas. In: de Supinski, B.R., Valero-Lara, P., Martorell, X., Mateo Bellido, S., Labarta, J. (eds.) IWOMP 2018. LNCS, vol. 11128, pp. 37–52. Springer, Cham (2018). https://doi.org/10.1007/978-3-319-98521-3_3
6. Kruse, M., Finkel, H.: User-directed loop-transformations in Clang. In: 2018 IEEE/ACM 5th Workshop on the LLVM Compiler Infrastructure in HPC (LLVM-HPC), pp. 49–58, November 2018. https://doi.org/10.1109/LLVM-HPC.2018.8639402
7. OpenACC-Standard.org: The OpenACC Application Programming Interface Version 4.0, November 2017
8. Pouchet, L.N., Yuki, T.: Polybench 4.2.1 beta. https://sourceforge.net/projects/polybench
9. Spiegel, J., Robie, J., Dyck, M.: XML Path Language (XPath) 3.1. W3C recommendation, W3C, March 2017. https://www.w3.org/TR/2017/REC-xpath-31-20170321/

Ompparser: A Standalone and Unified OpenMP Parser

Anjia Wang[1], Yaying Shi[1], Xinyao Yi[1], Yonghong Yan[1(✉)], Chunhua Liao[2], and Bronis R. de Supinski[2]

[1] University of South Carolina, Columbia, SC 29208, USA
{anjia,yaying,xinyaoy}@email.sc.edu, yanyh@cse.sc.edu
[2] Lawrence Livermore National Laboratory, Livermore, CA 94550, USA
{liao6,bronis}@llnl.gov

Abstract. OpenMP has been quickly evolving to meet the insatiable demand for productive parallel programming on high performance computing systems. Creating a robust and optimizing OpenMP compiler has become increasingly challenging due to the expanding capabilities and complexity of OpenMP, especially for its latest 5.0 release. Although OpenMP's syntax and semantics are very similar between C/C++ and Fortran, the corresponding compiler support, such as parsing and lowering are often separately implemented, which is a significant obstacle to support the fast changing OpenMP specification. In this paper, we present the design and implementation of a standalone and unified OpenMP parser, named ompparser, for both C/C++ and Fortran. ompparser is designed to be useful both as an independent tool and an integral component of an OpenMP compiler. It can be used for syntax and semantics checking of OpenMP constructs, validating and verifying the usage of existing constructs, and helping to prototype new constructs. The formal grammar included in ompparser also helps interpretation of the OpenMP standard. The ompparser implementation supports the latest OpenMP 5.0, including complex directives such as metadirective. It is released as open-source from https://github.com/passlab/ompparser with a BSD-license. We also demonstrate how it is integrated with the ROSE's open-source OpenMP compiler.

Keywords: OpenMP · Parser · Intermediate representation · Compiler

1 Introduction

To meet the demand of productive parallel programming on existing and emerging high-performance computing systems, the OpenMP standard has been evolving significantly in recent years [10]. Since the creation of the standard in 1997 that specified a handful of directives, substantial amount of new constructs have been introduced and most existing APIs have been enhanced in each revision.

© Springer Nature Switzerland AG 2019
X. Fan et al. (Eds.): IWOMP 2019, LNCS 11718, pp. 140–152, 2019.
https://doi.org/10.1007/978-3-030-28596-8_10

The latest version of OpenMP 5.0, released in 2018, has more than 60 directives. Compiler support thus requires more efforts than before [5]. Compilation of OpenMP programs for both C/C++ and Fortran includes parsing, syntax and semantics checking, generation of compiler intermediate representation (IR) of OpenMP constructs, and code transformation to support computing devices including CPUs, GPUs and SIMD units. A full compiler implementation of the latest OpenMP standard for both C/C++ and Fortran would involve a large amount of development efforts spanning multiple years.

Many OpenMP compilers use a high-level IR that is language neutral (or close to neutral) to represent C/C++ and Fortran OpenMP programs. For example, OpenMP support in GNU compiler [8] operates on its high-level and unified IR (named GENERIC and GIMPLE) for C/C++ and Fortran. OpenMP support in IBM XLC compiler [4] also uses its high-level AST-style and unified IR for C/C++ and Fortran for transformation. ROSE's OpenMP implementation [6] operates on the same unified AST representing both C/C++ and Fortran OpenMP input codes. It lowers the AST to generates standard C/C++ or Fortran code with calls to OpenMP runtime functions as its output. OpenMP support in LLVM is an exception so far. The OpenMP compilation for C/C++ are performed within the Clang frontend [1,3] and for Fortran within the Flang Fortran frontend [2,9]. There is however effort of extending LLVM IR with intrinsic [11] to perform OpenMP transformation in the LLVM IR, demonstrating the feasibility of OpenMP transformation in a unified and mid-level type of IR.

Our effort to create a standalone and unified OpenMP parser, named as ompparser, is motivated by the facts that (1) the differences in terms of syntax and semantics of OpenMP constructs between C/C++ and Fortran are minor, and (2) current OpenMP compilers develop their own parsers, which represent redundant work. The contribution of our work includes:

- ompparser can be used standalone for static source code analysis, e.g. tools for semantics checking or similarity analysis between C/C++ and Fortran programs.
- Integrating omppaser into an OpenMP compiler implementation can reduce the development efforts. There will be no need to create and maintain two separate parsers for C/C++ and Fortran, or separate parsers for different compilers.
- ompparser provides a complete reference OpenMP grammar in the Backus-Naur Form that formally describes the latest OpenMP language constructs. This will help users understand the rules and restriction of the OpenMP standard, which no longer contains a reference grammar in its recent versions.

In the rest of the paper, we describe the design and interface of the ompparser in Sect. 2, the ompparser implementation including lexer, grammars and intermediate representation in Sect. 3, and how it can be used as a standalone tool or to be integrated into a compiler in Sect. 4. The paper concludes in Sect. 5.

2   The Design and Interface of Ompparser

The ompparser is designed to work as an independent tool or to be integrated into a compiler to parse OpenMP constructs in both C/C++ and Fortran form. It takes a string of C/C++ pragma processing directive or Fortran comment as input and generates OpenMPIR object as its output representation. OpenMPIR is designed to be in the same form for semantically equivalent C/C++ and Fortran OpenMP constructs. ompparser does not parse the code regions affected by OpenMP constructs. In our current design, it does not parse C/C++ or Fortran expressions or identifiers. ompparser preserves them as plain strings in the OpenMPIR for the compiler to parse. It however provides a callback interface to allow a host compiler to parse expressions and identifiers. ompparser expects the callback to produce compiler-specific IR objects for expressions and identifiers and ompparser attaches those objects as opaque to the OpenMPIR generated for the OpenMP constructs.

The workflow is shown in Fig. 1 and the public interface is shown in Fig. 2. The parseOpenMP method accepts a string of an OpenMP directive to parse, e.g. pragma omp parallel shared (a, b). The optional _langParse parameter can be used by the caller of the parseOpenMP method to pass a language-specific callback function for parseOpenMP to parse language-specific expressions, identifiers, and variables. The _langParse callback should return a pointer to a compiler-specific IR object to ompparser which attaches that object as opaque object to the Open-MPIR. If no _langParse callback is provided when the parseOpenMP is called, language-specific expressions, identifiers, and variables are attached as literal string to the OpenMPIR object. When ompparser is used by a compiler, the compiler may choose to use the OpenMPIR directly returned by ompparser or translate OpenMPIR to the IR of the compiler. Section 3.3 provides the description of the IR and methods to access the IRs. ompparser can also be used as standalone library, used for source code analysis.

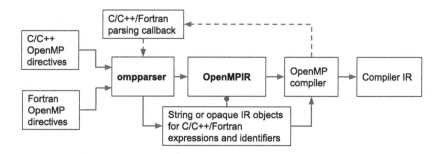

Fig. 1. Ompparser integration with an OpenMP compiler

```
typedef enum OMPLang {
    C, Cplusplus, Fortran,
} OMPLang_t;

//Set the base language for the paser
void OMPSetLang(OMPLang_t lang);

// _input: a string of an input OpenMP directive/commet
// _langParse: a callback function for expression parsing
OpenMPDirective* parseOpenMP(const char* _input,
    void * _langParse(const char*));
```

Fig. 2. Ompparser's interface functions

3   Implementation

To help describe the details of our work, we categorize the directives and clauses of the standard based on the complexity of the language constructs.

For directives, we have the following categories:

- A declare target region can contain multiple function declarations/definitions, which would result in multiple additional declarations. It has no association with the immediate execution of any user code. Declarative directives in the latest 5.0 standard include declare simd, declare target, declare mapper, declare reduction and declare variant.
- An executable directive has immediate executable code associated with it. Most executable directives have a simple structure with a directive name and a clause list.
- Metadirective is a special case of executable directive since the directive-variant parameter of the when and default clause could also be a directive construct.
- Each combined directives is considered as a single directive.

For clauses, we categorize them into three classes:

- clauses with no, one or multiple OpenMP-defined constant parameters, for example, nowait, untied, default in parallel.
- clauses with only a language expression or list as its parameters, e.g. num_threads, private, shared, etc, and
- clauses with one or multiple parameters of OpenMP-defined constants, and then a language expression or list, e.g. map, depend, allocate, reduction, etc.

3.1   Lexer for Tokenizing Keywords, Expressions and Identifiers

The first step of parsing uses a lexer or scanner to tokenize OpenMP keywords, as well as C/C++ or Fortran expressions and identifiers used in the directives and clauses. We use FLEX (Fast Lexical analyzer generator) lexer generator to generate the lexer based on the regular expressions and action rules for the matching tokens. For directives and clauses that require no parameters (class 1 and class 2 mentioned above) as well as OpenMP-defined constants, lexer returns the enum representation of the construct to the parser when the token is matched.

For clauses that have parameters, expression and identifiers (class 3 mentioned above), we use the Flex mechanism for conditionally activating rules based on state to process tokens. This feature makes the Flex rules better organized and versatile to deal with the large number of clauses in OpenMP. We take the reduction clause as an example and its Flex rules are shown in Fig. 3.

reduction([reduction-modifier,] reduction-identifier : list)

```
1   reduction       { yy_push_state(REDUCTION_STATE);return REDUCTION; }
2   <REDUCTION_STATE>inscan/{blank}*,      { return MODIFIER_INSCAN; }
3   <REDUCTION_STATE>task/{blank}*,        { return MODIFIER_TASK; }
4   <REDUCTION_STATE>default/{blank}*,     { return MODIFIER_DEFAULT; }
5   <REDUCTION_STATE>"("                   { return '('; }
6   <REDUCTION_STATE>")"                   { yy_pop_state(); return ')'; }
7   <REDUCTION_STATE>","                   { return ','; }
8   <REDUCTION_STATE>":"                   { yy_push_state(EXPR_STATE);
        return ':'; }
9   <REDUCTION_STATE>"+"                   { return '+'; }
10  ...
11  <REDUCTION_STATE>min/{blank}*:         { return MIN; }
12  <REDUCTION_STATE>max/{blank}*:         { return MAX; }
13  <REDUCTION_STATE>.                     { yy_push_state(EXPR_STATE);
        current_string = yytext[0]; }
```

Fig. 3. Flex rules for the reduction clause

To recognize expressions, we develop an expression tokenizer to identify individual expressions from a list without the need to fully parse the expression. A string for a list of expressions separated by "," is split into a list of strings of expressions. The same approach is used for handling shape expression or range-specification used in array sections (e.g. c[42][0:6:2][:]) and other places. While processing the string, the expression tokenizer pairs up brackets ("(", ")", "[", "]", etc) used in an expression and ignore other characters within a bracket pair. Using this approach, the expression tokensizer is able to handle all the cases of expressions in C/C++ and Fortran. For one special case, in some clauses we will encounter the form type id;. "type" refers to the data type, and "id" refers to the user-defined identifier. In this case, we take the type and id as one expression. Unlike the normal expression, we need to save the space as well. Then C compiler can compile this expression correctly for us.

3.2 Parser for OpenMP Constructs

This section describes the Bison grammar for OpenMP directives. With Flex rules and Bison grammar, a parser is automatically generated. Bison is a look ahead left to right (LALR) parser generator. Compared to Left to Right (LL) parser generators, an LALR parser parses the text by the flexible production rules, which enables developers to create a grammar for complex OpenMP structures. Besides, LALR parser is much easier than LL parser to construct grammar since it can be left-recursive.

The grammar structures for executable and declarative directives are very similar. Declare mapper is used to explain how the grammar was generated in Bison, since it represents other declarative directives as well as most executable directives. Figure 4 shows the grammar of declare mapper directive. The enum values of directive name, which is tokenized by the lexer, is used for start of directive grammar. Declare mapper has two directive-related parameters: mapper_identifier and type_var, which are considered as mapper_parameters. Mapper_identifier includes two identifiers: default and user defined identifier. Default identifier uses DEFAULT as terminal symbol, and user defined identifier uses EXPR_STRING as terminal symbol. For type_var, the reason why we use EXPR_STRING as token was introduced in last section. Mapper clauses are concluded into a declare_mapper_clause_optseq. All attributes must be stored into OpenMP intermediate representation (IR) by putting an action in the middle of a rule (Mid-Rule Actions in Bison's term).

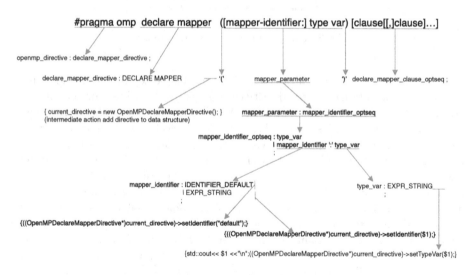

Fig. 4. The grammar for declare mapper directive

The grammar structure for most clauses are very similar. Schedule clause is used as an example to explain how grammar was generated for OpenMP clause. Figure 5 shows the grammar of schedule clause. Schedule clause has multiple parameters. In those schedule parameters, kind is the only non-optional parameter. Schedule clause should be added to its directive right after kind parameter since we have all parameters information after rule of kind parameter. The information of two modifiers should be stored separately as the Fig. 5 shows. Since those two modifiers are optional and different from each other, recursive grammar can not distinguished them. We use two global variables to store them. At last, chunk size is stored as independent attributes.

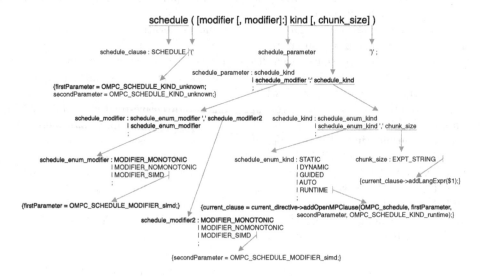

Fig. 5. The grammar for schedule clause

Metadirective is a special directive which contains nested directive and clause structure. Information of nested directives and clauses should be stored appropriately. As Fig. 6 shows, Metadirective has two kinds of clauses. The when clause is similar to other clauses, but it has a context selector and directive variant which may be a directive on its own. A context selector has two parts: specification and trait set selector. Especially, when construct is used as trait set selector, Construct directive will be added as current directive. Therefore, we have designed a nested directive structure. To solve this problem, information of directives and clauses should be stored via two global variables. After construct directive finished its parses, clause and directive should switch back to when and metadirective. Directive-variant also has own directive and clause, same method can be used to handle it. Additionally, it may nest with another directives, but grammar will handle nested directive automatically. Default clause only has one parameter – directive variant. Default clause can be parsed in same way of when clause.

For error handling, both syntax and semantic errors will be checked by grammar. Once an error is found, an corresponding error message will be printed. Then the program won't be crashed but a null pointer will be returned to host compiler/tool to indicates the parsing failed. In this project, a single clause can be used by several directives. And each directive maintains its own clause sequence. Each clause will be added to the directive through an intermediate action. A combined directive is considered as a new directive rather than a

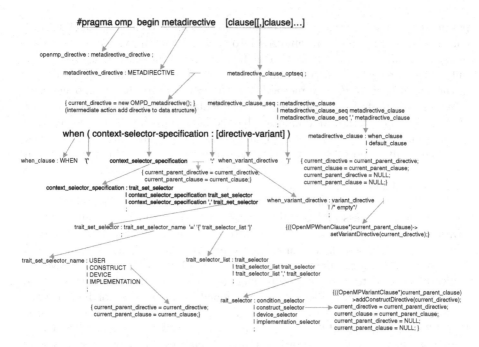

Fig. 6. The grammar for Metadirective

nested directive. If a combined directive is used as nested directive, Bison will report a reduce-reduce error.

3.3 OpenMP Intermediate Representation

The intermediate representation of ompparser is an abstract syntax tree for an OpenMP directive. The root node of the tree is the object of the directive and the child nodes are usually the objects for the clauses. Nodes for clauses are stored in a map structure with a clause type as its keys, and a vector of clause objects as its values. For the same kind of clauses that may be used multiple times, e.g. reduction(+:a) and reduction(-:b), the clause objects are stored in the vector of the clause map. With this data structure, searching clauses of a specific kind takes constant time. Searching a specific clause of a specific kind is also fast, since in general we anticipate users would not use the same kind of clause for many times in a directive. Cases where users include many clause in the same directive (e.g. map clause) are uncommon.

There are three methods that are related to how the clause objects are added to directive object – appendOpenMPClause, searchOpenMPClause and normalizeClause. appendOpenMPClause can be used to add a clause after the clause parameters are identified. searchOpenMPClause is used to search clauses of a specific kind and parameters from the OpenMPIR map. normalizeClause can be used to combine objects for the same kind of clause that also have identical parameters but variable list. For example, objects for two clauses reduction(+:a) and reduction(+:b) can be normalized into one object with two variables, reduction(+:a,b). Clause normalization can be performed alone after a directive is fully parsed or performed while adding a clause to the clause map of a directive in the appendOpenMPClause method. For the later approach, the appendOpenMPClause methods would call searchOpenMPClause methods to retrieve a list of clause objects of the same kind as the one being appended. It then searches to determine whether there's a matching clause to combine with. A new clause is created only if no such clause exist and the reference to this new clause is returned. Otherwise, the existing clause is updated with new information and reference to the clause is returned.

In ompparser, OpenMPIR is implemented with two main C++ classes, the OpenMPDirective class and OpenMPClause class, shown in Fig. 7. The OpenMPDirective class can be used to instantiate most OpenMP directives that only have OpenMP-defined clause names. For directives that may have extra parameters, such as declare variant variant_func_id clause1 clause2 ..., the OpenMPDirective class need to be extended to include more fields for those parameters. Similarly directives that allows for user-defined clause names, for instance the requires directive, it needs to be extended to include user-defined clause names. Figure 7 shows the OpenMPDeclareVariantDirective class. For clauses, the OpenMPClause class is used to instantiate OpenMP clauses that have no parameters (class 1 and 2 clauses). For clauses with parameters (class 3), a subclass is needed that includes the fields for the extra parameters of the clause. Figure 7 shows the OpenMPReductionClause class. The OpenMPClause class has a field of vector named as expressions for storing strings of expressions (or list items) specified for a clause. The expressionNodes field is a vector that can be used to store the opaque objects returned by the callback for parsing language expressions.

3.4   Unparsing and Testing

In ompparser, toString and generateDOT methods are provided to unparse the OpenMPIR to its original source code and in a DOT graphic file, respectively. An automated test driver is also implemented. The test driver takes test cases included in source files as its input, creates OpenMPIR, and unparses it to a text output for correctness checking. All the cases in the input file are checked automatically by the test driver and a summary will be printed in the end.

4   Preliminary Results

We are actively developing ompparser to add more OpenMP 5.0 support. Still, we have conducted preliminary evaluation of its current version.

4.1   Used as a Standalone Parser

To evaluate our initial implementation, we use two simple examples in Fig. 8, which are C and Fortran programs that share the same functionality. Ompparser

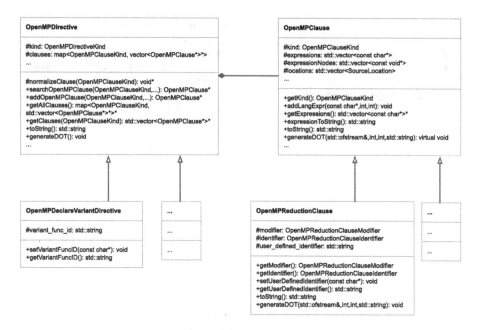

Fig. 7. OpenMPIR architecture

produces the identical OpenMPIR (Fig. 9a) except that the code in Fortran has a second OpenMPIR since the !$omp end parallel is considered as OpenMP code as well (Fig. 9b). Ompparser can merge the OpenMPIR for end with the IR for begin through a normalization step. In the source code, there are two shared clauses. But in the OpenMPIR, they are combined to one after normalization.

The metadirective in the latest OpenMP 5.0 is also supported in ompparser. The example shown in Fig. 10a can switch conditionally between sequential and parallel computing with metadirective. In its OpenMPIR, the parallel directive is attached to default clause as a child node (Fig. 10b).

Ompparser is also able to determine syntax errors existing in the input. For example, the OpenMP 5.0 code #pragma omp parallel if(task: n<3) is provided by user. In if clause, it can have an optional directive-name-modifier, such as task, parallel and so on. But it has to be the same as the directive. In this case, if clause cannot have task as modifier because it belongs to parallel directive. Only parallel modifier is allowed in this particular if clause. ompparser will report the syntax error and return null object to the host, which indicates that the parsing failed.

4.2 ROSE Integration

We have also integrated ompparser into the ROSE compiler framework. Developed at LLNL, ROSE [6,7] is an open source compiler infrastructure to build source-to-source program transformation and analysis tools for Fortran

```
1 | subroutine foo(m,n)
2 |   integer m,n
3 | !$omp parallel shared(m) shared(n)
4 |   if (OMP_GET_THREAD_NUM()<m) then
5 |     PRINT*, n
6 |   end if
7 | !$omp end parallel
8 | end subroutine foo
```

```
1 | void foo(int m,int n) {
2 | #pragma omp parallel shared(m)
  |        shared(n)
3 |     if (omp_get_thread_num() < m)
4 |       printf("%d\n",n);
5 | }
```

(a) C   (b) Fortran

Fig. 8. OpenMP source code in C/C++ and Fortran

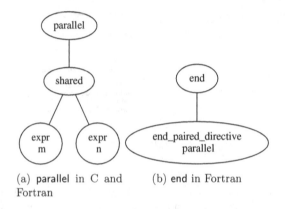

(a) parallel in C and   (b) end in Fortran
Fortran

Fig. 9. OpenMPIR for parallel in both C and Fortran

77/95/2003, C, C++, OpenMP, and UPC applications. Internally, ROSE generates a uniform abstract syntax tree (AST) as its intermediate representation (IR) for input codes. Sophisticated compiler analyses, transformations and optimizations are developed on top of the AST and encapsulated as simple function calls, which can be readily leveraged by tool developers.

Figure 11 shows how ompparser is integrated with ROSE. ROSE uses EDG to parse C/C++ codes, and OpenFortranParser (OFP) to parse Fortran codes. However, neither of these two frontends recognizes pragmas or comments for OpenMP constructs. As a result, OpenMP directives are represented as strings in ROSE's AST generated from these two frontends. A separate phase, called OpenMP parsing, is added after the two frontends to parse these OpenMP strings. Before using ompparser, two separate parsers were used for parsing C/C++ pragmas and Fortran comments for OpenMP constructs, respectively. The parsing results were first attached to AST as special OpenMP attributes and later translated to dedicated AST nodes representing OpenMP constructs. The ROSE AST has builtin support for OpenMP nodes representing both C/C++ and Fortran, as much as possible, in a uniform way. The unparser is able to parse

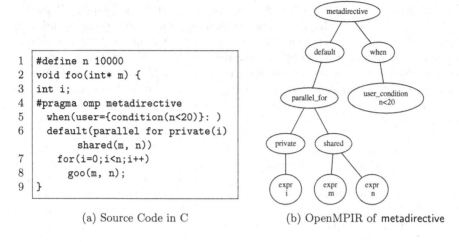

```
1   #define n 10000
2   void foo(int* m) {
3   int i;
4   #pragma omp metadirective
5     when(user={condition(n<20)}: )
6     default(parallel for private(i)
            shared(m, n))
7       for(i=0;i<n;i++)
8         goo(m, n);
9   }
```

(a) Source Code in C   (b) OpenMPIR of metadirective

Fig. 10. A metadirective example

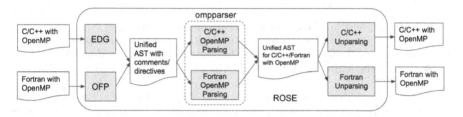

Fig. 11. OpenMP parsing and unparsing in ROSE and ompparser integration

the same AST into two different output languages (e.g. C or Fortran) as long as their semantics are equivalent.

We replaced the two OpenMP parsers in ROSE with ompparser, as shown in Fig. 11. A translator is implemented in ROSE to convert the OpenMPIR produced by omppaser to ROSE's OpenMP AST. The code size and complexity of translator is very similar with the original module in ROSE that generates OpenMP AST. During the conversion, the language expressions are parsed by ROSE's expression parser to produce their AST representation. We have tested the integrated ompparser inside ROSE, using the same examples mentioned in Sect. 4.1. The output of unparsed ROSE AST is identical to its input code when code in Fig. 9 is used. ROSE unparser's support for metadirective is still under development.

5   Conclusion

OpenMP is becoming more and more capable and complicated. It requires a significant amount of efforts for compiler developers to keep their implementations, including parsing, up-to-date. It is not cost effective for every OpenMP compiler to maintain its own parsers while all parsers share the very similar functionality.

In this paper, we have presented a standalone and unified OpenMP parser, named ompparser, which can be developed, maintained and used independently. We also took the ROSE compiler framework as an example to demonstrate how to integrate ompparser into other compiler and tools. The initial results show that ompparser's design can support the latest OpenMP 5.0 features such as metadirective. It can also be easily leveraged by an OpenMP compiler. We plan to add more features into ompparser and make it more useful to the OpenMP community.

Acknowledgment. This work was performed under the auspices of the U.S. Department of Energy by Lawrence Livermore National Laboratory under Contract DE-AC52-07NA27344, and supported by the U.S. Dept. of Energy, Office of Science, Advanced Scientific Computing Research (SC-21), under contract DE-AC02-06CH11357. LLNL-CONF-774801. This material is also based upon work supported by the National Science Foundation under Grant No. 1833332 and 1652732.

References

1. OpenMP Support in Clang/LLVM. https://openmp.llvm.org/
2. OpenMP Support in Flang/LLVM. https://github.com/flang-compiler
3. Antao, S.F., et al.: Offloading support for OpenMP in Clang and LLVM. In: Proceedings of the Third Workshop on LLVM Compiler Infrastructure in HPC, pp. 1–11 (2016)
4. Hayashi, A., Shirako, J., Tiotto, E., Ho, R., Sarkar, V.: Exploring compiler optimization opportunities for the OpenMP 4.x accelerator model on a POWER8+GPU platform. In: Proceedings of the Third International Workshop on Accelerator Programming Using Directives, WACCPD 2016, pp. 68–78. IEEE Press, Piscataway (2016). https://doi.org/10.1109/WACCPD.2016.7
5. Leontiadis, I., Tzoumas, G.: OpenMP C Parser, December 2001
6. Liao, C., Quinlan, D.J., Panas, T., de Supinski, B.R.: A ROSE-based OpenMP 3.0 research compiler supporting multiple runtime libraries. In: Sato, M., Hanawa, T., Müller, M.S., Chapman, B.M., de Supinski, B.R. (eds.) IWOMP 2010. LNCS, vol. 6132, pp. 15–28. Springer, Heidelberg (2010). https://doi.org/10.1007/978-3-642-13217-9_2
7. Liao, C., Yan, Y., de Supinski, B.R., Quinlan, D.J., Chapman, B.: Early experiences with the OpenMP accelerator model. In: Rendell, A.P., Chapman, B.M., Müller, M.S. (eds.) IWOMP 2013. LNCS, vol. 8122, pp. 84–98. Springer, Heidelberg (2013). https://doi.org/10.1007/978-3-642-40698-0_7
8. Novillo, D.: OpenMP and automatic parallelization in GCC. In: In the Proceedings of the GCC Developers (2006)
9. Ozen, G., Atzeni, S., Wolfe, M., Southwell, A., Klimowicz, G.: OpenMP GPU offload in Flang and LLVM. In: LLVM-HPC2018: The Fifth Workshop on the LLVM Compiler Infrastructure in HPC, pp. 1–9, November 2018
10. de Supinski, B.R., et al.: The ongoing evolution of OpenMP. Proc. IEEE **106**(11), 2004–2019 (2018)
11. Tian, X., et al.: LLVM framework and IR extensions for parallelization, SIMD vectorization and offloading. In: Third Workshop on the LLVM Compiler Infrastructure in HPC, LLVM-HPC@SC 2016, Salt Lake City, UT, USA, 14 November 2016, pp. 21–31 (2016). https://doi.org/10.1109/LLVM-HPC.2016.008

The TRegion Interface and Compiler Optimizations for OPENMP Target Regions

Johannes Doerfert$^{(\boxtimes)}$, Jose Manuel Monsalve Diaz, and Hal Finkel

Argonne Leadership Computing Facility, Argonne National Laboratory,
Argonne, IL 60439, USA
{jdoerfert,jmonsalvediaz,hfinkel}@anl.gov

Abstract. OPENMP is a well established, single-source programming language extension to introduce parallelism into (historically) sequential base languages, namely C/C++ and Fortran. To program not only multi-core CPUs but also many-cores and heavily parallel accelerators, OPENMP 4.0 adopted a flexible offloading scheme inspired by the hierarchy in many GPU designs. The flexible design of the offloading scheme allows to use it in various application scenarios. However, it may also result in a significant performance loss, especially because OPENMP semantics is traditionally interpreted solely in the language front-end as a way to avoid problems with the "sequential-execution-minded" optimization pipeline. Given the limited analysis and transformation capabilities in a modern compiler front-end, the actual syntax used for OPENMP offloading can substantially impact the observed performance. The compiler front-end will always have to favor correct but overly conservative code, if certain facts are not syntactically obvious.

In this work, we investigate how we can delay (target specific) implementation decisions currently taken early during the compilation of OPENMP offloading code. We prototyped our solution in LLVM/Clang, an industrial strength OPENMP compiler, to show that we can use semantic source code analyses as a rational instead of relying on the user provided syntax. Our preliminary results on the rather simple Rodinia benchmarks already show speedups of up to $1.55\times$.

Keywords: Compiler optimizations · GPU · Accelerator offloading

1 Introduction

Parallel execution and accelerator offloading are requirements for any HPC workload. Furthermore, it is now impossible to imagine anything, from mobile devices to supercomputers, without multi-cores and heavily parallel accelerators. It is only consequential that programming languages and language extensions evolved to help with massive parallel execution and accelerator offloading. A longstanding contender in this field is OPENMP. Its popularity is partially due to the

© Springer Nature Switzerland AG 2019
X. Fan et al. (Eds.): IWOMP 2019, LNCS 11718, pp. 153–167, 2019.
https://doi.org/10.1007/978-3-030-28596-8_11

single source approach that enables gradual adaption of parallel and offloaded execution (almost) seamlessly into existing C/C++ and Fortran projects.

According to the academic literature, as well as various "best practice guidelines", effective OPENMP accelerator offloading (for GPUs) requires combined OPENMP constructs [5,15–17]. Figure 1a shows the "inferior" case in which the OPENMP `target` (or `target teams`) pragma is used on its own, presumably with nested `parallel` directives that activate the threads of the created target team(s). A slightly modified version of the code, illustrating the "desirable" case, is shown in Fig. 1b. Here, the `parallel` is combined with the `target` construct causing each thread in the initial team to execute the outer loop on its own before the inner loop iterations are again shared among all threads in the team. While this conceptually changes the way the program is executed, it is not an externally observable difference. As such, it is not different from other program transformations that are performed by a compiler to bridge the gap between high-level programming abstractions and the actual hardware.

In this work we examine the current support of OPENMP target offloading directives in the LLVM/Clang [14] compiler, especially with the transformation sketched in Fig. 1 in mind. We discuss engineering challenges that arise when the legality of this transformation is determined in the current code generation scheme. To facilitate this optimization, as well as others to come, we introduce the TREGION interface, a new abstraction layer designed to eliminate various problems transformations for OPENMP offloaded code currently face. To showcase the potential of our solution, we evaluate our prototype implementation on four Rodinia v3.1 [6] benchmarks that come with OPENMP `target` directives. For three of them, LLVM/Clang falls back to a slower execution mode while we can apply a more elaborate version of the aforementioned transformation to achieve speedups up to 1.55× on a NVIDIA K40, and up to 1.36× on a NVIDIA V100.

The remainder of this paper is organized as follows: In Sect. 2, concepts relevant to this work are discussed. Afterwards, in Sect. 3, we introduce the TREGION abstraction layer to gradually lower OPENMP target offloading directives. In Sect. 4 we describe the two transformations we added to the LLVM middleend. One optimization aims to perform the optimization introduced with the motivating example in Fig. 1 while the other will eliminate overhead caused by the TREGION abstraction if that fails. Note that both are aware of the semantics of the TREGION abstraction and interact with it not only for analysis but also for transformation purposes. Our prototype implementation is evaluated in Sect. 6. After we compare this work to related approaches in Sect. 5, we provide a conclusion and discuss next steps in Sect. 7.

2   Background

This section briefly introduces key OPENMP offloading concepts as well as implementation details of the LLVM/Clang compiler front-end. For a more thorough description of the OPENMP directives and detailed semantics we recommend the OPENMP language standard [18]. For more information on the design decisions that shaped the LLVM/Clang front-end, we refer to the works of Bertolli et al. [3,4], Antão et al. [1], Bercea et al. [2], and Jacob et al. [10].

```
#pragma omp target                    #pragma omp target parallel
for(int i = 0; i < N; i++)            for(int i = 0; i < N; i++)
  #pragma omp parallel for              #pragma omp for
  for (int j = 0; j < M; j++)           for (int j = 0; j < M; j++)
    work(i, j);                           work(i, j);
```

(a) Code with standalone **target** direc- (b) Code with combined **target**
tive as found in the Rodinia v3.1 [6] nw   **parallel** directive as often recom-
(needleman-wunsch) benchmark.   mended to achieve high performance.

Fig. 1. Syntactically different but semantically equivalent code patterns that can easily result in significant performance differences. (**teams** omitted for simplicity)

2.1   OpenMP Target, Teams, and Parallel

Even though most accelerator are heavily parallel devices, the offloading and parallelization are separate concepts in OpenMP. The former is expressed with **#pragma omp target** while the latter is denoted either as **#pragma omp teams**, to spawn teams of threads with one concurrently running thread per team, or as **#pragma omp parallel**, to start parallel execution with all threads in the encountering team. Even though these directives regularly occur together, e.g., as a combined **#pragma omp target teams parallel**, it is unclear if that is due to the application design or because of the performance hit separate directives tend to cause (ref. Sect. 6). The existence and occasional use of the different concepts in separation, as well as the ubiquitous warnings to combine them, can arguably be interpreted as a hint towards the need for efficient support.

The general implementation of **target**, **teams**, and **parallel** is similar in all major C/C++ compilers. Each construct will cause the enclosed code to be outlined in (at least) a separate function. These functions are then passed to, and eventually called from, runtime functions that implement the respective directive semantics, e.g., orchestrate the offloading in case of **target**. In addition to outlining, the front-end will perform various other required tasks, e.g., emit code to communicate explicitly and implicitly captured variables [2].

This "early outlining" approach allows rapid integration of new features and bears little risk of miscompilations due to the function level abstraction and the indirection through the runtime library. Though, this approach will inevitably prevent any optimization to cross the boundary between sequential and parallel code as long as the semantics of the runtime library are not explicitly encoded [7].

2.2   Accelerator Execution Mode—SPMD Vs. Non-SPMD

While the single source approach taken by OpenMP is arguably beneficial for productivity and maintainability of the source, it makes it implicitly harder to achieve maximum performance when the accelerator execution model is substantially different from the one on the host. This problem is known especially when offloading to a GPU. These devices, in contrast to a CPU, expect to be utilized through multiple levels of parallelism, commonly via single-program-multiple-data (SPMD) execution. OpenMP provides a way to express this natively, namely outer-level parallelism through **teams**, SPMD execution through **parallel**, and inner-level parallelism through **simd**. Compound usage of all four directives (incl. **target**) often results in relatively good performance. However, any non-trivial separated usage of the directives might not. The reason is the (possible existence of) intermediate code which requires a different execution model. To implement single thread, host-like execution required for **target** regions (with or without **teams**) on SPMD (=GPU) devices, different schemes have been proposed [3,4]. Since they were mostly syntax driven, it is hard for the user to understand the performance differences of semantically equivalent OPENMP code. Even if the performance implications are clear, the combined directives are less flexible. They might simply not fit the needs of an application with a modular design that is developed for various different platforms.

3   The TRegion Interface

The TREGION interface is a simple, concise, and explicit interface for an OPENMP device runtime library, thus the part of the runtime that orchestrates OPENMP offloading related tasks on the device. The interface is constructed to be an easy target for OPENMP front-ends by minimizing the amount and complexity of code needed to use it. The idea is to avoid complex logic and target dependent code in the front-ends and instead use the compiler middle-end for the former and target specific device runtime implementations of the interface for the latter. In addition, the TREGION interface is designed to aid compiler analysis and transformation by encoding source code information, as well as implementation choices, explicitly. That means the interface calls have are various constant arguments to choose the runtime behavior. Assuming the runtime implementation is at some point inlined, the abstraction layer will be completely eliminated. Even if not, the overhead is limited to a (few) conditional(s) for each runtime call.

The general structure to be emitted by the front-end for an OPENMP **target** directive is depicted in Fig. 2. The interface call arguments are shown and discussed in Sect. 3.2. As illustrated, there are two distinct runtime calls surrounding the user code in the target region, one for initialization and one for deinitialization. When the target region code is translated, all **parallel** regions are outlined. These new functions, as well as the communicated values, are then passed to a **__kmpc_target_region_parallel** runtime call.

It is important to stress that the TREGION interface does not require logic or target specific code generation in the front-end. Instead, it should be possible to translate each OPENMP directive in isolation, without the need for much state kept in the front-end, and exactly the same way regardless of the actual target.

```
void kernel(/* mapped variables */) {
    int8_t ThreadKind = __kmpc_target_region_init(...);
    if (ThreadKind != 1) return;    // (surplus) worker thread
    // User defined target region code with parallel regions
    // replaced by __kmpc_target_region_parallel(...) calls.
    __kmpc_target_region_deinit(...);
}
```

Fig. 2. Code generated by the front-end for an OPENMP target region.

3.1 Design Rationale

The TREGION design has various consequences important for the performance and transformability of the code. First, the (device) runtime is required to provide a default implementation for each functionality necessary to orchestrate offloading (ref. Sect. 3.3). This is different than the current situation (in LLVM/ Clang) where a substantial part of the responsibility is carried by the language front-end. Second, the TREGION interface exposes source information and implementation choices as (constant) arguments (ref. Sect. 3.2). This allows analyses to easily pick up relevant source information from the runtime calls, and transformations to completely change the implementation by altering the arguments. Third, the TREGION code generated for the OPENMP directives is not (substantially) altering the original user code structure. Lastly, the TREGION abstraction will completely vanish once the device runtime library is linked into the user code and optimized through standard compiler techniques, e.g., inter-procedural constant propagation and subsequent dead code elimination.

3.2 Argument Semantic

Argument semantics are now discussed in the order they appear in Fig. 4: The `Ident` pointer specifies source location information. It is not used for semantic reasoning by the target region interface. The argument `IsSPMDMode`, which can be boolean or ternary to include the value -1 for "unknown", determines the logical execution mode (ref. Sect. 2.2). The bit-field `RequiredRTFeatures` informs the runtime which OPENMP features are potentially required in the target region to allow for limiting capabilities in favor of performance (ref. Sect. 3.4). The `NumThreads` argument determines the maximal number of threads allowed to participate in the subsequent parallel execution. The `WorkFn` function pointer identifies the code that will be executed in parallel, e.g., an outlined `parallel` region. The pointer and size pairs, `SharedValues`/`SharedValuesBytes`, and `PrivateValues`/`PrivateValuesBytes`, specify the values communicated between the sequential and parallel program part. The runtime has to make sure the values are accessible by all parallel threads, e.g., by copying them to shared memory[1]. Note that only shared values need to be copied back. If the boolean flag `AdjSharedMemPointers` is set, the caller placed shared and private values adjacent in a shared memory area, eliminating the need for copies.

Default Argument Values. The arguments for the TREGION interface can be set conservatively to the values shown in Fig. 3. This way front-ends can be kept simple, without the need to perform any source code analysis. Though, "smart" front-ends can still initialize the arguments based on syntactic reasoning.

---

[1] The current TREGION design (and its implementation) can deal with "first-level" shared variables, e.g., sharing and modifying a pointer to a global value. However, "higher-level" sharing, e.g., sharing a pointer to a master stack variable, is not possible. While there is no reason we could not reuse the existing scheme, as described by Bercea et al. [2], we are still in the process of determining if a middle-end solution is sensible.

While the "*varying*" arguments have to be set early, they are basically determined the same way as we do it for `parallel` directives on the host already. The `IsSPMDMode` flag conservatively `false` for the "init" and "deinit" calls, and -1, which represents "unknown", for "parallel" calls. If not specialized during the later optimization phase, an "unknown" value may require the implementation to determine the execution mode at runtime. The extra state is useful as orphaned "parallel" calls are then no different to the ones syntactically contained in a target region.

Argument	Default
Ident	nullptr
IsSPMDMode	false/-1
RequiredRTFeatures	(uint64_t)-1
NumThreads	*varying*
WorkFn	*varying*
SharedValues	*varying*
SharedValuesBytes	*varying*
PrivateValues	*varying*
PrivateValuesBytes	*varying*
AdjSharedMemPointers	false

Fig. 3. Conservative default argument values for the TREGION interface.

```
// Runtime initialization based on the arguments. Returns
// thread characterization, e.g., team master or worker.
int8_t __kmpc_target_region_init(ident_t *Ident,
        bool IsSPMDMode, uint64_t RequiredRTFeatures);

// Runtime de-initialization based on the arguments.
void __kmpc_target_region_deinit(ident_t *Ident,
        bool IsSPMDMode, uint64_t RequiredRTFeatures);

// Type for parallel region callbacks.
typedef void (*ParallelWorkFnTy)(void * /* SharedValues  */,
                                 void * /* PrivateValues */)

// Start parallel execution. The callback attribute allows
// LLVM to optimize across the sequential-parallel
// boundary (ref. Doerfert and Finkel [8]).
__attribute__((callback(WorkFn, SharedValues, PrivateValues)))
void __kmpc_target_region_parallel(ident_t *Ident,
        int16_t IsSPMDMode, uint64_t RequiredRTFeatures,
        uint16_t NumThreads, ParallelWorkFnTy WorkFn,
        void *SharedValues, uint16_t SharedValuesBytes,
        void *PrivateValues, uint16_t PrivateValuesBytes,
        bool AdjSharedMemPointers);
```

Fig. 4. The function declarations that make up the main target region interface.

3.3   Interface Semantic

The TREGION interface is a compiler internal abstraction layer designed to be targeted by different front-ends and implemented by different device runtime libraries. While the first part allows us to define the semantics on a high-level, the second requires a dependable contract linking front-ends and implementations. To this end, we detail the semantics of each interface function in the following, and also elaborate the freedom and guarantees implementations have.

The *init* function (__kmpc_target_region_init):
Any device runtime specific initialization code can be executed when the *init* function is called. This will happen before any other target region related code is executed. The arguments determine the execution mode and the runtime features (potentially) required during the target region execution. One such feature, discussed further in Sect. 4.2, is a generic state machine we added to our device runtime library to support this work. *All threads* of *all teams* (which were started by the host elsewhere) will enter the *init* function in order to be categorized via the return value. For now, we distinguish three types of threads:

0, for "surplus" threads that shall directly terminate.
1, for "executor" threads that execute the target region.
-1, for "worker" threads that help execute parallel sub-regions.

Note that all team masters have to be executor threads but there can be more. In SPMD-mode, hence if IsSPMDMode is true, all threads that participate in any execution are expected to be executors, all others have to be surplus threads.

The *de-init* function (__kmpc_target_region_deinit):
Any device runtime specific deinitialization (= tear down) code can be executed when the *de-init* function is called. This will happen for each executor thread after all user code in the target region was executed. Neither worker, nor surplus threads will reach the *de-init* function.

The *parallel* function (__kmpc_target_region_parallel):
The purpose of the *parallel* function is to orchestrate the parallel execution of the code region provided through the WorkFn argument. In SPMD-mode, hence if IsSPMDMode is true or if it is -1 (=unknown) and the runtime check determines SPMD-mode execution, all threads of a team that are supposed to participate in the parallel execution will reach the *parallel* function. Each encountering thread, up to a limit imposed by the NumThreads argument and potentially other factors, will then call the work function with the shared and private values, SharedValues and PrivateValues, as arguments. We delay the soundness discussion and other considerations to Sect. 4.1. In non-SPMD-mode, the implementation has to ensure that the shared and private values passed to the work function, stored in SharedValues[0:SharedValuesBytes] and PrivateValues[0:PrivateValuesBytes] respectively, are accessible by all participating threads[2]. If AdjSharedMemPointers is set, the implementation can assume this to be true.

The callback attribute, as known to LLVM and Clang, guarantees that the work function is called with the specified pointer arguments, or equivalent inputs, as arguments. Furthermore, neither is otherwise used, inspected, or modified in

---

[2] See also footnote 1 on Page 5.

a way that is observable from the outside. As a result, inter-procedural optimizations for scalar code, e.g., inter-procedural constant propagation, attribute
deduction, alias analysis, argument promotion, etc., can be applied *as-if* the
TREGION runtime call was not there but the work function was directly called [8].

3.4   Required Runtime Features

Any OpenMP runtime comes with various features necessary to ensure the functionality defined in the standard, but not always needed in actual code. Furthermore, our proposed solution will shift even more responsibilities to the runtime,
though mostly in the form of fallback implementations.

Given that many features require initialization and will cause overheads even
if they are not explicitly used, it comes naturally to disable the ones known not
required during the execution of a program (part). This is especially true for
target offloading because accelerators are often more resource-constraint than
general purpose CPUs.

Our prototype will, when SPMD-mode is enabled, follow the lead by the
current LLVM/Clang implementation and set the `RequiredRTFeatures` to the
most optimistic value. In the future, we expect to provide, and utilize, more fine
grained choices for non-SPMD-mode execution.

3.5   Reduction Support

Our prototype implementation already supports scalar reduction with builtin
types and operators through an interface in the same spirit as the one shown
in Fig. 4. Given that we are currently extending the capabilities towards a mix-
and-match system as described by Gonzalo et al. [9], we want to postpone the
interface description until all requirements have been determined.

4   Target Region Transformations

To showcase that the TREGION interface enables LLVM middle-end optimization
of `target` regions in a reasonable manner, we implemented two distinct transformations working directly on the TREGION encoding. Both optimizations are, to
some degree, already performed by LLVM/Clang. However, they are based on an
intra-procedural front-end analysis performed only on the immediate neighbor-
hood of the `target` directive. Our proposed alternatives work on the generated
LLVM-IR and are guided by an inter-procedural analysis. The key is awareness
of the TREGION interface semantics (ref. Sects. 3.2 and 3.3) and the interaction
with the runtime calls that exposed information and implementation choices.

4.1   SPMD-Mode Execution of Target Regions

As discussed in Sect. 2.2, SPMD-mode is the native execution model for GPUs.
If OPENMP target offloading code is written with a host-centric execution model

in mind, performance easily suffers. So far, the LLVM/Clang compiler only uses syntactic reasoning to justify execution of `target` (`teams`) regions in SPMD-mode. That means, if it is not syntactically known that there is a single `parallel` region nested at the outermost level of an `target` (`teams`) region, it is executed in non-SPMD mode and with a state machine for the worker threads (ref. Sect. 4.2). In contrast, our TREGION Clang front-end prototype does not (yet) perform any syntax based reasoning and instantiates the TREGION arguments with their conservative defaults (ref. Sect. 3.2). Thus, the `IsSPMDMode` argument set to `false`, or `-1` (=unknown) for "parallel" calls. As part of the code optimizations the middle-end "openmp-opt" pass will, if it determines SPMD-mode execution is sound, modify these arguments to change the behavior of the device runtime. Our prototype implementation uses an inter-procedural walk of the device code, starting at the `target` region entry point, to collect information about functions and potentially executed side-effects. During this process various OpenMP API functions, functions in the OpenMP runtime implementation, as well as compiler builtin functions are recognized. This allows us to refine the set of instructions that might actually result in an arbitrary side-effect and also to identify all instructions that cannot be reached without entering a `parallel` region.

Once all information is collected, our SPMD-mode soundness predicate is checked. The idea is that SPMD-mode execution is legal as long as it is not distinguishable for an (external) observer (through language defined channels). To simplify the following reasoning, we introduce two invariants which are preserved for instructions potentially reachable without entering a `parallel` region.

Uniform Control The path taken by any thread in SPMD-mode is equal to the path that the master would have taken in non-SPMD-mode.

Uniform Memory The memory, including the register file, visible to any thread in SPMD-mode at any program point is equal to the view the master would have had at that program point in non-SPMD-mode execution.

Note that both invariants initially hold. Hence, before any instruction was executed on the device, the memory accessible by any thread in the team is the same and all have the same control flow history.

SPMD-Mode Soundness Predicate. Instructions without direct externally visible side-effects[3], including branch instructions, are safe to be executed in SPMD-mode because the uniform memory invariant guarantees that all threads in the team will end up with the same result. This also preserves both invariants.

The invariants guarantee that all threads in a team encounter a "parallel" TREGION interface call together with their master and with the same memory state, at least if they are not already inside a parallel region. Furthermore, in SPMD-mode execution, the TREGION interface call lets all participating threads call the work function directly (ref. Sect. 3.3). The situation is therefore not

---

[3] Reading special registers, e.g., the block index register `thread.x` in CUDA, is modeled as a builtin call in LLVM-IR and considered a side-effect here.

distinguishable from a single master encountering the TREGION call and the implementation replicating its state across the required number of workers.

Given that the state at the beginning of the parallel region can be assumed indistinguishable, and the execution inside is the same, the state afterwards will also be. However, there is an implicit barrier at the end of the parallel execution in non-SPMD-mode, hence "at the end of" the TREGION runtime call. Assuming this barrier is replicated for SPMD-mode execution, and that the team threads not required for the parallel region will wait at this barrier, we can conclude that the outermost TREGION parallel call can safely be executed in SPMD-mode. As a result, all calls to the parallel TREGION runtime are SPMD-mode safe. They are either the outermost one for the team, or reached from within a parallel region in which the behavior is indistinguishable between both execution modes.

Lastly, we consider instructions that may cause side-effects and which are potentially encountered outside of parallel regions. While certain side-effects are safe, e.g., accesses to the local stack, it is generally not sound to execute them in SPMD-mode. There are various potential problems, including:

Data Races Replicating side-effects can introduce data race if the whole team is not executing the instructions in lock step.

Observable Effects Replication of certain side-effects, e.g., I/O, can be directly observed externally.

Divergence Replicating side-effects allows for the memory and control flow to diverge between threads, e.g., by querying the thread id from the runtime.

To avoid these problems in SPMD-mode execution the side-effects need to be guarded such that only a single thread encounters them. Since the side-effect has to be visible for all threads in the team, synchronization afterwards is necessary. Finally, the side-effect instruction could produce a result that needs to be shared between the team threads. Our prototype

```
#pragma omp barrier
#pragma omp master
shared_mem = side_effect();
#pragma omp barrier
result = shared_mem;
```

Fig. 5. Guard code generated for generic side-effects in target master only code.

"openmp-opt" pass will, assuming a call to the side_effect function, produce the code shown in Fig. 5. However, it will only do so if it can prove that the guarded code cannot distinguish between single-threaded execution in SPDM-mode and single-threaded execution in non-SPMD-mode. This basically means that the guarded code does not contain a nested parallel region. Such a region would in SPMD-mode not have the team threads available as they are stuck in the guard code barrier. Note that this only becomes a correctness issue if the *dyn-var* internal control variables (ICV) [18, Sect. 2.5.1] is set to *false*, a condition we can currently not exclude statically.

4.2   Specialized State Machine Generation

In case it is impossible to use SPMD-mode execution there is still optimization potential. A generic state machine implementation in the runtime, e.g. as shown in Fig. 6a, is far from optimal, especially for GPU targets. Similar to Clang right now, our prototype generate state machines specialized to a target region. This will replace the indirect call with an if-cascade that checks the work function pointer against known work functions. Unlike Clang, we can easily identify parallel work functions inter-procedurally and determine if a fallback indirect call is necessary. Furthermore, we plan to use control dependences which may allow chaining of known work functions without the need to traverse the if-cascade again. Figure 6b illustrates specialization if the target region contains exactly two parallel regions, outlined as KnownWorkFn0 and KnownWorkFn1, which are executed in this order once each.

```
void rt_state_machine() {
  barrier();                                    // activation signal
  bool IsActive = false;
  ParallelWorkFnTy WorkFn = rt_get_work_fn(&IsActive);
  if (!WorkFn) return;
  if (IsActive)
    WorkFn(rt_get_shared_values_ptr(),          // indirect call
           rt_get_private_values_ptr());
  barrier();                                    // finished signal
  rt_state_machine();                           // recursion or loop
}
```

(a) Generic state machine implementation in the device runtime.

```
void specialized_state_machine() {
  barrier();                                    // activation signal
  KnownWorkFn0(/* no shared values */ NULL,     // direct call
               rt_get_private_values_ptr());
  barrier();                                    // finished signal
  barrier();                                    // activation signal
  KnownWorkFn1(rt_get_shared_values_ptr(),      // direct call
               /* no private values */ NULL);
  barrier();                                    // finished signal
}
```

(b) Specialized state machine implementation in the user code.

Fig. 6. State machine implementations: generic (top) and specialized (bottom).

5 Related Work

Liao et al. [15] argue that combined OpenMP offloading directives are "more useful and more intuitive than their separate forms". They come to this conclusion because of "the native fit" of the execution model to the accelerator one and after discussing inferior implementations required for separate directives.

While the evaluation by Larkin [13] seems to show that various compilers perform better with a combined target construct than with separate ones, it is unclear if that was the (main) reason for the performance differences.

To enable compiler optimizations of parallel programs, various techniques have been proposed [11,12,19–23]. Most often they involve a new representation of parallel constructs to reuse existing analyses and transformations in the presence of parallelism. While the TREGION interface is certainly similar in thought, it serves a different purpose. Lowering to TREGION calls simplifies the front-end, allows easier adoption of new targets, and facilitates the development of new, explicitly "parallelism-aware" optimizations.

6   Evaluation

We evaluate our approach on four of the Rodinia v3.1[4] OPENMP benchmarks that feature `target` regions. With our prototype we could execute all in SPMD-mode. LLVM/Clang, our baseline, did so only for BFS, which has a single

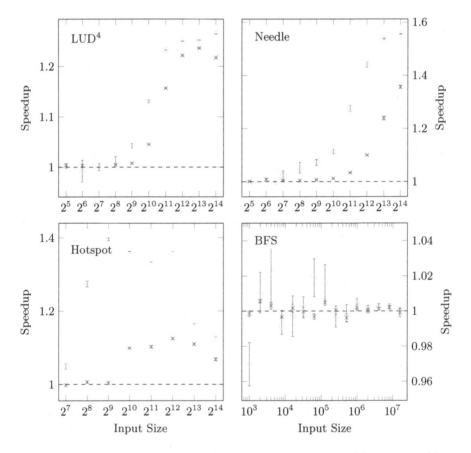

Fig. 7. Evaluation of four Rodinia v3.1 [6] on a NVIDIA K40 (○) and V100 (×).

---

[4] We removed `omp_set_num_threads` calls which were intended for specific hardware.

parallel region directly nested in the target region. The other benchmarks
are similar to Fig. 1, with Needle being even "simpler". Both LUD and Hotspot
feature calls in their target region outside of any parallel region. The call to
lud_diagonal_omp in LUD needed to be guarded (ref. Sect. 4.1) to allow execution
of the target region in SPMD-mode.

All benchmarks were executed 13 times with LLVM/Clang as a baseline. The
plots show the average as well as the standard deviation for various input sizes.
Overall, the performance consistently improved for both our targets, a NVIDIA
K40 (○) and V100 (×), if LLVM/Clang defaulted to non-SPMD-mode. BFS, which
is always executed in SPMD-mode, shows no significant performance difference
(Fig. 7).

7 Conclusion

In this work we discussed and removed a major shortcoming of state-of-the-
art OpenMP target offloading implementations. With the TREGION interface
we introduced a new step in the lowering of high-level directives that is well-
suited for compiler analyses and transformations. At the same time it is much
easier to lower to than the existing solution. The design of the TREGION interface
eliminates front-end complexity and also hides target details, thereby simplifying
the adoption of new ones. We have shown that transformations based on the
new interface are not only feasible but required to obtain good performance
if syntactic patterns are violated. We believe the latter to be too restrictive
to begin with and that middle-end compiler techniques will be able to justify
transformations much more reliably. The proposed scheme, if explored further,
will allow flexible use of OpenMP while delivering portable performance through
code transformations towards the native target execution model.

Acknowledgments. We would like to thank the reviewers for their helpful and extensive comments.

This research was supported by the Exascale Computing Project (17-SC-20-SC), a
collaborative effort of two U.S. Department of Energy organizations (Office of Science
and the National Nuclear Security Administration) responsible for the planning and
preparation of a capable exascale ecosystem, including software, applications, hardware,
advanced system engineering, and early testbed platforms, in support of the nation's
exascale computing imperative.

References

1. Antão, S.F., et al.: Offloading support for OpenMP in Clang and LLVM. In: Third
   Workshop on the LLVM Compiler Infrastructure in HPC, LLVM-HPC@SC 2016,
   Salt Lake City, UT, USA, 14 November 2016, pp. 1–11. IEEE Computer Society
   (2016). https://doi.org/10.1109/LLVM-HPC.2016.006
2. Bercea, G., et al.: Implementing implicit OpenMP data sharing on GPUs. In:
   Proceedings of the Fourth Workshop on the LLVM Compiler Infrastructure in
   HPC, LLVM-HPC@SC 2017, Denver, CO, USA, 13 November 2017, pp. 5:1–5:12.
   ACM (2017). https://doi.org/10.1145/3148173.3148189

3. Bertolli, C., et al.: Integrating GPU support for OpenMP offloading directives into Clang. In: Finkel, H. (ed.) Proceedings of the Second Workshop on the LLVM Compiler Infrastructure in HPC, LLVM 2015, Austin, Texas, USA, 15 November 2015, pp. 5:1–5:11. ACM (2015). https://doi.org/10.1145/2833157.2833161

4. Bertolli, C., et al.: Coordinating GPU threads for OpenMP 4.0 in LLVM. In: Finkel, H., Hammond, J.R. (eds.) Proceedings of the 2014 LLVM Compiler Infrastructure in HPC, LLVM 2014, New Orleans, LA, USA, 17 November 2014, pp. 12–21. IEEE Computer Society (2014). https://doi.org/10.1109/LLVM-HPC.2014.10

5. Bertolli, C., Bercea, G.: Performance portability with OpenMP on Nvidia GPUs. In: DOE Centers of Excellence Performance Portability Meeting (2016). https://asc.llnl.gov/DOE-COE-Mtg-2016/talks/2-19_Bertolli.pdf

6. Che, S., et al.: Rodinia: a benchmark suite for heterogeneous computing. In: Proceedings of the 2009 IEEE International Symposium on Workload Characterization, IISWC 2009, Austin, TX, USA, 4–6 October 2009, pp. 44–54 (2009). https://doi.org/10.1109/IISWC.2009.5306797

7. Doerfert, J., Finkel, H.: Compiler optimizations for OpenMP. In: de Supinski, B.R., Valero-Lara, P., Martorell, X., Mateo Bellido, S., Labarta, J. (eds.) IWOMP 2018. LNCS, vol. 11128, pp. 113–127. Springer, Cham (2018). https://doi.org/10.1007/978-3-319-98521-3_8

8. Doerfert, J., Finkel, H.: Compiler optimizations for parallel programs. In: 31th International Workshop on Languages and Compilers for Parallel Computing, LCPC 2018, Short Papers, Salt Lake City, UT, USA, 2–4 October 2018. Lecture Notes in Computer Science. Springer (2018)

9. Gonzalo, S.G.D., Huang, S., Gómez-Luna, J., Hammond, S.D., Mutlu, O., Hwu, W.: Automatic generation of warp-level primitives and atomic instructions for fast and portable parallel reduction on GPUs. In: Kandemir, M.T., Jimborean, A., Moseley, T. (eds.) IEEE/ACM International Symposium on Code Generation and Optimization, CGO 2019, Washington, DC, USA, 16–20 February 2019, pp. 73–84. IEEE (2019). https://doi.org/10.1109/CGO.2019.8661187

10. Jacob, A.C., et al.: Efficient fork-join on GPUs through warp specialization. In: 24th IEEE International Conference on High Performance Computing, HiPC 2017, Jaipur, India, 8–21 December 2017, pp. 358–367. IEEE Computer Society (2017). https://doi.org/10.1109/HiPC.2017.00048

11. Jordan, H., Pellegrini, S., Thoman, P., Kofler, K., Fahringer, T.: INSPIRE: the insieme parallel intermediate representation. In: Proceedings of the 22nd International Conference on Parallel Architectures and Compilation Techniques, Edinburgh, United Kingdom, September 7–11 2013, pp. 7–17 (2013). https://doi.org/10.1109/PACT.2013.6618799

12. Khaldi, D., Jouvelot, P., Irigoin, F., Ancourt, C., Chapman, B.M.: LLVM parallel intermediate representation: design and evaluation using openshmem communications. In: Proceedings of the Second Workshop on the LLVM Compiler Infrastructure in HPC, LLVM 2015, Austin, Texas, USA, 15 November 2015, pp. 2:1–2:8 (2015). https://doi.org/10.1145/2833157.2833158

13. Larkin, J.: Early results of OpenMP 4.5 portability on NVIDIA GPUs. In: DOE Centers of Excellence Performance Portability Meeting (2017). https://www.lanl.gov/asc/_assets/docs/doe-coe17-talks/S7_2_larkin_doe_portability.pdf

14. Lattner, C., Adve, V.S.: LLVM: a compilation framework for lifelong program analysis & transformation. In: 2nd IEEE / ACM International Symposium on Code Generation and Optimization (CGO 2004), San Jose, CA, USA, 20–24 March 2004, pp. 75–88 (2004). https://doi.org/10.1109/CGO.2004.1281665

15. Liao, C., Yan, Y., de Supinski, B.R., Quinlan, D.J., Chapman, B.: Early experiences with the openmp accelerator model. In: Rendell, A.P., Chapman, B.M., Müller, M.S. (eds.) IWOMP 2013. LNCS, vol. 8122, pp. 84–98. Springer, Heidelberg (2013). https://doi.org/10.1007/978-3-642-40698-0_7

16. Martineau, M., et al.: Performance analysis and optimization of Clang's OpenMP 4.5 GPU support. In: 7th International Workshop on Performance Modeling, Benchmarking and Simulation of High Performance Computer Systems, PMBS@SC 2016, Salt Lake, UT, USA, 14 November 2016, pp. 54–64. IEEE Computer Society (2016). https://doi.org/10.1109/PMBS.2016.011

17. Martineau, M., McIntosh-Smith, S., Price, J., Gaudin, W.: Writing performance portable OpenMP 4.5. In: OpenMP Booth Talk (2016). https://www.openmp.org/wp-content/uploads/Matt_openmp-booth-talk.pdf

18. OpenMP, A.: The OpenMP API Specification (2018). https://www.openmp.org

19. Schardl, T.B., Moses, W.S., Leiserson, C.E.: Tapir: embedding fork-join parallelism into LLVM's intermediate representation. In: Proceedings of the 22nd ACM SIG-PLAN Symposium on Principles and Practice of Parallel Programming, Austin, TX, USA, 4–8 February 2017, pp. 249–265 (2017). http://dl.acm.org/citation.cfm?id=3018758

20. Tian, X., Girkar, M., Bik, A.J.C., Saito, H.: Practical compiler techniques on efficient multithreaded code generation for OpenMP programs. Comput. J. **48**(5), 588–601 (2005). https://doi.org/10.1093/comjnl/bxh109

21. Tian, X., Girkar, M., Shah, S., Armstrong, D., Su, E., Petersen, P.: Compiler and runtime support for running OpenMP programs on pentium-and itanium-architectures. In: Eighth International Workshop on High-Level Parallel Programming Models and Supportive Environments (HIPS 2003), 22 April 2003, Nice, France, pp. 47–55 (2003). https://doi.org/10.1109/HIPS.2003.1196494

22. Tian, X., et al.: LLVM framework and IR extensions for parallelization, SIMD vectorization and offloading. In: Third Workshop on the LLVM Compiler Infrastructure in HPC, LLVM-HPC@SC 2016, Salt Lake City, UT, USA, 14 November 2016, pp. 21–31 (2016). https://doi.org/10.1109/LLVM-HPC.2016.008

23. Zhao, J., Sarkar, V.: Intermediate language extensions for parallelism. In: Conference on Systems, Programming, and Applications: Software for Humanity, SPLASH 2011, Proceedings of the Compilation of the Co-located Workshops, DSM 2011, TMC 2011, AGERE! 2011, AOOPES 2011, NEAT 2011, and VMIL 2011, Portland, OR, USA, 22–27 October 2011, pp. 329–340 (2011). https://doi.org/10.1145/2095050.2095103

Extensions

The Cooperative Parallel: A Discussion About Run-Time Schedulers for Nested Parallelism

Sara Royuela$^{(\boxtimes)}$, Maria A. Serrano$^{(\boxtimes)}$, Marta Garcia-Gasulla$^{(\boxtimes)}$,
Sergi Mateo Bellido$^{(\boxtimes)}$, Jesús Labarta$^{(\boxtimes)}$, and Eduardo Quiñones$^{(\boxtimes)}$

Barcelona Supercomputing Center, Barcelona, Spain
{sara.royuela,maria.serranogracia,marta.garcia,sergi.mateo,
jesus.labarta,eduardo.quinones}@bsc.es

Abstract. Nested parallelism is a well-known parallelization strategy to exploit irregular parallelism in HPC applications. This strategy also fits in critical real-time embedded systems, composed of a set of concurrent functionalities. In this case, nested parallelism can be used to further exploit the parallelism of each functionality. However, current run-time implementations of nested parallelism can produce inefficiencies and load imbalance. Moreover, in critical real-time embedded systems, it may lead to incorrect executions due to, for instance, a work non-conserving scheduler. In both cases, the reason is that the teams of OpenMP threads are a *black-box* for the scheduler, i.e., the scheduler that assigns OpenMP threads and tasks to the set of available computing resources is agnostic to the internal execution of each team.

This paper proposes a new run-time scheduler that considers dynamic information of the OpenMP threads and tasks running within several concurrent teams, i.e., concurrent parallel regions. This information may include the existence of OpenMP threads waiting in a barrier and the priority of tasks ready to execute. By making the concurrent parallel regions to *cooperate*, the shared computing resources can be better controlled and a work conserving and priority driven scheduler can be guaranteed.

Keywords: Resource allocation · Concurrency · Runtime scheduler

1 Introduction

OpenMP, widely used in the High Performance Computing (HPC) domain, is increasingly gaining attention in others domains [15,22,23,36] due to its efficient parallel execution model in shared memory systems, and also its support for heterogeneous computing. This is the case of critical real-time embedded systems, in which new computational intensive functionalities are being developed (e.g., autonomous driving). Here, OpenMP allows to efficiently exploit the performance capabilities of the newest highly parallel and heterogeneous embedded architectures, while benefiting from its programmability and portability capabilities. Moreover, OpenMP has been proven to be time predictable [35,36,38], a key aspect to introduce this model in the critical real-time embedded domain.

© Springer Nature Switzerland AG 2019
X. Fan et al. (Eds.): IWOMP 2019, LNCS 11718, pp. 171–185, 2019.
https://doi.org/10.1007/978-3-030-28596-8_12

OpenMP implements a fork-join model in which the parallel execution is initiated when a `parallel` construct is encountered. Then, a new team of threads (and implicit tasks) is created, associated to the corresponding parallel region. Moreover, OpenMP supports *nested parallelism* in which new parallel regions can be created in contexts that are already being executed in parallel.

Nested parallelism has a number of benefits in both HPC and critical real-time systems: (1) it is a well-known parallelization strategy to support irregular (imbalanced) applications, and (2) it can be used to boost performance at the different levels of a complex system or application, where parallelism is exposed. By using nested parallel regions, applications can benefit from an outer `parallel` construct for exploiting coarse-grain parallelism, and multiple inner `parallel` constructs for exploiting fine-grain parallelism.

However, this strategy presents two important issues: (1) it may result in load imbalance and hence, loss of performance [17], and (2) in the case of critical real-time systems, it may result in an incorrect (or too pessimistic) timing analysis [33,35,37,38]. The reason is that timing analysis is based on work-conserving scheduling policies [35], in which computing resources cannot be idle if there is pending work to do, and priority driven scheduling strategies, where the preference to execute is given to high priority tasks. These properties are not guaranteed between different concurrent parallel regions in OpenMP.

In both HPC and critical real-time systems, the reason to obtain worse or wrong results is that each parallel region operates independently, as a *black-box*, over a set of computing resources, either software resources (e.g., pthreads) or hardware resources (e.g., cores). The scheduler implemented at the OpenMP runtime level is agnostic of the internal execution of each team of threads. As a result, a team can have idle OpenMP threads waiting in a barrier, and occupying computing resources, while there is another team with pending work. The *black-box* problem in critical real-time systems was already identified [36], so the use of a unique team of threads was proposed to parallelize such systems.

In this paper, we propose a new run-time scheduler in which concurrent parallel regions *cooperate* by sharing internal execution information between different teams of threads, e.g., the highest priority among the ready tasks and whether there are idle OpenMP threads waiting in a barrier. This cooperation is used to (1) share computing resources among different (cooperative) teams by defining a new OpenMP thread scheduler, and (2) ensure a work-conserving and priority-driven scheduling, so the timing analysis for critical real-time systems, defined at analysis time, remains valid at runtime.

It is important to remark that our proposed run-time implementation is fully compatible with the current OpenMP specification [2]: the number of OpenMP threads within a parallel region remains fixed, the parallel work defined within each parallel region is executed exclusively by the corresponding team of OpenMP threads, and the thread affinity is preserved. Moreover, since the behavior of this implementation can be essential for some systems, e.g., critical real-time systems, we propose to provide the programmer with a new OpenMP feature to enforce parallel regions to cooperate.

```
1 #pragma omp parallel
2 {
3   if (th_work >= THRESLHOLD) {
4     #pragma omp parallel
5     ditribute_and_compute();
6   }
7   else {
8     compute();
9   }
10 }
```

Implicit parallel region

First parallel region

Nested parallel region

(a) Code snippet.   (b) Parallel regions.

Fig. 1. Example of nested parallelism with OpenMP.

2 Motivation: The Importance of Nested Parallelism

This section presents the use of nested parallelism in the HPC and critical real-time embedded domains, and motivates the need for a more flexible and controllable scheduler regarding computing resources and OpenMP teams.

2.1 Nested Parallelism in HPC

Before the introduction of the tasking model into OpenMP (specification v.3.0 [1]), nested parallelism was a well-known pattern used to address irregular HPC applications (e.g., tree traversal, adaptive mesh refinement [6], and dense linear algebra [25]). This strategy, which consists on creating new parallel regions in contexts that are already executed in parallel, may help to reduce load-balancing issues, because threads that get more work may decide to solve their work in parallel opening a new parallel region. Figure 1a illustrates this behavior, and Fig. 1b shows a diagram of the parallel execution of that code.

Although in several cases the tasking model has replaced nested parallelism to exploit irregular applications [3,39], the latter still outperforms the former in some cases. This is, for example, the case of imbalanced loops, where dynamic scheduling or tasking may suffer from poor cache behavior and low data reuse due to the inability to bind tasks to cores [8]. This, and the high overhead typically introduced by the runtime to manage the tasking model [26], makes nested parallelism a valid and still valuable mechanism. Particularly, for modern SMP machines with hierarchical memory systems, where outer teams can be created at core level, and inner teams can be created at hardware thread context [30].

The use of nested parallelism may however introduce problems by itself: on one hand, the overhead associated to the creation of parallel regions and the synchronizations [13]; on the other hand, the difficulty of tuning the number of threads of each parallel region. Regarding the former, different works try to mitigate the overhead of OpenMP parallel regions [13,21] by reusing structures when possible (the most significant techniques are introduced in Sect. 3). Regarding the latter, the problem explodes, because an inappropriate definition of the number of threads in nested parallel regions may entail several issues: (1) loss of programmability, because more responsibilities are pushed to the programmer; (2) loss of portability, because a particular set of values might be optimal for one architecture and mediocre in a different one; (3) situations of load imbalance, because threads are waiting at synchronization points while there might be work to do; and (4) oversubscription of the system resources.

Interestingly, the problem of load balancing nested parallel regions has been tackled widely, underscoring the importance of reusing the resources efficiently, reducing oversubscription and boosting data locality. Some solutions are based on a dynamic distribution of the resources between the different nested parallel regions [14], relieving the programmer from the burden of defining the number of threads of each parallel region, and thus enhancing programmability and portability. Others are based in work stealing strategies [29], crucial to ensure work-conserving schedulers that better exploit the possibilities of the system [7]. These works however, consider scheduling solutions in which the internal information about the execution status of the teams executed in parallel is not taken into account. This prevents teams to *cooperate* among them to, for example, avoid having idle threads when there is work to do in other teams.

Next paragraphs introduce an HPC application that presents limitations in the scheduling of different OpenMP parallel regions.

Human Respiratory Simulations: Alya

Coupled runs, consisting in simulations that solve different physics for a single run, are very common in HPC environments [10]. They can be found in a variety of examples from earth science, where some processes simulate the earth while other the ocean, to biological ones. This section describes the couple run applied to a biological simulation of the human respiratory system [18]. It is composed of the simulation of the air going through the human airways, and the simulation of the transport of particles inhaled through the bronchopulmonary tree.

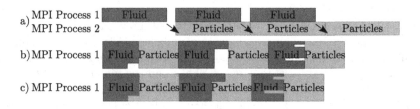

Fig. 2. Coupled run respiratory system.

Concretely, the simulation can be performed in two different instances of the program, one solving the fluid (air), and the other solving the transport of particles (particles inhaled). In this approach, shown in Fig. 2a, when the processes solving the fluid have computed its velocity, they send it to the processes computing the transport of particles, so both can be pipelined in parallel.

This simulation can also be performed by one instance, as shown Fig. 2b, where the program first solves the velocity of the fluid, and then the transport of particles. Considering that both phases include OpenMP parallel loops, and given that the computation is completely independent, each physics (fluid and particles) can be encapsulated within a high level task so they can run in parallel. This approach may result in a load imbalance scenario, however, if the workload is not properly distributed among the threads in the nested parallel.

If the concurrent parallel regions within each high level task are cooperative, the imbalance present in the fluid phase can be used to compute some of the particles parallel region, as shown in Fig. 2c.

2.2 Nested Parallelism in Critical Real-Time Systems

OpenMP is increasingly being considered as a convenient parallel programming model to develop the most advanced critical real-time systems. One of the main reasons is that the semantics of OpenMP tasks resembles the limited preemptive scheduling models [33,34,37]. The preemption strategy is an important factor in real-time scheduling because it determines when real-time functionalities, *real-time tasks*, can be stopped and resumed. Limited preemptive scheduling has been shown to reduce preemption-related overheads compared to *fully-preemptive* systems, while limiting the amount of blocking typical of *fully-non-preemptive* systems [5]. In this regard, OpenMP defines *Task Scheduling Points* (TSPs) as points in the execution of a program at which an OpenMP task can be suspended, allowing the associated computing resource to execute other OpenMP tasks. TSPs are therefore well-identified preemption points of parallel execution that can be considered in the timing analysis of real-time systems [33,34].

However, current timing analysis techniques are based on run-time schedulers with two important features: (1) a priority-driven execution, and (2) a work-conserving nature. Regarding the former, real-time systems typically assign priorities to real-time tasks and give preference to those tasks with a higher priority (based on the implemented preemption strategy) so that all tasks meet their deadlines. On the other hand, timing analysis for work non-conserving schedulers (i.e., there may be idle threads while there is still work to be done) have been proven to be very complex, and hence lead to unacceptable pessimistic results [35]. As a result, timing analysis techniques impose the real-time system to use a *single team of OpenMP threads* to execute all real-time tasks [36]. The reason lies in the black-box nature of concurrent parallel regions: the execution of each parallel region is governed by the team associated to that region, and each team has access only to the tasks associated to that team. Subsequently, two problems arise: (1) threads encountering a TSP can only schedule tasks that belong to its own team, so highest priority tasks from other teams might be delayed, and (2) threads waiting in a barrier cannot see there is work to do from other teams, so a work-conserving policy cannot be guaranteed.

```
1  // Real−time functionality T₁
2  #pragma omp parallel \
3                num_threads (2)
4  #pragma omp single
5  {
6    #pragma omp task priority (1)
7    { ... }
8    #pragma omp task priority (1)
9    { ... }
10   #pragma omp task priority (1)
11   { ... }
12 }
```

```
1  // Real−time functionality T₂
2  #pragma omp parallel \
3                num_threads (2)
4  #pragma omp single
5  {
6    #pragma omp task priority (2)
7    { ... }
8    #pragma omp task priority (2)
9    { ... }
10   #pragma omp task priority (2)
11   { ... }
12 }
```

(a) Low priority tasks   (b) High priority tasks

Fig. 3. Concurrent OpenMP parallel regions

As an example, Fig. 3 shows the OpenMP code implementing two concurrent real-time tasks[1]. Figures 3a and b correspond to the low-priority and high-priority real-time tasks respectively, set by means of the `priority` clause. Moreover, both parallel regions consider two OpenMP threads and a one-to-one mapping to physical resources (cores). Figure 4a shows the time diagram of the expected parallel execution of the OpenMP tasks, as considered by the timing analysis. Low priority OpenMP tasks are created at time instant t_1, and high priority tasks, at t_2, and so low priority tasks start the execution first in cores 1 and 2. The timing analysis considers that, when a low priority task finishes, a high priority task starts the execution, e.g., at time instant t_3. As a result, the system is considered to be schedulable because all deadlines are meet, i.e., the high-priority real-time task completes before t_5 and the low-priority real-time task before t_6.

However, due to the black-box nature of the two concurrent parallel regions, the run-time behavior may be different to that computed at analysis time. Figure 4b shows the time diagram of a compliant OpenMP execution of the two parallel regions, but not consistent with the timing analysis shown in Fig. 4a. The reason is that when the thread executing the low priority real-time task reaches the TSP at t_3, it is not aware of the pending high priority OpenMP tasks ready to execute in the other parallel region. As a result, the execution of the high-priority real-time task is delayed, missing its deadline at t_5. In this same scenario, a work-conserving strategy is not ensured, since at t_4, one of the OpenMP threads belonging to low-priority real-time task becomes idle and stays *busy-waiting* in the barrier while there is work to do in the other parallel region, instead of freeing the core to assign it to the other parallel team.

Next paragraphs present a real-time application where nested parallelism is useful, although its usage can cause the issues described in this section.

---

[1] The parallel region that encloses the two functionalities is not shown for simplicity.

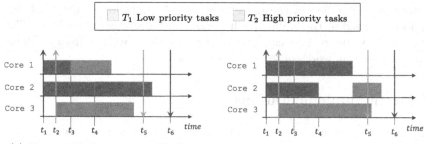

<table>
<tr><td>☐ T_1 Low priority tasks</td><td>☐ T_2 High priority tasks</td></tr>
</table>

(a) Expected behavior considered in the timing analysis.   (b) Possible behavior according to current OpenMP `parallel` implementations.

Fig. 4. Behavior of two real-time functionalities parallelized with OpenMP.

GPS-aided SINU

Global Positioning System (GPS)-aided Strapdown Inertial Navigation Unit (SINU) system is a low cost motion measurement device commonly used in real-time navigation systems. The system, depicted in Fig. 5, is composed of two functionalities: (1) obtain information from accelerometers, gyroscopes and magnetometers to generate outputs in terms of position, velocity and orientation, and (2) combine this information with that obtained from a Global Positioning System (GPS) to minimize errors by implementing a Kalman filter [20].

The Kalman filter is a common recursive application that estimates the internal state of a linear dynamic system from a series of noisy measurements. As depicted in Fig. 6, it is separated into two distinct phases: the prediction phase and the measurement phase. Both utilize the Cholesky decomposition to capture the mean and covariance of the system state.

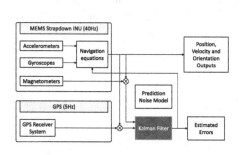

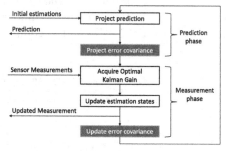

Fig. 5. Block diagram of the GPS-aided SINU system.   **Fig. 6.** Block diagram of the Kalman filtering algorithm.

Overall, the GPA-aided SINU is a real-time application that can exploit two levels of parallelism: in the outer level, the computation of the two functionalities (i.e., computing position, velocity and orientation, and estimating errors) can be performed in parallel; in the inner level, the computation of the Cholesky decomposition used in the Kalman Filter [39] can be further parallelized. The use of nested parallel regions can however prevent the scheduler from fulfilling priorities or ensuring work-conserving executions.

3   Current Implementations

The OpenMP [2] specification defines an *OpenMP thread* as an execution entity with a stack and associated static memory (so called threadprivate memory) that is managed by the OpenMP implementation. Then, this high-level concept may be implemented using different libraries, e.g., pthreads [4] and Windows threads [32]. Hence, when the specification states that a `parallel` construct causes the creation of a team of threads, and that the number of threads remains constant for the duration of that parallel region, it refers to the high-level concept of thread, and not the actual computing resources.

In that context, runtimes must consider the overhead introduced by multi-threading libraries [27] when using computing resources. This includes: (1) thread library startup overhead, that is one-time overhead occurring when the library starts; (2) thread startup overhead, that is time to create threads; (3) per-thread overhead, that is work scheduling overhead; and (4) lock management overhead, that is time spent managing locks. Two of them are particularly interesting when it comes to share resources among teams: the thread startup and the per-thread overheads. On the other hand, thread library startup overhead is usually negligible, and several works tackle lock management overhead [9,31].

Current OpenMP runtimes (e.g., LLVM [28], libgomp [19]) try to reduce the impact of thread startup overhead by using a *pool of threads* [13], and so avoid the costly creation and destruction of threads. For example, libgomp safely reuses idle threads, considering the processor binding and the thread affinity. As an illustration, for the code shown in Fig. 7, LLVM consistently creates $X * Y$ threads, while libgomp creates a number equal or (a bit) bigger than $X * Y$. Both results prove that LLVM and libgomp use pools of threads.

```
1  #pragma omp parallel num_threads(X)
2     for (int i=0; i<1000; i++) {
3        #pragma omp parallel num_threads(Y)
4           { ... }
```

Fig. 7. OpenMP example with nested parallelism.

Although OS-threads are reused, the overhead associated with these resources is still quite high in architectures with a large amount of cores (e.g., the Intel® Xeon Phi™ Coprocessor [12]), because more threads are potentially created. In this context, Intel® introduced the concept of *hot teams* [30]. This idea, implemented in the LLVM runtime for OpenMP, exploits the fact that OpenMP programs may execute many parallel regions with the same set of parameters (i.e., number of threads, internal control variables and information associated with the barrier). So, the runtime maintains one structure per team configuration. Intel also supports *nested hot teams*, that keep a pool of threads alive (but idle) during the execution of the non-nested parallel code [21]. This is very useful in cases such as the code presented in Fig. 7, where the use of hot teams allows to create the X inner teams once and not destroy them. Without this, the runtime would create and destroy them a thousand times.

These techniques, and the behavior they model, are not controllable at an specification level (and sometimes not even at a runtime level). This is because OpenMP takes the responsibility of scheduling parallel work out of the hands of the programmer. Just the scheduling of loop iterations can be tuned by means of the `schedule` clause, and the *run-sched-var* and *def-sched-var* internal control variables (as determined in Sect. 2.9.2.1 of the specification [2]). The scheduling of tasks is completely managed by the runtime following the Task Scheduling Constraints defined in the specification (Sect. 2.10.6).

Some runtime implementations, such as Nanos++ [11], allow a finer control of the scheduler by means of execution modifiers: *throttling policies* (i.e., define whether a new task is created and pushed into the scheduler system, or just a minimal description of the task is created and it is executed right away in the current context), *barrier algorithms* (i.e., how threads waiting at barriers execute remaining work), *traversal order* (i.e., how tasks are traversed, e.g., work-first and breadth-first), and *thread managers* (i.e., control the amount of resources needed for a specific amount of workload). Regarding the latter, there are specific libraries, e.g., Dynamic Load Balancing (DLB) [16], that, attached to the runtime system, allow dynamically managing threads to exploit work-conserving policies.

Overall, a constant behavior of current runtimes is that they tend to apply work-conserving scheduling policies because: (1) they are proven to be optimal for multi-threaded scheduling of Directed Acyclic Graphs [7] (as the ones generated by OpenMP tasks and their dependencies) because it helps load balance, and (2) they are used in the timing analysis performed for real-time systems in order to get not too pessimistic results. This policy defines a work queue for each thread; then, whenever a thread becomes idle, it may steal work from other busy threads. Both the Intel and the GNU OpenMP runtimes (i.e., KMP and libgomp) implement work-stealing for tasks (this aspect can be tuned in Intel by means of the environment variable KMP_TASKING). However, the time spent in busy-waiting is particular to each implementation.

4   Run-Time Scheduling Based on Cooperative Parallels

As introduced in Sect. 3, there exist two different kinds of *threads* involved in the execution of an OpenMP code. On one hand, the OpenMP threads are high-level abstractions associated to each team that remain fixed until the team completes. On the other hand, OS-level threads (e.g., pthreads, as used hereinafter) upon which OpenMP threads execute may exist along the execution of the whole application and be reused among different OpenMP teams (using thread pooling), even when the teams execute concurrently. For instance, the pthreads can be shared among two concurrent parallel regions, and so two (or more) OpenMP threads from different teams (or even the same team) could be mapped to the same pthread. The use of this technique can lead to incorrect executions, considered in Sect. 4.2.

It is OpenMP-compliant to have several OpenMP threads concurrently mapped to the same pthread. However, in current implementations, the OpenMP thread scheduler is not aware about the internal execution status of each of the parallel regions. As a result, different issues relevant for the HPC and real-time domains may arise, i.e., load imbalance, work non-conserving executions or the impossibility of honoring priorities across teams (see Sect. 2 for further details).

To address these issues and force a given implementation to provide the run-time behavior required by HPC or critical real-time systems, we define the *cooperative parallels*, in which concurrent parallel regions communicate to exchange information about their execution status. Concretely, the run-time thread scheduler will act as follows:

- Whenever there is an idle OpenMP thread waiting in a `barrier` or a `taskwait`, `barrier`), it will communicate with other concurrent parallel regions to check if there is pending work to do. If this is the case, the idle OpenMP thread will be suspended and the pthread will map to the parallel region with pending work to do. This will allow to provide better load balancing execution for HPC and real-time systems, as well as guaranteeing a work-conserving scheduling execution in case of real-time systems.
- Whenever an OpenMP thread arrives to a TSP, it will check the work pending in its team and will communicate with the other concurrent parallel regions to check the priority of the pending ready tasks. If the most priority ready task belongs to other team, the OpenMP thread will be suspended and the pthread will map to the parallel region in which the highest priority OpenMP task belongs to. OpenMP thread (and then the most priority task). This will allow to accomplish OpenMP tasks priorities as required by real-time systems.

Moreover, we propose to extend the `requires` directive with a new implementation defined requirement called `ext_cooperative_parallel`. This directive forces the implementation of OpenMP run-time to handle teams in such a way that the thread scheduler will take into account the work pending in all teams executing concurrently as described in this section.

Overall, the implementation of the cooperative parallels requires to have a global overview of the *running* OpenMP threads and the pending work of each team, while maintaining the compliance with the OpenMP execution model. Section 4.2 describes the properties that could be affected when implementing *cooperative parallels*, and must remain valid in the OpenMP specification. Before, Sect. 4.1 describes an example of the desired behavior of the *cooperative parallels*.

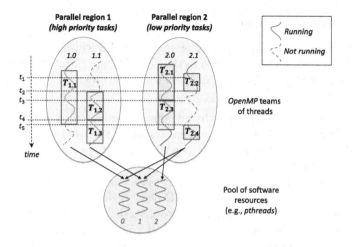

Fig. 8. Example of two *Cooperative parallels*.

4.1   Example

Figure 8 shows an example of two concurrent cooperative parallels, each with two OpenMP threads, that execute OpenMP tasks with a given priority. For simplicity, there are two priority levels for the OpenMP tasks, high and low, executed within the parallel region 1 and 2, respectively. There are three pthreads with IDs 0, 1, and 2. OpenMP threads have IDs 1.0 and 1.1 (parallel region 1), and 2.0 and 2.1 (parallel region 2).

Runtime Behavior of the Proposed Cooperative Parallels

1. Initially, at time instance t_1, we consider that all the OpenMP tasks of both teams are ready to be executed and the OpenMP threads 1.0, 2.0 and 2.1 are being executed in the available pthreads, with the following mapping: 1.0 mapped to 0, 2.0 mapped to 2 and 2.1 mapped to 1.
2. At time instant t_2, the OpenMP thread 2.1 reaches a TSP. Since task $T_{1,2}$ of parallel region 1 has a priority higher than any other ready tasks of the parallel region 2, the OpenMP thread 2.1 is suspended and the pthread 1 is mapped to the OpenMP thread 1.1, and so task $T_{1,2}$ can start executing.
3. At time instant t_3, the OpenMP thread 2.0 reaches a TSP. At this point, task $T_{1,3}$ has a priority higher than pending tasks $T_{2,3}$ and $T_{2,4}$. However, the two OpenMP threads of team 1 are already executing, and so the OpenMP thread 2.0 starts the execution of the task $T_{2,3}$.
4. At time instant t_4, the OpenMP thread 1.1 reaches a TSP but, since all the tasks in parallel region 2 have lower priority than $T_{1,3}$, OpenMP thread 1.1 starts the execution of $T_{1,3}$.
5. Finally, let's assume that at time instant t_5 the OpenMP thread 1.0 reaches a `taskwait`), and so it becomes idle. Therefore, since there is still a ready task pending to be executed in the parallel region 2, OpenMP thread 1.0 is suspended and the pthread 0 is mapped to the OpenMP thread 2.1 to start the execution of task $T_{2,4}$.

4.2   OpenMP Compliance

Possible implementations of the *cooperative parallels* concept must take into account some of the features defined in the OpenMP specification in order to be OpenMP compliant. This section analyses these features.

Thread Affinity Policy. The thread affinity policy (managed in OpenMP by the OMP_PROC_BIND environment variable, the *bind-var* ICV and the proc_bind clause) establishes how OpenMP threads are assigned to OpenMP places. If the thread affinity is enabled, the OpenMP implementation should not move OpenMP threads between OpenMP places once a thread in the team is assigned to a place. However, an OpenMP place is defined as "*an unordered set of processors on a device*", i.e., physical resources (hardware threads, cores, etc.), as described in Sect. 6.5 of the OpenMP API v5.0 [2]. Therefore, the OpenMP thread affinity, although compatible with the *cooperative parallels*, may break the desired behavior if a given computing resource is idle to execute work of an OpenMP thread that it is not assigned to it. In any case, the programmer is responsible of defining a thread affinity that does not break the properties brought by the cooperative parallels.

Deadlocks. The use of the same OS-level thread to execute different OpenMP regions associated with different OpenMP threads may generate deadlocks. We recognize two cases: one regarding barriers, and the other regarding locking routines. In the former case, if some OpenMP threads are blocked executing the implicit barrier of one parallel region, and some others are executing the implicit barrier of another parallel region, the OS-level threads may end up having in their call stack the execution of an implicit barrier that they are not going to be able to execute until they do not finish the execution of the current one. In order to solve this issue, our proposal should require an implementation that does not block the different contexts in the call stack of the OS-level, for instance implementing the OpenMP threads as user-level threads. In the latter case, when locking routines are used, compiler analysis [24] can be used to determine the possibility of a deadlock and hence inform the runtime not to safely share threads among OpenMP teams.

Threadprivate Variables. OpenMP provides Thread Local Storage mechanisms by means of the threadprivate directive, which allows to specify a list of variables that must be replicated for each OpenMP thread. Typically, current implementations use either mechanisms provided by the base language (e.g., the C/C++ __thread attribute), or mechanisms provided by POSIX (i.e., pthread_getspecific(), pthread_setspecific()), because it is the simpler way to go. However, this mechanisms are not valid if different OpenMP threads are mapped to the same OS-level thread, because the latter may end up having incoherent information coming from the different OpenMP threads. For that reason, when OS-level threads are to be reused among different cooperative parallel regions, the runtime must provide the mechanisms to determine to which parallel region a OS-level thread is assigned at a given point in time, so the proper threadprivate data is accessed.

5 Conclusions

Nested parallelism is a well-known strategy used in the HPC and the critical real-time domains to exploit irregular parallelism in systems exposing parallelism at different levels. However, due to the black-box nature of the parallel regions, nested parallelism may also result in an inefficient parallel execution because of load imbalance in the concurrent parallel regions. Moreover, in case of critical real-time systems, the computation may result incorrect from a timing perspective because of a work non-conserving execution, and the impossibility of fulfilling priorities among different parallel regions.

To address these problems, this paper introduces the concept of *cooperative parallels*, in which the information about the internal execution status of concurrent teams can be shared among them. Moreover, the possible scheduling solutions that can take benefit of this information are analyzed. From that discussion we conclude that a deeper control of the mapping between OpenMP threads and the underlying OS-level threads (e.g., pthreads) is needed to fulfill the work-conserving and priority driven strategies required in both HPC and critical safety systems to achieve better performance and meet timing constraints. An implementation of the cooperative parallel remains as a future work. Nonetheless, this paper discusses the compliance of the cooperative parallel concept with the current OpenMP specification, and provides tips to inspire future implementations.

Acknowledgments. This project has received funding from the European Union's Horizon 2020 research and innovation programme under grant agreement No 780622.

References

1. ARB: Openmp 3.0 specification (2008). https://www.openmp.org/wp-content/uploads/spec30.pdf
2. ARB: Openmp 5.0 specification (2018). https://www.openmp.org/wp-content/uploads/OpenMP-API-Specification-5.0.pdf
3. Ayguadé, E., Duran, A., Hoeflinger, J., Massaioli, F., Teruel, X.: An experimental evaluation of the new OpenMP tasking model. In: Adve, V., Garzarán, M.J., Petersen, P. (eds.) LCPC 2007. LNCS, vol. 5234, pp. 63–77. Springer, Heidelberg (2008). https://doi.org/10.1007/978-3-540-85261-2_5
4. Barney, B.: Posix threads programming (2017). https://computing.llnl.gov/tutorials/pthreads/
5. Bertogna, M., Xhani, O., Marinoni, M., Esposito, F., Buttazzo, G.: Optimal selection of preemption points to minimize preemption overhead. In: Procedings of the 23rd Euromicro Conference on Real-Time Systems (ECRTS) (2011)

6. Blikberg, R., Sørevik, T.: Load balancing and OpenMP implementation of nested parallelism. Parallel Comput. **31**(10–12), 984–998 (2005)
7. Blumofe, R.D., Leiserson, C.E.: Scheduling multithreaded computations by work stealing. J. ACM (JACM) **46**(5), 720–748 (1999)
8. Briggs, J.P., Pennycook, S.J., Fergusson, J.R., Jäykkä, J., Shellard, E.P.: Chapter 10 - cosmic microwave background analysis: nested parallelism in practice. In: High Performance Parallelism Pearls, vol. 2, pp. 171–190 (2015)
9. Caballero, D., Duran, A., Martorell, X.: An OpenMP* barrier using SIMD instructions for Intel® Xeon Phi™ coprocessor. In: Rendell, A.P., Chapman, B.M., Müller, M.S. (eds.) IWOMP 2013. LNCS, vol. 8122, pp. 99–113. Springer, Heidelberg (2013). https://doi.org/10.1007/978-3-642-40698-0_8
10. Cajas, J., et al.: Fluid-structure interaction based on HPC multicode coupling. SIAM J. Sci. Comput. **40**(6), C677–C703 (2018)
11. Center, B.S.: Ompss user guide (2019). https://pm.bsc.es/ftp/ompss/doc/user-guide/index.html
12. Chrysos, G.: Intel® Xeon Phi™ Coprocessor - The architecture. Intel Whitepaper 176 (2014)
13. Dimakopoulos, V.V., Hadjidoukas, P.E., Philos, G.C.: A microbenchmark study of OpenMP overheads under nested parallelism. In: Eigenmann, R., de Supinski, B.R. (eds.) IWOMP 2008. LNCS, vol. 5004, pp. 1–12. Springer, Heidelberg (2008). https://doi.org/10.1007/978-3-540-79561-2_1
14. Duran, A., Gonzalez, M., Corbalán, J.: Automatic thread distribution for nested parallelism in OpenMP. In: Proceedings of the 19th Annual International Conference on Supercomputing, pp. 121–130. ACM (2005)
15. Ferry, D., Li, J., Mahadevan, M., Agrawal, K., Gill, C., Lu, C.: A real-time scheduling service for parallel tasks. In: 2013 IEEE 19th Real-Time and Embedded Technology and Applications Symposium (RTAS), pp. 261–272. IEEE (2013)
16. Garcia, M., Corbalan, J., Labarta, J.: LeWI: a runtime balancing algorithm for nested parallelism. In: International Conference on Parallel Processing, pp. 526–533 (2009)
17. Garcia Gasulla, M.: Dynamic load balancing for hybrid applications (2017)
18. Garcia-Gasulla, M., Mantovani, F., Josep-Fabrego, M., Eguzkitza, B., Houzeaux, G.: Runtime mechanisms to survive new HPC architectures: a use case in human respiratory simulations. Int. J. High Perform. Comput. Appl. (2019)
19. GNU: libgomp (2019). https://gcc.gnu.org/onlinedocs/libgomp/
20. Hun, L.C., Yeng, O.L., Sze, L.T., Chet, K.V.: Kalman filtering and its real-time applications. In: Real-Time Systems (2016)
21. Jeffers, J., Reinders, J., Sodani, A.: Intel Xeon Phi Processor High Performance Programming: Knights, Landing edn. Morgan Kaufmann, Burlington (2016)
22. Kim, J., Kim, H., Lakshmanan, K., Rajkumar, R.R.: Parallel scheduling for cyber-physical systems: analysis and case study on a self-driving car. In: Proceedings of the ACM/IEEE 4th International Conference on Cyber-physical Systems, pp. 31–40. ACM (2013)
23. Knafla, B., Leopold, C.: Parallelizing a real-time steering simulation for computer games with OpenMP. In: Parallel Computing: Architectures, Algorithms, and Applications, vol. 15, p. 219 (2008)
24. Kroening, D., Poetzl, D., Schrammel, P., Wachter, B.: Sound static deadlock analysis for C/Pthreads. In: 31st International Conference on Automated Software Engineering, pp. 379–390. IEEE, September 2016

25. Kurzak, J., Dongarra, J.: Implementing linear algebra routines on multi-core processors with pipelining and a look ahead. In: Kågström, B., Elmroth, E., Dongarra, J., Waśniewski, J. (eds.) PARA 2006. LNCS, vol. 4699, pp. 147–156. Springer, Heidelberg (2007). https://doi.org/10.1007/978-3-540-75755-9_18
26. LaGrone, J., Aribuki, A., Chapman, B.: A set of microbenchmarks for measuring OpenMP task overheads. In: Proceedings of the International Conference on Parallel and Distributed Processing Techniques and Applications (PDPTA), p. 1. Citeseer (2011)
27. Lindberg, P.: Performance obstacles for threading: how do they affect OpenMP code. Intel Software Developer Zone (2009). https://software.intel.com/en-us/articles/performance-obstacles-for-threading-how-do-they-affect-openmp-code
28. LLVM: OpenMP*: Support for the OpenMP language (2019). https://openmp.llvm.org
29. Meadows, L., Pennycook, S.J., Duran, A., Wilmarth, T., Cownie, J.: Workstealing and nested parallelism in SMP systems. In: Maruyama, N., de Supinski, B.R., Wahib, M. (eds.) IWOMP 2016. LNCS, vol. 9903, pp. 47–60. Springer, Cham (2016). https://doi.org/10.1007/978-3-319-45550-1_4
30. Meadows, L., Kim, J.: Chapter 18 - exploiting multilevel parallelism in quantum simulations. In: High Performance Parallelism Pearls. Volume 2: Multicore and Many-Core Programming Approaches, pp. 335–354 (2015)
31. Nanjegowda, R., Hernandez, O., Chapman, B., Jin, H.H.: Scalability evaluation of barrier algorithms for OpenMP. In: Müller, M.S., de Supinski, B.R., Chapman, B.M. (eds.) IWOMP 2009. LNCS, vol. 5568, pp. 42–52. Springer, Heidelberg (2009). https://doi.org/10.1007/978-3-642-02303-3_4
32. Russinovich, M.E., Solomon, D.A., Ionescu, A.: Windows Internals. Pearson Education, London (2012)
33. Serrano, M.A., Melani, A., Bertogna, M., Quiñones, E.: Response-time analysis of DAG tasks under fixed priority scheduling with limited preemptions. In: Proceedings of the Design, Automation & Test in Europe Conference & Exhibition (DATE) (2016)
34. Serrano, M.A., Melani, A., Kehr, S., Bertogna, M., Quiñones, E.: An analysis of lazy and eager limited preemption approaches under DAG-based global fixed priority scheduling. In: Proceedings of the 20th IEEE International Symposium on Real-Time Distributed Computing (ISORC) (2017)
35. Serrano, M.A., Melani, A., Vargas, R., Marongiu, A., Bertogna, M., Quiñones, E.: Timing characterization of OpenMP4 tasking model. In: International Conference on Compilers, Architecture and Synthesis for Embedded Systems, pp. 157–166. IEEE (2015)
36. Serrano, M.A., Royuela, S., Quiñones, E.: Towards an OpenMP specification for critical real-time systems. In: de Supinski, B.R., Valero-Lara, P., Martorell, X., Mateo Bellido, S., Labarta, J. (eds.) IWOMP 2018. LNCS, vol. 11128, pp. 143–159. Springer, Cham (2018). https://doi.org/10.1007/978-3-319-98521-3_10
37. Sun, J., Guan, N., Wang, Y., He, Q., Yi, W.: Scheduling and analysis of real-time OpenMP task systems with tied tasks. In: Proceedings of Real-Time Systems Symposium (2017)
38. Vargas, R., Quiñones, E., Marongiu, A.: OpenMP and timing predictability: a possible union? In: Proceedings of the 2015 Design, Automation & Test in Europe Conference & Exhibition, pp. 617–620 (2015)
39. YarKhan, A., Kurzak, J., Luszczek, P., Dongarra, J.: Porting the PLASMA numerical library to the OpenMP standard. Int. J. Parallel Prog. **45**(3), 612–633 (2017)

Toward a Standard Interface
for User-Defined Scheduling in OpenMP

Vivek Kale[1(✉)], Christian Iwainsky[2], Michael Klemm[3],
Jonas H. Müller Korndörfer[4], and Florina M. Ciorba[4]

[1] Brookhaven National Laboratory, Upton, USA
vivek.lkale@gmail.com
[2] Technische Universität Darmstadt, Darmstadt, Germany
[3] Intel Deutschland GmbH, Feldkirchen, Germany
[4] University of Basel, Basel, Switzerland

Abstract. Parallel loops are an important part of OpenMP programs.
Efficient scheduling of parallel loops can improve performance of the programs. The current OpenMP specification only offers three options for
loop scheduling, which are insufficient in certain instances. Given the
large number of other possible scheduling strategies, standardizing each
of them is infeasible. A more viable approach is to extend the OpenMP
standard to allow a user to define loop scheduling strategies within her
application. The approach will enable standard-compliant application-
specific scheduling. This work analyzes the principal components required
by user-defined scheduling and proposes two competing interfaces as candidates for the OpenMP standard. We conceptually compare the two proposed interfaces with respect to the three host languages of OpenMP, i.e.,
C, C++, and Fortran. These interfaces serve the OpenMP community
as a basis for discussion and prototype implementation supporting user-
defined scheduling in an OpenMP library.

Keywords: OpenMP · Multithreaded applications ·
Shared-memory programming · Multicore · Loop scheduling ·
Self-scheduling · User-defined loop scheduling ·
Dynamic load balancing · High performance computing

1 Introduction

OpenMP [9] is the industry and academic standard for parallel programming
on shared memory platforms. Loop-level parallelism is a very important part of
many OpenMP applications that frequently contain *computationally-intensive*
and large *data parallel loops*. Such OpenMP applications are typically executed
on high performance computing (HPC) platforms which are increasingly complex, large, heterogeneous, and exhibit massive and diverse parallelism. The performance of applications executing on HPC platforms can be degraded due to

X. Fan et al. (Eds.): IWOMP 2019, LNCS 11718, pp. 186–200, 2019.
https://doi.org/10.1007/978-3-030-28596-8_13

various *overheads*, such as synchronization, management of parallelism, communication, and load imbalance [4]. Indeed, these overheads cannot be ignored by any effort to improve the performance of applications, such as the loop scheduling schemes [7]. The scheduling of those large and complex OpenMP loops can be a critical factor for the efficient use of those HPC platforms.

The optimal scheduling of parallel applications on parallel computing platforms is NP-hard [16]. No single loop scheduling technique can address all sources of *load imbalance* to effectively optimize the performance of all *parallel applications* executing on all types of *computing platforms*. Indeed, the characteristics of the loop iterations *compounded* with the characteristics of the underlying computing systems determine, typically during execution, whether a certain scheduling scheme outperforms another. The performance of parallel applications is impacted by system-induced variability (e.g., operating system noise, power capping) and results in additional irregularity that has often been neglected in loop scheduling research, particularly in the context of OpenMP scheduling [17,30]. Efficient loop scheduling can mitigate those variabilities, if a suitable schedule is available. However, choices for loop scheduling strategies in OpenMP are limited today to static, guided, or dynamic. These three scheduling strategies have been shown in previous work [8,22] not to offer the best performance possible. Moreover, fault-tolerant and energy-oriented OpenMP loop scheduling strategies require domain-specific knowledge to maintain correctness and energy-efficiency at large-scale, respectively [11,32], which is currently not exploited by the three standard OpenMP scheduling strategies.

More and novel loop scheduling strategies are needed in OpenMP given complexity of emerging applications and of supercomputer architectures. This is evident by the efforts of compiler developers, open-source and commercial alike, to support additional scheduling schemes. The efforts can be observed in LLVM [2] with the trapezoid self-scheduling [31] strategy, or in the Intel compiler with a static stealing scheme [24]. However, given the great body of work on loop scheduling, in general, standardizing all possible scheduling strategies in OpenMP is infeasible. Therefore, given the many different compilers supporting OpenMP, a standardized way of supporting additional scheduling strategies is mandatory for portability and use in today's frequently changing HPC landscape.

A more viable approach is to extend the OpenMP standard to allow for *user-defined loop scheduling* (UDS). Doing so will enable application-specific scheduling as well as a standard-compliant means to customize current loop schedulers. To this end, this work analyzes the principal operations of a loop scheduling scheme using a 'todo list' as a representation of the loop iteration space. Based on this modeling we identify four mandatory operations (init, enqueue, dequeue, and finalize). To support all currently available scheduling strategies, additional information may be necessary, which can be obtained through two measurement operations around the loop body. Using these principal components, we propose two complementary UDS specification interfaces for OpenMP, following the distinct styles of C, Fortran, and C++. One proposal supports a more modern programming style, such as that used in C++14 and later. The other proposal takes a classic approach, is suitable for C, Fortran and C++ programs and helps many types of applications to run on various architectures. The aim is that these proposals serve the OpenMP community and compiler developers as a basis for discussion and prototype implementation of UDS.

The core contributions of this work are: (1) an analysis of existing scheduling strategies and specifications of a minimal function set that is capable of implementing them and (2) an actual language-specific proposal of how to implement existing and future user-defined scheduling strategies.

The remainder of this paper is structured as follows. First, we provide the background and state of the art in recent loop scheduling strategies in Sect. 2. We then introduce our proposal for an interface in OpenMP to facilitate user-defined scheduling and its design rationale in Sect. 3. We present in Sect. 4.2 the two alternative proposals for the specification of user-defined loop scheduling for OpenMP. Finally, we summarize our experience in Sect. 5.

2   Scheduling Background and State of the Art

Scheduling, as broadly understood, refers to the orchestration of units of work onto units of execution, in space and time. It typically consists of three steps: partitioning, assignment, and load balancing. A computational application is *partitioned* into units of work to expose the software parallelism. This parallelism is expressed by *assigning* the units of work (e.g., problem sub-domains) to units of processing (e.g., processes, threads, tasks). The parallel units of processing are subsequently *assigned* to units of execution (e.g., nodes, processors, cores) to exploit the available hardware parallelism. *Load balancing* refers to evenly assigning the units of work to units of processing (software load balancing) or to evenly assigning the units of processing to units of execution (hardware load balancing). In load balancing, the transfer policy determines *whether* a unit of work should be transferred, while the location policy determines *where* it should be transferred. Based on the location policy, load balancing approaches can be *sender-initiated* (also called work sharing), *receiver-initiated* (also referred to as self-scheduling or work stealing), or *symmetrically-initiated* [23].

Load imbalance is the major performance degradation overhead in computationally-intensive applications [12,13]. It can result from the uneven assignment of units of computation to units of processing (e.g., threads) or the uneven assignment of units of processing to units of execution. At light and moderate load imbalance, sender-initiated and symmetrically-initiated algorithms outperform receiver-initiated algorithms. Conversely, at high loads, they perform poorly, possibly causing system instability and are outperformed by receiver-initiated algorithms [23]. A *load balanced execution* refers to the case when all units of execution complete their assigned work *at the same time.*

In this work, we concentrate on the scheduling and (software) load balancing of parallel OpenMP loops. In this context, we consider computational problems that contain parallel loops expressed using OpenMP *worksharing* constructs. The iterations of these loops are scheduled and load balanced, respectively, to achieve a load balanced execution.

It is important to note that many scientific, engineering, and industrial applications that use OpenMP contain worksharing loops. Therefore, scheduling of worksharing loops in OpenMP is not overshadowed by the recent advances and developments in OpenMP tasking. Worksharing loops and tasking represent two complementary parallel programming approaches that intersect when each iteration of a worksharing loop creates an OpenMP task to execute the loop body.

The term *loop scheduling strategy* denotes the technique (or policy) for assigning the loop iterations to threads in a team. A *loop scheduler* refers to the implementation of a particular loop scheduling strategy, while *loop schedule* represents the resulting assignment of loop iterations to threads in a team based on the particular scheduling strategy and its corresponding scheduler. In this work, the acronym UDS denotes *user-defined loop scheduling*. However, unless otherwise noted, the term UDS is also interchangeably used to denote either scheduling, scheduler, or schedule.

There exists a great body of work on loop scheduling and a taxonomy of loop scheduling strategies can be found in recent literature [8]. Loop scheduling strategies can broadly be classified into *static* and *dynamic*. The dynamic strategies can further be classified into *non-adaptive* and *adaptive*. The static scheduling strategies take the partitioning, assignment, and load balancing decisions *before* the loop executes, while dynamic scheduling strategies take most of or all these decisions during execution. Moreover, the dynamic adaptive scheduling strategies *adapt* these decisions as the loop executes based on the application, execution, and system states, to deliver a highly balanced execution.

The OpenMP specification [9] offers three scheduling options for worksharing loops: `static`, `dynamic`, and `guided`. Each can be directly selected as arguments to the OpenMP `schedule()` clause of a `for` directive. The first option falls into the *static* scheduling category, while the other two options belong to the *dynamic non-adaptive* scheduling category with *receiver-initiated* load balancing location policy. The loop scheduling strategies can also automatically be selected by the OpenMP runtime system via the `auto` argument to `schedule()` or their selection can be deferred to execution time via the `runtime` argument to `schedule()`.

The use of `schedule(static,chunk)` employs *straightforward parallelization* or *static block scheduling* [25] (STATIC) wherein N loop iterations are divided into P chunks of size $\lceil N/P \rceil$; P being the number of units of processing (e.g., threads). Each `chunk` of consecutive iterations is assigned to a thread, in a round-robin fashion. This is only suitable for *uniformly distributed* loop iterations and in the *absence* of load imbalance. The use of `schedule(static,1)` implements *static cyclic scheduling* [25] wherein single iterations are statically assigned consecutively to different threads in a cyclic fashion, i.e., iteration i is assigned to thread $i \bmod P$. For certain non-uniformly distributed parallel loop iterations, cyclic scheduling produces a more balanced schedule than block scheduling. Both versions achieve high locality with virtually no scheduling overhead, at the expense of poor load balancing if applied to loops with irregular loop iterations or in systems with high variability.

The dynamic version of `schedule(static,chunk)` that employs *dynamic block scheduling* is `schedule(dynamic,chunk)`. It differs in that the assignment of chunks to threads is performed during execution. The dynamic counterpart to `schedule(static,1)` is `schedule(dynamic,1)` which employs *pure self-scheduling* (PSS or simply SS), the easiest and most straightforward dynamic loop self-scheduling algorithm [29]. Whenever a thread is idle, it retrieves an iteration from a central work queue (receiver-initiated load balancing). SS achieves good load balancing yet may cause excessive scheduling overhead. The scheduling option `schedule(guided)` implements *guided self-scheduling* (GSS) [26], one of the early self-scheduling-based techniques that trades off load imbalance and scheduling overhead.

Further noteworthy dynamic non-adaptive loop scheduling techniques are *trapezoid self-scheduling* (TSS) [31], *factoring2* (FAC2) [15], and *weighted factoring2* (WF2) [14]. TSS, FAC2, and WF2 do not require additional information about loop characteristics and the allocated chunk sizes using these techniques decrease during the course of the execution from one work request to another. It is important to note that the FAC2 and WF2 evolved from the probabilistic analyses that conceived FAC [15] and WF [14], respectively, while TSS is a deterministic self-scheduling method. Moreover, WF2 can employ workload balancing information specified by the user, such as the capabilities of a heterogeneous hardware configuration.

TSS, FAC2, WF2, and RAND (random self-scheduling-based method that employs the uniform distribution between a lower and an upper bound to arrive at a randomly calculated chunk size between these bounds) [8] have been implemented in the LaPeSD libGOMP [3] based on the GNU OpenMP library. The LLVM OpenMP runtime [2] also provides an implementation of TSS [31] and *static stealing* (also referred to as fixed-size chunking [24]). FAC2 has also been recently implemented in the LLVM OpenMP runtime to offer further performance enhancement possibilities at higher loads [22].

This review of existing related efforts shows that there is a large amount of ad-hoc development of loop scheduling strategies and schedulers for OpenMP in various OpenMP runtime libraries (RTLs), yet none of these efforts comply with the OpenMP specification. While these implementations may remain helpful to certain users, applications, and systems, their broad practical usability may be limited, rendering them not useful for supporting the development of novel advanced loop scheduling strategies in OpenMP.

The main challenge is to *decouple* the loop scheduling strategy from its implementation strategy. Such a decoupling opens the door to a broad range of dynamic adaptive loop scheduling strategies that simply cannot be efficiently implemented in OpenMP RTLs, such as adaptive weighted factoring [6] and adaptive factoring [5] that adapt to changes during execution; strategies that mix static and dynamic scheduling to maintain a balance between data locality and load balance [10, 20]; and fault-tolerant and energy-oriented loop scheduling strategies that require domain-specific knowledge [11, 32].

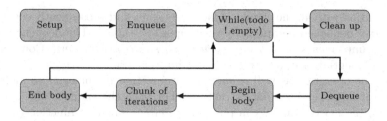

Fig. 1. Basic loop scheduler code structure.

3   Support for User-Defined Scheduling Strategies

Let us consider what is needed to specify an arbitrary scheduling strategy for a parallel loop. The strategy can use a combination of shared data structures, a collection of low-overhead steal work queues, exclusive queues meant for each core, or shared queues from which multiple threads can dequeue tasks each representing a chunk of loop iterations of a parallel loop. To enable the ability to learn from recent execution history, e.g., recent outer iterations, or to make decisions about the scheduling strategy based on information from libraries handling inter-node parallelism, e.g., slack from MPI communication [27], the scheduling strategy needs the ability to pass a call-site specific history-tracking object [19].

To adapt a loop scheduling strategy's parameters, e.g., chunk size, we provide a mechanism for a UDS to store the history of loop timings or other statistics across loop invocations in an application program, e.g., a simulation time-step of a numerical simulation. Such a mechanism improves productivity for the application programmer. The adjustment of the loop scheduling strategy during execution reduces the need for manual performance tuning and compiler-guided performance tuning, which for certain applications such as those involving sparse matrix vector multiplication is difficult, and for other applications such as a galaxy simulation involving an N-body computation, is nearly impossible.

In order to support UDS in OpenMP, we must first understand the principal components of loop scheduling. Figure 1 shows a control flow diagram of the basic loop scheduling code structure. In principle, an OpenMP loop scheduling problem can be represented as a *todo list* of loop iterations (or chunks of loop iterations), that must somehow be mapped to parallel execution units. To manage such a *todo list*, and assuming an undefined initial state, three specific operations are required:

(a) *a setup operation* to generate a known initial state, i.e., the todo list must be created and initialized,
(b) *an enqueue operation* to place the loop iterations on the todo list, and
(c) *a dequeue operation* to select the next loop iteration to be executed from the todo list.

As OpenMP requires that the precise iteration space is known before the loop execution starts, the todo list is conceptually completely filled at the beginning of loop execution with all the chunks of loop iterations, and subsequently consumed by iterative dequeue operations by each OpenMP thread. The dequeue operation then implements *an arbitrary scheduling strategy* or pattern. Constraints, such as sequential ordering or the scheduling pattern are solely an aspect of the dequeue operation as well as any synchronization mechanisms to maintain parallel safety of the used data structures. For both the enqueue and dequeue functions, the master thread can potentially serve a different function than the remaining threads in a loop scheduler. Also, the behavior of the threads needs to be specified either via function pointers or declaratively. Such specification must be done while preserving generality so that novel loop scheduling strategies have the ability to deal with the loop's iteration space in a controlled manner. As an example, we have shown how dynamic scheduling can be optimized by using a combination of statically scheduled and dynamically scheduled loop iterations [10], where the dynamic iterations still execute in consecutive order on a thread to the extent possible [18].

Good practice also recommends to clean up after performing work, as the OpenMP base languages do not offer automatic garbage collection. Hence, a clean-up, or post scheduling operation is needed.

Analyzing the current state of the art in loop scheduling in Sect. 2, we identified three categories of strategies:

(1) *static loop scheduling*: each thread is assigned a fixed workload,
(2) *dynamic non-adaptive loop scheduling*: each thread requests iterations according to a fixed pattern, and
(3) *dynamic adaptive loop scheduling*: each thread requests iterations according to a variable pattern, while the performance of work chunks is measured and scheduling pattern is adjusted accordingly.

For loop scheduling strategies of type (1) and type (2), in principle, only the three operations are required. For strategies of type (3), the execution behavior of previous iterations of the loop body is used as input to determine the scheduling strategy parameters, e.g., next chunk size, to use for scheduling chunks of loop iterations of the current loop iteration and/or invocation. To accommodate such scheduling strategies, a mechanism needs to be provided to *obtain* information during previous loop iterations and/or invocations and a mechanism to *store* this information.To obtain the information, measurement facilities for the loop body may be required, be it explicit operations, such as 'begin-loop-body'–'end-loop-body' to allow for measurements, or implicit facilities, e.g., as defined by the OpenMP tools interface.

To store information, i.e., a form of execution history that must be preserved across dequeue operations to account for past behavior, UDS must provide a mechanism to store and access the history of loop timings or other statistics across multiple loop iterations and/or invocations in an application program, e.g., across simulation time-steps of a numerical simulation.

With these functions and mechanisms, a user of OpenMP can declare in the code a `schedule` clause of kind X. In the declaration, the user would specify a function to *initialize* the scheduler, a function to *enqueue* chunks onto a shared queue, a function to *dequeue* chunks of iterations from a queue by a thread, a function for garbage collection (*finalize*) after loop scheduling is done, and, optionally, *begin* and *end* functions for a dynamic adaptive loop scheduling. Then, function X_init() allows a user-defined scheduling to allocate and initialize its data structures that are to be used commonly across parallel loops that use X. The functions X_enqueue() and X_dequeue() determine a loop's indices that a thread should work on based on the parameter values for the scheduling strategy and the loop. Every thread in the team should call X_dequeue() repeatedly. For adaptive loop scheduling, one needs to have an X_begin() and X_end() function for measurements of the current invocation of a loop used for history used for adapting the parameters of the scheduling strategy used in subsequent iterations and/or invocations of the loop. Finally, a user can optionally define a data structure to store timings of a loop or other data to enable persistence over invocations of an OpenMP parallel loop.

As long as one is allowed to define the four functions (init, enqueue, dequeue, and finalize), together with the begin and end functions for gathering per-loop invocation data and data structure for storing history of the data, one can implement *any user-defined loop scheduling* through a loop scheduler. Formally, the four functions together with begin and end functions and class declaration and definition for the history object are *necessary and sufficient* to fully express an arbitrary user-defined loop scheduling strategy.

4   An Interface for User-Defined Loop Scheduling

As described in Sect. 3, only six operations, i.e., init, enqueue, dequeue, finalize, begin-loop-body, and end-loop-body must be defined in order to implement all existing loop scheduling strategies. While not all of those operations must be implemented by a given loop scheduling strategy, it must be possible to implement those operations. An interface for a UDS in OpenMP must enable such definitions from the user program without having to alter the OpenMP runtime library. However, due to a programmer's desire for brevity, such an interface should avoid verbosity and enable efficient and quick specification of new scheduling strategies.

Due to the restriction and requirements of the OpenMP language on loops, the set of six operations can further be reduced. As the iteration space of loops with OpenMP parallel for must be fixed prior to loop execution, the enqueue function must only be executed prior of the actual loop execution. It, therefore, can be merged with the init operation. The dequeue operation and the begin-loop-body operations are executed, if defined, always back-to-back. Hence, these operations can also be implemented in a single merged operation. The conceptional code transformation (see Fig. 1) in combination with a loop similarly provides a way to merge the end-loop-body operation with the dequeue operation.

This results in *only three* operations that must be defined by a UDS developer in the context of OpenMP loop scheduling: a *start* routine implementing the setup and enqueue operation, a *get-chunk* operation implementing the end-body, dequeue and begin-loop-body operation, and a *finish call* for the finalize operation.

The concept of a todo list of loop iterations is rather impractical for OpenMP loops, as the iteration space may be large and an explicit enumeration of all iterations is not practical. Thus, the todo list is typically implemented as a set of shared or thread-private loop counters.

For current implementations of OpenMP parallelized loops in Intel, LLVM and GNU Runtime Libraries, we observe a common implementation pattern. Using the three fundamental operations of init, dequeue and finalize, these compilers transform an OpenMP 'parallel for' as follows using the following pattern: a setup operation, a while loop with a dequeue function and a tailing end operation, which implements cleanup of residual stack data (see code at the top of this page). The three OpenMP loop scheduling strategies, i.e. static, guided, and dynamic, are implemented using similar patterns [22].

```
#pragma omp parallel for
  for (i=0;i<iMax;i++)
      {
      ... LOOP BODY ...
  }
```
→
```
#pragma omp parallel
{
  init(...);
  #pragma omp barrier
  while(!done){
     for (each item in dequeue(...))
        ... LOOP BODY ...
  }
  finalize(...);
}
```

A UDS specification must allow a loop scheduling implementer to access critical loop parameters and program data: *(a)* lower bound, *(b)* upper bound, *(c)* stride, *(d)* custom data, e.g. loop history data or NUMA information, and *(e)* chunk size. The 'chunk size' here is not the **chunksize** parameter frequently referred to in the OpenMP **schedule()** clause, but an optimization parameter used to group multiple iterations into a single loop scheduling item.

We currently propose two complementary proposals for an interface for a UDS, enabling a user specification for those three functions. However, the design of these interfaces substantially differs at the OpenMP host language level: (1) a C++-geared interface using a concept similar to lambdas and (2) a more classic C/Fortran-geared interface similar to user-defined reductions in OpenMP.

4.1   Lambda-Style Specification for UDS

Using a lambda-style syntax, a scheduling implementer can define code to implement the setup, dequeue, and finalize operations.

```
#pragma omp parallel for \
  schedule(UDS[:chunkSize, [monotonic| non-monotonic]) \
  [init(@@INIT_LAMDA@@)] dequeue(@@DEQUEUE_LAMDA@@)    \
  [finalize(@@FINISH_LAMDA@@)] [uds_data(void*)]
```

To access the critical loop parameters, we propose compiler-generated getter and setter functions.

```
inline unsigned int OMP_UDS_loop_start();
inline unsigned int OMP_UDS_loop_end();
inline unsigned int OMP_UDS_loop_step();
inline unsigned int OMP_UDS_chunksize();
inline unsigned int OMP_UDS_user_ptr();
```

```
void OMP_UDS_loop_chunk_start(int start_iteration);
void OMP_UDS_loop_chunk_end(int end_iteration);
void OMP_UDS_loop_chunk_step(int step_size);
void OMP_UDS_loop_dequeue_done();
```

To compile a loop scheduled using a UDS, the compiler mixes the lambda code into the respective regions in the loop transformation pattern. The setter and getter functions can furthermore be inlined and their values propagated by constant value propagation, to further reduce and optimize the specific loop code.

As this interface would require a definition for every use of a specific loop scheduling approach, a template-like directive defines reusable schedules without the need to repeat the actual UDS code at every usage.

```
#pragma omp declare schedule_template (mystatic)  \
  [init(@@INIT_LAMDA@@)] dequeue(@@DEQUEUE_LAMDA@@)  \
  [finalize(@@FINISH_LAMDA@@)] [uds_data(void*)]
```

```
#pragma omp parallel for schedule(UDS,template(mystatic))
  for (int i = 0; i < n; i++) { ... LOOP BODY ... }
```

The availability of both UDS templates and localized UDS allows for implementation of libraries supported UDSs, but preserves the ability to either specify localized single use loop scheduling strategies or to overwrite specific elements of an existing UDS template for a specific loop. An example of how the user could implement the above mystatic is provided in Fig. 2 where the left side illustrates a naive implementation of the OpenMP static scheduling clause using *lambda-style UDS* based on the chunksize specified by the programmer.

4.2   Specifying UDS via declare Directives

The second variant for specifying UDS derives from the existing syntax for a user-defined reduction, or UDR, in OpenMP. Here, the declare schedule clause defines a new named scheduling using user-defined functions with positional arguments:

```
#pragma omp declare schedule(mystatic) arguments(2)  \
  init(my_init(omp_lb, omp_ub, omp_inc, omp_arg0, omp_arg1))  \
  next(my_next(omp_lb_chunk, omp_ub_chunk, omp_arg0, omp_arg1))  \
  fini(my_fini(omp_arg1))
```

The arguments sub-clause allows to specify the number of additional arguments beyond the required arguments. The reserved keywords omp_lb, omp_ub, omp_inc, omp_lb_chunk, and omp_ub_chunk serve as markers for the compiler what information about the loop iteration space to pass to the UDS, as the user code expects this information as a function argument. The compiler generates `omp_arg0` .. `omp_argN` as necessary, based on the count in the `arguments` sub-clause. However, the OpenMP-defined arguments must always be the first arguments, followed by any user-defined arguments. This allows, for example, simpler scheduling strategies to omit unused information. The additional user-provided arguments use the type of the argument at the use-site of the user-defined scheduling, similar to the `auto`-type in C++. The function implementations must then use the appropriate types and provide the implementation of the scheduling strategy. Please note, that a definition of the `next` function must return a non-zero value if unprocessed loop chunks remain, and zero if the loop has been completed.

```
void mystatic_init(int lb, int ub, int inc, loop_record_t * lr);
int mystatic_next(int * lower, int * upper, loop_record_t * lr);
void mystatic_fini(loop_record_t * lr);
```

To generate code from such a UDS specification, the compiler employs the standard loop transformation pattern it uses today and replaces the calls to its scheduling function with user-supplied functions of the UDS. The compiler may then match the types defined by the scheduling implementing function definitions to generate error messages, if a type mismatch is detected, or apply inlining to remove the function call.

The following example showcases how a user-defined scheduling strategy would be used and how parameters are passed to the scheduler:

```
#pragma omp parallel for schedule(mystatic(&lr))
  for (i = 0; i < sz; i++) {
#pragma omp atomic
    array[i]++;
  }
}
```

An example of how the user could implement the above schedule `mystatic` is provided in Fig. 2, where the right side shows a naive implementation of the OpenMP `static` scheduling clause using *declare-style UDS* based on the `chunksize` specified by the programmer.

4.3   Discussion

We consider both proposals sufficient as a UDS specification layer. As OpenMP targets three separate host languages, we must consider the implications of each interface to the host language and use in daily programming work[1].

The *lambda-style* interface easily fits into the language canon of C++, where the concept of lambdas already exists and can easily be reused in the context of UDS. Also, the use of getter and setter functions does not present a source of

---

[1] We consider the utility of each of the proposals to application programs in an extended version of this work, accessible at the following link: https://arxiv.org/abs/1906.08911.

```
typedef struct {
  int * next_lb;
} loop_record_t;

void mystatic_init() {
  int tid = omp_get_thread_num();
  #pragma omp single
  {
    OMP_UDS_user_ptr()->next_lb =
      malloc(sizeof(int)*omp_get_num_threads());
  }
  OMP_UDS_user_ptr()->next_lb[tid] =
    lb+tid * chunksz;
}

void mystatic_next() {
  int tid = omp_get_thread_num();
  if (OMP_UDS_user_ptr()->next_lb[tid] >=
  OMP_UDS_loop_end()) return 0;
  OMP_UDS_loop_chunk_start(
  OMP_UDS_user_ptr()->next_lb[tid]);
  if (OMP_UDS_user_ptr()->next_lb[tid] +
  OMP_UDS_chunksize() >=
  OMP_UDS_loop_end()) {
  OMP_UDS_loop_chunk_end(OMP_UDS_loop_end());
  }
  else {
    OMP_UDS_loop_chunk_end(
    OMP_UDS_user_ptr()->next_lb[tid] +
    OMP_UDS_chunksize());
  }
  OMP_UDS_user_ptr()->next_lb[tid] =
  OMP_UDS_user_ptr()->next_lb[tid] +
  omp_get_num_threads()*OMP_UDS_chunksize();
  OMP_UDS_loop_chunk_step(
  OMP_UDS_loop_step());
  return 1;
}

void mystatic_fini(){
  free(OMP_UDS_user_ptr()->next_lb);
}

#pragma omp declare \
  schedule_template(mystatic)\
  init(mystatic_init())\
  next(mystatic_next())\
  finalize(mystatic_fini())
```

```
typedef struct {
  int lb;
  int ub;
  int incr;
  int chunksz;
  int * next_lb;
} loop_record_t;

void mystatic_init(int lb, int ub, int incr,
    int chunksz,loop_record_t * lr) {
  int tid = omp_get_thread_num();
  #pragma omp single
  {
    lr->lb = lb;
    lr->ub = ub;
    lr->incr = incr;
    lr->next_lb = malloc(sizeof(int)*
        omp_get_num_threads());
    lr->chunksz = chunksz;
  }
  lr->next_lb[tid] = lb + tid * chunksz;
}

int mystatic_next(int * lower, int * upper,
    int * incr, loop_record_t * lr) {
  int tid = omp_get_thread_num();
  if (lr->next_lb[tid] >= lr->ub) return 0;
  *lower = lr->next_lb[tid];
  if (lr->next_lb[tid] +
    lr->chunksz >= lr->ub)
    *upper = lr->ub;
  else
    *upper = lr->next_lb[tid] + lr->chunksz;
  lr->next_lb[tid] = lr->next_lb[tid] +
    omp_get_num_threads()*lr->chunksz;
  *incr = lr->incr;
  return 1;
}

int mystatic_fini(loop_record_t * lr) {
  free(lr->next_lb);
}

#pragma omp declare schedule(mystatic) \
  arguments(1) init(mystatic_init(omp_lb, \
  omp_ub,omp_incr,omp_chunksz,omp_arg0) \
  next(mystatic_next(omp_lb_chunk, \
  omp_ub_chunk,omp_chunk_incr,imp_arg0)) \
  fini(mystatic_fini(imp_arg0)
```

Fig. 2. Naive example for implementing the OpenMP `static` scheduling clause using both proposed UDS strategies. Left side presents the implementation following the *lambda-style* specification, Sect. 4.1, while the right side follows the *declare-directives* style, Sect. 4.2.

overhead, as existing compiler optimizations, such as inlining and constant-value propagation and folding, will enable removal of all explicit function calls. As some operations, i.e., setup and finalize, are also not required for all implementations of a UDS, this avoids the verbose, potentially empty argument list of positional arguments, required by the second proposal. However, the flexibility and ease of iteration in C++ conflicts with C and Fortran, where lambda constructs are not (yet) available. While the concept of lambdas is likely to be added to Fortran in the future, the specific syntax and semantics are currently not known. At this point, we are also not aware of any efforts to add lambdas to C. The *UDR-style* specification has, in principle, a precedence-case in the UDR specification in OpenMP. While this approach relies on a more frumpy fixed position syntax style, it remains compatible with all three OpenMP host languages.

A potential solution would allow the use of the lambda-style syntax for C++, and the UDR-style for C and Fortran codes.

Our suggested UDS approach for supporting novel loop scheduling strategies and two alternative interfaces for it have much work related to it, which we mention here to distinguish our idea and its development from the existing work. Work on an OpenMP runtime scheduling [30,33] system automatically chooses the schedule. The problem with this scheme is that it does not work for all application-architecture pairs: it allows no domain knowledge or architecture knowledge to be incorporated into it, which only a user would know. Methods such as setting the schedule of an OpenMP loop to 'auto' are insufficient because the methods do not allow a user to take control of any decision of loop scheduling that the OpenMP RTL makes [21]. The emergence of threaded runtimes such as Argobots [28] and QuickThreads [1] are frameworks containing novel loop scheduling strategies, and they actually argue in favor of a flexible specification of scheduling strategies. In comparison, our work on the UDS specification is the first proposal that works at the OpenMP standard specification level.

5   Conclusion

OpenMP's loop scheduling choices do not always offer the best performance, and standardization of all existing scheduling strategies is infeasible. In this work, we showed that an OpenMP standard-compliant interface is needed to implement an arbitrary user-defined loop scheduling strategy. We presented two competing standard-compliant UDS interface proposals to support this need. We conceptually compare the two proposed UDS interfaces in terms of feasibility and capabilities regarding the programming languages C, C++, and Fortran that host OpenMP.

The immediate next step is the implementation of the UDS interfaces as a prototype in an open source compiler, such as GNU or LLVM, to explore the performance-related capabilities and benefits of the proposed approaches. As the Intel and LLVM OpenMP RTLs offer schedules choices beyond those in the OpenMP standard, we will work to expose those schedules using either or both UDS proposals and evaluate their practical use for various application-architecture pairs. We welcome and value the feedback from the OpenMP community as we proceed in this direction.

Acknowledgments. We thank Alice Koniges from Maui HPCC for providing us with NERSC's cluster Cori for experimenting with machine learning applications using OpenMP, which helped us consider a relevant platform for user-defined scheduling. This work is partly funded by the Hessian State Ministry of Higher Education by granting the "Hessian Competence Center for High Performance Computing" and by the Swiss National Science Foundation in the context of the "Multi-level Scheduling in Large Scale High Performance Computers" (MLS) grant, number 169123.

References

1. QuickThread: A New C++ Multicore Library, November 2009. http://www.drdobbs.com/parallel/quickthread-a-new-c-multicore-library/221800155
2. LLVM's OpenMP Compiler, April 2019. https://openmp.llvm.org/
3. An Enhanced OpenMP Library, January 2018. https://github.com/lapesd/libgomp. Accessed 27 Apr 2018
4. Banicescu, I.: Load balancing and data locality in the parallelization of the fast multipole algorithm. Ph.D. thesis, New York Polytechnic University (1996)
5. Banicescu, I., Liu, Z.: Adaptive factoring: a dynamic scheduling method tuned to the rate of weight changes. In: Proceedings of 8th High performance computing Symposium, pp. 122–129. Society for Computer Simulation International (2000)
6. Banicescu, I., Velusamy, V., Devaprasad, J.: On the scalability of dynamic scheduling scientific applications with adaptive weighted factoring. Cluster Comput. 6(3), 215–226 (2003). https://doi.org/10.1023/A:1023588520138
7. Bast, H.: Dynamic scheduling with incomplete information. In: Proceedings of the Tenth Annual ACM Symposium on Parallel Algorithms and Architectures, SPAA 1998, pp. 182–191. ACM, New York (1998)
8. Ciorba, F.M., Iwainsky, C., Buder, P.: OpenMP loop scheduling revisited: making a case for more schedules. In: de Supinski, B.R., Valero-Lara, P., Martorell, X., Mateo Bellido, S., Labarta, J. (eds.) IWOMP 2018. LNCS, vol. 11128, pp. 21–36. Springer, Cham (2018). https://doi.org/10.1007/978-3-319-98521-3_2
9. Dagum, L., Menon, R.: OpenMP: an industry-standard API for shared-memory programming. IEEE Comput. Sci. Eng. 5(1) (1998)
10. Donfack, S., Grigori, L., Gropp, W.D., Kale, V.: Hybrid static/dynamic scheduling for already optimized dense matrix factorizations. In: 2012 IEEE International Parallel and Distributed Processing Symposium (IPDPS), Shanghai, China (2012)
11. Dong, Y., Chen, J., Yang, X., Deng, L., Zhang, X.: Energy-oriented OpenMP parallel loop scheduling. In: 2008 IEEE International Symposium on Parallel and Distributed Processing with Applications, pp. 162–169, December 2008
12. Dongarra, J., Beckman, P., et al.: The international exascale software roadmap. Int. J. High Perform. Comput. Appl. 25(1), 3–60 (2011)
13. Flynn Hummel, S., Banicescu, I., Wang, C.T., Wein, J.: Load balancing and data locality via fractiling: an experimental study. In: Szymanski, B.K., Sinharoy, B. (eds.) Languages, Compilers and Run-Time Systems for Scalable Computers, pp. 85–98. Springer, Boston (1996). https://doi.org/10.1007/978-1-4615-2315-4_7
14. Flynn Hummel, S., Schmidt, J., Uma, R.N., Wein, J.: Load-sharing in Heterogeneous Systems via Weighted Factoring. In: Proceedings of the Eighth Annual ACM Symposium on Parallel Algorithms and Architectures, SPAA 1996, pp. 318–328. ACM, New York (1996)
15. Flynn Hummel, S., Schonberg, E., Flynn, L.E.: Factoring: a method for scheduling parallel loops. Commun. ACM 35(8), 90–101 (1992)
16. Garey, M.R., Johnson, D.S.: Computers and Intractability: A Guide to the Theory of NP-Completeness. W. H. Freeman & Co., New York (1990)
17. Govindaswamy, K.: An API for adaptive loop scheduling in shared address space architectures. Master's thesis, Mississippi State University (2003)
18. Kale, V., Donfack, S., Grigori, L., Gropp, W.D.: Lightweight scheduling for balancing the tradeoff between load balance and locality. Poster at International Conference on High Performance Computing, Networking, Storage and Analysis (2014)

19. Kale, V., Gamblin, T., Hoefler, T., de Supinski, B.R., Gropp, W.D.: Abstract: slack-conscious lightweight loop scheduling for improving scalability of bulk-synchronous MPI applications. In: High Performance Computing, Networking Storage and Analysis, SC Companion, p. 1392, November 2012

20. Kale, V., Gropp, W.: Load balancing for regular meshes on SMPs with MPI. In: Keller, R., Gabriel, E., Resch, M., Dongarra, J. (eds.) EuroMPI 2010. LNCS, vol. 6305, pp. 229–238. Springer, Heidelberg (2010). https://doi.org/10.1007/978-3-642-15646-5_24

21. Kale, V., Gropp, W.D.: Composing low-overhead scheduling strategies for improving performance of scientific applications. In: Terboven, C., de Supinski, B.R., Reble, P., Chapman, B.M., Müller, M.S. (eds.) IWOMP 2015. LNCS, vol. 9342, pp. 18–29. Springer, Cham (2015). https://doi.org/10.1007/978-3-319-24595-9_2

22. Kasielke, F., Tschüter, R., Iwainsky, C., Velten, M., Ciorba, F.M., Banicescu, I.: Exploring loop scheduling enhancements in OpenMP: an LLVM case study. In: Proceedings of the 18th International Symposium on Parallel and Distributed Computing (ISPDC 2019), Amsterdam, June 2019

23. Krueger, P., Shivaratri, N.G.: Adaptive location policies for global scheduling. IEEE Trans. Softw. Eng. **20**(6), 432–444 (1994)

24. Kruskal, C.P., Weiss, A.: Allocating independent subtasks on parallel processors. IEEE Trans. Softw. Eng. **SE–11**(10), 1001–1016 (1985)

25. Li, H., Tandri, S., Stumm, M., Sevcik, K.C.: Locality and loop scheduling on NUMA multiprocessors. In: Proceedings of the 1993 International Conference on Parallel Processing, ICPP 1993, Washington, DC, USA, vol. 2, pp. 140–147. IEEE Computer Society (1993)

26. Polychronopoulos, C.D., Kuck, D.J.: Guided self-scheduling: a practical scheduling scheme for parallel supercomputers. IEEE Trans. Comput. **C–36**(12), 1425–1439 (1987)

27. Rountree, B., Lowenthal, D.K., de Supinski, B.R., Schulz, M., Freeh, V.W., Bletsch, T.: Adagio: making DVS practical for complex HPC applications. In: Proceedings of the 23rd International Conference on Supercomputing, ICS 2009, Yorktown Heights, NY, USA, pp. 460–469. ACM (2009)

28. Seo, S., et al.: Argobots: a lightweight low-level threading and tasking framework. IEEE Trans. Parallel Distrib. Syst. **29**(3), 512–526 (2018)

29. Tang, P., Yew, P.C.: Processor self-scheduling for multiple-nested parallel loops. In: Proceedings of International Conference on Parallel Processing, pp. 528–535. IEEE, December 1986

30. Thoman, P., Jordan, H., Pellegrini, S., Fahringer, T.: Automatic OpenMP loop scheduling: a combined compiler and runtime approach. In: Chapman, B.M., Massaioli, F., Müller, M.S., Rorro, M. (eds.) IWOMP 2012. LNCS, vol. 7312, pp. 88–101. Springer, Heidelberg (2012). https://doi.org/10.1007/978-3-642-30961-8_7

31. Tzen, T.H., Ni, L.M.: Trapezoid self-scheduling: a practical scheduling scheme for parallel compilers. IEEE Trans. Parallel Distrib. Syst. **4**(1), 87–98 (1993)

32. Wang, Y., Nicolau, A., Cammarota, R., Veidenbaum, A.V.: A fault tolerant self-scheduling scheme for parallel loops on shared memory systems. In: 2012 19th International Conference on High Performance Computing, pp. 1–10, December 2012

33. Zhang, Y., Voss, M.: Runtime empirical selection of loop schedulers on hyper-threaded SMPs. In: Proceedings of the 19th IEEE International Parallel and Distributed Processing Symposium (IPDPS 2005) - Papers - Volume 01, IPDPS 2005, Washington, DC, USA, p. 44.2. IEEE Computer Society (2005)

Extending OpenMP Metadirective Semantics for Runtime Adaptation

Yonghong Yan[1(✉)], Anjia Wang[1], Chunhua Liao[2], Thomas R. W. Scogland[2], and Bronis R. de Supinski[2]

[1] University of South Carolina, Columbia, SC 29208, USA
yanyh@cse.sc.edu,anjia@email.sc.edu
[2] Lawrence Livermore National Laboratory, Livermore, CA 94550, USA
{liao6,scogland1,bronis}@llnl.gov

Abstract. OpenMP 5.0 introduces the metadirective to support selection from a set of directive variants based on the OpenMP context, which is composed of traits from active OpenMP constructs, devices, implementations or user-defined conditions. OpenMP 5.0 restricts the selection to be determined at compile time, which requires that all traits must be compile-time constants. Our analysis of real applications indicates that this restriction has its limitation, and we explore extension of user-defined contexts to support variant selection at runtime. We use the Smith-Waterman algorithm as an example to show the need for adaptive selection of parallelism and devices at runtime, and present a prototype implemented in the ROSE compiler. Given a large range of input sizes, our experiments demonstrate that one of the adaptive versions of Smith-Waterman always chooses the parallelism and device that delivers the best performance, with improvements between 20% and 200% compared to non-adaptive versions that use the other approaches.

Keywords: OpenMP 5.0 · Metadirective · Dynamic context

1 Introduction

OpenMP 5.0 [5] introduces the concept of OpenMP contexts and defines traits to describe them by specifying the active construct, execution devices, and functionality of an implementation. OpenMP 5.0 further introduces the metadirective and declare variant to support directive selection based on the enclosing OpenMP context as well as user-defined conditions. This feature enables programmers to use a single directive to support multiple variants tailored for different contexts derived from the hardware configuration, software configuration or user defined conditions. With context traits that are available to the compiler when performing OpenMP transformations, a user can much more easily optimize their application for specific architectures, possibly resolving to multiple different directives in the same compilation in different call chains or different contexts.

© Springer Nature Switzerland AG 2019
X. Fan et al. (Eds.): IWOMP 2019, LNCS 11718, pp. 201–214, 2019.
https://doi.org/10.1007/978-3-030-28596-8_14

OpenMP 5.0 restricts context traits to be fully resolvable at compile time. Thus, the ability to optimize OpenMP applications based on their inputs and runtime behavior is severely constrained, even with user-defined conditions. The semantics of context selection are naturally applicable to support both compile time and runtime directive selection. Given a low overhead runtime selection mechanism, the extension for enabling runtime adaptation would improve performance of an application based on system architecture and input characteristics. Applications that would benefit from this feature include those that use traits based on problem size, loop count, and the number of threads. For example, most math kernel libraries parallelize and optimize matrix multiplication based on input matrix sizes.

In this paper, we extend the semantics of user-defined contexts to support runtime directive selection. We use the Smith-Waterman algorithm as an example to demonstrate that the extensions enable runtime adaptive selection of target devices, depending on the size of the input. We develop a prototype compiler implementation in the ROSE compiler and evaluate the performance benefits of this extension. Our experiments demonstrate that one of the adaptive versions of Smith-Waterman always chooses the parallelism and device that delivers the best performance for a large range of input sizes, with improvements between 20% and 200% over the non-adaptive versions.

The remainder of this paper is organized as follows. Section 2 presents the current syntax and semantics of OpenMP context and metadirective in the latest standard. A motivating example is given in Sect. 3 to demonstrate the need to support dynamic selection of directives at runtime based on user defined conditions. Section 4 introduces our extension to allow dynamic user-defined context. We discuss a prototype compiler implementation for the dynamic extension in Sect. 5. Section 6 evaluates performance of our prototype that automates adaptation of the Smith-Waterman algorithm. Finally, we mention related work in Sect. 7 and conclude our paper in Sect. 8.

2   Variant Directives and Metadirective in OpenMP 5.0

Variant directives is one of the major features introduced in OpenMP 5.0 to facilitate programmers to improve performance portability by adapting OpenMP pragmas and user code at compile time. The standard specifies the traits that describe active OpenMP constructs, execution devices, and functionality provided by an implementation, context selectors based on the traits and user-defined conditions, and the metadirective and declare directive directives for users to program the same code region with variant directives. A metadirective is an executable directive that conditionally resolves to another directive at compile time by selecting from multiple directive variants based on traits that define an OpenMP condition or context. The declare variant directive has similar functionality as the metadirective but selects a function variant at the call-site based on context or user-defined conditions. The mechanism provided by the two directives for selecting variants is more convenient to use than the C/C++ preprocessing since it directly supports variant selection in OpenMP and allows an

OpenMP compiler to analyze and determine the final directive from variants and context.

In this paper, we use metadirective to explore the runtime adaptation feature since it applies to structured user code region (instead of a function call as in declare variant), which poses more adaptation needs based on the program inputs. The metadirective syntax for C and C++ is:

#pragma omp metadirective [clause[[,]clause]...]new-line

The clause in a metadirective can be either
when(context-selector-specification:[directive-variant]) or default (directive-variant).

The expressiveness of a metadirective to enable conditional selection of a directive variant at compile time is due to the flexibility of its context selector specification. The context selector defines an OpenMP context, which includes a set of traits related to active constructs, execution devices, functionality of an implementation and user defined conditions. Implementations can also define further traits in the device and implementation sets.

```
1   context_selector_spec : trait_set_selector
2                         | context_selector_spec trait_set_selector;
3   trait_set_selector : trait_set_name '=' '{' trait_selector_list '}';
4   trait_set_name : CONSTRUCT | DEVICE | IMPLEMENTATION | USER;
5   trait_selector_list : trait_selector
6                       | trait_selector_list trait_selector;
7   trait_selector : construct_selector
8                  | device_selector
9                  | implementation_selector
10                 | condition_selector;
11  condition_selector : CONDITION '(' trait_score const_expression ')';
12  device_selector : context_kind | context_isa | context_arch;
13  context_kind : KIND '(' trait_score context_kind_name ')';
14  context_kind_name : HOST | NOHOST | ANY | CPU | GPU | FPGA;
15  context_isa : ISA '(' trait_score const_expression ');
16  context_arch : ARCH '(' trait_score const_expression ')';
17  implementation_selector : VENDOR '(' trait_score context_vendor_name ')'
18                          | EXTENSION '(' trait_score const_expression ')'
19                          | const_expression '(' trait_score ')';
20                          | const_expression;
21  context_vendor_name : AMD  | ARM | BSC | CRAY | FUJITSU | GNU | IBM |
22                        INTEL | LLVM | PGI | TI | UNKNOWN;
23  construct_selector : parallel_selector;
24  parallel_selector : PARALLEL | PARALLEL '(' parallel_parameter ')';
25  parallel_parameter : trait_score parallel_clause_optseq;
26  trait_score : | SCORE '(' const_expression ')' ':';
27  const_expression : EXPR_STRING;
```

Fig. 1. Context selector grammar

Figure 1 shows the grammar for context selectors in Backus-Naur Form. A context selector contains one or more trait set selectors. Each trait set selector may contain one or more trait selectors. Each trait selector may contain one or more trait properties. All traits must be resolved to constant values at compile time, as indicated by condition_const_expression at line 12. The upper case tokens throughout the grammar are enum names that the lexer returns.

Figure 2(b) shows an example that uses a metadirective to specify a variant to use for NVIDIA PTX devices, and a variant that is applied in all other cases by default. Figure 2(a) shows the code using C/C++ macro to achieve the same goal. In Fig. 2(b), a trait selector named arch from the device trait set specifies the context selector. If the trait's property is resolved to be nvptx at compile-time then the directive variant that has one thread team and the loop construct is applied. Otherwise, a target parallel loop directive is applied. Using metadirective has two major benefits. One is that compiler could be aware of more context information. In Fig. 2(a), the preprocessor will prune one of the conditional statement before passing the source code to compiler. However, in Fig. 2(b), compiler has all the information of branches. The other advantage is that the redundant code is optimized. The two lines of for loop only appear once while using metadirective.

```
1  int v1[N], v2[N], v3[N];
2  #if defined(nvptx)
3    #pragma omp target teams distribute
           parallel loop map(to:v1,v2)
           map(from:v3)
4      for (int i= 0; i< N; i++)
5        v3[i] = v1[i] * v2[i];
6  #else
7    #pragma omp target parallel loop
           map(to:v1,v2) map(from:v3)
8      for (int i= 0; i< N; i++)
9        v3[i] = v1[i] * v2[i];
10 #endif
```

(a) Original code

```
1  int v1[N], v2[N], v3[N];
2  #pragma omp target map(to:v1,v2)
          map(from:v3)
3    #pragma omp metadirective
4      when(device={arch(nvptx)}:
           teams distribute
           parallel loop)
5      default(target parallel
           loop)
6    for (int i= 0; i< N; i++)
7      v3[i] = v1[i] * v2[i];
```

(b) Using metadirective

Fig. 2. An example using metadirective

3   A Motivating Example

While the metadirective can be used to specify multiple variants in a program, it requires the corresponding traits to be resolved at compile time, which limits customization of the user code at runtime. In this section, we use the Smith-Waterman algorithm to demonstrate the need for customization and dynamic adaptation.

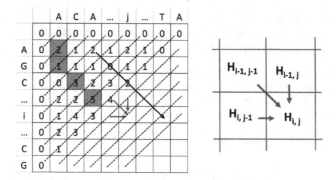

Fig. 3. Wavefront computation pattern of the Smith-Waterman algorithm

The Smith-Waterman algorithm performs local sequence alignment [8] to find the optimal occurrence of a sub-sequence within a DNA or RNA sequence. The algorithm compares segments of all possible lengths and optimizes the similarity measure. Similarity is represented by a score matrix H. The update of the score is derived from one-to-one comparisons between all components in two sequences from which the optimal alignment result is recorded. Figure 3 shows the scoring step of the algorithm. Arrows in the figure denote data dependency between points of the computation. The scoring process is a wavefront computation pattern. Figure 4 shows a typical OpenMP implementation of the scoring wavefront pattern by parallelizing the computation that iterates on a wavefront line. The implementation of the algorithm has O(M*N) time complexity in which M and N are the lengths of the two sequences that are being aligned. The space complexity is also O(M*N) since the program must store two string sequences and two matrices, one for scoring and the other for backtracking.

```
1   long long int nDiag = M + N - 3;
2   for (i = 1; i <= nDiag; ++i) {
3     long long int nEle, si, sj;
4     nEle = nElement(i); calcFirstDiagElement(i, &si, &sj);
5   #pramga omp parallel for shared (nEle, si, sj, H, P, maxPos) private(j)
6     for (j = 0; j < nEle; ++j)
7       similarityScore(si-j, sj+j, H, P, &maxPos);
8   }
```

Fig. 4. An OpenMP implementation of the Smith-Waterman algorithm

One can add OpenMP device constructs to create a version for GPUs, shown in Fig. 5. In our early evaluation, we compare the performance of three baseline versions of the algorithm: CPU sequential, OpenMP parallel with 56 threads, and OpenMP offloading on a NVIDIA V100 GPU. Figure 6 shows that the performance of three versions varies dramatically with regards to the length of one

```
1    long long int nDiag = M + N - 3;
2    #pragma omp target enter data map(to:a[0:m],...) map(to:H[0:asz],...)
3    for (i = 1; i <= nDiag; ++i) {
4        long long int nEle, si, sj;
5        nEle = nElement(i); calcFirstDiagElement(i, &si, &sj);
6        #pragma omp target teams distribute parallel for map (...)
7        for (j = 0; j < nEle; ++j)
8            similarityScore(si-j, sj+j, H, P, &maxPos);
9    }
10   #pragma omp target exit data map(from:H[0:asz],...)
```

Fig. 5. An OpenMP implementation using offloading on GPUs

sequence (N), indicated by the cross points of the three plotted lines. Thus an algorithm that adapts between the three versions based on the lengths of the input sequences would perform best overall.

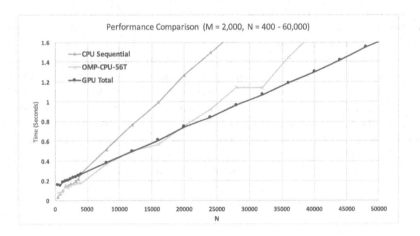

Fig. 6. Smith-Waterman execution times (Fixed M, Varying N)

We consider two adaptive versions. First, we optimize the program such that it automatically selects one of the three versions, i.e. CPU sequential, or CPU parallel or GPU based on the lengths of the sequences, which can be represented by the outer loop count nDiag. A typical use case of this approach could be that a user wants to align a large number of sequences of varying lengths (N) with a sequence of fixed length (M). From Fig. 6, the best choice among the three versions clearly depends on the evaluation of the length of N against a threshold. Since all the three versions exhibit good weak scaling, the two thresholds are the value of N at which the performance crossover occurs. These two thresholds separate the three versions according to the problem size.

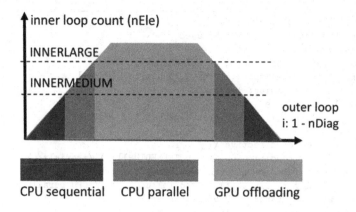

Fig. 7. The relationship between the outerloop index and inner loop count

For the second version, we observe that when computing the scoring matrix, the inner loop count varies between outer loop iterations. One can optimize the inner loop such that it uses one of the three versions based on the inner loop count. Figure 7 shows the relationship between the outer loop index, the inner loop count and the two hypothetical thresholds for inner loop count (INNER-MEDIUM and INNERLARGE) for determining which parallelism approach to use for the inner loop.

In either approach, the dynamic nature of the outer loop count (nDiag), inner loop count (nEle) and their impact on performance would benefit from metadirective's support of runtime selection of different code variants.

4   Extension of the Metadirective Semantics and Its Application to Smith-Waterman

We present an initial exploration of extending metadirective by relaxing its restriction of compile-time only selection. We allow runtime evaluation of user-defined conditions. Our future work includes exploration of semantic extensions of other selectors to allow for combined compile-time and the runtime selection of variants. We anticipate that those extensions may require new clauses to facilitate low overhead selection.

4.1   Adaptation Based on the Outer Loop Count

Figure 8 shows the first version which uses the metadirective to adapt the algorithm based on the outer loop count (nDiag) to control the switch between the three versions. OpenMP 5.0 provides a scoring mechanism for the directive variants to guide the compiler's selection among them. In our prototype, the variants and their conditions are evaluated in the order that they appear in the metadirective construct. The first variant for which its condition is true is chosen and

```
1    long long int nDiag = M + N - 3;
2    //Copy the data if GPU will be used
3    #pragma omp metadirective \
4      when(user={condition(nDiag >= OUTERLARGE)}: \
5      target enter data map(to:a[0:m],...) map(to:H[0:asz],...))
6    for (i = 1; i <= nDiag; ++i) {
7      long long int nEle, si, sj;
8      nEle = nElement(i);  calcFirstDiagElement(i, &si, &sj);
9
10     #pragma omp metadirective \
11       when (user={condition(nDiag < OUTERMEDIUM)}: ) /*serial*/ \
12       when (user={condition(nDiag < OUTERLARGE)} : \
13         parallel for private(j) shared (nEle, ...)) /*CPU parallel*/ \
14       /*nDiag>=OUTERLARGE, GPU offloading*/ \
15       default (target teams distribute parallel for ...)
16       for (j = 0; j < nEle; ++j)
17         similarityScore(si-j, sj+j, H, P, &maxPos);
18   }
19   //Copy data back to CPU if GPU is used
20   #pragma omp metadirective \
21     when (user={condition(nDiag >= OUTERLARGE)}: \
22     target exit data map(from:H[0:asz],...)
```

Fig. 8. Selection via metadirective based on the outer loop count (nDiag)

the following variants are ignored by the runtime. These semantics are familiar to programmers since standard programming languages use them to evaluate the conditions of if-else and switch-case statements.

To identify the two thresholds (OUTERMEDIUM and OUTERLARGE) in this version, we can profile each of the three versions, using a small data set. Since they all have good weak scaling, as demonstrated in Fig. 6, we can easily extrapolate the performance to find the crossover points of the three versions, which represent the two thresholds.

4.2   Adaptation Based on the Inner Loop Count

Figure 9 shows the version of using metadirective and INNERMEDIUM and INNERLARGE thresholds shown in Fig. 7 to control switching the execution between CPU and GPU. Since the inner loop is offloaded across consecutive outer loop iterations, we optimize data movement with target enter data and target exit data directives such that it is copied only once when the INNERLARGE threshold is met.

For both of the adaptive versions, an OpenMP compiler must generate three versions of the inner loop for the three base versions. The runtime uses the condition checks in the when clause of the directive to determine which version to invoke.

```
1   bool GPUDataCopied = false;
2   for (i = 1; i <= nDiag; ++i) {
3     long long int nEle, si, sj;
4     nEle = nElement(i);   calcFirstDiagElement(i, &si, &sj);
5
6     //Copy the data for the first time GPU will be used
7     if (nEle >= INNERLARGE && !GPUDataCopied) {
8       #pragma omp target enter data map(to:a[0:m],...) map(to:H[0:asz],...)
9       GPUDataCopied = true;
10    }
11    //Copy data back to CPU after the last time GPU is used
12    if (GPUDataCopied && nEle < INNERLARGE ) {
13      GPUDataCopied = false;
14      #pragma omp target exit data map(from:H[0:asz],...)
15    }
16    #pragma omp metadirective \
17     when (user={condition(nEle < INNERMEDIUM)}:  ) /*serial*/ \
18     when (user={condition(nEle < INNERLARGE)} : \
19       parallel for private(j) shared (nEle, ...)) /*CPU parallel*/ \
20     default (target teams distribute parallel for \
21         map (to:a[0:m], b[0:n], ...) map(tofrom: H[0:asz], ...) \
22         shared (nEle, ...)) //GPU offloading
23    for (j = 0; j < nEle; ++j)
24      similarityScore(si-j, sj+j, H, P, &maxPos);
25  }
```

Fig. 9. Selection via metadirective based on the inner loop count (nEle)

5   Prototype Implementation

We use ROSE to prototype our metadirective implementation and extension. Developed at LLNL, ROSE [7] is an open source compiler infrastructure to build source-to-source program transformation and analysis tools for Fortran and C/C++ applications. ROSE supports OpenMP 3.0 [1] and part of 4.0 [2]. It parses OpenMP directives and generates an Abstract Syntax Tree (AST) representation of OpenMP constructs. The OpenMP AST is then lowered and unparsed into multithreaded CPU or CUDA code. A backend compiler, such as GCC or NVCC, compiles the CPU or CUDA code and links the generated object files with a runtime to generate the final executable. Our prototype implementation includes the following components:

- A new OpenMP parser for metadirective, which is treated as nested directives;
- An extension of the internal ROSE AST to represent metadirective;
- A new phase of OpenMP lowering as the first step to translate the AST of metadirective into the OpenMP 4.0 AST using if-else statement as Fig. 10 shows for the input code in Fig. 9;
- Existing OpenMP lowering phase that generates CUDA code and connections to a thin layer of the XOMP runtime [1]; and
- Generated CUDA code compilation with NVCC and linking with XOMP.

```
1    ...
2
3    if (nEle < INNERMEDUIM) {    //serial
4      for (j = 0; j < nEle; ++j) similarityScore(si-j, sj+j, H, P, &maxPos);
5    } else if (nEle < INNERLARGE) {    //CPU parallel
6      #pragma omp parallel for private(j) shared (nEle, ...) )
7      for (j = 0; j < nEle; ++j)
8        similarityScore(si-j, sj+j, H, P, &maxPos);
9    } else {    //GPU offloading
10     #pragma omp target teams distribute parallel for \
11         map (to:a[0:m], b[0:n], ... ) \
12         map(tofrom: H[0:asz], ...) shared (nEle, ... ))
13     for (j = 0; j < nEle; ++j)
14       similarityScore(si-j, sj+j, H, P, &maxPos);
15   }
16   ...
17 }
```

Fig. 10. Lowering metadirective with dynamic conditions to an if statement

6   Experimental Results

Our experimental platform has 2 CPUs, each with 28 cores, and one NVIDIA Telsa V100 GPU with 16 GB of HBM. The system has 192 GB of main memory and runs Ubuntu 18.04 LTS, GCC 8.2.0 and NVIDIA CUDA SDK 10.1.105.

6.1   Evaluation of Adaptation Based on Outer Loop Count

To evaluate performance of the version that Fig. 8 shows, we performed the following experiment. First, we measured individual performance of CPU sequential, CPU parallel and GPU versions. As in Fig. 6, we identified the crossover points for the OUTERMEDIUM and OUTERLARGE thresholds as 3200 and 22000. Figure 11 shows the performance results. The adaptive version always chooses the parallelism and device that delivers the best performance for a large range of input sizes, with improvements between 20% and 200% over the non-adaptive versions.

6.2   Evaluation of Adaptation Based on Inner Loop Count

As Fig. 7 shows, this version tries to adaptively divide the inner loop iterations among CPU sequential, CPU parallel and GPU such that it could perform better than any individual version alone. In the experiments, we decide to use just the INNERLARGER to switch the computation between CPU parallel and GPU since the impact of CPU sequential is minimal. We evaluated the performance using five different M-N configurations: 45,000-45,000, 2,000-200,000, 200,000-2,000, 20,000-40,000, 40,000-20,000. In each configuration, we experiment with different

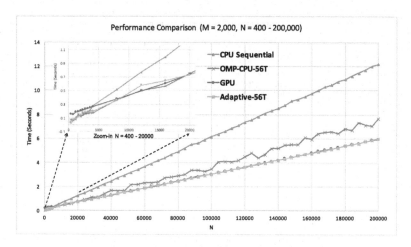

Fig. 11. Adaptive Smith-Waterman performance using outer loop count

INNERLARGE threshold values to control the switch between CPU parallel and GPU.

Our experiment shows that the benefits of using the adaptive version of the Smith-Waterman (SW) algorithm can be observed for M = 20,000 and N = 200,000, shown in Fig. 12. However, the performance advantage (when the inner loop count threshold is at 200, 1300, 1600, etc) is very small compared to the best non-adaptive GPU version.

For all other configurations, the adaptive version is not able to improve the overall performance over the best non-adaptive baseline version. Figure 13 shows one example for M = 45,000 and N = 45,000.

To understand our results, we profiled the execution to break down the GPU time into GPU kernel time and GPU data transfer time (shown in both Figs. 12 and 13). For M = N = 45,000, the profiling results show that the GPU data transfer overhead dominates the GPU offloading time, about 80%. Instead of only transferring the wavefront that needed for calculation, it always transfers all the data unnecessarily. Also, as we increase the inner loop count's threshold value, the compute time for the adaptive version also slightly increase, making it difficult to outperform its non-adaptive baseline version. Further investigation is still needed to make this adaptive version more effective.

6.3   Overhead Discussion

Since the transformation of metadirective simply uses the if-else statement and the overhead is expected to be negligible. However, the multi-version fat-binary code generated by the compiler may have a large code footprint in both disk and instruction memory when being executed.

From Fig. 11, we observe that the execution time of adaptive version is not significantly different from the individual version. With configurations that

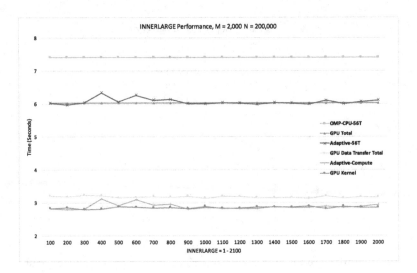

Fig. 12. Adaptive SW's performance using inner loop count (M != N)

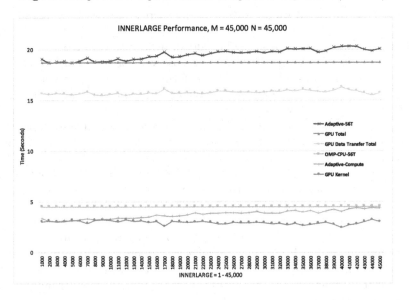

Fig. 13. Adaptive SW's performance using inner loop count (M == N)

M = 2,000 and N = 20,000–200,000, the execution overheads are measured. By average among all those configurations, the adaptive version is slower than individual GPU version by 0.28%, which is unnoticeable.

We also measured code size of different versions, as shown in Table 1. The object file of adaptive version is 18.37% to 34.9% larger than the individual non-adaptive versions. For the final executable files, the GPU executable files are significantly larger since they incorporate more supportive object files for both CPU and GPU execution. As a result, our transformation has much less impact on the code size.

Table 1. Code size overhead of adaptive Smith Waterman

Smith Waterman version		Object file size/KB	Executable file size/KB
Non-adaptive	Serial	43	14
	CPU Parallel	49	18
	GPU	44	751
Adaptive		58	751

7 Related Work

In [6], the authors explored the benefits of using two OpenMP 5.0 features, including metadirective and declare variant, for the miniMD benchmark from the Mantevo suite. The authors concluded that these features enabled their code to be expressed in a more compact form while maintaining competitive performance portability across several architectures. However, their work only explored compile-time constant variables to express conditions.

Many researchers have studied using GPUs to speedup Smith-Waterman algorithm, beginning as far back as Liu et al. in 2006 [3]. Our implementation resembles some of these early attempts in terms of data motion and synchronization behavior, mainly as a simple case study. Later work uses a variety of techniques to reduce the data movement and memory requirement by doing backtracking on the GPU [9] and even exploring repeating work to accomplish the backtrace in linear space [4]. These techniques would likely make the inner-loop optimization we discussed more attractive by removing the high cost of moving the complete cost matrix to and from the device, and may be worth exploring in the future.

8 Conclusion

Metadirectives in OpenMP 5.0 allow programmers to easily apply multiple directive variants to the same code region in order to meet the need of different software and hardware contexts. However, the context must be resolved at compile time. In this paper, we have used the Smith-Waterman algorithm to demonstrate the need for runtime adaptation. We propose to relax the compile-time restriction to allow dynamic adaptation of user-defined contexts. Our experimental results with a prototype compiler implementation show that dynamic evaluation of user-defined conditions can provide programmers more freedom to express a range of adaptive algorithms that improve overall performance. In the future, we would like to explore more complex user-defined conditions and extend other context selectors to support dynamic adaptation of metadirective at runtime, including dynamic work partitioning between CPUs and GPUs.

Acknowledgment. This work was performed under the auspices of the U.S. Department of Energy by Lawrence Livermore National Laboratory under Contract DE-AC52-07NA27344, and supported by the U.S. Dept. of Energy, Office of Science, Advanced Scientific Computing Research (SC-21), under contract DE-AC02-06CH11357. The manual reference codes were supported by LLNL-LDRD 18-ERD-006. LLNL-CONF-774899. This material is also based upon work supported by the National Science Foundation under Grant No. 1833332 and 1652732.

References

1. Liao, C., Quinlan, D.J., Panas, T., de Supinski, B.R.: A ROSE-based OpenMP 3.0 research compiler supporting multiple runtime libraries. In: Sato, M., Hanawa, T., Müller, M.S., Chapman, B.M., de Supinski, B.R. (eds.) IWOMP 2010. LNCS, vol. 6132, pp. 15–28. Springer, Heidelberg (2010). https://doi.org/10.1007/978-3-642-13217-9_2
2. Liao, C., Yan, Y., de Supinski, B.R., Quinlan, D.J., Chapman, B.: Early experiences with the OpenMP accelerator model. In: Rendell, A.P., Chapman, B.M., Müller, M.S. (eds.) IWOMP 2013. LNCS, vol. 8122, pp. 84–98. Springer, Heidelberg (2013). https://doi.org/10.1007/978-3-642-40698-0_7
3. Liu, Y., Huang, W., Johnson, J., Vaidya, S.: GPU accelerated Smith-Waterman. In: Alexandrov, V.N., van Albada, G.D., Sloot, P.M.A., Dongarra, J. (eds.) ICCS 2006. LNCS, vol. 3994, pp. 188–195. Springer, Heidelberg (2006). https://doi.org/10.1007/11758549_29
4. de O Sandes, E., de Melo, A.: Smith-Waterman alignment of huge sequences with GPU in linear space. In: 2011 IEEE International Parallel Distributed Processing Symposium, pp. 1199–1211, May 2011. https://doi.org/10.1109/IPDPS.2011.114
5. OpenMP Architecture Review Board: OpenMP Application Programming Interface 5.0, November 2018. https://www.openmp.org/wp-content/uploads/OpenMP-API-Specification-5.0.pdf
6. Pennycook, S.J., Sewall, J.D., Hammond, J.R.: Evaluating the impact of proposed OpenMP 5.0 features on performance, portability and productivity. In: 2018 IEEE/ACM International Workshop on Performance, Portability and Productivity in HPC (P3HPC), pp. 37–46, November 2018. https://doi.org/10.1109/P3HPC.2018.00007
7. Quinlan, D., Liao, C.: The ROSE source-to-source compiler infrastructure. In: Cetus Users and Compiler Infrastructure Workshop, in Conjunction with PACT, vol. 2011, p. 1. (2011)
8. Smith, T.F., Waterman, M.S., et al.: Identification of common molecular subsequences. J. Mol. Biol. **147**(1), 195–197 (1981)
9. Xiao, S., Aji, A.M., Feng, W.C.: On the robust mapping of dynamic programming onto a graphics processing unit. In: 2009 15th International Conference on Parallel and Distributed Systems, pp. 26–33. IEEE (2009)

Tasking

Teaching

On the Benefits of Tasking with OpenMP

Alejandro Rico[1]([✉])(iD), Isaac Sánchez Barrera[2,3](iD), Jose A. Joao[1](iD),
Joshua Randall[1](iD), Marc Casas[2](iD), and Miquel Moretó[2,3](iD)

[1] Arm Research, Austin, TX, USA
{alejandro.rico,jose.joao,joshua.randall}@arm.com
[2] Barcelona Supercomputing Center, Barcelona, Spain
{isaac.sanchez,marc.casas,miquel.moreto}@bsc.es
[3] Universitat Politècnica de Catalunya, Barcelona, Spain

Abstract. Tasking promises a model to program parallel applications
that provides intuitive semantics. In the case of tasks with dependences,
it also promises better load balancing by removing global synchronizations (barriers), and potential for improved locality. Still, the adoption of
tasking in production HPC codes has been slow. Despite OpenMP supporting tasks, most codes rely on worksharing-loop constructs alongside
MPI primitives. This paper provides insights on the benefits of tasking
over the worksharing-loop model by reporting on the experience of taskifying an adaptive mesh refinement proxy application: miniAMR. The
performance evaluation shows the taskified implementation being 15–
30% faster than the loop-parallel one for certain thread counts across
four systems, three architectures and four compilers thanks to better
load balancing and system utilization. Dynamic scheduling of loops nar-
rows the gap but still falls short of tasking due to serial sections between
loops. Locality improvements are incidental due to the lack of locality-
aware scheduling. Overall, the introduction of asynchrony with tasking
lives up to its promises, provided that programmers parallelize beyond
individual loops and across application phases.

Keywords: Tasking · OpenMP · Parallelism · Scaling

1 Introduction

Tasking is an important feature of multiple parallel programming models targeting both shared and distributed memory, such as Thread Building Blocks
(TBB), Chapel, OmpSs, OpenACC, Kokkos, among others. OpenMP, main-
stream programming model in the high performance computing (HPC) space,
includes tasking since version 3.0 (2008) [2,5] and tasking with dependences
since version 4.0 (2013) through `task` constructs [6,17,18]. OpenMP also supports tasking for distributed memory with `target` constructs. Tasking is widely
used to offload computation to accelerators in heterogeneous systems. CUDA,
OpenCL and OpenACC kernels, and OpenMP target concepts are examples
of this. However, the adoption of tasking for shared memory (threading) has

© Springer Nature Switzerland AG 2019
X. Fan et al. (Eds.): IWOMP 2019, LNCS 11718, pp. 217–230, 2019.
https://doi.org/10.1007/978-3-030-28596-8_15

been slow. Many HPC codes include threading with OpenMP alongside MPI, mostly through the use of worksharing-loop constructs with fork-join semantics. For more developers to taskify their codes, the effort required and the resulting benefits need to be considered.

This paper is an assessment of the benefits promised by tasking. These benefits include an intuitive parallel work unit—a task—which can be defined as a piece of computation on a piece of data that could be run in parallel. They also include the ability to define data-flow semantics between tasks using dependences and remove expensive global synchronizations and their potential load imbalance. We contribute to the discussion on tasking adoption in the community with our experience taskifying an adaptive mesh refinement (AMR) proxy-app: miniAMR [12,16]. This proxy-app is part of the Mantevo [10] project and the Exascale Computing Project Proxy Apps Suite [7] and models the refinement and communication phases of AMR codes. It is programmed in MPI and OpenMP, the OpenMP parallelization using worksharing-loop constructs only. Our taskification focuses on removing global synchronization between communication and computation phases to reduce the inherent load imbalance of working on blocks at different refinement levels. A previous paper [14] improves miniAMR load imbalance at the MPI level by changing its algorithmic implementation. In this work, we focus on maintaining the algorithmic properties of the reference miniAMR implementation and replacing loop-level parallel regions by task regions. The goal is to quantify the resulting performance benefits and report on our experience to give guidance on how to taskify such type of parallel work and give a sense of the effort required.

We report better performance using tasks on multiple systems including Marvell ThunderX2, IBM POWER9, Intel Skylake-SP and AMD EPYC. Overall, the taskification experience shows that developers need to think on parallel work across application phases, which involves larger code sections than only focusing on individual loops. The results show that tasking provides 15–30% better performance for certain thread counts and across the evaluated platforms. These improvements are mainly due to removal of load imbalance and avoidance of serial sections leading to a higher thread utilization.

2   The miniAMR Proxy Application

Adaptive mesh refinement (AMR) was developed as a way to model the physical domain with different levels of precision in numerical problems [3,4], with the goal of achieving higher precision in regions where it is needed (such as boundaries, points of discontinuity or steep gradients [4]). The physical domain is a rectangle (a rectangular prism in 3D space) that is represented as nested rectangular grids that share boundaries, with denser (finer) grids where higher precision is required.

The numerical algorithm is applied to each of the rectangles of the grid, with the corresponding communication on the boundaries between grid elements. The grid is updated when the conditions of the domain change: an error formula is

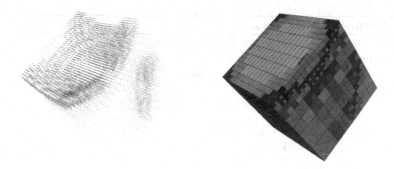

Fig. 1. Visualization of a unit cube with a domain defined by two empty spheres, using the vertices (left) and boundaries (right) of the grids. Colors have no special meaning.

defined to force the use of a finer grid when a threshold value is reached. The refinement is carried out by splitting the elements of the grid into two equal parts in all dimensions. This means that, in 2D, each rectangle is split into 4 other rectangles (quadrants) and, in 3D, each prism is split into 8 prisms (octants).

MiniAMR is a proxy application released as part of version 3.0 of the Mantevo suite [10,11] that is used to model the refinement/coarsening and communication routines of parallel AMR applications using MPI. The physical domain is modelled as a unit cube in 3D space divided in blocks in all three dimensions, which define the coarsest level of the grid.

To simulate the changes in the domain, miniAMR provides up to 16 different types of objects (both solid and surfaces), which include spheroids, cylinders, rectangles and planes. These objects can interact with the domain in different ways: moving at a constant speed, bouncing on the boundaries of the outside prism and growing on the X, Y or Z directions. Their positions determine the regions of the domain that need more precision and, therefore, a finer grid.

To simplify the communications, miniAMR forces neighboring blocks to be at distance 1 in the refinement level. This means that every face of a 3D block is a neighbor of a whole face (at the same refinement level), four other faces (which are finer) or a quarter of another face (which is coarser). A sample domain at a given time step can be seen in Fig. 1. All these blocks occupy the same bytes in memory; when refinement happens for a block, the resolution is doubled in each dimension by replacing that block by 8 new blocks.

The sample computations are modeled using different stencil algorithms, applying them to the different variables that are defined. For simplicity, we will focus on the 7-point stencil, where each discrete point is the average of itself and its six neighbor points in 3D space (up, down, north, south, east, west).

2.1   Baseline Parallelization of the miniAMR Code

To understand the changes to the code for taskification in Sect. 3, we first introduce how the application works originally according to the source code available in the Mantevo repository [12].

Algorithm 1. miniAMR main loop

```
foreach time step or simulation time finished do
    foreach stage in time step do
        foreach communication group do
            communicate;
            foreach variable in communication group do
                stencil;
                if time for checksum then
                    checksum;
                    validate checksum;
                end
            end
        end
    end
    if time for refinement then
        refine;
    end
end
```

The initial, coarsest grid is given by the number of MPI ranks in each dimension and the number of initial blocks (grid cells) per MPI rank per dimension. The application does an initial allocation for all the blocks that can be used (limited by a user-specified parameter). In the original code, this is implemented as an array of structs, where each block struct contains a quadruple pointer to `double` (i.e., `double****`) with the first indirection for the total amount of variables, one indirection per dimension, and memory contiguity only in the Z axis. Each dimension has two extra elements to allow for an extra face on each side of the block to account for *ghost values* (as the values in the boundaries of neighbor blocks are called in the miniAMR code). Blocks that are not in use are marked as such so that they can be used in future refinements.

Algorithm 1 shows the pseudo-code of the main loop that is executed after initialization. The main loop runs for a total number of time steps or a given simulation time. This loop is divided in stages that start with the communications between neighboring cells followed by the stencil updates, sometimes followed by a checksum calculation. These pairs of communication and stencil are grouped by a certain number of variables (communication group). For example, the total number of variables is 40, while communications and stencil updates are done in groups of 10 variables. Every few stages, the objects in the domain are moved according to the parameters, the domain is refined/coarsened following the settings, and the main loop starts again.

The communications are done for both local (intraprocess) and external (interprocess) neighboring blocks, MPI non-blocking calls being used for the second case. When the blocks are of the same size, the ghost values are simply copied. If a face has four neighbors, because the neighbor grid is finer, the values

Table 1. MiniAMR versions developed in this work

Label	Description
Orig	Original code from Mantevo repository with stencil parallel loop fixed
Orig-dyn	Orig with dynamically scheduled comm
Loop	Transformation of main data structure into contiguous array
Loop-dyn	Loop with dynamically scheduled comm
Task-1	Data-flow parallelization of comm and stencil. Taskloop for checksum
Task-2	Data-flow parallelization of comm, stencil and checksum

are replicated four times and the variables are divided by 4 to keep the total value constant. Similarly, all ghost values received by the coarser face are added up in groups of four to a single discrete point.

When splitting a block in the refinement process, each original point is replicated 8 times and its variables are divided by 8 in order to preserve the total value, as when communicating. The coarsening process is equivalent: 8 blocks are joined to form a coarser block, so the points are added up in groups of 8 to form a coarser point.

3   Taskification of MiniAMR

Table 1 lists the versions developed in this work towards the taskification of mini-AMR using OpenMP. The parallelization of miniAMR in the reference code of the Mantevo project is based on MPI and OpenMP. Message passing between processes occurs mainly in the communication phase when the faces of blocks (ghost values) are transferred in a process commonly known as halo exchange. An `MPI_AllReduce` primitive coordinates all processes to calculate the overall checksum. MPI is also used in other parts of the code outside of the main phases that are outside of the scope of this analysis, such as a plotting phase to visualize the simulated grid like the one shown in Fig. 1. OpenMP is used in the communication phase to exchange halos between threads, the computation phase (stencil) and checksum calculation. The refinement phase is serial.

The first transformation of the code (labeled as Orig) is to correct the original stencil OpenMP parallelization, which gives incorrect results as of February 14th, 2019 (the latest commit in the master branch at the time of writing). This issue was communicated to miniAMR developers. Listing 1 shows the resulting OpenMP annotation on the 7-point stencil code.

The taskification strategy is that a task communicates (`comm`) or computes (`stencil`) the variables of one block. It is beneficial for the data belonging to the variables of a block to be contiguous in memory so task dependencies can be expressed as array sections. To prepare the code towards taskification, the second transformation is to change the main data structure from a quadruple

```
#pragma omp parallel for default(shared)
//loop over blocks
for (int in = 0; in < sorted_index[num_refine+1]; in++) {
  block *bp = &blocks[sorted_list[in].n];
  block3D_t array = (block3D_t)&bp->array[var*block3D_size];
  double work[x_block_size+2][y_block_size+2][z_block_size+2];
  memcpy(work, array, sizeof(work)); //save in temp storage
  for (int i = 1; i <= x_block_size; i++)
    for (int j = 1; j <= y_block_size; j++)
      for (int k = 1; k <= z_block_size; k++)
        array[i][j][k] = (work[i-1][j  ][k  ] +
                          work[i  ][j-1][k  ] +
                          work[i  ][j  ][k-1] +
                          work[i  ][j  ][k  ] +
                          work[i  ][j  ][k+1] +
                          work[i  ][j+1][k  ] +
                          work[i+1][j  ][k  ])/7.0;
}
```

Listing 1. 7-point stencil code with correct worksharing construct.

```
double *barray  = bp->array;
double *barray1 = bp1->array;
#pragma omp task \
    depend(inout: barray[start*bsize:num_comm*bsize], \
                  barray1[start*bsize:num_comm*bsize]) \
    firstprivate(...) default(none)
{
  //loop over variables in communication group
  for (int m = start; m < start+num_comm; m++) {
    block3D_t array  = (block3D_t)&barray[m*bsize];
    block3D_t array1 = (block3D_t)&barray1[m*bsize];
    //exchange face ghost values
    for (int j = 1; j <= y_block_size; j++)
      for (int k = 1; k <= z_block_size; k++) {
        array1[x_block_size+1][j][k] = array[1][j][k];
        array[0][j][k] = array1[x_block_size][j][k];
      }
  }
}
```

Listing 2. Communication task between blocks at the same refinement level. bp and bp1 are pointers to the blocks exchanging faces. bsize is the 3D block size. Blocks are laid out contiguously for each variable

pointer (double****) with disaggregated arrays for each block, variable, and X, Y and Z dimensions, into a contiguous array (double*). This version (labeled as Loop) is our reference loop-parallel version using worksharing-loop constructs only. Having a contiguous array improves performance over the original code thanks to better prefetching coverage and accuracy due to improved locality. To isolate this improvement from that provided by taskification, the performance results in Sect. 5 are normalized to Loop.

The third version (labeled Task-1) is the taskification of the communication, stencil and checksum phases on top of Loop. In the original code, the loop in the communication phase traverses all blocks and each iteration performs

```
#pragma omp taskwait
//original: #pragma omp parallel for reduction(+: sum)
#pragma omp taskloop
for (int in = 0; in < sorted_index[num_refine+1]; in++) {
  block *bp = &blocks[sorted_list[in].n];
  double block_sum = 0.0;
  block3D_t array = (block3D_t)&bp->array[var*bsize];
  for (int i = 1; i <= x_block_size; i++)
    for (int j = 1; j <= y_block_size; j++)
      for (int k = 1; k <= z_block_size; k++)
        block_sum += array[i][j][k];
  //update check sum
#pragma omp atomic
  sum += block_sum;
}
```

Listing 3. Checksum task for Task-1 using taskloop

ghost value exchanges between a block face and a neighbor face at the same or different refinement level. This loop is distributed across threads with an omp parallel for construct. In this taskification, this worksharing-loop construct is removed and a task is defined for each exchange inside the loop. Listing 2 shows the task code for a face exchange at same refinement level. Tasks read and write to a part of the block and the dependence is set for the whole block. This could be improved by arranging halos with ghost values in separate arrays and having dependences only on halos instead, or by adding a separate dependence for each halo and variable. However, both of these solutions add complexity either to the data structure or to the directive readability, so this is not included in the version evaluated here. We expect support for multidependences [8,17] in OpenMP 5.0 to help with the directive readability issue (we must restrict this effort to OpenMP 4.5 features due to current compiler support). Stencil computations are taskified with an inout dependence on the block they operate on, and therefore depend on the previous communication tasks that write to that block. With this data-flow dependence strategy, a pair of parallel and single directives surround the loop iterating over the stages in the main loop, therefore removing the implicit barrier between the communication and stencil phases that worksharing-loop constructs in the original code imply.

At this point there is data flow between communication and stencil computation. Due to being inside a parallel-single pair, the worksharing-loop construct around checksum executes serially on one thread. Given that checksum does not execute on every iteration, this taskification uses a taskloop construct [15], which executes the iterations of checksum over the blocks in tasks, and therefore has the same implicit barrier after the checksum loop as the previous worksharing-loop construct. Listing 3 shows the corresponding task code. To make sure prior tasks complete before checksum, a taskwait primitive is placed before the checksum task loop. The refinement phase is outside of the task region and therefore remains serial as in the original code. Taskifying the refinement phase to overlap iterations across timesteps is a potential improvement left for future work.

```
for (int in = 0; in < sorted_index[num_refine+1]; in++) {
  block *bp = &blocks[sorted_list[in].n];
  double *barray = bp->array;
#pragma omp task \
  depend(in: barray[var*bsize:number*bsize]) \
  firstprivate(...) default(none)
  {
    //loop over variables in communication group
    for (int v = var; v < var+number; ++v) {
      block3D_t array = (block3D_t)&barray[v*bsize];
      double block_sum = 0.0;
      for (int i = 1; i <= x_block_size; i++)
        for (int j = 1; j <= y_block_size; j++)
          for (int k = 1; k <= z_block_size; k++)
            block_sum += array[i][j][k];
      //update check sum for a given variable
#pragma omp atomic
      sum[v] += block_sum;
    }
  }
}
#pragma omp taskwait
```

Listing 4. Checksum task for Task-2 using data-flow dependences

The fourth version (labeled as Task-2) builds on top of Task-1 and replaces the `taskloop`-based taskification of checksum by data-flow using dependencies. Listing 4 shows the task code. The loop iterating over the variables in the block is brought inside the task and the partial checksum variable becomes an array with an entry for each variable. This removes the `taskwait` before the checksum phase and allows hoisting the checksum for a given block as soon as its stencil is complete. The `taskwait` moves down after the creation of checksum tasks so checksum validation happens once all checksum tasks are complete.

Given the intrinsic load imbalance of the communication phase due to different block communications happening at different refinement levels, Table 1 includes two more versions of the code. Orig-dyn and Loop-dyn use dynamic scheduling by adding the clause `schedule(dynamic)` to the parallel loop in the communication phase to mitigate this imbalance and have another point of comparison between statically-scheduled loops and tasking.

This effort covers the shared memory portion of the application by replacing loop-level parallelization of communication, stencil and checksum with task-level parallelization to compare both models. The taskification of the MPI part promises further improvements given that it already uses asynchronous message passing. The evaluation of MPI communication tasking is left as future work.

4   Experimental Methodology

The experiments focus on comparing the worksharing-loop parallel and task-based implementations of miniAMR described in Sect. 3. As in prior work [1], they are run on multiple systems with different architectural and microarchitectural features and using different OpenMP C/C++ compiler and runtime

Table 2. Systems used for evaluation

System				
Name	Marvell ThunderX2	IBM POWER9	Intel Skylake-SP	AMD EPYC
Part no	CN9975	8335-GTH	Xeon Platinum 8160	7401P
Processors	2	2	2	1
Memory	16xDDR4-2666	16xDDR4-2666	12xDDR4-2666	8xDDR4-2666
Processor				
Cores	28	20	24	24
L1D cache	32 KB/core	32 KB/core	32 KB/core	32 KB/core
L2 cache	256 KB/core	512 KB/2 cores	1 MB/core	512 KB/core
L3 cache	32 MB	120 MB	33 MB	64 MB
NoC	Ring	-	Mesh	4-die MCM
Software				
Compilers	GNU-8.2	GNU-8.1	GNU-8.1	GNU-8.2
	Arm 19.1	IBM XL 16.1	Intel 19.0	

systems to quantify the sensitivity to the underlying system features and runtime implementation. Table 2 shows the testbed systems and compilers used in this work.

We run miniAMR with multiple variations of input parameters that affect different parts of the application. We test multiple block sizes and number of variables, which directly affect parallel work duration - often a performance limiting factor [9,13]. The default block size in miniAMR is $10 \times 10 \times 10$ and previous papers used $64 \times 64 \times 64$ [14]. We use $16 \times 16 \times 16$ as a reasonable input and $8 \times 8 \times 8$ as a deliberately small block size to stress tasking overheads. The default number of variables is 40. We use 40 and 160 as a deliberately large input to isolate tasking overheads. We test checksum frequencies of one every five, and one every ten stages, which affects tasking look ahead as checksum validation implies a barrier. We test 10 and 40 stages per time step which affects refinement frequency—more stages per time step means less relative time spent in the refinement phase. The number of overall refinements is 4, maximum blocks is 3000 and simulation starts with 1 block. The simulated object, position, direction and speed is defined with parameters: `--num_objects 1 --object 2 0 -1.1 -1.1 -1.1 0.060 0.060 0.060 1.1 1.1 1.1 0.0 0.0 0.0`. The memory footprint of these runs is between 900 MB and 20 GB.

Experiments compare the execution time of the multiple variants (lower is better) varying the number of OpenMP threads in one MPI rank. The execution time of each phase is measurable only for the worksharing-loop versions, and therefore not relevant in this study because when global synchronizations are removed the execution of multiple phases overlap. The executions are done multiple times to mitigate variation across runs. Most systems show a small variation between runs, so one of them is shown here except for EPYC. This system showed the largest variation, so experiments were run 10 times and the results shown are the average after removing outliers ($\pm 2 \times$ standard deviation).

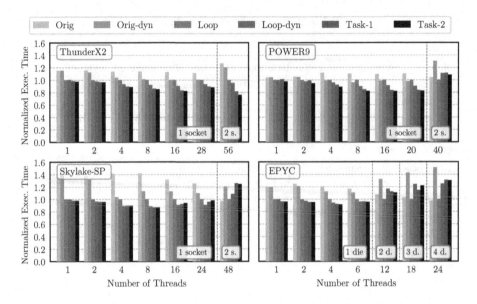

Fig. 2. Execution time of multiple miniAMR implementations on testbed systems; normalized to Loop

5 Performance Evaluation

Figure 2 shows the normalized execution time (lower is better) of the multiple implementations of miniAMR, each subplot corresponding to a different platform, and each cluster of bars being for a different number of threads. All results are using the GNU compiler and normalized to the Loop implementation. The parameters for this execution are: checksum frequency is every 5 stages, number of refinements is 4, blocks are $16 \times 16 \times 16$, with 40 variables and 40 stages per timestep. We focus on this configuration as it is a representative input after discussion with application developers. A discussion of the performance variations of sweeping parameters is included later in this section.

In all cases, Loop is faster than the original version of the code (Orig) because of improved locality while accessing the main data structure, which is a contiguous array instead of being segregated per dimension. The two task implementations are generally better than the Loop version due to load imbalance mitigation in the communication phase and, for the larger core counts, also the stencil phase. Loop-dyn also improves over Loop due to better load balancing and outperforms tasking in some cases. However, in most cases, tasking is superior to dynamically-scheduled loops due to the serial portion in between parallel loops becoming increasingly important with increasing thread counts (Amdahl's Law).

When crossing socket or die boundaries (e.g., 56 cores in ThunderX2 are in two sockets, see Table 2), the dynamically-scheduled configurations (Orig-dyn, Loop-dyn, Task-1 and Task-2) show worse performance than statically-scheduled

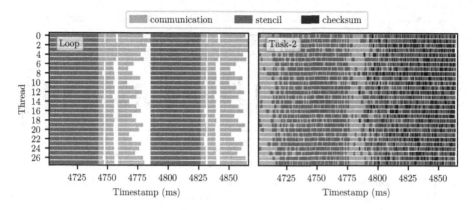

Fig. 3. Execution timelines of Loop (left) and Task-2 (right). White color is idle time

ones (Orig and Loop) in most cases. This is due to a large drop in performance of execution of both stencil and communications due to NUMA/NUCA effects. Static scheduling suffers heavily from load imbalance at the large core counts tested across sockets but has better caching behavior due to the same blocks being processed in the same threads across stages. With dynamic scheduling, each block is processed in potentially different threads across stages. The result is that the drop in instructions per cycle (IPC) on each thread for static scheduling is smaller than for dynamic scheduling when going from one socket to two sockets. In the case of EPYC, this is noticeable already at 12 threads because only 6 threads are co-located within the same die so over 6 threads is already a cross-chiplet execution paying larger NUMA latencies. Given the lack of performance counters that measure accesses to remote NUMA domains in the evaluated platforms, we plan to further analyze the impact of cross-socket/cross-chiplet accesses using simulated platforms in future work.

Figure 3 shows a timeline of the Loop (left) and Task-2 (right) versions showing execution of parallel loops and tasks, respectively, on the 28 threads of one ThunderX2 socket. Both timelines show the same duration. In the Loop timeline, light green is communication and turquoise is stencil compute. In the Task-2 timeline, the colors are the same and dark purple refers to checksum tasks. The Loop timeline shows a clear imbalance across threads in the communication phase, with certain threads consistently doing less work than others due to working on blocks at different refinement levels. The Task-2 timeline shows communication, stencil and checksum tasks concurrently executing as they become ready, leading to incidental locality improvement and little idle time. This incidental locality improvement happens more often with lower thread counts (4–8). Some consumer tasks execute faster due to executing back-to-back with their producer, e.g., communications of a block happening right after its stencil computation, or vice versa. In the absence of a locality-aware scheduler, this is less likely on larger thread counts and we observe a larger drop in task performance.

Looking across systems, the Task-2 version results in over 90% useful time on threads, i.e., communication/stencil/checksum, with a few threads achieving

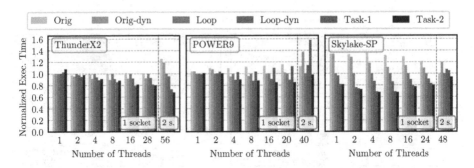

Fig. 4. Execution time with proprietary compilers: Arm Compiler on ThunderX2 (left), IBM XL on POWER9 (middle) and Intel Compiler on Skylake-SP (right)

just over 80% utilization due to task creation time not being accounted as useful. The Loop version gets a lower utilization of between 40% and 80%. The threads that spend more than half of the time idle are those that repeatedly operate on blocks at the lower refinement levels.

Figure 4 shows the normalized execution time on ThunderX2 using Arm Compiler, on POWER9 using IBM XL, and on Skylake-SP using Intel compiler. The tasking versions achieve similar gains on ThunderX2 with the exception of dual socket which performs better. On POWER9, tasking gets smaller gains and Loop-dyn performs the same in certain thread counts. On Skylake-SP, the tasking advantage over the loop-parallel versions is even larger than with GNU.

Testing other application parameters to verify the sensitivity of this analysis showed some variations in the results, but they do not change the conclusions above. Going to arbitrarily small 8 × 8 × 8 blocks to stress task creation overhead, indeed shows smaller benefit of the task versions and they scale worse overall, especially across sockets where they perform significantly worse, but still work better than Loop within single socket cases. Going to 160 variables to isolate task creation overhead, and a checksum frequency of 10 for larger task-scheduling look-ahead, shows a bit better results for tasking but not significantly better than the ones using 40 variables or a checksum frequency of 5. Going to a checksum frequency of 10 instead of 5 also shows a bit better results for tasking and the benefit of Task-2 over Task-1 is also larger.

6   Conclusion

The benefits of tasking come mainly from a higher level view of parallelization by the programmer. Introducing asynchrony by parallelizing across program phases enables a higher utilization of threads thanks to removing global synchronizations, not having serial code between loops and, compared to static scheduling, avoiding load imbalance. Due to the lack of locality-aware scheduling in the tested runtimes (to the best of our knowledge), locality improvements by consumer tasks executing after producer tasks was incidental. Also, tasking suffers from worse NUCA/NUMA behavior because tasks operating on the same blocks may execute on different threads across sockets and chiplets. Our experiments suggest that locality/affinity semantic extensions for tasking in OpenMP have potential for significant performance improvement and scaling across NUMA domains if paired with balanced data allocation.

Parallelizing across program phases requires a mindset change if the programmer tends to parallelize loops or small sections after having parallelized at the MPI level. This strategy of focusing on small code portions when parallelizing with OpenMP limits scaling because sections between parallel regions remain serial. Tasking helps think in terms of larger code sections thanks to task dependences—a task can execute anytime during the task region as soon as its dependencies are satisfied.

A potentially-beneficial extension to the OpenMP standard for this taskification effort would have been the ability to specify dependences in taskloops. This way the Task-2 implementation could have been written in a easier and clearer way building on top of Task-1 code. This is an extension that is on-going work by the OpenMP committee and this paper shows a potential use case for it.

Lastly, we encountered several compiler issues with tasks that were reported to developers. Some compilers failed to compile certain constructs or generated incorrect results. These issues did not happen with worksharing-loop constructs, which shows the different maturity of both models.

Acknowledgments. This work was in collaboration with Cray and funded in part by the DOE ECP PathForward program. It has been partially supported by the Spanish Government through Programa Severo Ochoa (contract SEV-2015-0493), by the Spanish Ministry of Economy and Competitiveness (contract TIN2015-65316-P), by the Generalitat de Catalunya (contracts 2017-SGR-1414 and 2017-SGR-1328), by the European Unions's Horizon 2020 Framework Programme under the Mont-Blanc project (grant agreement number 779877), and by the Arm-BSC Centre of Excellence initiative. I. Sánchez Barrera has been partially supported by the Spanish Ministry of Education, Culture and Sport under Formación del Profesorado Universitario fellowship number FPU15/03612. M. Casas has been partially supported by the Spanish Ministry of Economy, Industry and Competitiveness under Ramón y Cajal fellowship number RYC-2017-23269. M. Moretó has been partially supported by the Spanish Ministry of Economy, Industry and Competitiveness under Ramón y Cajal fellowship number RYC-2016-21104.

References

1. Atkinson, P., McIntosh-Smith, S.: On the performance of parallel tasking runtimes for an irregular fast multipole method application. In: de Supinski, B.R., Olivier, S.L., Terboven, C., Chapman, B.M., Müller, M.S. (eds.) IWOMP 2017. LNCS, vol. 10468, pp. 92–106. Springer, Cham (2017). https://doi.org/10.1007/978-3-319-65578-9_7
2. Ayguadé, E., et al.: A proposal for task parallelism in OpenMP. In: Chapman, B., Zheng, W., Gao, G.R., Sato, M., Ayguadé, E., Wang, D. (eds.) IWOMP 2007. LNCS, vol. 4935, pp. 1–12. Springer, Heidelberg (2008). https://doi.org/10.1007/978-3-540-69303-1_1

3. Berger, M.J., Colella, P.: Local adaptive mesh refinement for shock hydrody-namics. J. Comput. Phys. **82**, 64–84 (1989). https://doi.org/10.1016/0021-9991(89)90035-1

4. Berger, M.J., Oliger, J.: Adaptive mesh refinement for hyperbolic partial differ-ential equations. J. Comput. Phys. **53**, 484–512 (1984). https://doi.org/10.1016/0021-9991(84)90073-1

5. Duran, A., Corbalán, J., Ayguadé, E.: Evaluation of OpenMP task scheduling strategies. In: Eigenmann, R., de Supinski, B.R. (eds.) IWOMP 2008. LNCS, vol. 5004, pp. 100–110. Springer, Heidelberg (2008). https://doi.org/10.1007/978-3-540-79561-2_9

6. Duran, A., Perez, J.M., Ayguadé, E., Badia, R.M., Labarta, J.: Extending the OpenMP tasking model to allow dependent tasks. In: Eigenmann, R., de Supinski, B.R. (eds.) IWOMP 2008. LNCS, vol. 5004, pp. 111–122. Springer, Heidelberg (2008). https://doi.org/10.1007/978-3-540-79561-2_10

7. ECP Proxy Apps Suite. https://proxyapps.exascaleproject.org/

8. Garcia-Gasulla, M., Mantovani, F., Josep-Fabrego, M., Eguzkitza, B., Houzeaux, G.: Runtime mechanisms to survive new HPC architectures: a use case in human respiratory simulations. Int. J. High Perform. Comput. Appl. (2019). https://doi.org/10.1177/1094342019842919

9. Gautier, T., Perez, C., Richard, J.: On the impact of OpenMP task granularity. In: de Supinski, B.R., Valero-Lara, P., Martorell, X., Mateo Bellido, S., Labarta, J. (eds.) IWOMP 2018. LNCS, vol. 11128, pp. 205–221. Springer, Cham (2018). https://doi.org/10.1007/978-3-319-98521-3_14

10. Heroux, M.A., et al.: Improving performance via mini-applications. Techni-cal report. SAND2009-5574, Sandia National Laboratories (2009). http://www.mantevo.org/MantevoOverview.pdf

11. Mantevo Project. https://mantevo.org/

12. MiniAMR Adaptive Mesh Refinement (AMR) Mini-app. https://github.com/Mantevo/miniAMR

13. Rico, A., Ramirez, A., Valero, M.: Available task-level parallelism on the cell BE. Sci. Program. **17**(1–2), 59–76 (2009). https://doi.org/10.3233/SPR-2009-0269

14. Sasidharan, A., Snir, M.: MiniAMR - a miniapp for adaptive mesh refinement. Technical report. University of Illinois Urbana-Champaign (2016). http://hdl.handle.net/2142/91046

15. Teruel, X., Klemm, M., Li, K., Martorell, X., Olivier, S.L., Terboven, C.: A proposal for task-generating loops in OpenMP*. In: Rendell, A.P., Chapman, B.M., Müller, M.S. (eds.) IWOMP 2013. LNCS, vol. 8122, pp. 1–14. Springer, Heidelberg (2013). https://doi.org/10.1007/978-3-642-40698-0_1

16. Vaughan, C.T., Barrett, R.F.: Enabling tractable exploration of the performance of adaptive mesh refinement. In: 2015 IEEE International Conference on Cluster Computing, pp. 746–752 (2015). https://doi.org/10.1109/CLUSTER.2015.129

17. Vidal, R., et al.: Evaluating the impact of OpenMP 4.0 extensions on relevant parallel workloads. In: Terboven, C., de Supinski, B.R., Reble, P., Chapman, B.M., Müller, M.S. (eds.) IWOMP 2015. LNCS, vol. 9342, pp. 60–72. Springer, Cham (2015). https://doi.org/10.1007/978-3-319-24595-9_5

18. Virouleau, P., et al.: Evaluation of OpenMP dependent tasks with the KASTORS benchmark suite. In: DeRose, L., de Supinski, B.R., Olivier, S.L., Chapman, B.M., Müller, M.S. (eds.) IWOMP 2014. LNCS, vol. 8766, pp. 16–29. Springer, Cham (2014). https://doi.org/10.1007/978-3-319-11454-5_2

Detecting Non-sibling Dependencies in OpenMP Task-Based Applications

Ricardo Bispo Vieira[1(✉)], Antoine Capra[2], Patrick Carribault[3], Julien Jaeger[3], Marc Pérache[3], and Adrien Roussel[3]

[1] Exascale Computing Research Lab, Bruyères-le-Châtel, France
`ricardo.bispo-vieira@exascale-computing.eu`
[2] Bull/Atos SAS, Les Clayes-sous-Bois, France
`antoine.capra@atos.net`
[3] CEA, DAM, DIF, 91297 Arpajon, France
`{patrick.carribault,julien.jaeger,marc.perache,adrien.roussel}@cea.fr`

Abstract. The advent of the multicore era led to the duplication of functional units through an increasing number of cores. To exploit those processors, a shared-memory parallel programming model is one possible direction. Thus, OpenMP is a good candidate to enable different paradigms: data parallelism (including loop-based directives) and control parallelism, through the notion of tasks with dependencies. But this is the programmer responsibility to ensure that data dependencies are complete such as no data races may happen. It might be complex to guarantee that no issue will occur and that all dependencies have been correctly expressed in the context of nested tasks. This paper proposes an algorithm to detect the data dependencies that might be missing on the OpenMP task clauses between tasks that have been generated by different parents. This approach is implemented inside a tool relying on the OMPT interface.

Keywords: OpenMP task · Nested task · OMPT · Data dependency · Data-race

1 Introduction

The advent of multi-core processors occurred more than a decade ago, bringing processors scaling from a few cores to several hundreds. To exploit those functional units, the OpenMP programming model [1] became the *defacto* standard leveraging the programmability and the performance of such systems. Based on compiler directives and the fork-join model, it spawns threads and implies a synchronization *rendez-vous* at the end of parallel regions. Mainly oriented to structured and regular parallelism first, it has been extended with a task programming model to enable efficient use of irregular and nested parallelism. Even if this tasking model has proven to provide good performance, global synchronizations are expensive and may prevent scheduling of upcoming tasks. Therefore, the notion of *data dependency* has been introduced, to provide a lighter

© Springer Nature Switzerland AG 2019
X. Fan et al. (Eds.): IWOMP 2019, LNCS 11718, pp. 231–245, 2019.
https://doi.org/10.1007/978-3-030-28596-8_16

local synchronization between successive dependent tasks. These dependencies can be expressed only between sibling tasks (i.e., created by the same parent task). The execution order of these tasks is given by the creation sequence (task directives order in the code) and the depend clauses. We call the sets of tasks spawned from the same parent a *dependency domain*.

Combining nested tasks with data dependencies may lead to some issues because of the parallel execution of tasks between dependency domains. Indeed, dependencies only apply between sibling tasks. However, these dependencies are not passed on the next generation of tasks. Hence, two dependency domains issued from sibling tasks with dependencies will not inherit their parent order. In this case, race conditions may occur even if the programmer thinks the dependencies are correctly expressed in the depend clauses. Correctly specifying a large number of dependencies across multiple dependency domains implies a non negligible burden to the developer and remains error prone.

In this paper, we aim at detecting such dependency declaration errors. The contribution of this paper is threefold: (1) we develop an algorithm to detect possible data races based on declared task dependencies, (2) we propose new extensions to the OMPT interface for keeping track of the memory scope of dependency variables and, (3) we implement the OMPT extensions in an OpenMP implementation and the algorithm in a tool to effectively detect data races.

The remaining of the paper is organized as follows: Sect. 2 presents some motivating examples. Related work regarding nested tasks with data dependencies and their correctness is presented in Sect. 3. Then, Sect. 4 explains the main contribution through the dynamic detection of race conditions among data dependencies in non-sibling tasks. Section 5 describes the implementation of our approach while Sect. 6 illustrates our tool output and its overhead on some applications, before concluding in Sect. 7.

2 Motivating Examples

When considering nested tasks, each task in a dependency domain generates its own children tasks, hence its own dependency domain. By representing each task with a vertex, and linking each task to its children with an edge, it results a tree structure. We call such tree a *spawn-tree*. Since dependencies can only induce scheduling constraints inside a dependency domain (i.e., between sibling tasks), there is no ordering between tasks from different domains. Thus, these tasks can run concurrently in any order, even if they are at different levels in the spawn-tree. Indeed, specifying a dependency clause at a given level in the task nest does not propagate it to deeper levels (i.e., to children tasks). This might become tricky as, from the user point of view, dataflow information has been expressed. However, the resulting behavior and scheduling may not be the one expected. We present very simple test cases to illustrate such possible data races with misleading depend clauses.

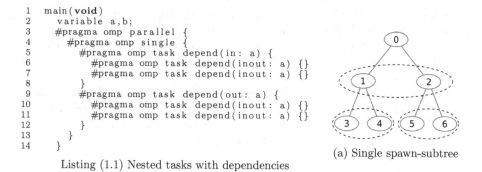

```
1   main(void)
2       variable a,b;
3       #pragma omp parallel {
4           #pragma omp single {
5               #pragma omp task depend(in: a) {
6                   #pragma omp task depend(inout: a) {}
7                   #pragma omp task depend(inout: a) {}
8               }
9               #pragma omp task depend(out: a) {
10                  #pragma omp task depend(inout: a) {}
11                  #pragma omp task depend(inout: a) {}
12              }
13          }
14      }
```

Listing (1.1) Nested tasks with dependencies

(a) Single spawn-subtree

Fig. 1. An OpenMP code with nested tasks with dependencies and its corresponding spawn-subtree. Dotted ellipses in the tree are for dependency domains.

Wrongly Expressed Dependencies. Listing 1.1 presents a test case based on nested tasks with data dependencies. The first task (**single** directive - task 0 in the spawn-tree represented in Fig. 1a) spawns two children tasks with dependencies (**task** constructs lines 5 and 9 with **depend(in)** and **depend(out)** clauses - tasks 1 and 2 in the spawn-tree). These tasks belong to the same dependency domain (dotted ellipse around task 1 and 2 in the spawn-tree). Each of these tasks spawns two other children tasks with dependencies (**task** constructs with **depend(inout)** clauses - tasks 3, 4, 5 and 6 in the spawn-tree).

The parents tasks 1 and 2 have serialized dependencies over a, ensuring an order. However, their children don't inherit this dependency. Without any **taskwait** directive at the end of task 1 to ensure that all its children tasks have finished before task 1 ends, all the tasks at the last level of the tree can run concurrently. Moreover, the children of task 1 can run concurrently with task 2. If the variable a is effectively written as suggested in the depend clauses, a race condition on a may happen.

```
1   main(void)
2       variable a,b;
3       #pragma omp parallel {
4           #pragma omp single {
5               #pragma omp task depend(in: a) {
6                   #pragma omp task depend(inout: a) {}
7               #pragma omp taskwait
8               }
9               #pragma omp task depend(in: a) {
10                  #pragma omp task depend(inout: a) {}
11              #pragma omp taskwait
12              }
13          }
14      }
```

Listing 1.2. Unexpressed/Hidden dependencies

Unexpressed/Hidden Dependencies. Listing 1.2 presents a similar test case, except that parent tasks don't express a data dependency over a. In this case, adding a **taskwait** directive is not enough to order all tasks. Since there is no inferred writing of a between the parent tasks, they can be executed in any order, and even concurrently. Hence, ensuring that all children tasks are finished does not enforce an order between other tasks at the same tree level, as the tasks from the two lower dependency domains can run concurrently, also causing data races. One possibility to solve this issue is to apply children dependency clauses to the parent tasks. Thus, these dependencies are said to be *unexpressed* (or *hidden*).

Listing 1.3 presents the same behavior: two tasks are spawned inside **parallel** construct. Even without nested tasks, the same problem occurs due to implicit tasks. Indeed, the **parallel** construct first spawns implicit tasks (one per OpenMP thread). Due to these implicit tasks, the explicit task creations (**task** constructs) represents the second level in the spawn-tree. For example, if one considers 2 OpenMP threads, thus two implicit tasks, this listing produces the same spawn-tree as depicted in Fig. 1a. The implicit task level cannot accept **depend** clauses. Hence, the dependencies expressed on the explicit tasks are hidden to the implicit ones, causing the ordering issue as before. The same applies when creating explicit tasks with dependencies in a worksharing-Loop construct.

```
1   variable a;
2   main(void)
3     #pragma omp parallel {
4       #pragma omp task depend(in: a) {}
5       #pragma omp task depend(inout: a) {}
6     }
```

Listing 1.3. Tasks with dependencies in implicit task

3   Related Work

The OpenMP support for tasks with dependencies has shown a growing interest from the community of developers and researchers, in various topics such as scheduling [4], data locality [3] and more generally performance optimization [6,7]. Thus, Perez et al. propose an extension of the OpenMP task directive to apply dependencies between different family lineage of domain dependencies [2]. The new clauses **weakwait**, **weakin**, **weakout**, **weakinout** and **release** refine the dependency relationship in a two-step process starting by applying inner-task dependencies directly to the outer-task successors at a **weakwait** synchronization point. Early processing is possible as the **release** clause indicates that no more dependencies will be expressed on the listed variables. Then, outer tasks with a **weak** dependency clause pass down predecessors dependencies to inner subtasks. The results obtained with these new extensions are coherent with the theoretical study conducted by Dinh et al. [8]. In the nested dataflow model (ND), they showed that modified scheduling algorithms achieve better locality reuse and higher performance on large number of processors. ND is the extension of the nested parallel model (NP) with dependencies, where the **fire** construct completes the **parallel** and **sequential** constructs representing partial dependencies between two dependency domains. They introduced a methodology called DAG rewriting system (DRS) to translate from NP to ND and use it to revisit existing linear algebra algorithms, providing material for the modified scheduling proof. But these approaches do not enable debugging of current

OpenMP task-based applications. For this purpose, data-race detection methods exist, based on either static, dynamic, or post-mortem approaches. Nonetheless, the majority only provides support for tasking model without data dependencies. Some tools support tasks with dependencies. Protze et al. [9] proposed an efficient and scalable OpenMP data-race detection tool called Archer based on a static-dynamic method for large HPC applications: relying on a LLVM compilation pass for static analysis and on ThreadSanitizer for dynamic analysis via code instrumentation and *Happens-before* relation. They annotated the OpenMP runtime to reduce false positives arising from synchronizations points and locking. They defined three detection states resulting from static analysis, race free, certainly racy and potentially racy regions. On top of that information, they extend ThreadSanitizer to take as input a blacklisted set of race-free regions, notably reducing amount of instrumentation at dynamic analysis. In [10], they detailed how they reported OpenMP runtime annotations into OMPT events callbacks, providing a portable data race detection tool with support for tasks with dependencies. Matar et al. [11] conducted a similar study mainly oriented to tasking programming model, relying on ThreadSanitizer and the *Happens-before* relation for dynamic analysis. They proved that their tool, Tasksanitizer, is more efficient at task level to detect determinacy races. However, when combining nested tasks with dependencies, their respective solutions might be related to task scheduling, missing some possible race conditions. Our approach does not instrument every memory access, but it tracks dependency clauses and deals with the hierarchy of tasks, whatever the scheduling of those tasks. It is therefore complementary to methods like Archer and Tasksanitizer.

4 Detecting Dependencies Between Non-sibling Tasks

Section 2 showed how unexpressed dependencies or the absence of `taskwait` directive in descendant tasks may lead to data races, despite the expression of dependencies on some tasks. In this Section, we present our approach to detect such wrong behavior. First, we will describe our approach with our main algorithm to detect potential data races based on the expressed dependencies. Then, since dependencies in OpenMP are passed through variables (i.e., logical memory addresses), we present in a second part how we detect that the `depend` clauses on the same address indeed concern the same variable.

4.1 Main Approach

Our main approach to detect potential data races in nested tasks is based on spawn-tree subgraph and their isolation. Each task t in a dependency domain will generate its own subtree in the spawn-tree. This subtree regroups all the tasks having the task t as an ancestor. All the tasks from the subtree of t should be compared with the subtree spawned from the siblings of t. However, these subtrees may not be compared in one case: if the t subtree is *isolated*.

A subtree is *isolated* if all the tasks in the subtree are enforced to be finished before any subtree from a subsequent sibling is started. Thus, the t subtree is isolated from another t' subtree if, and only if, there is an ordering between t and t', and all tasks in t subtree are done before starting task t' and its own subtree. This isolation can be achieved with several methods. The first method consists in putting a `taskwait` directive after the last task of each level in the t spawn-tree. The second method encapsulates task t in a `taskgroup` construct ending before task t'. A third method inserts a `if(0)` clause on each task of the subtree.

If the subtree is isolated, no tasks from the t subtree may run concurrently with t subsequent sibling tasks. On the other hand, if the t subtree is not isolated from the subtrees of t subsequent siblings, tasks of multiple subtrees may run concurrently. In such case, it is necessary to test each task in all subtrees in a pairwise manner to detect **depend** clauses on same addresses. If this occurs, and the address in the multiple **depend** clauses refers to the same variable, then a data race may occur.

Algorithm 1. Resolve Non Sibling Dependencies

---

1 **ResolveNonSiblingDependencies**
    inputs: vertex *root* of the spawn-tree
2   **if** $root.children \neq \emptyset$ **then**
3   **for** $v \in root.children$ **do**
4              $DoDectectionConflicts = true$
5   **for** $v' \in root.children \smallsetminus \{v\}$ **do**
6   **if** $DependencyPath(v, v') = true$ **then**
7                      $Synched = \text{CheckSynch}(v)$
8   **if** $Synched = true$ **then**
9                          $DoDectectionConflicts = false$
10   **if** $DoDectectionConflicts = true$ **then**
11   **for** $w \in subtree(v) \cup v$ **do**
12   **for** $w' \in subtree(v') \cup v'$ **do**
13                         $\text{DetectConflicts}(w, w')$
14   ResolveNonSiblingDependencies(v)

Algorithm 1 presents these different steps. We will describe it on a small example. Listing 1.4 presents a task-based Fibonacci kernel extracted from the BOTS benchmarks [14] and modified to express dependencies. In this new program, each invocation of the `fib` function creates three tasks: one for each new invocation of the `fib` function, and a third task to realize the sum of the two sub-results. The two `fib` invocations are independent (`depend(out:x)` and `depend(out:y)` clauses respectively), but the last task depends from the two

```
1   fib (n)
2      int x, y, s;
3      if( n < 2 ) return n;
4      #pragma omp task shared(x) depend(out:x) {
5         x = fib( n - 1 );
6      }
7      #pragma omp task shared(y) depend(out:y) {
8         y = fib( n - 2 );
9      }
10     #pragma omp task shared(s,x,y) depend(in:x,y) {
11        s = x + y;
12     }
13     #pragma omp taskwait
14     return s;
```

Listing 1.4. Task-Based Fibonacci with dependencies

previous tasks (depend(in:x,y) clause). The computation of fib(4) with this new algorithm produces the spawn-tree displayed in Fig. 2a.

In our algorithm, we study each pair of tasks in each dependency domain, starting with the set of tasks generated by the root of the spawn-tree (l.3 and l.5 in the algorithm). Applied to the fib(4) example, we start by studying the tasks fib(3) and fib(2) at the first level. For each pair, we check if there is an isolation between their subtrees, hence if these tasks are ordered and all descendant tasks of the first task are enforced to be finished before starting the other task. We start by looking if the two tasks are ordered. To do so, for each dependency domain, we build a *Directed Acyclic Graph* (e.g., DAG) representing the complete ordering of tasks, thanks to depend and if clauses, taskwait and taskgroup directives. Then detecting if two tasks are ordered in a dependency graph is equivalent to find a path between the two tasks in the DAG (l.6). If there is a path, then the two tasks are ordered.

Figure 2b depicts the DAG generated for the dependency domain formed by the leaf tasks in subtree B. Since the two fib invocations are independent, there is no link between them. However, two links come from these tasks towards the third (sum) task, due to the depend(in) expressed dependencies. Hence, an order exists between fib(0) and (sum), and an order also exists between fib(1) and (sum).

We then check if the first subtree is isolated. If so, it is useless to detect potential conflicts between these subtrees (l.7–9). In the example, if the subtrees from fib(3) and fib(2) are isolated, no data race can happen between (sum) and the subtrees. However, it will not prevent data races between the subtrees, as they can be executed in any order, and even concurrently.

If no isolation is detected, we need to compare every pair of tasks in the tested subtrees (l.11–12). We check each depend clause from the two tasks to detect potential conflicting memory access (l.13). Once all the current sibling tasks are tested, we do the same procedure with the next level in the spawn-tree.

4.2 Tracking Memory Scope

The OpenMP runtime only uses the address of memory storage to express the dependencies. When detecting conflict with addresses, two cases arise. First, the address always identifies the same variable throughout the program execution. It is the case for global variables. On the other hand, some addresses can be reused throughout the program to store different variables. It is the case for heap and stack addresses, through function calls and return statements or memory allocation/deallocation. To ensure that the detected conflict on addresses passed to depend clauses can actually lead to a data race, we have to ensure that the same address relates to the same variable.

The fibonacci example can illustrate such behavior. With the dataflow based fibonacci algorithm, we can see that the same pattern of tasks may be replicated in the spawn-tree. It is the case for the subtrees **B** and **C** in Fig. 2a.

When the program is running, the following behavior can happen. First, a thread runs the task which is the root node of subtree **B**. This task declares dependencies on stack addresses for variables x, y and s for the children task. Upon completion of the task, stack memory is recycled for the next instructions. If the root node of subtree **C** is then scheduled on this same thread, as it is the same task as the root of subtree **B**, it will map the same variables to the same stack addresses. The executing task will also declares dependencies for variables x, y and s, which happen to have the exact same stack addresses than the dependencies declared for the previous task. However, they are not related, and the reuse of addresses only relates to this specific scheduling. It is necessary to check if the use of the same addresses in multiple depend clauses are indeed related to the same variables.

Data scoping is a key element in OpenMP, and more generally in shared memory programming models. It describes if a specific data is shared among threads or is local to a thread. By default, scope attribute is set to shared for threads and implicit tasks, and to firstprivate for explicit tasks. OpenMP provides clauses to modify the scope attribute of data: shared exhibits data's memory address to all threads, and private, firstprivate or lastprivate create a thread's local data copy (different memory address). The firstprivate clause is a special case, the value of the variable is passed on to the local copy. By this way, if the variable value is an address, it violates the private attribute since all threads having the local data copy can simultaneously access the same memory storage. If the variable is used later in a depend clause, it may lead to a concurrent access.

To ensure that the same address in multiple depend clauses relates to the same variable, we record the data scoping attributes at task creation. We then study the data scoping path, i.e. the variable's scope attribute at each level between a task and a child task of its lineage. A color c is associated with each tested pair of tasks and each tested address. For the two tested tasks, we go up in the spawn-tree and check at each level if the address is a shared data, or if it was a value passed in a firstprivate clause. In both cases, the link to the checked level is colored with the color c. Once a common ancestor for the two tasks is found in the spawn tree, we obtain a direct path between the two tasks. If all the links in the path have the same color c, it means that the tested address was passed by the common ancestor down to the two tested tasks, and that the address relates to the same variable. Hence, the tested **depend** clauses may actually cause a data race, and the *DetectConflicts* phase in our algorithm raises an issue.

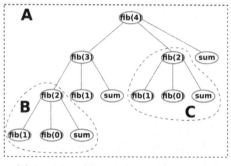

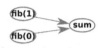

(a) Spawn-tree instance of fibonacci(4)

(b) DAG generated from the dependency domain formed by the leaf tasks in subtree B.

Fig. 2. Data structures related to the task-based Fibonacci example

To illustrate this coloring search, we focus on x variables from **fib(1)** invocations. To both tasks **fib(1)** from subtrees **B** and **C** for variable x, we use the color c_0. Since the variable is in a **shared** clause for both tasks, the links between these tasks and their parents (respectively roots of subtrees **B** and **C**) are colored with c_0. However, the variable passed in the **shared** clause is a newly created variable and does not come from a previous **shared** clause (or **firstprivate** clause). Hence, the upward links are colored with a new color c_1 (from root node of subtree **B** to **fib(3)** task, and from root node of subtree **C** to **fib(4)** task). For the same reason, the last link from **fib(3)** to **fib(4)** will have a new color c_2. Once this link is colored, we obtain a colored path between the two tested tasks. However the path has multiple colors, hence the two addresses don't relate to the same variable. No potential data race will be raised, even if the **depend** clauses use the same memory address.

4.3 Method Limitations

Our method uses the same information as the OpenMP dependencies mechanism, i.e, the memory address. We do not aim to detect nor instrument actual memory access, but only to check if the dependencies declared in the OpenMP task constructs are coherent. As we are based on the addresses passed in the dependency clauses, our method may miss some data races or report false positive.

The false positive arises when the task constructs declares dependencies on variables which are not used in the task, or in its descendant tasks. In these cases, our method returns a potential data race. However, since the variables are not used in the tasks, it is not a data race. These variables might just have been used to infer ordering between tasks with no actual read or write.

In the same way, if variables are used in a task but do not appear in a **depend** clause, our method will not consider the variable. The same also happens if a variable a variable is used in the task spawning a dependency domain, with tasks declaring dependencies on the same variable. In these cases, out method will not detect the potential data race.

```
1    #pragma omp task depend(in:a)
2      #pragma omp task depend(out:a) {
3        a = some_value; }
4      local = a;
```

Listing 1.5. Nested tasks with potential race conditions

The test case in Listing 1.5 presents such scenario. Based only on the dependency declarations, there is no way to detect when the actual memory access is performed in the parent task, i.e, before or after the child task.

5   Tool Implementation

Our detection method is based on the task spawn-tree and the *DAG* built from dependency clauses information. Building and maintaining such structures requires accessing information from the OpenMP directives and internals in addition to those provided by its API: e.g., when a parallel region starts and ends, when synchronizations occur at multiple levels, be informed of tasks creation and retrieve their dependencies set if any. These information are tightly linked to the OpenMP API and runtime implementation.

The OMPT [12] interface aimed at developing portable performance and analysis tools for OpenMP. Recently released as part of the OpenMP specification, it provides an instrumentation-like portable interface for tool callbacks. A callback is a function that is registered during the tool initialization to be triggered at corresponding events. In addition, OMPT specifies a collection of inquiry functions to probe the OpenMP runtime for internal information.

Our tool can either be used at runtime or post-mortem through the generation of a trace. Both versions use the same information that can be gathered through the set of OMPT callbacks listed below. Implementation has been done inside the MPC framework [15], a hybrid MPI/OpenMP runtime which support the OMPT interface. During the initialization phase, we create the internal structures and the root task of the spawn tree. Then, to instrument all OpenMP tasks in the application, the tool registers the following OMPT callbacks to the OpenMP runtime:

- **ompt_callback_parallel_{begin/end}_t:** callbacks to register the entry and exit points of parallel regions. We use the *begin* event to retrieve the number of threads inside the parallel team. During the *end* event, we deallocate all nodes of the spawn tree, if any, and its related dependencies. Only the root task remains as the code returns to the initial task.

- **ompt_callback_implicit_task_t:** callback triggered during the creation of implicit tasks. We use it to add nodes representing the implicit tasks of the parallel region into the spawn tree.

- **ompt_callback_sync_region_t:** callback to register region synchronization. Its parameters contain the synchronization type (*i.e.* a barrier, a taskgroup or a taskwait) and the endpoint scope (*i.e.* the beginning or the end of the synchronization). We use it for partitioning the dependency domain at the explicit task level. In the runtime version, the main Algorithm 1 for data race detection is triggered. This allows to reduce memory consumption by only keeping and applying resolution on one instance of the spawn-tree at the time. In post-mortem version, trace generation is performed by dumping local buffers to output files.

- **ompt_callback_task_create_t:** callback to register the creation of an explicit task. We use this callback to add a task node to our internal spawn tree representation at the creation of an explicit task. Such informations are stored in local buffers in the post-mortem version.

- **ompt_callback_dependences_t:** callback to register all dependencies specified on a new task. We retrieve the dependencies of the newly created task, and update the dependency *DAG* of the parent task node. Such informations are stored in local buffers in the post-mortem version.

OMPT Extensions. Section 4 highlights that it is necessary to know the data sharing attribute of a dependence to detect data races in the context of nested tasks with dependencies. The current OMPT interface exposes the scope of a parallel region, the spawning sequence of tasks and the dependencies between these tasks. But it lacks a way to provide information about data-sharing attributes at constructs, needed in our method to detect false positives. To do so, we propose the following extensions to the OMPT interfaces.

```
1   typedef void (*ompt_callback_task_create_t) (
2      ompt_data_t *          encountering_task_data ,
3      const ompt_frame_t *   encountering_task_frame ,
4      ompt_data_t *          new_task_data ,
5      int                    flags ,
6      int                    has_dependences ,
7      size_t                 array_data_attributes_size ,
8      void *                 array_data_attributes
9      const void *           codeptr_ra ,
10  );
```

Listing 1.6. Extension to ompt_callback_task_create_t

The data sharing attributes of each variable are retrieved at task creation. We extend the callback to also store an array with the data collection inherited from outer scope to the new task (see Listing 1.6). This array contains values for each variable: if a variable is shared, the array contains its address. If a variable is firstprivate, the array contains the variable value.

```
1  typedef struct ompt_dependence_s
2     ompt_data_t              variable;
3     ompt_dependence_type_t dependence_type;
4     int                      address_location;
5  ) ompt_dependence_t;
```

Listing 1.7. Extension to ompt_task_dependence_t

The location of the address variable used in the **depend** clause is required to eliminate false positive in our data race detection method. We extended the structure exposed in Listing 1.7 to include an *int* value to store this location.

6   Experimental Results

An enumeration of available applications using nested tasks with dependencies lead to a small set of candidates. Upon *ad hoc* test cases based on those presented throughout the whole paper and the modified Fibonacci, the Kastors benchmarks suite [13] provided a suitable candidate. The *Strassen* benchmark is a well-known algorithm for matrix multiplication that achieves lower execution bound than the regular method $O(n^3)$. It recursively splits the matrices and applies the Strassen method in a *divide and conquer* manner, until a specified cutoff is reached where the regular method turns back to be more efficient. We present the output format of our tool and its associated overhead on these benchmarks.

Output Description. The generated output goes along with the approach described as follows: the nodes of the spawn tree are numbered in a breadth-first search manner, therefore, the root has the number 0, each implicit task has the number between $[1, ..., N]$ where N is the number of threads participating to the parallel region, and the explicit tasks have a number between $[N, ..., M]$ where M is the total number of nodes in the spawn tree. Two conflicting nodes n and n' respectively belonging to the subtree where nodes rn and rn' are the roots and with dependencies d and d' on a variable address $addr$ generate the following output: $* addr<rn, n, d><rn', n', d'>$

```
> OMP_TOOL_LIBRARIES=Ompt_tool.so OMP_NUM_THREADS=2 mpcrun ./testCase3
* 0x2b7730422e70 < 1, 3, in >< 2, 6, out >
* 0x2b7730422e70 < 1, 4, out >< 2, 5, in >
* 0x2b7730422e70 < 1, 4, out >< 2, 6, out >
```

The small example above is the output of our tool for Listing 1.3. The corresponding spawn-tree is depicted in Fig. 1a. Our tool returns three potential data races: task 3 with task 6, task 4 with task 5 and task 4 with task 6. Theses pairs of tasks have dependencies on the same variable, with at least one being a write, so the analysis is true. A data race is possible as implicit tasks may run concurrently. Task 3 and task 5 have both read dependencies on the same variable, hence no order is required. Hence no issue is raised for this pair.

We also applied the Archer and the Tasksanitizer tools on this example. Tasksanitizer correctly unveils a data race, whereas for Archer, the analysis being

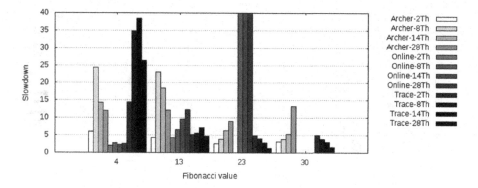

Fig. 3. Overhead for multiple fibonacci values and number of threads.

applied on the current execution scheduling, the data race is not detected on every run. Both tools, upon detection of a race condition, only retrieve a subset of possible cases/scheduling leading to the race condition. In our ad-hoc cases, Tasksanitizer did find many false positives, mainly arising from poorly support of *taskwait* and *dependencies* in nested tasks with dependencies context.

Study of Overhead. We evaluated our tool overhead on the Fibonacci and the Strassen benchmarks. The tests were conducted on an Intel XEON node with 28 physical cores and 186 GB of memory ram. In our results, we illustrate the slowdown factor (*i.e.* execution time with a tool divided by the time of the standard version of the code) for different tools: Archer, our tool with both online and post-mortem analysis. Tasksanitizer exhibited very high overhead for Fibonnacci (from one hundred to several thousands) and was segfaulting on Strassen, hence its results are not displayed.

Archer is more complete and performs more analyses than our tool. We use this time as an upper bound overhead to not overcome.

The evaluation of the modified Fibonacci was conduct on the Fibonacci values $fib(x)$, where $x \in \{4, 13, 23, 30\}$, representing respectively the creation of 12, 1128, 139101 and 4038804 tasks at runtime (see Fig. 3). For a small number of tasks, the online version is efficient, whereas the trace-based version is slower than Archer. This is due to our tracing mechanism which is very basic (no I/O delegation or asynchronism), and the cost of waiting to write the trace is too high regarding the benchmark execution time. For a large number of tasks the online version spends to much time checking each pair of tasks, and has prohibitive overhead. On the other hand, tracing becomes very competitive. The evaluation of the Strassen benchmark was conducted on square matrices with power of two sizes from 512 to 8192. Two cutoffs were set for the switching value to regular method and for the max depth, controlling the task nesting up to four levels. On Strassen (Fig. 4), overheads of both online and trace-based methods are lower than Archer. The slowdown is up to 7.7 for online resolution and a maximum of 4.6 for trace generation. With online resolution, only size 4096 provides high overheads. Further investigation is needed to understand these results.

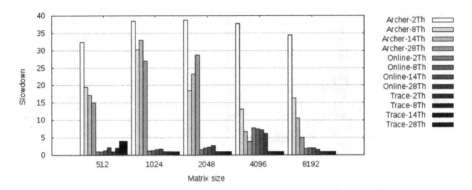

Fig. 4. Overhead for multiple Strassen matrix sizes and number of threads.

7 Conclusion

Since version 4.0, the OpenMP standard includes the notion of data dependencies between tasks created by the same parent (either another task or a thread). But combining nested tasks with data dependencies may lead to race conditions, some uncovering unexpressed/hidden dependencies. This paper proposed an algorithm to detect such problems based on the **depend** clauses exposed by the programmer. We implemented this method in a tool providing both dynamic and post mortem approaches, based on the recently released OMPT interface and our extensions for data sharing attributes. We demonstrated that this method can effectively detect race conditions with a reasonable slowdown compared to existing tools. The proposed OMPT extension for data sharing attributes can be useful for any tools relying on addresses passed in clauses. For future work, we plan to study a restricted use of code instrumentation to detect data accesses inside OpenMP tasks, and then be able to detect any data races between **depend** clauses and actual variable accesses.

Acknowledgments. This work was performed under the Exascale Computing Research collaboration, with the support of CEA, Intel and UVSQ.

References

1. OpenMP Architecture Review Board: OpenMP Application Program InterfaceVersion 5.0, November 2018
2. Pérez, J., Beltran, V., Labarta, J., Ayguadé, E.: Improving the integration of task nesting and dependencies in OpenMP. In: IEEE International Parallel and Distributed Processing Symposium, IPDPS 2017, pp. 809–818. IEEE Computer Society, Orlando, FL, USA (2017)
3. Virouleau, P., Roussel, A., Broquedis, F., Gautier, T., Rastello, F., Gratien, J.-M.: Description, implementation and evaluation of an affinity clause for task directives. In: Maruyama, N., de Supinski, B.R., Wahib, M. (eds.) IWOMP 2016. LNCS, vol. 9903, pp. 61–73. Springer, Cham (2016). https://doi.org/10.1007/978-3-319-45550-1_5

4. Rana, V.S., Lin M.: A scalable task parallelism approach for LU decomposition with multicore CPUs. In: Proceedings of Second International Workshop on Extreme Scale Programming Models and Middleware (ESPM2 2016), Salt Lake City, November 2016

5. Podobas, A., Brorsson, M., Vlassov, V.: TurboBŁYSK: scheduling for improved data-driven task performance with fast dependency resolution. In: DeRose, L., de Supinski, B.R., Olivier, S.L., Chapman, B.M., Müller, M.S. (eds.) IWOMP 2014. LNCS, vol. 8766, pp. 45–57. Springer, Cham (2014). https://doi.org/10.1007/978-3-319-11454-5_4

6. Ghane, M., Malik, A.M., Chapman, B., Qawasmeh, A.: False sharing detection in OpenMP applications using OMPT API. In: Terboven, C., de Supinski, B.R., Reble, P., Chapman, B.M., Müller, M.S. (eds.) IWOMP 2015. LNCS, vol. 9342, pp. 102–114. Springer, Cham (2015). https://doi.org/10.1007/978-3-319-24595-9_8

7. Agullo, E., Aumage, O., Bramas, B., Coulaud, O., Pitoiset, S.: Bridging the gap between OpenMP and task-based runtime systems for the fast multiple method. IEEE Trans. Parallel Distrib. Syst. (TPDS) **28**, 2794–2807 (2017)

8. Dinh, D., Harsha, S., Tang, Y.: Extending the nested parallel model to the nested dataflow model with provably efficient schedulers. In: Proceedings of the 28th Symposium on Parallelism in Algorithms and Architectures, SPAA 2016, pp. 49–60. ACM, Asilomar State Beach/Pacific Grove, CA, USA (2016)

9. Protze, J., et al.: Towards providing low-overhead data race detection for large OpenMP applications. In: Proceedings of the 2014 LLVM Compiler Infrastructure in HPC, LLVM 2014, pp. 40–47. IEEE Computer Society, New Orleans, LA, USA (2014)

10. Protze, J., Hahnfeld, J., Ahn, D.H., Schulz, M., Müller, M.S.: OpenMP tools interface: synchronization information for data race detection. In: de Supinski, B.R., Olivier, S.L., Terboven, C., Chapman, B.M., Müller, M.S. (eds.) IWOMP 2017. LNCS, vol. 10468, pp. 249–265. Springer, Cham (2017). https://doi.org/10.1007/978-3-319-65578-9_17

11. Matar, H.S., Unat, D.: Runtime determinacy race detection for OpenMP tasks. In: Aldinucci, M., Padovani, L., Torquati, M. (eds.) Euro-Par 2018. LNCS, vol. 11014, pp. 31–45. Springer, Cham (2018). https://doi.org/10.1007/978-3-319-96983-1_3

12. Eichenberger, A.E., et al.: OMPT: an OpenMP tools application programming interface for performance analysis. In: Rendell, A.P., Chapman, B.M., Müller, M.S. (eds.) IWOMP 2013. LNCS, vol. 8122, pp. 171–185. Springer, Heidelberg (2013). https://doi.org/10.1007/978-3-642-40698-0_13

13. Virouleau, P., et al.: Evaluation of OpenMP dependent tasks with the KASTORS benchmark suite. In: DeRose, L., de Supinski, B.R., Olivier, S.L., Chapman, B.M., Müller, M.S. (eds.) IWOMP 2014. LNCS, vol. 8766, pp. 16–29. Springer, Cham (2014). https://doi.org/10.1007/978-3-319-11454-5_2

14. Duran, A., Teruel, X., Ferrer, R., Martorell Bofill, X., Ayguadé Parra, E.: Barcelona OpenMP tasks suite: a set of benchmarks targeting the exploitation of task parallelism in OpenMP. In: Proceedings of the International Conference on Parallel Processing (ICPP) (2009)

15. Carribault, P., Pérache, M., Jourdren, H.: Enabling low-overhead hybrid MPI/OpenMP parallelism with MPC. In: Sato, M., Hanawa, T., Müller, M.S., Chapman, B.M., de Supinski, B.R. (eds.) IWOMP 2010. LNCS, vol. 6132, pp. 1–14. Springer, Heidelberg (2010). https://doi.org/10.1007/978-3-642-13217-9_1

A Proposal for Supporting Speculation in the OpenMP `taskloop` Construct

Juan Salamanca$^{(\boxtimes)}$ and Alexandro Baldassin

São Paulo State University, São Paulo, Brazil
{juan,alex}@rc.unesp.br

Abstract. Parallelization constructs in OpenMP, such as `parallel for` or `taskloop`, are typically restricted to loops that have no loop-carried dependencies (DOALL) or that contain well-known structured dependence patterns (e.g. reduction). These restrictions prevent the parallelization of many computational intensive *may* DOACROSS loops. In such loops, the compiler cannot prove that the loop is free of loop-carried dependencies, although they may not exist at runtime. This paper proposes a new clause for `taskloop` that enables speculative parallelization of *may* DOACROSS loops: the `tls` clause. We also present an initial evaluation that reveals that: (a) for certain loops, slowdowns using DOACROSS techniques can be transformed in speed-ups of up to 2.14× by applying speculative parallelization of tasks; and (b) the scheduling of tasks implemented in the Intel OpenMP runtime exacerbates the ratio of order inversion aborts after applying the `taskloop-tls` parallelization to a loop.

Keywords: `taskloop` · DOACROSS · Thread-Level Speculation

1 Introduction

Code parallelization is a research problem for which there are partial solutions. Loops account for most of the execution time of programs and thus much research has been dedicated to parallelizing the iterations of loops, including DOALL [9], DOACROSS [3], and DSWP [15] algorithms. Often these efforts are hindered by false dependencies that cannot be resolved by a compiler.

Although modern compilers implement many loop parallelization techniques, their application is typically restricted to loops that have no loop-carried dependencies (DOALL) or that contain well-known dependence patterns (e.g. reduction). These restrictions prevent the parallelization of many computational intensive non-DOALL loops. In such loops, the compiler can either: (a) find at least one loop-carried dependence (DOACROSS loop); or (b) cannot prove, at compile-time, that the loop is free of loop-carried dependencies, even though they might never show up at runtime. Theses dependencies are called *may* dependencies and the loop a *may* DOACROSS loop. In any case, most compilers assume

X. Fan et al. (Eds.): IWOMP 2019, LNCS 11718, pp. 246–261, 2019.
https://doi.org/10.1007/978-3-030-28596-8_17

that an actual loop-carried dependence occurs and give up parallelizing these loops, thus eliminating any possibility of extracting speed-ups from them.

Speculative techniques based on Thread-Level Speculation (TLS) of loop iterations have recently [19,20] demonstrated speed-ups that have not been achieved before for loops that have unpredictable loop-carried dependencies. Unfortunately, implementing such algorithms is a very complex and cumbersome task that demands an extensive re-writing of the loop. For this reason, most programmers and compilers typically do not use these algorithms, opting for not parallelizing (*may*) DOACROSS loops.

In addition to loops, there are other hot-code regions that the programmer or the compiler tries to parallelize. Task-based programming model simplifies it by providing annotations of dependencies between function calls (tasks). Thus, a runtime system manages these dependencies and schedules tasks to execute on cores. Differently from thread parallelism, task parallelism does not focus on mapping parallelism to threads, but it is oblivious of the physical layout and focuses on exposing more parallelism. Task parallelism was implemented to be more versatile than thread-level parallelism [2] and was added to OpenMP in version 3.0.

OpenMP 4.5 specification [13] added a new construct called `taskloop` that allows programmers to use the task-based programming model to parallelize loops in a similar fashion to the old `parallel for` construct. However, like `parallel for`, the use of the `taskloop` construct is restricted to loops that have no loop-carried dependencies (DOALL loops) or that contain well-known reduction patterns through the `reduction` clause (recently added in the OpenMP 5.0 specification [14]). These restrictions specifically preclude the acceleration of *may* DOACROSS loops with no dependencies at runtime.

This paper proposes a clause called `tls` that extends the OpenMP `taskloop` construct, enabling programmers to mark the loop as speculative when he/she or the compiler cannot prove that the loop is DOALL. The clause allows the parallelization of (*may*) DOACROSS loops using the Hardware-Transactional-Memory-based Thread-Level Speculation (TLS) algorithm described in [19], but reusing the mechanism of `taskloop` to create OpenMP explicit tasks and to divide the iterations between them. The TLS mechanism uses explicit tasks instead of threads as units of speculative parallelization.

For instance, the listing of Fig. 1 shows the code of a loop from susan_corners benchmark where, depending on the value of variable x, it updates a position of an array of corners indexed by n and increases by one the value of the variable n (initialized to 0). The loop is *may* DOACROSS because depending on the benchmark's input a loop-carried dependence on n can be generated, however it could also be free of dependencies at runtime.

According to the OpenMP API 5.0 [14], this loop is non-conforming for `taskloop` because it relies on the execution order of the iterations and must be serialized. Thus a compiler or programmer gives up parallelizing this loop, or parallelizes this using DOACROSS (for example, OpenMP `ordered` clause) yielding slowdowns respect to the serial execution. Figure 3 shows the

```
1    n=0;
2    #pragma omp parallel for ordered(1)...
3    for(i=5;i<y_size-5;i++){//loopV
4        #pragma omp ordered depend (sink:i-1)
5        for(j=5;j<x_size-5;j++){
6            x = r[i][j];
7            if (x>0 &&(/*compare x*/)){
8                corner_list[n].info=0;
9                corner_list[n].x=j;
10               ...
11               n++;
12           }
13       }
14       #pragma omp ordered depend (source)
15   }
```

```
1    n=0;
2    #pragma omp parallel num_threads(N_CORES)
3    #pragma omp single
4    #pragma omp taskloop tls(STRIP_SIZE)...
5    for(i=5;i<y_size-5;i++){//loopV
6        for(j=5;j<x_size-5;j++){
7            x = r[i][j];
8            if (x>0 &&(/*compare x*/)){
9                corner_list[n].info=0;
10               corner_list[n].x=j;
11               ...
12               n++;
13           }
14       }
15   }
```

Fig. 1. Fragment of susan_corners's loop (loopV) using ordered depend

Fig. 2. The same loop using tls clause and taskloop

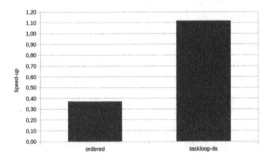

Fig. 3. Performance of loopV using ordered depend and taskloop-tls

speed-ups (with respect to sequential execution) of loopV (compiled with Clang and linked against the Intel OpenMP runtime) for the following cases: (a) when using ordered clause (left); and (b) when using taskloop and the proposed tls clause (right). Speed-ups measurements were performed in a quad-core Intel Skylake machine with TSX-NI support (Fig. 2).

As shown, the ordered serializes the execution of the iterations resulting in performance degradation due to the synchronization overhead. In the case of taskloop tls, TLS is used to parallelize the loop dividing the iterations to be executed speculatively in tasks, producing an improvement of 12%.

In this paper we make the following contributions:

- We propose a novel OpenMP clause (Sect. 3) that extends the taskloop construct and enables the programmer to parallelize (*may*) DOACROSS loops using TLS.
- We evaluate the taskloop tls clause. The initial experimental results (Sect. 5) shows the effectiveness of our proposed clause. We further compare against parallel for tls implemented in [19].

This paper is divided as follows. Section 2 describes the background to introduce our proposal. Section 3 details the design and implementation of the new clause `tls`. Benchmarks, methodology and settings are described in Sect. 4. Section 5 evaluates the performance of the clause. Section 6 discusses work related to this paper. Finally, Sect. 7 concludes the work.

2   Background

This section presents related works and the main concepts used in this paper: Task-based Parallelism, Transactional Memory, and Thread-Level Speculation.

2.1   Task-Based Parallelism

In this model the execution can be modeled as a directed acyclic graph, where nodes are tasks and edges define data dependencies between tasks. A runtime system schedules tasks whose dependencies are resolved over available worker threads.

To explore task-based programming models, OpenMP and Intel TBB are increasing their popularity thus confirming that the task abstraction is an intuitive construct. StarSs programming model family introduces the ability to extract task parallelism in the presence of data dependencies. These models use programmer annotations of input and output operands to tasks (kernel functions) to construct an inter-task data dependence graph dynamically. Calls to tasks are checked at runtime for dependencies by analyzing the addresses of their parameters and by using programmer annotations [4].

At runtime, task creation code packs the kernel code pointer and the task operands and puts them in the task pipeline; in this way, the generating thread can continue creating additional tasks. The pipeline decodes task dependencies, generates the dependence graph, and schedules tasks when they are ready [16].

OpenMP Tasks. Tasks in OpenMP are blocks of code that the compiler envelops and provides to be executed in parallel. Tasks were introduced to OpenMP in version 3.0 [2]. In OpenMP 4.0 [13] were introduced the `depend` clause and the `taskgroup` construct, and OpenMP 4.5 introduced the `taskloop` construct [13]. Like work-sharing constructs, tasks must be created inside of a `parallel` region. To spawn each task once, the `single` construct is used. The ordering of tasks is not defined, but there are ways to specify ordering: (a) with directives such as `taskgroup` and `taskwait`; and (b) with task dependencies (`depend` clause). The `depend` clause takes a type (`in`, `out`, or `inout`) followed by a variable or a list of variables. These types establish an order between sibling tasks. A `taskwait` clause waits for the child tasks of the current task. `taskgroup` is similar to `taskwait` but it waits for all descendant tasks created in the block.

The `taskloop` construct was proposed in [24] and allows parallelizing a loop by dividing its iterations into a number of created tasks, with each task being assigned to one or more iterations of the loop. The `grainsize` clause specifies how many iterations are assigned for each task and the number of tasks can be calculated automatically. OpenMP brings another clause called `priority` to specify the level of priority of each task used by the runtime scheduler [13]. `taskloop` is compliant with the `parallel for` construct, the main difference is the lack of schedule clause in the `taskloop` [17].

2.2 Transactional Memory

Transactional memory (TM) was proposed as architectural support to make lock-free synchronization as efficient as conventional parallelization approaches based on mutual exclusion [6]. TM simplifies parallel programming by enabling a mechanism to ensure the consistency of shared data. Transactional memory systems must provide transaction *atomicity* and *isolation*, which require the implementation of the following mechanisms: *data versioning management*, *conflict detection*, and *conflict resolution* [11]. In Transactional Memory, version management decides where new (speculative) and old data are stored. Conflict detection determines whether two operations executed in separate transactions cause a conflict, *i.e.* if they access a common memory location and at least one of the operations is a write. Conflict detection can be eager (detection is done immediately when the conflict occurs) or lazy (detection is done when transactions attempt to commit) [11]. A conflict causes at least one of the transactions involved in the conflict to abort and it may re-execute. Other actions could also be carried out to support a conflict-resolution policy. Resolution can happen eagerly when the conflict occurs or lazily when the transaction attempts to commit.

Intel TSX-NI. Intel TSX-NI provides developers an instruction-set interface to specify transactional execution [8] with two software interfaces: *Hardware Lock Elision* (HLE) and *Restricted Transactional Memory* (RTM). The RTM is an instruction-set extension that includes the instructions `xbegin`, `xend`, and `xabort`. When a transaction aborts, the state of the program immediately before the `xbegin` instruction is recovered, all speculatively written data are dismissed, and the values stored in registers are rolled back to their values prior to the transaction. The execution restarts at a program point specified by the address given as argument to the `xbegin` instruction. Data written transactionally are not visible to other transactions until the transaction commits by executing the `xend` instruction.

Intel TSX-NI does not guarantee that a conflict-free transaction will commit. Aborts may be caused by excess transactional reads or writes, conflicts due to false sharing, and instructions that cause aborts (*e.g.* system calls). All data conflicts are detected at the granularity of the 64-byte cache line because the implementation of TSX uses the L1 data cache to track transactional states using physical addresses and the cache coherence protocol.

2.3 Thread-Level Speculation

Torrellas defines Thread-Level Speculation (TLS) as an environment where execution threads operate speculatively, performing potentially unsafe operations, and temporarily buffering the state that they generate in a buffer [25]. Then, the operations of a thread are declared to be correct or incorrect. If they are correct, the thread commits; if they are incorrect, the thread is rolled back and typically restarted from its beginning. The term TLS is most often associated to a scenario where the goal is to parallelize a sequential application. However, in general, TLS can be applied to any environment where speculative threads are executed and can be squashed and restarted [25].

When a compiler cannot prove that a loop can be executed in parallel but it can estimate with high probability that the loop iterations will be independent at runtime, it can schedule the parallel execution of the loop speculatively. A mechanism is then necessary to detect when a dependence does occur at runtime and to re-execute the loop iterations that were compromised. This technique is known as Thread-Level Speculation. TLS has been widely studied [21–23]. For performance, TLS requires hardware mechanisms that support four primary features: conflict detection, speculative storage, in-order commit of transactions, and transaction roll-back. However, to this day there is no off-the-shelf processor that provides direct support for TLS. Speculative execution is supported, however, in the form of Hardware Transactional Memory (HTM) available in processors such as the Intel Core and the IBM POWER. HTM implements three out of the four key features required by TLS: conflict detection, speculative storage, and transaction roll-back. And thus these architectures have the potential to be used to implement TLS.

3 Our Proposal

This section presents the proposed extension to OpenMP that enables programmers to easily annotate loops that should speculatively execute explicit tasks generated by `taskloop`. This extension allows programmers to parallelize *may* DOACROSS loops and to tune parameters such as strip size to improve performance.

3.1 Use of the Clause

The use of the `tls` clause for `tasklooop` is syntactically similar to the `grainsize` clause, thus they are mutually exclusive and should not appear on the same `taskloop` directive. The syntax is the same of *taskloop*:

```
#pragma omp taskloop tls(strip_size) [clause[[, ] clause] ... ]
for-loops
```

where:

- *clause* can be any clause allowed for `taskloop` except `grainsize` and `num_tasks`.

- *strip_size* is the number of iterations assigned to each speculative task generated by `taskloop`. In compiler parlance, it is said that the loop is partitioned into strips, and thus this size is often called the *strip size* of the loop.

```
1   #pragma omp parallel num_thread(N_CORES)
2   #pragma omp single
3   #pragma omp taskloop tls(STRIP_SIZE) shared(glob,A) firstprivate(n)
4   for (i = INI; i < n; i++) {
5       if (cond)
6           glob++;
7       else
8           glob=i;
9       A[i]= glob*i;
10  }
```

Fig. 4. Code using OpenMP `taskloop` and `tls` clause

```
1   int next_strip_to_commit=INI;
2
3   #pragma omp parallel num_thread(N_CORES)
4   #pragma omp single
5   #pragma omp taskloop grainsize(1) shared(glob,A) firstprivate(n)
6   for (i = INI; i < n; i+=STRIP_SIZE) {
7       int speculative = BEGIN(&next_strip_to_commit,i)
8       // if speculative is 1, the explicit task starts a transaction T which runs STRIP_SIZE
            speculative iterations
9
10      for (int ii=i; ii < n && ii - i < STRIP_SIZE; ii++) {
11          // previous loop body replacing i with ii
12      }
13
14      END(speculative, &next_strip_to_commit, i);
15      next_strip_to_commit+=STRIP_SIZE;
16  }
```

Fig. 5. Resulting code converted to standard OpenMP

3.2   Implementation of the Clause

Clang 4.0 was adapted to generate the AST(*Abstract Syntax Tree*) to support the new clause. For the following discussion consider Fig. 5, which shows the OpenMP translated code from Fig. 4. The translation mechanism consists of the following steps:

(a) Create a new `int` variable called `next_strip_to_commit` which is `shared` for the construct and controls the order of transaction commits. This variable is initialized to the value of the first iteration, `INI` in this case (Line 1);

(b) Set `grainsize` to 1 (Line 5). Now it is the `tls` clause that controls the chunk of iterations that each explicit task will execute;

(c) Create variable `ii` (`private` for the construct) and apply strip mining transformation to the loop using `ii` and a size of strips equal to `STRIP_SIZE` (Lines 6 and 10). The resulting loop body of the inner loop, `i` is replaced by `ii`;

(d) Insert a call to the BEGIN function at the entry of the loop body (Line 7). At runtime, each explicit task created by `taskloop` will execute the BEGIN function, thus the task will create a transaction T that encapsulates STRIP_SIZE speculative iterations. The size of the strip is specified as parameter of the clause;

(e) Insert a call to END function at the end of the loop body (Line 14). Thus, the task will try to commit the transaction T if all task with previous strips have already committed and no conflict is detected, otherwise the task will abort and re-start T;

(f) Insert a statement to increment `next_strip_to_commit` by STRIP_SIZE and thus enable other tasks to commit (Line 15).

3.3   How the Clause Works

The `parallel` construct creates a team of OpenMP threads that execute the explicit tasks created by `taskloop`. The number of threads in the example is equal to the number of physical cores because, as explained in previous work [18], to achieve performance in TLS it is necessary to bound each software thread to one hardware thread since it avoids aborts due to the interference between threads when executing on the same core. With the `single` construct, the taskloop construct is executed by only one of the threads in the team. This thread encounters the `taskloop` which partitions the iterations of the loop into explicit tasks which are scheduled at runtime to be executed by the team of threads.

The data environment of each generated task follows the data-sharing attribute clauses defined in the `taskloop` construct. For the example, variables `glob` and A are declared as `shared` and variable n as `firstprivate`. Other variables are `shared` by default. The `grainsize` clause is set to 1 because if a value greater than 1 is defined the performance degrades since more transactions are created and therefore aborted by the task. As explained in previous work [20], the overhead of starting, finishing and aborting transactions is high.

Figure 6 shows some possible executions of the `taskloop tls` for the loop of Fig. 4, more details about how coarse-grained TLS is implemented on HTM can be found in previous work [18].

The order of creation of tasks is not specified in OpenMP. The `taskloop` construct does not include a `schedule` clause, although it was proposed by Teruel et al. [24]. Therefore, the scheduling of tasks completely depends on the runtime. When using threads, TLS takes advantage of a schedule similar to `static` because it has to be ensure the in-order commits of transactions (Fig. 6a–b). When `static` is defined in the `schedule` clause, for `parallel for` for example, the iterations are divided into chunks of a specified size, and these chunks are assigned to threads in a round-robin (in the order of thread numbers) and `monotonic` fashion (in the increasing iteration order). Similarly, depending on the loop and the load balancing of iterations, `dynamic` could work well in TLS but just in a `monotonic` way.

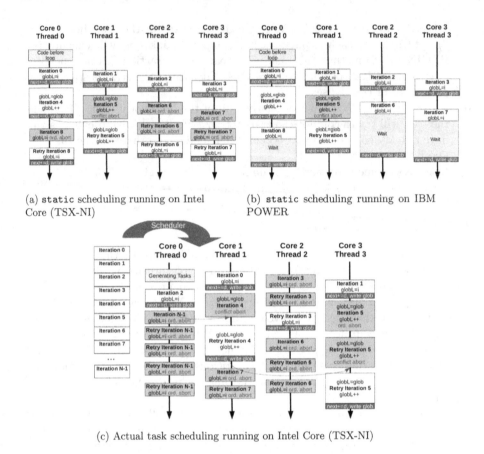

(a) `static` scheduling running on Intel Core (TSX-NI)

(b) `static` scheduling running on IBM POWER

(c) Actual task scheduling running on Intel Core (TSX-NI)

Fig. 6. Possible execution flows of Fig. 4 with `STRIP_SIZE`=1 and `N_CORES`=4

However, no kind of schedule is implemented for `taskloop` in OpenMP. This fact could cause a loss of performance in TLS for `taskloop` since the scheduling could be non-monotonic (Fig. 6c), meaning that explicit tasks executing higher iterations could be scheduled before than lower ones. Hence, transactions executed by explicit tasks of higher iterations will abort by ordered inversion—a kind of abort where a transaction that completes execution out of order is rolled-back using an explicit abort instruction (`xabort`) [20].

For instance, Fig. 6a shows how `taskloop tls` could work if the tasks were scheduled in a `static` fashion like used in the thread-level model in OpenMP. Thus, it is similar to `parallel for tls` proposed in [19]. Nevertheless, as mentioned before the task-level model relies on the runtime scheduler to distribute tasks onto cores and thus enabling load balancing and work stealing. In this way, no scheduling policy has been integrated and a more realistic execution flow is shown in Fig. 6c.

Table 1. Loops extracted from `cBench` applications.

Loop ID	Benchmark	Location	Function/Method	%Cov	Invocations
A	`automotive_bitcount`	`bitcnts.c,65`	`main1`	100%	560
E	`automotive_susan_s`	`susan.c,725`	`susan_smoothing`	100%	22050
H	`automotive_susan_e`	`susan.c,1117`	`susan_edges`	18%	374
I	`automotive_susan_e`	`susan.c,1056`	`susan_edges`	56%	374
V	`automotive_susan_c`	`susan.c,1614`	`susan_corners`	7%	782

Aborts by order inversion are a problem when using TLS on TSX-NI due to the lack of suspended transactions as previous works showed [20]. However, the problem is exacerbated in task-parallelism model by a possible non-monotonic scheduling as shown in Fig. 6c. A solution for this problem would be to implement a `schedule` clause for `taskloop` (as proposed in [24]) that supports `monotonic:dynamic` modifier.

The problem of aborts caused by order inversion is mitigated in IBM POWER since this architecture implements instructions to suspend and to resume a transaction which can be used to implement ordered transactions (Fig. 6b). This fact can be exploited by the task scheduler because OpenMP tasks can then be suspended. The idea would be to force a *task scheduling point* inside the non-transactional fragment that implements ordered transactions in a task $T1$ generated by `taskloop tls`, thus the thread executing $T1$ may switch to another task $T2$. $T1$ would be suspended but the transaction executing the assigned iterations would not be aborted. Thus, parallelism could be increased because other tasks would be executed instead of only waiting. In the example of Fig. 6b, iterations 9 or 10 could be executed in the range of time that Thread 2 is waiting.

4   Benchmarks, Methodology and Experimental Setup

The performance assessment in this work reports speed-ups and abort/commit ratios (transaction outcome) for the `taskloop-tls` and `for-tls` [19] parallelizations of *may* DOACROSS loops[1] from the Collective Benchmark (`cBench`) benchmark suite [5] running on Intel Core. For all experiments the default input is used for the `cBench` benchmarks. The baseline for speed-up comparisons is the serial execution of the same benchmark program compiled at the same optimization level. Loop times are compared to calculate speed-ups. Each software thread is bounded to one hardware thread (core). Each benchmark was run twenty times and the average time is used. Runtime variations were negligible and are not presented.

Loops were annotated with the proposed clause `taskloop tls`, following the syntax described in Sect. 3. They were then executed using an Intel Core

---

[1] Small %lc. `ordered` results in performance degradation respect to serial execution for these loops [10].

Table 2. Characterization and TLS execution of loops.

Loop ID	Loop Characterization			Execution				
	N	%lc	Average Iteration Size	Speculative Privatization	taskloop-tls		parallelfor-tls	
					ss	Speed-up	ss	Speed-up
A	1125000	0%	12 B	Reduction	502	1.71	502	1.77
E	600	0%	14 B	Array	25	1.03	15	1.70
H	442	0%	3 KB	Array	1	2.14	1	3.06
I	444	0%	4 KB	Array	1	1.08	2	1.55
V	440	34%	1 KB	Scalar	4	1.12	1	1.14

i7-6700HQ machine, and their speed-ups measured with respect to sequential execution. Table 1 lists the loops used in the study. The table shows (1) the ID of the loop in this study; (2) the benchmark of the loop; (3) the file/line of the target loop in the source code; (4) the function where the loop is located; (5) %Cov, the fraction of the total execution time spent in the loop; and (6) the number of invocations of the loop in the whole program.

This study uses an Intel Core i7-6700HQ processor with 4 cores with 2-way SMT, running at 2.6 GHz, with 16 GB of memory on Ubuntu 16.04.6 LTS (GNU/Linux 4.4.0-146-generic x86_64). The cache-line prefetcher is enabled by default. Each core has a 32 KB L1 data cache and a 256 KB L2 unified cache. The four cores share an 6144KB L3 cache. The benchmarks are compiled with customized Clang 4.0[2] at optimization level -O3 and with the set of flags specified in each benchmark program. Code compiled by clang -fopenmp was linked against the Intel OpenMP Runtime Library. To guarantee that each software thread is bound to one hardware thread (core), the environment variable KMP_AFFINITY is set to granularity=fine,scatter.

5   Experimental Results

The features used to characterize the loops are shown in the first part of Table 2: (1) N, the average number of loop iterations; (2) %lc, the percentage of iterations that have actual RAW loop-carried dependencies (excluding dependencies due to reduction operations) for the default input; and (3) the average size in bytes read/written by an iteration. The parameters in the right side of Table 2 describe: (1) the type of privatization within each transaction used in TLS implementation [19][3]; (2) ss, the *strip size* used for the experimental evaluation of taskloop tls; (3) the average speed-ups with four threads for taskloop tls; (5) the ss for for tls; and (6) the speed-ups for for tls.

For loop A and V, the parallelization with taskloop tls achieves almost the same for-tls speed-ups when a team with 4 threads is used. When a team with less than 4 threads is created, the taskloop-tls performance degrades, specially with 2 threads. The cause of this effect, which we call the *lost thread effect*, is

---

[2] Clang 4.0 was adapted to generate AST to support the new clause as explained in Sect. 3.

[3] Speculative privatizations described in [19] were implemented manually.

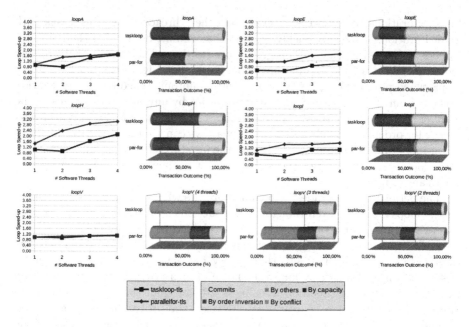

Fig. 7. Speed-ups and Abort ratios for `taskloop-tls` and `parallel-for-tls` execution on Intel Core (TSX-NI)

```
4 threads
=========
Core | Event0 | Event1 | Event2 | Event3
   0     8 K    1029 K    5768    1022 K
   1    391 K    123 K    6649     116 K
   2    404 K    126 K    6529     119 K
   3    403 K    126 K    6435     118 K

2 threads
=========
Core | Event0 | Event1 | Event2 | Event3
   0     5 K    2957 K    6232    2939 K
   1    122        7        7        0
```

```
3 threads
=========
Core | Event0 | Event1 | Event2 | Event3
   0     5 K    1405 K    5792    1394 K
   1    552 K     12 K    4277       4 K
   2    594 K     13 K    4595       4 K



Event0: Commits
Event1: Aborts
Event2: Conflict aborts
Event3: Order-inversion aborts
```

Fig. 8. Number of aborts for each thread (core) after executing loop A using `taskloop tls` (measured by `PCM-TSX` [8])

due to the Intel OpenMP Runtime, which schedules one thread (probably the generator that encounters `single`) to execute tasks that only manipulates higher iterations (for example, $N-1$), thus it aborts due to order inversion all the time as described in the example shown in Fig. 6c of Sect. 3. To confirm this hypothesis, we measured the aborts varying the number of threads. The results for loop V are shown as abort ratios in Fig. 7, and for loop A as number of transactions aborted for each core in Fig. 8.

In both cases, order-inversion aborts significantly increase as the number of threads is reduced, specifically the thread bounded to core 0 (the lost thread) as shown in Fig. 8. It makes sense since when a thread is executing tasks with higher iterations, it is necessary that the other threads (executing tasks with lower iterations) progress quickly to start the commit; however, if there are less threads in the team, they will progress more slowly and the lost thread will stay more time aborting due to order inversion. For loop V, Fig. 7 also shows the abort ratios when `parallel-for-tls` (static and monotonic schedule) parallelization is carried out; and, as expected, the abort ratios by any reason decreases as the number of threads is reduced. For `taskloop tls`, the abort ratios also decreases except for order-inversion aborts. In this way, we can see that Intel runtime uses a non-monotonic scheduling of tasks and the lost-thread effect is analogue in the other loops, and thus is the main cause to not achieving a better performance with `taskloop tls`.

The performance degrades with `taskloop tls` with a team of only one thread for the loops E and I—even though no transactions is started—because speculative privatizations of arrays are used. As explained in [19], temporal arrays are created to avoid false sharing; however, it just generates overhead when only one thread is executing. Notice also that loop V has actual loop-carried dependencies as shown in Table 2, making the choice of ss a critical decision. `taskloop tls` parallelization of this loop uses an ss greater than that of `for tls` to be more performant, but a coarser strip increases the probability of loop-carried dependencies as more iterations could conflict, thus causing the increase of the conflict-abort ratio.

In general, the implementation of a dynamic and monotonic scheduling for `taskloop` could achieve results closer to `for tls`, or even better, because `taskloop tls` can take advantage of the ability of the scheduler to suspend tasks which could be used in ordered transactions implemented with the suspend/resume instructions (POWER PC) to increase task parallelism. We intend to investigate this hypothesis in future works.

Furthermore, as explained in previous works, coarse-grained TLS algorithm results in a poor performance for actual DOACROSS loops ($\%lc = 100\%$) due to the large conflict-abort ratios [10,12,19]. Thus, DOACROSS techniques (e.g. `ordered`) perform better than TLS for this kind of loops [10].

6 Related Work

Salamanca *et al.* use TLS to speculate a (strip-mined) iteration and perform conflict detection and resolution at the end of the iteration to detect RAW dependence violations [18,20]. They describe how speculation support designed for HTM can also be used to implement TLS [18]. They focused their work on the impact of false sharing and the importance of judicious strip mining and privatization to achieve performance. They also provide a detailed description of the additional software support that is necessary for both the Intel Core and the IBM POWER8 architectures to enable TLS. Moreover, in [19], they also propose a implementation of fine-grained TLS and explain how to implement it on HTMs. Furthermore, they introduce an OpenMP extension to enable the implementation of coarse-grained TLS in [19]. This paper extends [19] by providing programmers a new clause to parallelize loops using `taskloop tls`.

Teruel *et al.* propose a worksharing-like construct called `taskloop` that distributes iterations of a loop in explicit tasks thus increasing opportunities for exploiting parallelism. They present an initial evaluation that demonstrates that the construct improves performance for some, but not all, applications [24]. This paper extends `taskloop` by enabling the speculative parallelization of tasks generated by the construct.

Podobas *et al.* study performance differences between `parallel for` and `taskloop` constructs. They introduce an efficient implementation for load balancing of task-loop iterations. They show that their `taskloop` implementation achieved an improvement of 3.2% when compared to `parallel for`.

XL C/C++ compiler for BG/Q supports a `speculative for` directive to speculatively parallelize `for` loops [7]. Aldea *et al.* propose to augment OpenMP capabilites by adding Sofware-based Thread-Level Speculation (STLS) support through a new STLS runtime library and a new clause called `speculative` to ensure the order of loop-carried dependencies [1]. This paper also proposes an extension to OpenMP—the clause `tls` for `taskloop`—that supports the specification of a loop strip size.

7 Conclusions

This paper introduces a novel clause to OpenMP, `taskloop tls`, that enables programmers to parallelize *may* DOACROSS loops using speculative task execution without imposing any significant burden. The parameter to specify strip size in the clause allows for selecting suitable strip mining strategies for TLS. Moreover, a preliminary evaluation of the performance of the clause was carried out, comparing it against `for tls` and providing interest insights on the issues in the task scheduler of Intel runtime that limit performance.

Acknowledgments. The authors would like to thank the anonymous reviewers for the insightful comments. This work is supported by FAPESP (grants 18/07446-8 and 18/15519-5).

References

1. Aldea, S., Estebanez, A., Llanos, D.R., Gonzalez-Escribano, A.: An OpenMP extension that supports thread-level speculation. IEEE Trans. Parallel Distrib. Syst. **27**(1), 78–91 (2016)
2. Ayguade, E., et al.: The design of OpenMP tasks. IEEE Trans. Parallel Distrib. Syst. (TPDS) **20**(3), 404–418 (2009)
3. Cytron, R.: Doacross: beyond vectorization for multiprocessors. In: International Conference on Parallel Processing (ICPP), pp. 836–844 (1986)
4. Etsion, Y., et al.: Task superscalar: an out-of-order task pipeline. In: International Symposium on Microarchitecture, Washington, DC, USA, pp. 89–100 (2010)
5. cTuning Foundation: Cbench: collective benchmarks (2016). http://ctuning.org/cbench

6. Herlihy, M., Moss, J.E.: Transactional memory: architectural support for lock-free data structures. In: International Symposium on Computer Architecture (ISCA), San Diego, CA, USA, pp. 289–300, May 1993
7. IBM: IBM XL C/C++ for Blue Gene/Q, V12.1 Compiler Reference (2012). http://www-01.ibm.com/support/docview.wss?uid=swg27027065&aid=1
8. Intel Corporation: Intel architecture instruction set extensions programming reference. Chapter 8: Intel transactional synchronization extensions (2012)
9. Lamport, L.: The parallel execution of do loops. Commun. ACM **17**(2), 83–93 (1974)
10. Mattos, L., Cesar, D., Salamanca, J., de Carvalho, J.P.L., Pereira, M., Araujo, G.: Doacross parallelization based on component annotation and loop-carried probability. In: International Symposium on Computer. Architecture and High Performance Computing (SBAC-PAD), Lyon, France, pp. 29–32 (2018)
11. Moore, K.E., Bobba, J., Moravan, M.J., Hill, M.D., Wood, D.A.: LogTM: log-based transactional memory. In: High-Performance Computer Architecture (HPCA), pp. 254–265 (2006)
12. Murphy, N., Jones, T., Mullins, R., Campanoni, S.: Performance implications of transient loop-carried data dependences in automatically parallelized loops. In: International Conference on Compiler Construction (CC), Barcelona, Spain, pp. 23–33 (2016)
13. OpenMP-ARB: OpenMP application program interface version 4.5 (2015)
14. OpenMP-ARB: OpenMP application program interface version 5.0 (2018)
15. Ottoni, G., Rangan, R., Stoler, A., August, D.I.: Automatic thread extraction with decoupled software pipelining. In: International Symposium on Microarchitecture (MICRO), p. 12, November 2005
16. Perez, J.M., Badia, R.M., Labarta, J.: A dependency-aware task-based programming environment for multi-core architectures. In: 2008 IEEE International Conference on Cluster Computing, Tsukuba, Japan, pp. 142–151 (2008)
17. Podobas, A., Karlsson, S.: Towards unifying OpenMP under the task-parallel paradigm. In: International Workshop on OpenMP (IWOMP), Nara, Japan, pp. 116–129 (2016)
18. Salamanca, J., Amaral, J.N., Araujo, G.: Evaluating and improving thread-level speculation in hardware transactional memories. In: IEEE International Parallel and Distributed Processing Symposium (IPDPS), Chicago, USA, pp. 586–595 (2016)
19. Salamanca, J., Amaral, J.N., Araujo, G.: Using hardware-transactional-memory support to implement thread-level speculation. IEEE Trans. Parallel Distrib. Syst. **29**(2), 466–480 (2018)
20. Salamanca, J., Amaral, J.N., Araujo, G.: Performance evaluation of thread-level speculation in off-the-shelf hardware transactional memories. In: Rivera, F.F., Pena, T.F., Cabaleiro, J.C. (eds.) Euro-Par 2017. LNCS, vol. 10417, pp. 607–621. Springer, Cham (2017). https://doi.org/10.1007/978-3-319-64203-1_44
21. Sohi, G.S., Breach, S.E., Vijaykumar, T.N.: Multiscalar processors. In: International Symposium on Computer Architecture (ISCA), Santa Margherita Ligure, Italy, pp. 414–425 (1995)
22. Steffan, J., Mowry, T.: The potential for using thread-level data speculation to facilitate automatic parallelization. In: High-Performance Computer Architecture (HPCA), Washington, USA, pp. 2–13 (1998)

23. Steffan, J.G., Colohan, C.B., Zhai, A., Mowry, T.C.: A scalable approach to thread-level speculation. In: International Conference on Computer Architecture (ISCA), Vancouver, British Columbia, Canada, pp. 1–12 (2000)
24. Teruel, X., Klemm, M., Li, K., Martorell, X., Olivier, S.L., Terboven, C.: A proposal for task-generating loops in OpenMP*. In: International Workshop on OpenMP (IWOMP), Camberra, Australia (2013)
25. Torrellas, J.: Speculation, thread-level. In: Padua, D. (ed.) Encyclopedia of Parallel Computing, pp. 1894–1900. Springer, Boston (2011). https://doi.org/10.1007/978-0-387-09766-4_170

OpenMP Task Generation for Batched Kernel APIs

Jinpil Lee[1]([✉]), Yutaka Watanabe[2], and Mitsuhisa Sato[1,2]

[1] RIKEN Center for Computational Science, Kobe, Japan
{jinpil.lee,msato}@riken.jp
[2] Graduate School of Systems and Information Engineering, University of Tsukuba, Tsukuba, Japan
ywatanabe@hpcs.cs.tsukuba.ac.jp

Abstract. The demand for calculating many small computation kernels is getting significantly important in the HPC area not only for the traditional numerical applications but also recent machine learning applications. While many-core accelerators such as GPUs are power-efficient compute platforms, a large amount of code modification is required. Batched kernel APIs such as batched BLAS can schedule numerical kernels efficiently on the target hardware while it still needs manual code modification. In this paper, we propose a code translation technique to generate batched kernel APIs in a high-level programming model. We use OpenMP task parallelism to specify dependency among numerical kernels. The user adds the *task* directives to specify tasks so that the compiler can recognize numerical kernels. The compiler detects conventional numerical kernels in the code and creates a unique batch ID for each kernel. When the task runtime detects tasks with the same batch ID, they are merged into a batch. The current implementation supports NVIDIA GPUs and batched BLAS in cuBLAS. DGEMM kernels can be detected and translated into batched DGEMM. A trivial DGEMM loop and blocked Cholesky decomposition code are used for performance evaluation. The evaluation result shows that batched DGEMM improves the performance when the matrix size is small and the number of DGEMM kernels is large. The time for DGEMMs in blocked Cholesky decomposition is 4 times faster than sequential execution when using batched DGEMM (4096×4096 matrix, tile size 128), however the overall performance is improved 36% because of task/batch management overhead.

Keywords: OpenMP · Task parallelism · Accelerator · Batched BLAS

1 Introduction

Numerical applications such as calculating large linear algebra problems can be decomposed into smaller kernels. For example, a large matrix-matrix multiplication can be solved by calculating multiplication of their submatrices. With the growth of machine learning, researchers find that some Artificial Intelligent (AI)

© Springer Nature Switzerland AG 2019
X. Fan et al. (Eds.): IWOMP 2019, LNCS 11718, pp. 262–273, 2019.
https://doi.org/10.1007/978-3-030-28596-8_18

applications generate hundreds of independent computation kernels of small data size, as a result, the demand for calculating a large number of small computation kernels is getting significantly important in the High Performance Computing (HPC) area. Many researches have been conducted to handle this situation efficiently with many architectures including current many-core accelerators.

Accelerators with many-core architecture such as GPUs are widely used in HPC since increasing the number of cores is an efficient way to build an energy efficient hardware. High-performance numerical libraries such as Basic Linear Algebra Subprograms (BLAS) are widely used to program those accelerators. Since these libraries are carefully designed to achieve high performance on the target architecture, it is often the best choice to use them if it can program the target application. Since each routine is designed to use the entire hardware resources, it cannot exploit the parallel architecture of current many-core accelerators with small data sizes.

The batched kernel Application Programming Interface (API) such as batched BLAS provide a programming interface to gather multiple compute kernels and calculate them in a single task, called a *batch*. The implementation of batched APIs for many-core architectures are designed to exploit the target parallel architecture by scheduling compute kernels on multiple cores. It requires code modification such as translation from the conventional kernel API (e.g. BLAS DGEMM, matrix-matrix multiplication in double precision) into the batched kernel API (e.g. batched DGEMM). How to rewrite the code depends on the target architecture because there is no standard specification or high-level programming model for batched kernel APIs.

The aim of our research is to invent a code translation technique from conventional numerical kernel APIs into the batched versions. We use OpenMP task parallelism to provide a high-level programming model for this purpose. OpenMP has been the de facto standard for thread-level parallel programming. In the early version of the OpenMP specification, data parallelism is the only way to exploit the performance of the target parallel architecture. OpenMP directives such as *parallel for* describe work sharing of loops with the global synchronization after the parallel execution. Along with the trend of many-core architecture, synchronization overhead gets bigger and load imbalance among cores causes significant performance degradation. Dynamic task parallelism has been introduced in OpenMP 3.0 to deal with imbalanced workload. In OpenMP 4.0, dependency among tasks can be specified using the *depend* clause.

The rest of the paper is organized as follows: Sect. 2 shows related work. In Sect. 3, we give a brief overview of batched BLAS and its interoperability with OpenMP. In Sect. 4, we propose a code translation technique for batched kernel APIs by using OpenMP task parallelism. After that, we show how our implementation translates OpenMP task directives into batched kernel API function calls. In Sect. 5, two benchmark codes are evaluated using batched BLAS in NVIDIA cuBLAS. Finally, we discuss the future work and conclude the paper and in Sect. 6 (Fig. 1).

```
1  void calc_dgemms(const int num_kernels, const int n,
2                   double **A, double **B, double **C,
3                   double *DMONE, double *DONE) {
4    for (int i = 0; i < num_kernels; i++) {
5      cublasDgemm(handle, CUBLAS_OP_N, CUBLAS_OP_N,
6                  n, n, n, &DMONE, A[i], n, B[i], n, &DONE, C[i], n);
7      cudaDeviceSynchronize();
8    }
9  }
```

Fig. 1. Calculating multiple DGEMM kernels in a loop

2 Related Work

Task parallelism can exploit potential parallelism in irregular applications and reduce synchronization overhead by fine-grain synchronization among dependent tasks [6,7,9]. Watanabe et al. [12] has investigated the trade-off between the matrix size and the number of DGEMM kernels, which has inspired us to use batched kernel APIs with OpenMP tasks.

Batched BLAS is the only batched kernel API currently available at the time. Intel Math Kernel Library (MKL) [5] implements batched BLAS for Intel CPU architectures. The NVIDIA CUDA programming environment provides its own BLAS implementation, named cuBLAS [8] for their GPU architectures. cuBLAS has batched BLAS kernel APIs including batched DGEMM. One of the difficulties in using batched BLAS is that there is no standard specification. Relton et al. [11] have compared several batched kernel APIs to establish a standard API for batched BLAS. Dongarra et al. [2–4] have proposed a batched BLAS interface for solving linear algebra kernels which can be decomposed into smaller submatrices. The effort is extended to cover whole BLAS APIs supporting various architectures including general-purpose CPUs and many-core accelerators. These researches have been conducted to provide a standard for batched kernel APIs, which still requires manual code modification. There is no programming model to generate batched kernel code from high-level description such as OpenMP directives.

3 Batched APIs on Accelerators

This section gives a brief overview of batched kernel APIs. We have chosen batched BLAS as the target API, however the code translation technique itself is general and can be adapted to other APIs.

Listing 1 shows an example code that uses cuBLAS with NVIDIA GPUs. The code calculates multiple DGEMM kernels in a loop. If we can assume that each kernel is independent to the others, we can make them calculated in parallel by using existing parallel programming models (Fig. 3).

Figure 2 shows parallel execution on a GPU using various programming models. Assume that there is a workload that can be divided equally into multiple smaller chunks. When the user writes a sequential code, each workload will be processed sequentially on the GPU (1 in Fig. 2).

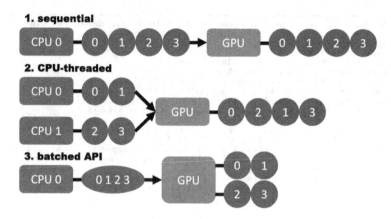

Fig. 2. Parallel execution on a GPU

```
1  void calc_dgemms_batched(const int num_kernels, const int n,
2                           double **A, double **B, double **C,
3                           double *DMONE, double *DONE) {
4    cublasDgemmBatched(handle, CUBLAS_OP_N, CUBLAS_OP_N,
5                       n, n, n, &DMONE, A, n, B, n,
6                       &DONE, C, n, num_kernels);
7    cudaDeviceSynchronize();
8  }
```

Fig. 3. Calculating multiple DGEMM kernels with batched BLAS API

To write a parallel code, the first choice would be OpenMP. The user can add the *parallel for* directive to the loop statement so that the workload will be distributed onto CPU cores (2 in Fig. 2). However, the performance will not be improved by this approach. It is because that the execution of DGEMM kernels are serialized in the same GPU stream even if each kernel is invoked by a different host thread[1]. If you are using CPUs and BLAS routines such as Intel MKL, OpenMP can make DGEMM kernels executed in parallel on the target CPU and the performance will be improved.

Batched APIs can solve this problem. Listing 3 shows an example code of batched DGEMM in cuBLAS. The main difference between *cublasDgemm()* and *cublasDgemmBatched()* is that the batched version takes the lists of array pointers as arguments. batched DGEMM in cuBLAS exploits GPU architecture by using parallelism in a batch. Each independent DGEMM kernel in a batch is scheduled on separate GPU cores (3 in Fig. 2) so that the computation time will be reduced[2].

---

[1] The *target* directive cannot deal with this situation because cuBLAS routines should be called from the CPU side and it offloads the calculation onto the GPU internally.

[2] Another choice is using multiple streams on GPUs by modifying code with CUDA APIs. Since there is no standard high-level programming interface, the code modification requires deep understanding of target GPU architecture and significant coding time.

```
1  void cholesky_decomposition(const int tile_size , const int num_tiles ,
2                              double* A[nt][nt]) {
3  #pragma omp parallel
4  #pragma omp single
5    for (int k = 0; k < num_tiles; k++) {
6  #pragma omp task depend(out:A[k][k])
7        dpotrf(A[k][k], tile_size , tile_size);
8        for (int i = k + 1; i < num_tiles; i++) {
9  #pragma omp task depend(in:A[k][k]) depend(out:A[k][i])
10           dtrsm(A[k][k], A[k][i], tile_size , tile_size);
11       }
12       for (int i = k + 1; i < num_tiles; i++) {
13           for (int j = k + 1; j < i; j++) {
14  #pragma omp task depend(in:A[k][i], A[k][j]) depend(out:A[j][i])
15               dgemm(A[k][i], A[k][j], A[j][i], tile_size , tile_size);
16           }
17  #pragma omp task depend(in:A[k][i]) depend(out:A[i][i])
18           dsyrk(A[k][i], A[i][i], tile_size , tile_size);
19       }
20    }
21 }
```

Fig. 4. Blocked Cholesky decomposition code in OpenMP task

Batched BLAS in CUDA has some drawbacks: first, it cannot describe parallelism among different kinds of numerical kernels, second, it still requires code modification from conventional cuBLAS routines to the batched version. The aim of the research is to provide a high-level programming model to generate batched kernel APIs for offloading accelerators (Fig. 4).

4   Design of Task-Based Batched Code Generation

In this section, we explain how the compiler generates batched kernel APIs from OpenMP *task* directives. We suppose that the user describes the application with numerical library routines in the C language and OpenMP directives. The target architecture is general offloading accelerators such as GPUs, where thread-level parallelism on the host side does not improve the performance.

4.1   Overview of the Programming Model

Listing 4 shows an example code which implements blocked Cholesky decomposition. The code uses OpenMP task parallelism with cuBLAS routines which calculate linear algebra kernels of submatrices. As you can see in the Listing 1, some applications have obvious parallelism so that the use can easily make it executed in parallel by using traditional data parallelism. In that case, the user can use batched kernel APIs manually as shown in Listing 3.

On the other hand, there are some applications which the traditional approach cannot be easily applied to Cholesky decomposition in Listing 4 consists of tasks with irregular dependency. Dependency among tasks is described by *depend* clauses, which can be shown as Fig. 5. In Fig. 5, kernels in the same row are independent to the others. Even they can be calculated in parallel, it is not

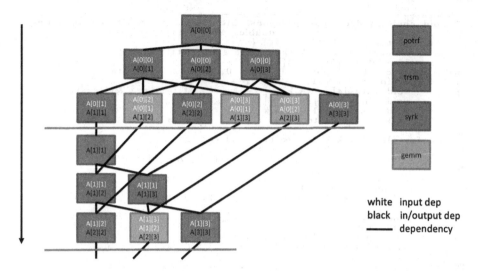

Fig. 5. Task dependency graph in blocked Cholesky decomposition

that obvious for the user to find and gather them into a batch by using batched BLAS manually.

Our approach is that the OpenMP compiler detects pre-registered numerical kernels in tasks and makes a batch instead of the user. The later part of the section consists of two parts: code translation that the compiler detects pre-registered kernels and the runtime implementation that makes batches from the detected tasks.

4.2 Code Translation

We have implemented the *task* directive using the Omni compiler infrastructure [10], which provides source-to-source code translation. A sequential code written in the C language with OpenMP directives is translated into a C code with OpenMP runtime function calls. Listing 6 shows the generated code translated from Listing 4[3]. The compiler translates the *task* directive into its runtime function, *task_create()*. The target code region of the task is translated into a function and its pointer and arguments are given to the runtime function. When it has a *depend* clause, the values in the clause are also given to the runtime function.

If the target code region only contains a numerical kernel, it will be a candidate for batch creation. The compiler has API information about batched BLAS. At the time the compiler can detect cuBLAS DGEMM routines in a task. If the compiler finds a DGEMM routine, it creates a unique batch ID for each batched BLAS routine. The first argument of *task_create()* indicates a batch ID. If it is 0, the function call will not be merged into a batch. When it has a value

---

[3] The code is simplified to make it easy to understand.

```
1   void cholesky_decomposition(const int tile_size, const int num_tiles,
2                               double* A[nt][nt]) {
3     for (int k = 0; k < nt; k++) {
4       void *args[3] = {A[k][k], &tile_size, &tile_size};
5       void *out_data[1] = {A[k][k]};
6       task_create(0, potrf, 3, args, 0, NULL, 1, out_data);
7       for (int i = k + 1; i < nt; i++) {
8         void *args[4] = {A[k][k], A[k][i], &tile_size, &tile_size};
9         void *in_data[1] = {A[k][k]};
10        void *out_data[1] = {A[k][i]};
11        task_create(0, trsm, 4, args, 1, in_data, 1, out_data);
12      }
13      for (int i = k + 1; i < nt; i++) {
14        for (int j = k + 1; j < i; j++) {
15          void *args[5] = {A[k][i], A[k][j], A[j][i],
16                           &tile_size, &tile_size};
17          void *in_data[2] = {A[k][i], A[k][j]};
18          void *out_data[1] = {A[j][i]};
19          task_create(1, gemm, 5, args, 2, in_data, 1, out_data);
20        }
21        void *args[4] = {A[k][i], A[i][i], &tile_size, &tile_size};
22        void *in_data[1] = {A[k][i]};
23        void *out_data[1] = {A[i][i]};
24        task_create(0, syrk, 4, args, 1, in_data, 1, out_data);
25      }
26    }
27    task_waitall();
28  }
```

Fig. 6. Transleted OpenMP Cholesky decomposition code

more than 0, the function call will be merged into a batch with the same number. The IDs should be unique when DGEMM routines use different values as arguments, which requires compiler analysis. For simplicity's sake, the current implementation creates the same ID 1 for every DGEMM (Fig. 6).

4.3   Runtime Implementation

Merging detected DGEMMs into a batch is done at runtime. Figure 7 shows that how the OpenMP task runtime is modified for batched kernel APIs. The OpenMP task runtime has a task queue where tasks are scheduled after resolving dependency and ready for execution. How to select a next task from the task

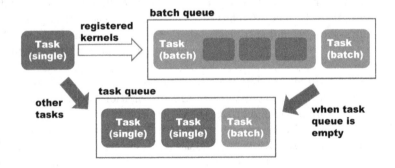

Fig. 7. Modified task runtime for batched kernel APIs

queue depends on the scheduling algorithm of the runtime implementation. We added a new queue in the task runtime, named batch queue as shown in Fig. 7.

Before resolving dependency, the runtime works as usual regardless of its kind (DGEMM or non-DGEMM task). The task runtime selects a queue to put a task when its dependency has been resolved and ready for execution. If the task does not include a pre-registered numerical kernel (DGEMM), it is scheduled to the task queue as usual.

When the task has only a registered numerical kernel and is given a batch ID by the compiler, it is scheduled to the batch queue. The task is merged into a existing batch when there is a batch which has the same batch ID. Runtime has information about batched DGEMM and knows how to translate the arguments of conventional DGEMM routines for batched DGEMM. For example, the pointer of array A, B and C are merged into the pointer arrays for the batched DGEMM. If there is no existing batch, a new batch is created and scheduled into the batch queue.

Batch has the same structure with the OpenMP task so that it can be scheduled and executed by the task runtime. Batch task in the batch queue is not scheduled if there is a ready task in the normal task queue. When the task queue is empty, the task runtime takes a batch task from the batch queue. This is for delaying batch execution until there is enough tasks in a batch. By using this scheme, all independent DGEMMs in the same row in Fig. 5 can be merged into a single batch.

We used Argobots [1] which has been being developed by Argonne National Laboratory to implement our task runtime. Argobots provides programming interface to create user-level lightweight threads implemented upon OS thread library. The current runtime implementation creates a single thread when creating batches from OpenMP tasks. This is because we assumed that multiple CPU threads does not improve the single stream GPU performance[4]. Another reason is that it is easier to estimate the performance breakdown.

5   Performance Evaluation

In this section, we evaluate our OpenMP implementation by using two benchmark codes. The first benchmark is DGEMM loop that calculates multiple DGEMMs in a loop statement. The second benchmark is blocked Cholesky decomposition already shown in Listing 4. Table 1 shows the evaluation environment. We used a NVIDIA Tesla K20 GPU as an offloading accelerator and cuBLAS in CUDA 9.1 (Fig. 8).

5.1   DGEMM Loop

Listing 8 shows a synthetic benchmark code which calculates independent DGEMM kernels. Each DGEMM kernel is implemented by cuBLAS DGEMM.

---

[4] Actually it improves the performance as shown in Sect. 5.

```
1  void dgemm_loop(const int num_kernels, const int n,
2                  double **A, double **B, double **C) {
3  #pragma omp parallel
4  #pragma omp single
5     for (int k = 0; k < num_kernels; k++) {
6  #pragma omp task
7        dgemm(A[k], B[k], C[k], n, n);
8     }
9  }
```

Fig. 8. DGEMM kernels in OpenMP task

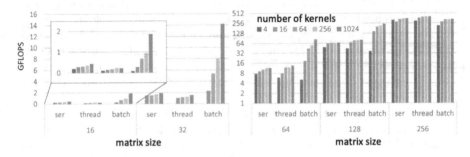

Fig. 9. Performance of DGEMM loop

Although it is a simple benchmark, it is useful to show the ideal case that most of the kernels in the application are merged into a single batch.

Figure 9 shows the performance of DGEMM loop. *ser* shows the performance of sequential execution. *thread* is the performance of CPU-threaded OpenMP task execution (2 in Fig. 2) using the normal OpenMP runtime. 16 threads are created for the evaluation. *batch* is the performance of the modified OpenMP runtime creating batched DGEMM. In this case, a single thread manages tasks/batches and executes all of them. The performance basically shows the performance of batched DGEMM since all DGEMM kernels are merged into a single batch at runtime. When the matrix size is small (16×16 and 32×32), the performance has been improved by batched DGEMM with a large number of kernels. When increasing the matrix size, the performance gap between sequential

Table 1. Evalustion environment

Item	Name/Value
CPU	Intel (R) Xeon (R) CPU E5-2680, 2 sockets 8 cores with HT, 2.70 GHz
Memory	DDR4 64 GB
GPU	NVIDIA Tesla K20
Back-end Compiler	Intel Compiler 18.0.3
CUDA Library	CUDA 9.1 with cuBLAS

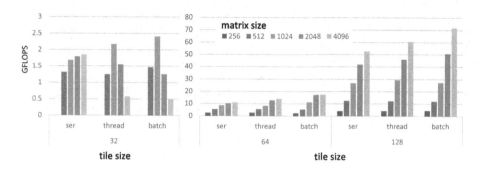

Fig. 10. Performance of blocked Cholesky decomposition

execution and batched DGEMM becomes smaller. This is because each DGEMM kernel can exploit entire GPU architecture so that batched DGEMM does not have performance advantage. Note that the performance with normal OpenMP runtime (*thread* in Fig. 9) shows the better performance than sequential execution. This is because some internal processes in the DGEMM kernel can be overlapped by multi-threading and reduce the synchronization time between CPU and GPU.

5.2   Blocked Cholesky Decomposition

Unlike the DGEMM loop, blocked Cholesky decomposition has less parallelism and irregular dependency. It can show more practical usage of the runtime implementation. We used the blocked Cholesky decomposition code shown in Listing 4 for the evaluation. It decomposes the entire matrix into smaller square matrices (tiles). *tile_size* in Listing 4 indicates the size of the tiles. Each DGEMM kernel calculates the matrix-matrix multiplication of two tiles.

Figure 10 shows the performance of the blocked Cholesky decomposition code. *ser, thread, batch* has the same meaning with the labels in Fig. 9. We have increased the matrix size while fixing the tile size, which increases the number of tiles (increases the number of DGEMM kernels eventually). When the tile size is small, batched DGEMM shows better performance in some cases but lower than sequential execution with the large matrix size. When we increase the tile size, which makes the DGEMM calculation bigger, batched DGEMM shows the best performance in most cases.

Figure 11 shows the performance breakdown of some cases in Fig. 10[5]. *dgemm* and *dgemm batch* shows the performance ratio of conventional/batched DGEMM kernels. *math* shows the ratio of non-DGEMM BLAS kernels and the LAPACK potrf kernel. *system* shows the ratio of the remaining execution time, which is mainly the runtime overhead including task scheduling and batch generation.

---

[5] *thread* is not given in this Figure. Since it is hard to estimate because of overlapped calculation among CPU threads and is not the main topic of the research.

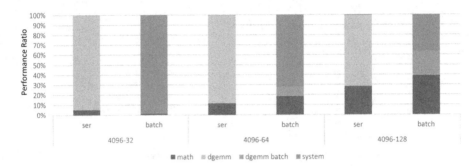

Fig. 11. Performance breakdown: blocked Cholesky decomposition

4096-32 shows the case of matrix size 4096 and tile size 32. It is the case that has the most numerous DGEMM kernels in Fig. 10. The execution time of DGEMM kernels is reduced from 11.8s to 0.27s as batched DGEMM can exploit the GPU hardware using the large number of small DGEMMs. The reason of performance degradation when using batched runtime comes from the task/batch management overhead. The system overhead dominates the total execution time in batch runtime because the DGEMM calculation time is relatively small compared to task/batch management.

In the case of *4096-64* and *4096-128*, we have increased the tile size while fixing the matrix size. It decreases the total number of DGEMM kernels and makes each DGEMM kernel calculation bigger than the case of *4096-32*. As a result, we can see that the ratio of system overhead becomes smaller. Although the effect of using batched DGEMM becomes lower than the small matrices, the case of *4096-128* shows the most improved performance because of low system overhead.

From the evaluation result, we can see that the DGEMM performance has been improved by the modified task runtime. However, the runtime achieves poor performance when there is many small computations because of the system overhead increases in proportion to the number of tasks. Currently, we are implementing multi-threaded runtime to create/manage tasks and batches in parallel to reduce the overhead.

6   Conclusion

In this research, we have proposed the task generation techniques for batched kernel APIs on accelerators. The performance evaluation using a NVIDIA GPU shows that modified OpenMP runtime can improve the performance when there is moderate number of mergeable tasks. While the current implementation is focused on GPUs and the BLAS DGEMM routine, the task generation techniques can be adapted any kind of offloading accelerators and batched kernel APIs.

We are currently investigating the following features to improve our compiler:

- batching frequently used level-3 BLAS routines
- multi-threaded runtime to reduce task/batch management overhead
- multi stream implementation for task parallelism on GPUs
- batch scheduling among multiple GPUs
- cooperate task scheduling on both CPU and GPU.

References

1. Argobots - Official Repository on Github. https://github.com/pmodels/argobots
2. Dongarra, J., et al.: Batched BLAS (basic linear algebra subprograms) 2018 specification, July 2018
3. Dongarra, J., Hammarling, S., Higham, N.J., Relton, S.D., Valero-Lara, P., Zounon, M.: The design and performance of batched blas on modern high-performance computing systems. Procedia Comput. Sci. **108**, 495–504 (2017). https://doi.org/10.1016/j.procs.2017.05.138. http://www.sciencedirect.com/scien ce/article/pii/S1877050917307056. International Conference on Computational Science, ICCS 2017, Zurich, Switzerland, 12–14 June 2017
4. Dongarra, J.J., et al.: A proposed API for batched basic linear algebra subprograms (2016)
5. Intel Math Kernel Library - Batched DGEMM Interface. https://software.intel. com/en-us/mkl-developer-reference-c-cblas-gemm-batch
6. Jin, C., Baskaran, M.: Analysis of explicit vs. implicit tasking in OpenMP using kripke, pp. 62–70, November 2018. https://doi.org/10.1109/ESPM2.2018.00012
7. Muddukrishna, A., Jonsson, P.A., Vlassov, V., Brorsson, M.: Locality-aware task scheduling and data distribution on NUMA systems. In: Rendell, A.P., Chapman, B.M., Müller, M.S. (eds.) IWOMP 2013. LNCS, vol. 8122, pp. 156–170. Springer, Heidelberg (2013). https://doi.org/10.1007/978-3-642-40698-0_12
8. NVIDIA cuBLAS - Batched DGEMM Interface. https://docs.nvidia.com/cuda/ cublas/index.html#cublas-lt-t-gt-gemmbatched
9. Olivier, S.L., Prins, J.F.: Evaluating OpenMP 3.0 run time systems on unbalanced task graphs. In: Müller, M.S., de Supinski, B.R., Chapman, B.M. (eds.) IWOMP 2009. LNCS, vol. 5568, pp. 63–78. Springer, Heidelberg (2009). https://doi.org/10. 1007/978-3-642-02303-3_6
10. Omni Compiler Infrastructure. https://omni-compiler.org/
11. Relton, S.D., Valero-Lara, P., Zounon, M.: A comparison of potential interfaces for batched BLAS computations (2016)
12. Watanabe, Y., Lee, J., Boku, T., Sato, M.: Trade-off of offloading to FPGA in OpenMP task-based programming. In: de Supinski, B.R., Valero-Lara, P., Martorell, X., Mateo Bellido, S., Labarta, J. (eds.) IWOMP 2018. LNCS, vol. 11128, pp. 96–110. Springer, Cham (2018). https://doi.org/10.1007/978-3-319-98521-3_7

Introducing the Task-Aware Storage I/O (TASIO) Library

Aleix Roca Nonell$^{(\boxtimes)}$ (ID), Vicenç Beltran Querol (ID), and Sergi Mateo Bellido (ID)

Barcelona Supercomputing Center, Barcelona, Spain
{aleix.rocanonell,vbeltran,sergi.mateo}@bsc.es
https://www.bsc.es

Abstract. Task-based programming models are excellent tools to parallelize and seamlessly load balance an application workload. However, the integration of I/O intensive applications and task-based programming models is lacking. Typically, I/O operations stall the requesting thread until the data is serviced by the backing device. Because the core where the thread was running becomes idle, it should be possible to overlap the data query operation with either computation workloads or even more I/O operations. Nonetheless, overlapping I/O tasks with other tasks entails an extra degree of complexity currently not managed by programming models' runtimes. In this work, we focus on integrating storage I/O into the tasking model by introducing the Task-Aware Storage I/O (TASIO) library. We test TASIO extensively with a custom benchmark for a number of configurations and conclude that it is able to achieve speedups up to 2x depending on the workload, although it might lead to slowdowns if not used with the right settings.

Keywords: Task-based programming models · I/O · OmpSs-2 · OpenMP · HPC

1 Introduction

In the road to exascale, it is essential to ensure the most efficient use of hardware resources. The increasing number of cores and hardware threads in modern computers requires an extra effort for application programmers to properly distribute work among cores. In particular, the penalization for not properly balancing an application workload is aggravated given that a single core in the application's critical path is able to keep all the other cores idle until its work finishes.

Programming models have proven to be a powerful tool to ease the processes of parallelizing applications regardless of their use case. Notably, task-based programming models are especially suitable to perform transparent load balancing by simply adjusting the size and/or number of tasks. However, because of its generality, programming models refrain from specifying use cases for I/O intensive applications.

© Springer Nature Switzerland AG 2019
X. Fan et al. (Eds.): IWOMP 2019, LNCS 11718, pp. 274–288, 2019.
https://doi.org/10.1007/978-3-030-28596-8_19

I/O intensive applications have a huge impact on the system's resource usage. Typically, I/O operations require of operating system assistance to interface with a particular hardware device. Such devices are slower than the main processing units which force the thread issuing the I/O request to either continuously poll for the completion or to block inside the operating system. In the first case, power and time is wasted in not truly productive work. In the second case, the core becomes idle allowing other system threads to run on it. However, because I/O operations are usually more expensive than the system's threads computing requirements, most of the time the core will be idling anyways. Typically, this problem is solved by using asynchronous functions to avoid the thread blocking on the operation. However, the application's design complexity increases substantially when trying to combine asynchronous calls with task-based programming models effectively.

OmpSs-2 is a task-based programming model (see Sect. 2.1) whose runtime is "asynchronous-aware", which means that provides an interface to register tasks performing asynchronous operations. In order to make use of such interface, in this paper we present a new library named TASIO which replaces synchronous I/O system calls by their asynchronous counterparts and notifies the runtime to schedule other tasks on the core while the operation is being serviced.

Hence, in this article we present the following contributions: (1) We propose the TASIO library to enable the conversion of synchronous to asynchronous operations and integrate it with "asynchronous-aware" runtimes (2) We present a task-based synthetic benchmark which simulates interleaved computation and I/O workloads and (3) We explore the results space of the synthetic benchmark for a number of configurations and detail the conclusions learned.

2 Background

2.1 The OmpSs-2 Programming Model

OmpSs-2 [6,9] is a task-based programming model developed at the Barcelona Supercomputing Center (BSC) with the objective of early-testing novel features for the tasking model that might influence the development of the OpenMP programming model [2,7]. The main focus of OmpSs-2 is in both asynchronous parallelism and device heterogeneity (distribute work among different devices such as systems' cores, GPUs, and FPGAs). The source to source Mercurium compiler and the Nanos6 runtime are the BSC's implementation of the OmpSs-2 model. Mercurium translates source code pragmas into Nanos6 library calls while Nanos6 manages the application's execution flow at runtime.

In a task-based programming model, all units of parallelism are expressed as tasks. A task is an enclosed sequence of instructions specified by the developer that must be executed sequentially. Multiple tasks can be executed in parallel as long as all their dependencies have been fulfilled. Dependencies express which data is required by tasks to perform its computation and which data it produces. Dependencies are expressed simply by specifying which variables a task uses as input, output or both. The actual execution sequence of tasks is determined by the runtime.

2.2 Linux Kernel Asynchronous I/O Interfaces

Synchronous I/O requests typically block[1] while the request is being processed. Instead, asynchronous I/O requests are intended to avoid blocking by separating the operation into two parts: submission of the request and check for completion. There are two standard implementations for asynchronous I/O in modern Linux machines: The Linux Kernel native AIO and the POSIX AIO.

The Linux Kernel native asynchronous I/O interface [3] consists in a set of system calls to submit and monitor I/O requests independently from the set of typical synchronous system calls. AIO requests are submitted in a context [2] created beforehand. When the submission operation returns, it is possible to check for the request status and to explicitly block until any of the requests in the context have finished. The POSIX AIO, instead, simulates Kernel AIO support by simply delegating synchronous I/O operations to a pool of threads.

Similarly to the synchronous approach, it is likely that the submission of an asynchronous request is completed just after it is submitted because of the effects of the page cache. For this reason, Linux AIO is only useful when the page cache is bypassed (non-buffered I/O). However, there are other system specific factors that might prevent the AIO requests to actually be asynchronous such as filesystem limitations. For instance, the ext4 filesystem mandates that the AIO operation should not modify the file metadata [4] such as when enlarging a file due to a write operation.

3   Related Work

Scientific application codes have historically used custom thread implementations to manage parallelism. Because these applications are usually complex and moving from the classic thread paradigm to a task-based solution is not usually simple, most of them refrain from changing their parallel scheme. Also, storage I/O has been traditionally implemented in sequential bursts due to constraints associated with legacy hard disks. Moreover, asynchronous I/O usually imposes strict constraints that are not always easy to meet. In consequence, there is not much literature focusing on the interaction of task-based programming models and asynchronous parallel I/O at the node level.

However, the Message Passing Interface (MPI) library is widely adopted and previous research exists on overlapping MPI communications with computation in task-based programming models. The Task-Aware MPI library (TAMPI) [10]

---

[1] The operation might return immediately, i.e. not block, if the system page cache already holds the requested data in the case of reads or if the page cache has enough free space as to defer the operation for a later time in the case of writes.

[2] A context is basically a queue of requests.

tackles the problem of overlapping network communications with other workloads. It uses the OmpSs-2 pause/resume, external events and polling services APIs (see Sect. 4) to minimize the time cores are idling while communicating over network. The TASIO library presented in this paper is highly inspired by TAMPI.

4   Computation and I/O Overlapping with OpenMP and OmpSs-2

I/O operations usually rely on blocking system calls that stall the execution of work in cores. On task-based programming models, this entails a performance degradation because runtimes are not aware of when cores became idle and hence, are not able to run other tasks on them while I/O is being serviced. A common technique to overlap I/O and computation is to run asynchronous I/O operations instead of blocking ones. Yet the integration of asynchronous calls with task-based programming models is usually tedious. Task-based programming models work on the abstraction of data dependencies and execution flow. Data consumed or generated asynchronously needs to be tracked by the dependency system which means that a task must generate or consume the data. Nonetheless, asynchronous operations need to be checked for completion by either polling or callback, but neither of them are trivial to wrap within a task.

This section explores the proposals of both the OpenMP and OmpSs-2 programming models and it introduces the TASIO library based on the OmpSs-2 APIs.

4.1   OpenMP

The OpenMP 5.0 specification [8] introduces the `detach` clause to the task construct with the purpose of delaying the completion of a task (possibly) long after its body has been executed. To complete a task with a detach clause it is necessary to, on the one hand, run it and, on the other hand, mark its event object (provided within the detach clause) as completed using an OpenMP API call. A task submitting an asynchronous operation will define the consumed or generated data in its dependencies and those will only be released when the task finishes. However, the task will not be completed until the code responsible to check for the asynchronous completion operation marks the associated detach event as satisfied.

The OpenMP specification gives complete freedom to the developer to decide how and when the completion checking code should be run. When working with frameworks providing callback support such as CUDA, running the OpenMP detach completion function is simple. However, when polling or blocking is needed the user needs to create its own thread and care must be taken to prevent this thread from overlapping with the computation of the other OpenMP threads.

4.2 OmpSs-2

OmpSs-2 features two APIs[3] to deal with blocking operations:

The *pause/resume API* allows to pause the execution of the current task and to resume it later on. Pausing deschedules the current task and returns control back to the runtime which is able to run other tasks in the core where the first task was running. Once a task is paused, the next task could be run either on the same thread as the previous task or on a new thread. In the first case, the stack of the paused stack becomes buried below the stack of the next task and, hence it cannot be resumed until the second task finishes. This could lead to a deadlock for tasks that use two-sided messages APIs such as MPI, therefore, the Nanos6 runtime implements the second approach because of its genericity.

The *external events API* does not stop the execution of a task, but it simply delays the release of its dependencies until all registered events have been fulfilled (similarly to the OpenMP detach clause). In other words, during the execution of a task, a number of events can be registered within Nanos6. Even if the task code finishes, it will not unblock the tasks that depend on this task until all events are satisfied. In consequence, asynchronously requested data cannot be used inside the same task that requests it, because its fulfillment is likely to occur after the task body is finished.

Both APIs rely on the OmpSs-2 *polling services API* to periodically run a user-registered function within Nanos6. This function is run at strategic points to avoid disturbing other tasks. A possible use case for this functions is to poll for completion of registered asynchronous events. The exact method to check for completion depends on the kind of submitted asynchronous operation and is the (library developer) user responsibility to code. Once a completion event is detected, the polling function must either resume a task (in case using the pause/resume API) or decrement the event counter (for the external events API).

4.3 The Task-Aware Storage I/O (TASIO) Library

The TASIO library is similar to the TAMPI library; it provides both blocking and non-blocking APIs through OmpSs-2. The basic functionality is shown in Fig. 1.

The TASIO blocking API (which uses the OmpSs-2 pause/resume API) defines wrappers for the `pread()`, `pwrite()`, `preadv()` and `pwritev()` syscalls (all Linux Kernel native AIO supported syscalls) which transparently call the asynchronous version of the intercepted syscall instead of the original one when applications are linked against it. After TASIO submits an AIO request it checks whether it has immediately completed or not and, if it is the case, the wrapper returns immediately as well. Otherwise, it sets the current task to the list of blocked tasks and transfers control to the runtime. The runtime is then able to execute other tasks in the current core while the I/O operation is being resolved.

---

[3] The low level details of such APIs can be consulted in [10].

In this work, we focus on studying the pause/resume OmpSs-2 implementation that relies on creating extra threads on task pause because as explained in Sect. 4.2 it is the most generic one. However, it is worth noting that the storage I/O does not suffer from the network I/O constraints and, therefore, would also work on the extra-thread-free version.

The TASIO non-blocking API (which uses the OmpSs-2 external events API) defines its own ta_pread(), ta_pwrite(), ta_preadv() and ta_pwritev() that behave as the pause/resume variant but instead of blocking the current thread it increments a task event counter and return immediately after submitting the AIO request.

At startup, TASIO registers a polling function within the Nanos6 runtime through the polling services API. Once a previously submitted asynchronous I/O request is completed, the polling function will retrieve it and either unlock the associated task if submitted through the pause/resume API or decrement its event counter for the external events API. The maximum amount of AIO petitions that TASIO can withstand at the same time is configured at 1000 by default. If at some point the maximum number of requests is reached, the offending request sleeps for 1ms and tries again[4].

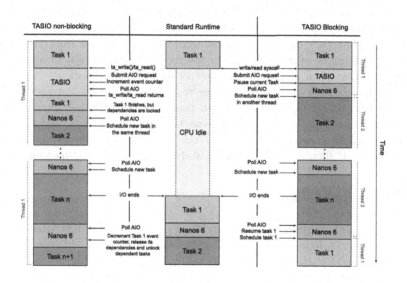

Fig. 1. TASIO runtime execution flow example on a single core system.

It is worth noting that because TASIO uses the Linux Kernel AIO interface, all submitted I/O operations must be non-buffered and comply with the O_DIRECT constraints as explained in Sect. 2.2.

---

[4] Smarter techniques could be used, but because this is a corner case we have simplified it for now.

Finally, we would like to point out that both TASIO and TAMPI can be combined in the same application and, in fact, this approach could be extended to other blocking mechanisms as long as asynchronous submission and non-blocking polling for completion mechanisms are supplied.

4.4   OpenMP and TASIO/TAMPI Support

OpenMP support could be added to both the TASIO and TAMPI libraries (TAL hereinafter) non-blocking API by relying on the detach clause but it would not be possible to implement the TAL blocking API without a compatible pause/resume API. Nonetheless, there are three implementation limitations that would affect the non-blocking API performance and/or slightly increase its complexity.

First and foremost, an additional thread would have to be created and managed by TAL to poll for AIO completions. The user would need to configure the thread's polling rate or at least be aware of the default one. However, as explained in Sect. 4.2, a runtime-aware completion thread would be more efficient.

Second, the OpenMP detach object has boolean semantics. Therefore, keeping track of multiple AIO submissions within a task requires an external counter. Also, a mechanism would be needed to associate detach objects and counters, such as a private TAL hash table. Even though, it would be particularly complex to combine multiple I/O functions of different task-aware non-blocking libraries within the same task because counters would be private per library. Keeping track of the number of requests within the detach OpenMP object and release its dependencies when zero is reached would simplify this detail.

And third (a minor detail), the user would need to feed the task context (detach object) to TAL functions when needed. OpenMP does not currently provide any means to obtain such context through an API call and therefore, it is not possible to retrieve it within TAL. However, adding such an API call within OpenMP should not be complex and would simplify the interface.

5   Experimentation

The TASIO exploitable benefits are highly dependent on the test environment. More precisely, it depends on the storage device, the number of cores and the application's I/O pattern. To cover as many cases as possible, we decided to implement a synthetic benchmark which we used to perform a deep scan on a number of configurations.

5.1   The Task I/O Meter Benchmark (TIOM)

The Task I/O Meter Benchmark (TIOM) is a simple OmpSs-2 application that interleaves computation and I/O operations wrapped in tasks. The number of tasks, I/O block size per task, computation time per task and I/O pattern is configurable. I/O operations are performed on a user file and computation work is simulated by busy waiting in a loop. There are four main modes of operation that simulate different application's I/O patterns. Each mode creates a configurable amount of "task series" that can be completely run in parallel to other series. A task series is a chain of tasks that are bound by their dependencies.

In the mix mode, each task performs both computation and I/O, in this order. The 1to1 mode is similar, but computation and I/O are separated in different tasks bound with dependencies. In the fjio (fork-join I/O) and fjc (fork-join computation) modes, computation and I/O are also performed in separated tasks but, in fjio, each computation task depends on four I/O tasks and each I/O task depends on a single computation task. The fjc mode is similar to fjio but interchanging I/O per computation tasks.

The mix and 1to1 modes define an interleaved sequence of computation and I/O operations. However, only mix actually enforces this sequence. Instead, the more fine-grained 1to1 might allow sustaining more I/O operations in flight if a core happens to run multiple I/O tasks of different series instead of consistently alternating I/O and computation of the same series (as long as there are more task series than cores).

The modes fjio and fjc consider the case of unbalanced amounts of I/O and computation tasks. fjio mode is particularly interesting as it allows to sustain more I/O requests per core when TASIO is in use. As long as the disk bandwidth is not saturated, running an I/O task with TASIO appears to be free because immediately after submitting the AIO requests, the runtime is able to run another task. The more I/O tasks that can be run sequentially in the same core, the more I/O petitions in flight the system will have a chance to optimize and process. When a computation task is encountered, the core is "stalled" and no more I/O requests can be issued from there until the task finishes. When the storage device is saturated, the TASIO effect is to only queue more I/O tasks and to run computation tasks earlier. However, when no more tasks are available, cores will idle until I/O petitions complete.

5.2   Test Environment

All tests have been run in a single node of Intel's Scalable System Framework (SSF) "Cobi" machine which features two Xeon E5-2690 v4 sockets with a total of 28 cores (56 hardware threads), 32 KiB L1i and L1d caches, 256 KiB L2 cache, 35840 KiB L3 cache, 128 GiB at 2400 MHz of main memory, a 960 GB SSD Intel Optane 905P [5] used for the tests I/O operations and a SATA SSD which holds the system installation. The Linux kernel version is 4.10 and core frequency scaling is disabled system-wide.

SSD Optane 905P Profiling. We have profiled the Intel's 905P Optane SSD maximum random read and write speeds using the Flexible I/O tester (fio) [1]. The used fio configuration runs 56 threads (one per hardware thread) which issue up to four AIO requests of 4 KiB and 1 MiB. The results obtained in the 1 MiB configuration closely resembles the official device specifications for sequential Read 2600 MB/s (2579.5 MiB/s) and sequential write (up to) 2200 MB/s (2098 MiB/s) as shown in Table 1.

Table 1. Intel 905P Optane SSD throughput in MiB/s for block sizes of 4 KiB (left) and 1 MiB (right) and up to four (1, 2, 3, 4) AIO petitions in flight

Block size	4 KiB				1 MiB			
AIO depth	1	2	3	4	1	2	3	4
Rand write	2255	2277	2285	2285	2278	2282	2283	2285
Rand read	2265	2264	2264	2264	2548	2548	2547	2547

5.3 Results

We have run the TIOM benchmark for all combinations of computation time ranging from 1 ms to 128 ms with block sizes ranging from 4 KiB to 8 MiB in power of two steps. We have repeated this sequence for sequential read, sequential write, random read (rr), and random write (rw). Also, we have run the experiments using two configurations for the maximum number of tasks that can be run in parallel at the same time (this directly affect the number of task series as described in 5.1). The configurations correspond to 128 and 256 which roughly corresponds to twice and four times the number of hardware threads respectively. Each configuration is repeated for the four TIOM operation modes mix, 1to1, fjio, fjc, except for sequential read and write tests which were run only for the mix mode. Three versions of TIOM are benchmarked: a standalone version, a version preloaded with TASIO in blocking mode (bq) and a version linked with TASIO in non-blocking mode (nb). Each test finishes when a 20 GiB file has been processed entirely (hence, the number of both I/O and computation tasks depends on the specified block size) and four repetitions are executed per configuration. However, we limited the execution time to 60 s for each repetition.

Figures 3 and 4 show speedup for a selected subset of relevant mix and fjio configurations respectively. We are not showing the results for fjc and 1to1 because they did not prove to be relevant enough. In fjc, simulated computation is throttling too much I/O for TASIO to be effective, and in 1to1, the results are quite similar to mix. Figure 2 shows bandwidth readings for both of the presented modes. The z-axis of all graphs either shows bandwidth (bw) readings in MiB/s for the standalone version or speedup (sp) readings in percentage achieved when comparing the standalone version with either the blocking (bq) or non-blocking (nb) versions. The left axis shows computation time in milliseconds and the right axis shows block size in KiB. White areas are close to 0% speedup, green areas to positive speedup and red areas to slowdown. Bandwidth graphs have their own coloring scheme.

The bandwidth graphs of Fig. 2 show that read operations are mostly able to saturate the disk consistently once the ratio $\frac{block\_size}{comput\_time} \geq 64$ is achieved. Write operations also reach the maximum speed rated by the manufacturer, but fail to keep it up as the block size increases.

As can be seen in both speedup Figs. 3 and 4, small blocks followed by long computation time lead to an underused storage device which is shown as a white triangle with its right angle pointing to the reader. As expected by the Amdahl's law, when computation far extends the I/O needs of an application, there is no point in using TASIO as the improvement is minimal.

Because read operations easily saturate the disk, we can only see the effect of using TASIO in the narrow and leaning diagonal region that drives the disk from underusage to saturation. Hence, TASIO non-blocking version is generally helping to saturate the disk in these cases. However, the blocking version sometimes leads to slowdown, quite likely because of the overhead introduced by creating and managing extra threads.

The difficulties presented to achieve sustained saturation throughput in write operations give TASIO the slack needed to actually improve the application performance. All write graphs show three common peculiarities: the first is, similarly to read operations, a diagonal of improvement that coincides with the device saturation ramp. The second is a moderate wavefront present after the diagonal for the biggest blocks which overlaps the throughput decrease seen in the bandwidth graphs. The third and last is a prominent peak standing at the smallest computation time values and between approximately 32 and 128 KiB that usually ranges between 40% and 80% but that it eventually reaches up to 100% of speedup in cases such as Fig. 3c.

Sequential I/O operations are slightly faster than random I/O operations. This leads to more room for TASIO to bring the device to saturation in the random case. In consequence, TASIO is, in general, able to achieve more performance (around 5% increase) on the random I/O case. However, we are not showing the sequential I/O graphs because of their similarity with the random case. It is worth noting that a few sequential read tests reported slowdown around 15%.

Although both TASIO modes achieve considerable speedups, the non-blocking mode is generally more efficient than the blocking mode. For instance, compare Fig. 3a with c or b with d. This is particularly true when a high degree of parallelism is present (256 parallel I/O tasks) and enough outstanding I/O requests are available as seen when comparing the fjio tests Fig. 4e with f. This makes sense as the higher the number of parallel tasks, the bigger the number of threads that are needed to processes more I/O operations in-flight, which leads to more overhead to manage them. Instead, no extra threads are required in non-blocking mode because tasks are not paused inside a thread context (blocking the entire thread), but tasks are detached of threads and remain in a "zombie" state until its associated pending events finishes.

Because write operations are more interesting than read operations (in this particular environment) from the TASIO point of view, Figs. 3 and 4 only show random write tests when using 256 parallel tasks series. Read tests generally reported either minor speedup or slowdown when increasing parallelism. More parallelism means more overhead and because read improvements are limited, overhead exceeds the margin for improvement.

As mentioned before, the results obtained in both 1to1 and mix modes are quite similar. In practice, 1to1 tasks might be executed in a similar sequence as to how they would have been in mix mode, so there is not much difference appreciated. The fjio results shown in Fig. 4 achieve the highest speedups for specific write cases as seen in Fig. 4f, but also show consistent slowdown regions. In general, this mode performs poorly on read operations such as in Fig. 4b, hitting slowdown mostly in blocking mode but also in the non-blocking one.

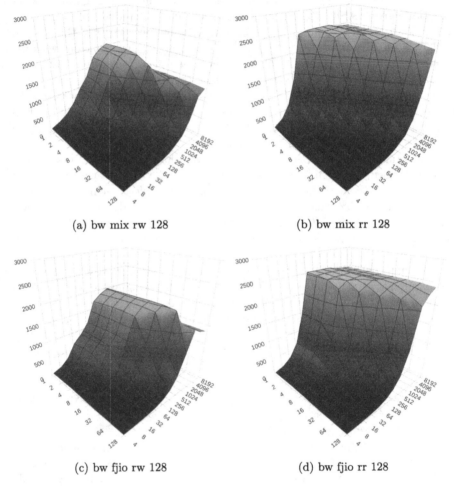

(a) bw mix rw 128   (b) bw mix rr 128

(c) bw fjio rw 128   (d) bw fjio rr 128

Fig. 2. TIOM storage I/O bandwidth tests for the standalone version. The upper axis shows bandwidth in MiB/s, the left axis shows simulated computational time in ms and the right axis shows block size in KiB.

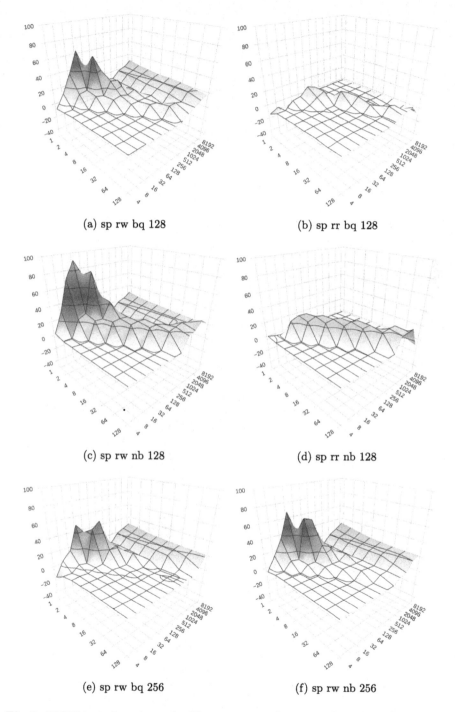

(a) sp rw bq 128

(b) sp rr bq 128

(c) sp rw nb 128

(d) sp rr nb 128

(e) sp rw bq 256

(f) sp rw nb 256

Fig. 3. TIOM tests for mix mode. The upper axis shows speedup, the left axis shows simulated computational time in ms and the right axis shows block size in KiB.

286   A. Roca Nonell et al.

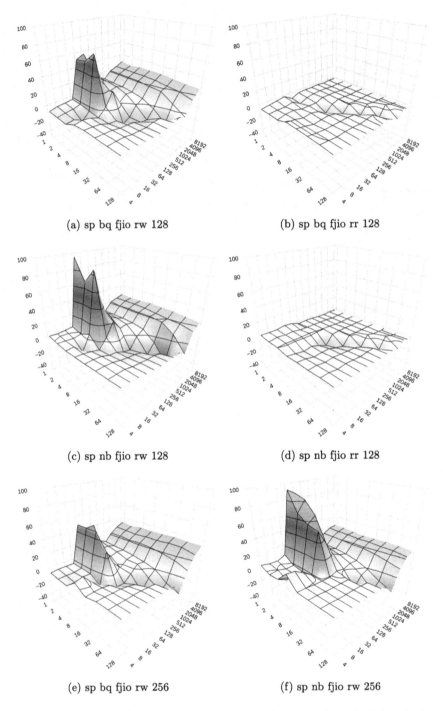

(a) sp bq fjio rw 128

(b) sp bq fjio rr 128

(c) sp nb fjio rw 128

(d) sp nb fjio rr 128

(e) sp bq fjio rw 256

(f) sp nb fjio rw 256

Fig. 4. TIOM tests for fjio mode. The upper axis shows speedup, the left axis shows simulated computational time in ms and the right axis shows block size in KiB.

6 Conclusions and Future Work

In this work, we have explored the state of the art of techniques to integrate storage I/O with the tasking model. We have presented the TASIO library to exploit such techniques in the context of read and write system calls and we have done exhaustive testing using a custom benchmark.

Both the blocking and non-blocking TASIO APIs have proved to improve the performance of the benchmark in most cases, although the blocking version's performance suffers due to the extra thread management overhead. Hence, the use of the library is encouraged but a previous analysis is needed to determine whether the application characteristics meet both TASIO and the system's AIO requirements which, in summary, are: (1) the application uses the disk intensively but (2) it is not already saturating it and (3) it does not benefit from the system's page cache and (4) I/O operation's meet the alignment and length requirements imposed by direct I/O and, finally, (5) there is enough computation work to be overlapped with I/O operations.

The exact parameters that fully exploit the library benefits are highly dependent on the system, with a primary focus on the number of cores, the storage device throughput and its capacity to sustain multiple parallel I/O requests. But for the particular set case tested in this work, we have found out that TASIO is able to achieve performance improvements between 40% and 80% (with peaks of up to 100%) for write operations of around 32 KiB to 128 KiB interleaved with computation blocks of 1ms, but also speedups between 10% to 40% for block sizes greater than 1 MiB run along computation tasks of any of the tested durations. The benefits of read operations are more discrete and its scope is limited to the narrow transition that leads to disk saturation, but still, a 20% speedup is easily achievable when moving in this ranges. However, the question remains of which points that have been explored are really relevant to real applications.

Regarding our future work, we intend to test TASIO with real applications and to study the combined effect with the TAMPI library. We also plan to test an extra-thread-free TASIO blocking version.

Acknowledgment. This project is supported by the European Union's Horizon 2021 research and innovation programme under the grant agreement No 754304 (DEEP-EST), the Ministry of Economy of Spain through the Severo Ochoa Center of Excellence Program (SEV-2015-0493), by the Spanish Ministry of Science and Innovation (contract TIN2015-65316-P) and by the Generalitat de Catalunya (2017-SGR-1481). Also, the authors would like to acknowledge that the test environment (Cobi) was ceded by Intel Corporation in the frame of the BSC - Intel collaboration.

References

1. Axboe, J.: Fio-flexible io tester (2014). http://freecode.com/projects/fio
2. Ayguade, E., et al.: A proposal to extend the OpenMP tasking model for heterogeneous architectures. In: Müller, M.S., de Supinski, B.R., Chapman, B.M. (eds.) IWOMP 2009. LNCS, vol. 5568, pp. 154–167. Springer, Heidelberg (2009). https://doi.org/10.1007/978-3-642-02303-3_13

3. Bhattacharya, S., Pratt, S., Pulavarty, B., Morgan, J.: Asynchronous I/O support in linux 2.5. In: Proceedings of the Linux Symposium, pp. 371–386 (2003)
4. E Community: Clarifying direct IO's semantics (2019). https://ext4.wiki.kernel.org/index.php/Clarifying_Direct_IO%27s_Semantics#Allocating_writes. Accessed 7 May 2019
5. Intel Corporation: Intel SSD 905P series (2019). https://www.intel.com/content/www/us/en/products/memory-storage/solid-state-drives/gaming-enthusiast-ssds/optane-905p-series/905p-960gb-aic-20nm.html. Accessed 7 May 2019
6. Duran, A., et al.: Ompss: a proposal for programming heterogeneous multi-core architectures. Parallel Process. Lett. **21**(02), 173–193 (2011)
7. Duran, A., Perez, J.M., Ayguadé, E., Badia, R.M., Labarta, J.: Extending the OpenMP tasking model to allow dependent tasks. In: Eigenmann, R., de Supinski, B.R. (eds.) IWOMP 2008. LNCS, vol. 5004, pp. 111–122. Springer, Heidelberg (2008). https://doi.org/10.1007/978-3-540-79561-2_10
8. OpenMP Architecture Review Board: OpenMP application program interface version 5.0 (2018). http://www.openmp.org. Accessed 7 May 2019
9. Perez, J.M., Beltran, V., Labarta, J., Ayguadé, E.: Improving the integration of task nesting and dependencies in OpenMP. In: 2017 IEEE International Parallel and Distributed Processing Symposium (IPDPS), pp. 809–818. IEEE (2017)
10. Sala, K., Teruel, X., Perez, J.M., Peña, A.J., Beltran, V., Labarta, J.: Integrating blocking and non-blocking MPI primitives with task-based programming models. Parallel Comput. **85**, 153–166 (2019). https://doi.org/10.1016/j.parco.2018.12.008. http://www.sciencedirect.com/science/article/pii/S0167819118303326

Using OpenMP

Optimization of Condensed Matter Physics Application with OpenMP Tasking Model

Joel Criado[1]([✉]), Marta Garcia-Gasulla[1], Jesús Labarta[1], Arghya Chatterjee[2], Oscar Hernandez[2], Raül Sirvent[1], and Gonzalo Alvarez[2]

[1] Barcelona Supercomputing Center, Barcelona, Spain
{joel.criado,marta.garcia,jesus.labarta,raul.sirvent}@bsc.es
[2] Oak Ridge National Laboratory, Oak Ridge, USA
{chatterjeea,oscar,alvarezcampg}@ornl.gov

Abstract. The Density Matrix Renormalization Group (DMRG++) is a condensed matter physics application used to study superconductivity properties of materials. It's main computations consist of calculating hamiltonian matrix which requires sparse matrix-vector multiplications. This paper presents task-based parallelization and optimization strategies of the Hamiltonian algorithm. The algorithm is implemented as a mini-application in C++ and parallelized with OpenMP. The optimization leverages tasking features, such as dependencies or priorities included in the OpenMP standard 4.5. The code refactoring targets performance as much as programmability. The optimized version achieves a speedup of 8.0× with 8 threads and 20.5× with 40 threads on a Power9 computing node while reducing the memory consumption to 90 MB with respect to the original code, by adding less than ten OpenMP directives.

Keywords: OpenMP · Tasks · Dependencies · Optimization · Analysis

1 Introduction and Related Work

Nowadays the High Performance Computing (HPC) community is focusing on the Exascale race. To succeed in this race, efforts are needed from all the

This manuscript has been co-authored by UT-Battelle, LLC under Contract No. DE-AC05-00OR22725 with the U.S. Department of Energy. The United States Government retains and the publisher, by accepting the article for publication, acknowledges that the United States Government retains a non-exclusive, paid-up, irrevocable, world-wide license to publish or reproduce the published form of this manuscript, or allow others to do so, for United States Government purposes. The Department of Energy will provide public access to these results of federally sponsored research in accordance with the DOE Public Access Plan (http://energy.gov/downloads/doe-public-access-plan).
G. Alvarez—Contributed in explaining the DMRG algorithm and its implementation, not in the OpenMP use and evaluation.

© Springer Nature Switzerland AG 2019
X. Fan et al. (Eds.): IWOMP 2019, LNCS 11718, pp. 291–305, 2019.
https://doi.org/10.1007/978-3-030-28596-8_20

actors, i.e., more powerful and efficient systems from architects, more flexible and scalable programming models and system software and, last but not least, applications that can exploit all the parallelism and computing power.

From the system architecture point of view, and looking at the current top systems in the top500 list, they are pushing into two clear directions: heterogeneous accelerator-based (e.g., GPUs) and many-core systems. Also, from the programming models and system software point of view, the efforts go to more flexible approaches [9,12], e.g., the tasking model in OpenMP.

Looking into scientific applications, their development pushes towards two directions: their scientific field and their performance [7]. For this reason, programmability is crucial, since applications cannot be written from scratch each time the architecture where they run changes. To avoid this, they must rely on programming models and runtime systems [10].

In this paper, we will focus on optimizing a critical computational kernel, a Hamiltonian sparse matrix-vector multiplication, of the Density Matrix Renormalization Group (DMRG++) application parallelized with OpenMP, which is currently a directive-based de-facto standard to program a shared memory programming model. We present an alternative parallelization with OpenMP using the tasking model to improve its performance and memory consumption, and at the same time maintain its programmability.

The optimization has been an iterative process of performance analysis, code optimization, and evaluation. This process ensures that we target the main source of inefficiency and we improve the performance with each change. We prove the benefits of our approach evaluating it on a POWER9 cluster hosted at Barcelona Supercomputing Center (BSC) since the objective of this research is to improve the performance of DRMG++ on the Summit supercomputer at the Oak Ridge Leadership Facility (OLCF)[1], that has the same architecture.

The main contribution of this paper is not only the optimization of the DMRG++ mini-application using the OpenMP tasking model, but also, the demonstration that the tasking model has huge benefits with very irregular applications concerning their load imbalance, offering a flexible, powerful and performant yet easy approach to parallelize code. The work presented in this paper can be considered a best practice or guide for programmers when dealing with similar problems.

The remaining of this document is organized as follows: Sect. 2 introduces the DMRG++ application and its scientific background, how the mini-application has been extracted, the original code and its main performance issues. In Sect. 3 we describe the environment in which the experiments have been conducted both in hardware and software terms and explain step by step the optimizations performed in the code and their impact. Finally, in Sect. 5 we will summarize the conclusions we extract from this work.

---

[1] World's fastest and smartest supercomputer with a theoretical performance of 200 petaflops at Oak Ridge National Laboratory as of Novemeber 2018.

2   Application Context and Background

The Density Matrix Renormalization Group (DMRG) algorithm, used in this work, is the preferred method to study quasi-one-dimensional systems. Strongly correlated materials are at the heart of current scientific and technological interest. These are a wide class of materials that show unusual, often technologically useful, electronic and magnetic properties, such as metal- insulator transitions or half-metalicity.

DMRG++ is a fully developed application that has been written entirely at Oak Ridge National Laboratory [4–6], and uses a sparse-matrix algebra computational motif for the simulation of Hubbard-like models and spin systems. By bringing DMRG++ to Exascale, condensed matter theorists will be able to solve problems such as correlated electron models of ladder geometries as opposed to just chain geometries, and multi-orbital models instead of just one-orbital models.

As an on-ramp to porting the DMRG++ application to OpenPOWER, a mini-application capturing the core algorithmic and computational structure of the application (Kronecker Product) was developed as the foundation for the exascale-ready implementation of DMRG++. In [8], the authors use OpenMP for on-node parallelization to manage the node complexity, by exploiting various "programming styles" in OpenMP 4.5 [13] (such as, SPMD style, multi-level tasks, accelerator programming and nested parallelism).

One goal of DMRG++ is to compute the lowest eigenvalue λ (which is related to the "ground-state" energy of the system) and the eigenvector Ψ of the full Hamiltonian (H_{full}) with N sites

$$H_{\text{full}}\Psi = \lambda\Psi, \text{ or } \lambda = \text{minimize}_{v \neq 0}\frac{v'H_{\text{full}}v}{v'v} \tag{1}$$

where the unit norm vector attaining the minimum value of Rayleigh quotient λ is eigenvector Ψ. The full Hamiltonian can then be written as Kronecker product of operators on left and right

$$H_{\text{full}} = H_L \otimes I_R + I_L \otimes H_R + \sum_{k=0}^{K} C_L^k \otimes C_R^k \tag{2}$$

where $H_L(H_R), I_L(I_R), C_L(C_R)$ are the Hamiltonian, identity, and interaction operators on the left (right).

The critical computational kernel in DMRG++ for computing the lowest eigenvector is the evaluation of matrix-vector products of the Hamiltonian matrix (H_{full}) in an iterative method such as the Lanczos algorithm.

2.1   Mini-application Code Structure and Initial Analysis

The DMRG++ mini-application (Kronecker Product) consists of 12k lines of C++ code parallelized with OpenMP. The mini-application comes with three

294   J. Criado et al.

input sets, each one representing a typical problem size (small, medium and large) of the real application (solving real science). The original parallelization of the mini-application is shown in Listing 1.1, which consisted of three OpenMP nested loops.

Figure 1 shows the data layout and main computations performed in the Kronecker Product. The Hamiltonian matrix is a 2-D matrix with each cell consisting of two, 1-D vector of vectors (A's and B's). The length of each of the vectors in a cell will be same, but will differ across the cells. The length of each element in vector's A and B, determines the sparsity or the density of the cell in the Hamiltonian Matrix. By property of the Hamiltonian Matrix in DMRG++, the data is primarily associated in the principal axis of the matrix and the den-

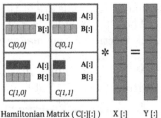

Fig. 1. Data layout in the Hamiltonian Matrix and computation for DMRG++

sity of the cells increase as we move closer to the center of the matrix, and the sparsity of the cells increase as we move away from the primary diagonal. This data layout gives rise to a significant load imbalance across the entirety of the matrix.

In Fig. 2, we can see a trace obtained from an execution of the mini-application with the second parallel pragma active (corresponding to jpatch). The x axis represents the time, and the y axis OpenMP threads, 40 in this case. The color indicates the duration of useful computation bursts; dark blue represents high values, whereas light green shows low computation, and the white areas represent idle time due to lack of parallelism or load imbalance. The bottom plot outlines the total number of actives threads as a function line, with values ranging between 1 and 40 in this figure and all the following ones.

```
1  #pragma omp parallel for schedule(dynamic,1)
2  for(int ipatch=0; ipatch<npatches; ipatch++){
3    std::vector<double> YI(vsize[ipatch], 0.0);
4    #pragma omp parallel for schedule(dynamic,1) reduction(vec_add:YI)
5    for(int jpatch=0; jpatch<npatches; jpatch++){
6      std::vector<double> YIJ(vsize[ipatch], 0.0);
7      #pragma omp parallel for schedule(dynamic,1) reduction(vec_add:YI)
8      for(int k=0; k<CIJ.cij[ipatch][jpatch].size()){
9        std::vector<double> Y_tmp(vsize[ipatch], 0.0);
10       Matrix A = CIJ.cij[ipatch][jpatch]->A[k];
11       Matrix B = CIJ.cij[ipatch][jpatch]->B[k];
12       int has_work = (A->nnz() && B->nnz());
13       if(!has_work) continue;
14       A->kron_mult('n','n', *A, *B, &X[j1], &Y_tmp[0]);
15       for(int i=0; i<vsize[ipatch]; i++) YIJ[i] += Y_tmp[i];
16     }
17     for(int i=0; i<vsize[ipatch]; i++) YI[i] += YIJ[i];
18   }
19   for(int i=i1; i<i2; i++) Y[i] = YI[i-i1];
20 }
```

Listing 1.1. Original code

In this trace, one must note that the workload in different parallel loops (arranged in columns) is not uniform across the execution. We also observe that the main bottleneck is the load imbalance (marked as the white space on

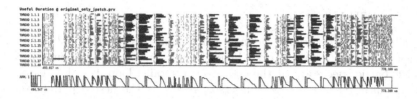

Fig. 2. Original code time line showing useful duration (Color figure online)

each column of threads) since the variability of the workload happens within the parallel loop, too. The important load imbalance within each loop results in very poor overall efficiency, while in reality, we know there is potential concurrency between many of these loops. The core of the problem lies at the too synchronous structure of the *parallel do* OpenMP construct. We will explore code refactoring based on medium or coarse grain tasks to expose the potential concurrency.

3 Code Optimization and Evaluation

In this section, we are going to explain the different steps we have taken to improve the performance of the Kronecker Product mini-app. For each stage, we include the proposed source code, explain the modifications together with their motivation, and show the performance evaluation and memory consumption of that version. The optimization process has been iterative and incremental, and for this reason, all the new versions are based on modifications from the previous one and their performance is also compared with it.

3.1 Environment and Methodology

All the experiments have been performed on the CTE-Power cluster [3,15] hosted at BSC. The cluster consists of 2 login and 52 compute nodes, each of them with 2 IBM Power9 8335-GTH 2.4 GHz processors (20 cores per processor, 4 SMT per core adding 160 SMTs per node), 512 GB of main memory at 2666 MHz distributed in 16 dimms and 4 NVIDIA V100 GPUs with 16 GB HBM2 memory. In all our experiments we have not used the GPUs nor the SMT, therefore we will use maximum 40 threads per core.

We have used GCC 8.1.0 as C and C++ compiler and its OpenMP runtime implementation and linked with IBM ESSL 5.4 library. Traces have been obtained using Extrae 3.5.4 [1,11] and visualized with Paraver [2,14].

All numbers reported (both for time and memory) are the average of 5 independent runs of 10 consecutive iterations, to be able to compare all versions to each other. In all cases, the relative error is below 5%, therefore, we do not show error bars on the charts for the sake of clarity. All experiments have been performed in one compute node of CTE-Power.

3.2   First Taskification

As we have seen from Fig. 2, the main performance issue is load imbalance. The
current parallelization using nested parallelism worsens this problem due to the
implicit barrier necessary at the end of each parallel loop. For this reason, the
first modification of the code consists of removing the nested parallelism and
using a task approach instead. In previous work, Chatterjee et al. [8] already
explored a task version of this Kernel, but there is minimal overlap with this
new version, illustrated in Listing 1.2.

```
1  #pragma omp parallel
2  #pragma omp single
3  for(int ipatch=0; ipatch<npatches; ipatch++){
4     for(int jpatch=0; jpatch<npatches; jpatch++){
5        for(int k=0; k<CIJ.cij[ipatch][jpatch].size(); k++){
6           double* Y_tmp = new double[vsize[ipatch]]();
7           Matrix A = CIJ.cij[ipatch][jpatch]->A[k];
8           Matrix B = CIJ.cij[ipatch][jpatch]->B[k];
9           int has_work = (A->nnz() && B->nnz());
10          if(has_work){
11             //Tasks in charge of dgemms. Red.
12 #pragma omp task depend(inout:Y_tmp[0:vsize[ipatch]]) firstprivate(A,B)
13             A->kron_mult('n','n', *A, *B, &X[j1], &Y_tmp[0]);
14             //Reduction tasks. Green.
15 #pragma omp task depend(inout: Y[i1:i2]) depend(in: Y_tmp[0:vsize[ipatch]])
16             {
17                int ilocal=0;
18                for(int i=i1; i<i2; i++) Y[i] += Y_tmp[ilocal++];
19                delete[] Y_tmp;
20 } } } } }
```

Listing 1.2. First Taskification

We keep only one parallel region (line 1) and add a single region (line 2)
where the tasks will be created. We define two kinds of tasks: a **computation
task**, that perform *dgemm* operations, and a **reduction task**, that accumulates
partial results from the first one into the return array. To pass intermediate
results from a *dgemm* task to its corresponding reduction task, we use temporal
arrays which are allocated sequentially by the same thread that creates the tasks.
To guarantee the correctness of the program the first task has an *out* dependence
on the temporary array and the second one has an *in* dependence. Additionally,
we define an *inout* dependence on a fraction of the return array to avoid several
tasks reducing on the same portion of Y simultaneously.

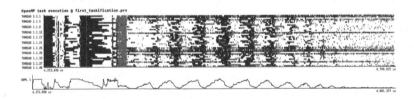

Fig. 3. First Taskification: Task Execution Timeline (Color figure online)

Figure 3 shows a trace of this version. In this case, the color represents which
task is being executed by each thread: the computing task is labeled as red
and the reduction task as green. This version allows exploiting more parallelism,

with many pink tasks running concurrently and avoiding periodic barriers. Nevertheless, we can still see other problems: (a) the duration of *computation tasks* has a considerable variability, with some tasks taking $18\,\mu s$ while the average is $150\,\mu s$, and (b) a single thread must allocate all the buffers before creating the corresponding task, which adds significant overhead. The second situation can be better appreciated with the pulsations of the bottom function plot in the figure, that shows the total number of pending tasks generated. When it starts executing regions with fine grain tasks, the number of ready tasks decrease quickly, and there are not enough tasks to fill every thread.

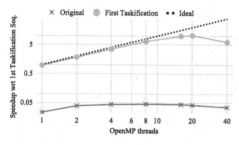

Fig. 4. Original vs first taskification

In Fig. 4, we can observe the speedup of the *Original* version with the nested work sharing and the taskified code. On the x axis we plot the number of OpenMP threads used, and the y axis shows the speedup with respect to the *First Taskification* version executed sequentially (i.e., with no OpenMP pragmas). Comparing one version to the other, we can see a speedup of $41.65\times$ with one thread when using the taskified version, which reveals the huge impact on the performance introduced by the nested worksharings. We can see the biggest difference at 20 OpenMP threads, with a value of $457.82\times$. Comparing the performance of the *First Taskification* version with respecto to ideal, it goes up to $10.55\times$ using 20 OpenMP threads, which indicates that there is still margin to improve the performance in subsequent versions. On the other hand, the speedup of the original code is around $0.045\times$ for 4 threads and above.

Memory usage [GB]	OpenMP Threads						
Code version	1	2	4	8	16	20	40
Original	1.39	1.40	1.40	1.42	1.46	1.47	1.55
First Taskification	1.39	1.43	1.44	1.47	1.62	1.64	1.61
Three Tasks	1.39	1.43	1.45	1.52	1.64	1.61	1.61
Priorities & Buffer Reuse	1.39	1.40	1.41	1.42	1.44	1.46	1.50
Overlap Iterations	1.39	1.41	1.41	1.47	1.47	1.48	1.49
Nested Tasks	1.39	1.39	1.40	1.41	1.43	1.41	1.46

Fig. 5. Total memory usage in GB for each version and different number of threads

In Fig. 5, we observe the total memory used in GB by each version depending on the number of OpenMP threads used. As we can see, the memory consumption is not a critical factor in our situation, but we want to demonstrate that this techniques don't increase the memory usage. In addition, memory usage is indeed a critical factor to scientifics using DMRG++, so porting this changes to the original application will allow them to use bigger inputs. In the *First Taskification* version since all the buffers are allocated at the beginning, the memory usage is higher than in the original one, and when using 20 threads the memory increases from $1.47\,GB$ to $1.64\,GB$. The rest of versions will be presented in the following sub-sections.

3.3 Tasks Distinction Based on Grain Size

In the *First Taskification* version, we see an issue with the very fine-grained tasks, which introduce a relevant overhead. To address this, in *Tasks' Size Distinction* version we define 3 kinds of tasks: **Fine grain tasks** with a low computational load, will do both the *computation* and the *reduction* (line 11); **Coarse grain compute task** (line 16); and the corresponding **reduction task** (line 19). The decision if a task has a high or a low load is taken based on a threshold that can be set by the user. The code corresponding to this version can be seen in Listing 1.3.

```
1 #pragma omp parallel
2 #pragma omp single
3 for(int ipatch=0; ipatch<npatches; ipatch++){
4    for(int jpatch=0; jpatch<npatches; jpatch++){
5       for(int k=0; k<CIJ.cij[ipatch][jpatch].size(); k++){
6          Matrix A = CIJ.cij[ipatch][jpatch]->A[k];
7          Matrix B = CIJ.cij[ipatch][jpatch]->B[k];
8          if(A->nnz() && B->nnz()){
9             if(vsize[ipatch] <= Threshold){
10               //Create single task for small pieces of work
11 #pragma omp task depend(inout: Y[i1:i2]) firstprivate(A, B)
12               A->kron_mult('n','n', *A, *B, &X[j1], &Y[i1]);
13            }else{
14               //Create compute task and reduction task for larger pieces
15               double* Y_tmp = new double[vsize[ipatch]]();
16 #pragma omp task depend(inout: Y_tmp[0:vsize[ipatch]]) firstprivate(A, B)
17               A->kron_mult('n','n', *A, *B, &X[j1], &Y_tmp[0]);
18 #pragma omp task depend(inout: Y[i1:i2]) depend(in: Y_tmp[0:vsize[ipatch]])
19               {
20                  int ilocal=0;
21                  for(int i=i1; i<i2; i++) Y[i] += Y_tmp[ilocal++];
22                  delete[] Y_tmp;
23 } } } } } }
```

Listing 1.3. Tasks' Size Distinction

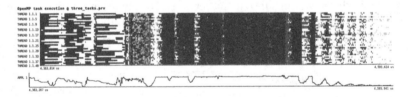

Fig. 6. Tasks' Size Distinction: Task Execution Timeline (Color figure online)

In Fig. 6, we plot a trace showing the behavior of this version. In this case, fine grain tasks are represented in red, compute tasks in green and reduction tasks in grey. Using this strategy, the application can exploit more parallelism, and there is less overhead of task creation, since the average task size has increased and the total number of tasks has decreased. The function at the bottom shows how this version can make better usage of the threads, reducing the number of pulsations from Fig. 3 of *First Taskification*.

In Fig. 7 (left), we plot the speedup obtained by the *Tasks' Size Distinction* version, which is computed with respect the *First Taskification* version when executed sequentially. As it can be seen, the previous version has a better performance when using a single thread, due to the if-else structure introduced in *Tasks' Size Distinction* version. Nevertheless, this fact allows for a better scaling, reaching a speedup of 1.19× and 1.6× when using 20 and 40 OpenMP threads, respectively.

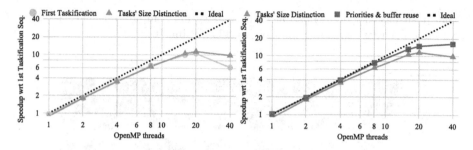

Fig. 7. First Taskification vs Tasks' Size Distinction (Left). Tasks' Size Distinction vs Priorities (Right)

3.4 Priorities and Buffer Reuse

In this version, we are going to address two problems from the *Tasks' Size Distinction* version: (a) the scheduling of the tasks to improve the performance, and (b) reusing buffer to improve the memory consumption. The new code is shown in Listing 1.4. To decrease memory consumption, instead of allocating one Y_tmp array for each task, we allocate a buffer of N arrays (line 1) that are reused by the different tasks. Each buffer establishes the dependence between compute and reduction tasks (previously Y_tmp), and also creates an anti-dependence between two compute tasks that use the same buffer.

```
 1  double*  buffers[NBUFF];  //Set of buffers to limit memory usage
 2  #pragma omp parallel
 3  #pragma omp single
 4  for(int ipatch=0; ipatch<npatches; ipatch++){
 5    for(int jpatch=0; jpatch<npatches; jpatch++){
 6      for(int k=0; k<CIJ.cij[ipatch][jpatch].size(); k++){
 7        Matrix A = CIJ.cij[ipatch][jpatch]->A[k];
 8        Matrix B = CIJ.cij[ipatch][jpatch]->B[k];
 9        if(A->nnz() && B->nnz()){
10          if(vsize[ipatch] <= Threshold){
11  #pragma omp task depend(inout: Y[i1:i2]) firstprivate(A, B) priority(0)
12            kron_mult('n','n', A, B, &X[j1], &Y[i1]); //New kron_mult call
13          }else{
14            mybuff = next = (next+1)%NBUFF;
15            int prio = vsize[ipatch] > PrioThreshold; //Dynamic priority
16  #pragma omp task depend(inout: buffers[mybuff]) \
17                   firstprivate(mybuff,ipatch,A,B) priority(prio)
18            {
19              double* Y_tmp = new double[vsize[ipatch]]();
20              buffers[mybuff] = Y_tmp;
21              kron_mult('n','n', A, B, &X[j1], Y_tmp);
22            }
23  #pragma omp task depend(inout:Y[i1:i2],buffers[mybuff]) \
24                   firstprivate(mybuff) priority(10)
25            {
26              double* Y_tmp=buffers[mybuff];
27              int ilocal=0;
28              for(int i=i1; i<i2; i++) Y[i] += Y_tmp[ilocal++];
29              delete[] Y_tmp;
30  } } } } }
```

Listing 1.4. Priorities and Buffer Reuse

Task priorities have also been added to help on improving the schedule of the tasks (i.e., schedule the bigger tasks first, followed by the smaller ones). Reduction tasks (line 23) have been assigned with the highest priority, to free buffer positions as soon as possible. The coarse grain compute tasks are assigned a variable priority depending on their workload (line 16).

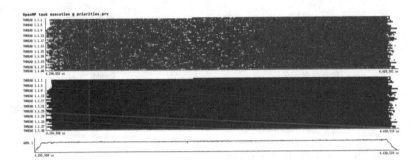

Fig. 8. Priorities and Buffer Reuse: Task Execution and Task Order Timelines (Color figure online)

Figure 8 shows a task execution timeline of this version (top), where the task coloring corresponds to the one in Fig. 6, and the task execution order (middle), where green stands for older tasks (instantiated early) and blue for younger ones. We can see the execution of tasks instantiated "late" (dark blue) are intermixed with the execution of tasks instantiated "early" (light green). Coalescing the priorities of the tasks as explained earlier, the execution timeline is now more compact, thereby leveraging more parallelism and almost removing pulsations of tasks (bottom function plot).

In Fig. 7(right), we plot the speedup obtained of the *Priorities and Buffer Reuse* version compared with the *Tasks' Size Distinction*. The speedup has been computed in both cases with respect to the *First Taskification* version executed sequentially. One should note that this new version performs better than the previous one, in particular for a high number of thread count. With 16 OpenMP threads, the execution is 1.28× faster than the *Tasks' Size Distinction* version. We can also see that the performance improves for 20 and 40 threads, although it is still far from the ideal one. Despite this fact, this is the first version which performance improves when using 40 OpenMP threads. Regarding the memory usage, it has been reduced achieving values equal to the *Original* version, as shown in Fig. 5.

3.5   Overlap Iterations

One of the issues detected in the *Priorities and Reuse Buffer* version is the imbalance at the end of the iteration, produced by the lack of parallelism and coarse grained tasks that need to be executed at that moment. Taking into account that the real application performs several iterations of this kernel, overlapping different iterations can reduce the impact of the imbalance. To achieve this, we move the parallel region up to include several iterations, as can be seen in Listing 1.5.

```
1 #pragma omp parallel
2 #pragma omp single
3 for(int its=0; its<NITS; its++){
4   //same code from Listing 1.4
5 }
```

Listing 1.5. Overlap iterations

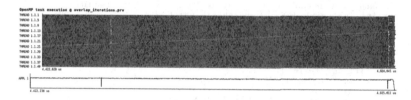

Fig. 9. Overlap Iterations: Task Execution Timeline (Color figure online)

In Fig. 9 we can see a trace of this version including 5 iterations. The color represents the task being executed: red for **fine grain tasks** including computation and reduction, green for **coarse grain compute tasks**, and grey for **reduction tasks**. Although we can visually detect the five iterations, we can see that the tasks belonging to different iterations are executed concurrently, thereby increasing the parallelism and reducing the imbalance.

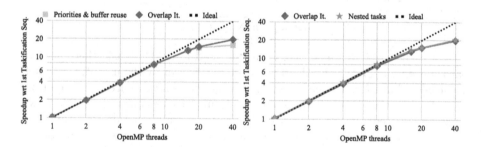

Fig. 10. Priorities vs Overlap It. (Left). Overlap It. vs Nested Tasks (Right)

Figure 10 (left) shows the speedup for the *Overlap Iterations* version. We can see that its performance is slightly better than the *Priorities* version, except in the case of 40 threads, where it obtains an improved gain of 1.24×. Because the unbalance increase as we add more threads, we will have a better benefit from overlapping iterations.

3.6 Nested Tasks

Upon further analysis of the *Overlap Iterations* version, we observe that grey tasks, with an average duration of few microseconds, are limiting the scalability. To address this issue, we implement a new task decomposition, with two levels of tasks. This strategy takes into account that the load only depends on ipatch.

```
1  char* sentinel = new char[npatches](); //Dependence token
2  #pragma omp parallel
3  #pragma omp single
4  for(int its=0; its<NITS; its++){
5    for(int ipatch=0; ipatch<npatches; ipatch++){
6      int fine_grain = vsize[ipatch] <= Threshold;
7      //New external task. It will generate more tasks based on size of ipatch
8  #pragma omp task depend(inout: sentinel[ipatch]) priority(10)
9      for(int jpatch=0; jpatch<npatches; jpatch++){
10       for(int k=0; k<CIJ.cij[ipatch][jpatch].size(); k++){
11         Matrix A = CIJ.cij[ipatch][jpatch]->A[k];
12         Matrix B = CIJ.cij[ipatch][jpatch]->B[k];
13         if(A->nnz() && B->nnz()){
14           //Fine_grain branch. Each task will always take the same path
15           if(fine_grain){
16             kron_mult('n','n', A, B, &X[j1], &Y[i1]);
17           }else{
18             double** buffer = new double*;
19  #pragma omp task depend(out:buffer)firstprivate(A,B,buffer,ipatch)priority
       (0)
20           {
21             double* Y_tmp = new double[vsize[ipatch]]();
22             buffer[mybuff] = Y_tmp;
23             kron_mult('n','n', A, B, &X[j1], Y_tmp);
24           }
25  #pragma omp task depend(inout:Y[i1:i2])depend(in:buffer)firstprivate(buffer)
       priority(5)
26           {
27             double* Y_tmp=buffer[mybuff];
28             int ilocal=0;
29             for(int i=i1; i<i2; i++) Y[i] += Y_tmp[ilocal++];
30             delete[] Y_tmp;
31             delete[] buffer;
32         } } } }
33         #pragma omp taskwait
34  } } }
```

Listing 1.6. Nested Tasks

For each ipatch, a single task is created, and inside this task, there are two paths depending on the threshold of the ipatch size set by the user. If the ipatch is considered fine grain, then the computation and reduction are computed (line 16). On the other hand, if the ipatch is deemed to be coarse grain, then two tasks are created: the compute task (line 19) and the reduction task (line 25). To guarantee that ipatches from different iterations are executed in the correct order (i.e., they do not overtake each other) a sentinel is used to generate a dependence (line 8).

Fig. 11. Nested Tasks: Task Execution Timeline (Color figure online)

In Fig. 11, we can see a task execution timeline of this version with five iterations overlapped. Here, the **external task** is red, while grey and green are the **reduction** and **compute tasks** respectively, like in the previous versions. This version has reduced the number of tasks created and parallelized the tasks' creation, which reduces the overhead from *Overlap Iterations* version. However, it presents a severe imbalance at the end, caused by the creation of tasks near the end, which limits its performance and will be addressed in future work.

Figure 10 (right), shows the speedup obtained with the *Nested Tasks* version over the *Overlap Iterations*. We can see a slight gain of performance of 1.06× and 1.05× using 8 and 16 OpenMP threads respectively; with 40 OpenMP threads the gain is even smaller, reaching 1.03×, caused by the big unbalance at the end of the execution shown in Fig. 11. Besides, this version reduces the memory usage for all the number of threads, with the higher difference from *Original* version at 90 MB when using 40 OpenMP threads, being the best one both in terms of execution time and memory usage, as illustrated in Fig. 5.

4 Summary and Best Practices

In this section, we summarize all the results obtained by the different optimizations and we present the lessons learned with this work as some best practices and guidelines for developers facing similar challenges.

In Fig. 12 we can see the speedup of the different versions presented with respect to the sequential execution of the *First Taskification* code. The performance of the *Original* code is not shown because its performance is too far from the optimized versions to be displayed on the same scale; nevertheless, it can be found in Fig. 4.

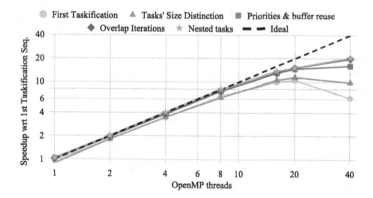

Fig. 12. Performance summary of the different versions

The most important improvement was obtained when adding the tasking model instead of the nested loop parallelism (585× with 40 threads). The following optimizations provided incremental gain, less spectacular but significant in global and especially when scaling to a high number of threads. Comparing the *First Taskification* and *Nested Tasks* versions we observe a speedup of 1,24× with 8 threads and 3,32× with 40 threads. We conclude that these fine grain optimizations are necessary when scaling applications to a high number of cores.

The limiting factor of the last version (*Nested Tasks*) seems to be the NUMA effect when using two sockets and the late instantiation of some "big" tasks, leaving a significant load imbalance at the end. As future work, we can try to mitigate this effect by using higher priorities for tasks that will create more tasks.

The main lesson learned with this work is the potential of the tasking model to address irregular problems, even for codes with a regular structure with loops, where a `parallel loop` construct can be used straight forward. Also, we have seen the high impact on the performance of synchronizations imposed by the parallel construct. We highlight how using clauses like `priorities` or `dependences` to fine tune the parallelization are crucial to achieving good scalability to a high number of threads while keeping the flexibility of the runtime to schedule them.

5   Conclusions

In this study, we have presented the modifications done to the Kronecker Product mini-application with the OpenMP tasking model. We have demonstrated the benefits of using this model, both in terms of performance and programmability for algorithms with such irregular computation. Besides, this work can be considered as a best practice for other researchers dealing with similar algorithms, including uneven workloads, huge imbalances or granularity problems.

Applying the described changes to the mini-application, we report a speedup of 8.0× with 8 OpenMP threads of the *Nested Tasks* version with respect to the serial code and 20.5× with 40 threads. Also, the memory usage decreases 90 MB, from *Original* version. The optimization has been done keeping the number of changes to the source code to a minimum. Moreover, the number of pragmas has been reduced increasing the programmability and maintainability of the code.

We consider this kind of work, not only an optimization and best practice programming guidelines, but also useful for co-design effort to the OpenMP community. For example, the if-else structure to generate a different kind of tasks depending on its load is not as elegant as one would want. The compiler could generate the code for the two branches given the corresponding syntax.

As future work, imbalances from *Nested Tasks* version will be addressed. Also, some features from OpenMP 5.0 may be used, like the *mutexinoutset* dependence type. Finally, a hybrid approach with MPI may help to reduce the NUMA effect detected when scaling from 20 to 40 cores.

Acknowledgments. This work is partially supported by the Spanish Government through Programa Severo Ochoa (SEV-2015-0493), by the Spanish Ministry of Science and Technology (project TIN2015-65316-P), by the Generalitat de Catalunya (contract 2017-SGR-1414) and by the BSC-IBM Deep Learning Research Agreement, under JSA "Application porting, analysis and optimization for POWER and POWER AI". This work was partially supported by the Scientific Discovery through Advanced

Computing (SciDAC) program funded by U.S. Department of Energy, Office of Science, Advanced Scientific Computing Research and Basic Energy Sciences, Division of Materials Sciences and Engineering. This research used resources of the Oak Ridge Leadership Computing Facility at the Oak Ridge National Laboratory, which is supported by the Office of Science of the U.S. Department of Energy under Contract No. DE-AC05-00OR22725.

References

1. Extrae website. https://tools.bsc.es/extrae. Accessed May 2019
2. Paraver website. https://tools.bsc.es/paraver. Accessed June 2019
3. Power9 CTE User's Guide. https://www.bsc.es/support/POWER_CTE-ug.pdf. Accessed May 2019
4. Alvarez, G.: DMRG++ website. https://g1257.github.com/dmrgPlusPlus
5. Alvarez, G.: Implementation of the SU(2) Hamiltonian symmetry for the DMRG algorithm. Comput. Phys. Commun. **183**, 2226–2232 (2012)
6. Alvarez, G.: The density matrix renormalization group for strongly correlated electron systems: a generic implementation. Comput. Phys. Commun. **180**(9), 1572–1578 (2009)
7. Cajas, J.C., et al.: Fluid-structure interaction based on HPC multicode coupling. SIAM J. Sci. Comput. **40**(6), C677–C703 (2018)
8. Chatterjee, A., Alvarez, G., D'Azevedo, E., Elwasif, W., Hernandez, O., Sarkar, V.: Porting DMRG++ scientific application to OpenPOWER. In: Yokota, R., Weiland, M., Shalf, J., Alam, S. (eds.) ISC High Performance 2018. LNCS, vol. 11203, pp. 418–431. Springer, Cham (2018). https://doi.org/10.1007/978-3-030-02465-9_29
9. Garcia, M., Labarta, J., Corbalan, J.: Hints to improve automatic load balancing with lewi for hybrid applications. J. Parallel Distrib. Comput. **74**(9), 2781–2794 (2014)
10. Garcia-Gasulla, M., Mantovani, F., Josep-Fabrego, M., Eguzkitza, B., Houzeaux, G.: Runtime mechanisms to survive new HPC architectures: a use case in human respiratory simulations. Int. J. High Perform. Comput. Appl. (2019, online)
11. Llort, G., Servat, H., González, J., Giménez, J., Labarta, J.: On the usefulness of object tracking techniques in performance analysis. In: Proceedings of the International Conference on High Performance Computing, Networking, Storage and Analysis, p. 29. ACM (2013)
12. Martineau, M., McIntosh-Smith, S.: The productivity, portability and performance of OpenMP 4.5 for scientific applications targeting Intel CPUs, IBM CPUs, and NVIDIA GPUs. In: de Supinski, B.R., Olivier, S.L., Terboven, C., Chapman, B.M., Müller, M.S. (eds.) IWOMP 2017. LNCS, vol. 10468, pp. 185–200. Springer, Cham (2017). https://doi.org/10.1007/978-3-319-65578-9_13
13. OpenMP Architecture Review Board: OpenMP 4.5 Specification. Technical report, November 2015. https://www.openmp.org/wp-content/uploads/openmp-4.5.pdf
14. Pillet, V., Labarta, J., Cortes, T., Girona, S.: PARAVER: a tool to visualize and analyze parallel code. In: Proceedings of WoTUG-18: Transputer and OCCAM Developments, vol. 44, pp. 17–31. IOS Press (1995)
15. Sadasivam, S.K., Thompto, B.W., Kalla, R., Starke, W.J.: IBM Power9 processor architecture. IEEE Micro **37**(2), 40–51 (2017)

Cache Line Sharing and Communication in ECP Proxy Applications

Joshua Randall$^{(\boxtimes)}$ ⓘ, Alejandro Rico ⓘ, and Jose A. Joao ⓘ

Arm Research, Austin, TX, USA
{joshua.randall,alejandro.rico,jose.joao}@arm.com

Abstract. Scientific computing codes rely on efficient parallelization to achieve performance. This parallel efficiency is reduced by factors such as communication, serialization, and data sharing. In this work, we examine interactions between OpenMP threads in the context of a Chip-multiprocessor (CMP). We first analyze cache line sharing to observe how often multiple threads are accessing the same data. We then look at producer-consumer and write-invalidation interactions between these threads. These interactions are implemented with cache coherence operations and demonstrate interference between threads. We find that none of the codes studied show prohibitive amounts of communication and many interactions between threads follow simple patterns. Our work discovers opportunities to increase parallel efficiency in the analyzed codes and provides motivating data for research into CMP design.

Keywords: Cache-communication · Coherence · Multi-core · Performance analysis · Scalability

1 Introduction

Multi-core processors with an increasing number of cores have potential to significantly boost performance of parallel applications, including high-performance computing (HPC) codes, by running multiple MPI processes and OpenMP threads in parallel. However, that potential may be thwarted by inter-thread communication, which can reduce single thread performance by disrupting cache locality. We identify two examples of inter-thread communication.

First, *producer-consumer communication* happens when one thread (producer) writes data that another thread (consumer) reads through a cache-to-cache transfer from the producer private cache to the consumer private cache. Second, *write invalidation communication* is when one thread running on core A writes to a cache line that is held in one or more remote private caches. These remote caches must be invalidated before the cache line can be brought in exclusive state and written to in core A's cache. Write invalidations can occur due

---

This work was in collaboration with Cray and funded in part by the DOE ECP Path-Forward program.

ⓒ Springer Nature Switzerland AG 2019
X. Fan et al. (Eds.): IWOMP 2019, LNCS 11718, pp. 306–319, 2019.
https://doi.org/10.1007/978-3-030-28596-8_21

to writes to truly shared data or due to writes to thread-private data that is on different words within the same cache line, which is called *false sharing*.

Application developers may improve parallel performance by reducing inter-thread communication. False sharing can be eliminated by allocating shared data and private data for different threads on different cache lines through alignment and padding. However, producer-consumer communication and write invalidations of truly shared data is intrinsic to the algorithm and can only be avoided with algorithmic changes.

In this paper, we study OpenMP inter-thread communication of HPC Proxy-Apps with a characterization of the following interactions:

- **Cache line sharing** among OpenMP threads to understand how inter-thread code and data sharing occurs on the cache hierarchy.
- **Producer-consumer communication** that results in direct cache-to-cache transfers.
- **Write invalidation communication** that occurs when shared data is modified.

Frequency of communication interactions indicate their likelihood of impacting performance and scalability of the applications, while interaction patterns visualize data movement between cores and provide insight into possible data movement optimizations.

2   Experimental Setup

2.1   ECP Proxy Apps

This Exascale Computing Project (ECP) [5] provides a collection of proxy applications that demonstrate a variety of multi-threading characteristics from HPC codes.

These proxy applications model characteristics of large scale HPC codes without the large code bases and problem sizes that are inherent to production HPC codes. These miniaturized codes enable detailed analysis of how these HPC codes run on single nodes or clusters. For our analysis, we examined behavior of these proxy apps from the perspective of a single CMP. Specifically, we evaluated the coherence behavior that these proxy apps demonstrate as the number of OpenMP threads increases.

Two of the proxy applications we evaluate, CoMD and miniFE, are no longer part of the latest release of the proxy application suite, but are still interesting to software developers. LULESH [7] is not part of the ECP proxy application suite, but has been a widely studied proxy app in multiple DOE exascale initiatives.

Inputs and Scaling. Table 1 shows the scaling strategy and base input sets used in this paper. Weak scaling, i.e., scaling problem sizes proportionally with the number of threads, was used when possible, in order to keep the amount of data per thread constant. For AMG, CoMD, ExaMiniMD, and LULESH, we maintained a cubic input size and doubled the volume as thread counts doubled. Therefore, doubling threads scaled each dimension by a factor of the cube root of 2. For miniFE, we maintained a constant z dimension and alternated doubling the y and x dimensions as thread counts doubled. For the other proxy applications, we applied strong scaling, where we problem size remains the same when increasing the number of threads.

Table 1. Inputs and scaling for proxy applications

Proxy App	Scaling Used	Parameters (2 threads)
ExaMiniMD	Weak	50 50 50
AMG	Weak	-n 94 94 94 -P 1 1 1
miniFE	Weak	-nx 32 -ny 16 -nz 128
LULESH	Weak	-s 25 -i 10
CoMD	Weak	-e -x 20 -y 20 -z 20 -T 4000 -N 2 -n 1
miniAMR	Strong	--nx 16 --ny 16 --nz 16 --num_vars 40
SWFFT	Strong	2 512
XSBench	Strong	-t 2 -l 5000000 -s large
miniVite	Strong	-n 150000

2.2 DynamoRIO

We measured data accesses and data sharing of the proxy apps using DynamoRIO [4]. DynamoRIO is a dynamic binary instrumentation tool that includes a cache simulator. This tool does not include a detailed core model, so it does not simulate cycles and timing, but it can produce an accurate estimation of cache behavior. While multithreaded simulation is supported in DynamoRIO, we had to implement coherence support on top of the latest open source version to properly track cache line sharing. Our results were collected during the parallel phase of execution for each proxy application. We statically mapped one logical thread per core in our simulations.

2.3 Compiler and Runtime System

All proxy applications were compiled using GCC version 7.1.0 and memory traces were gathered for AARCH64 code running the libgomp OpenMP runtime included with GCC. All of the proxy applications use OpenMP with the exception of ExaMiniMD, which is parallelized using Kokkos. We measured cache line communication during the entire parallel execution phase of each proxy apps.

2.4   Evaluation of Cache Line Sharing

We simulated three levels of cache in DynamoRIO. A shared LLC with 2 MB per core backs up coherent 512 KB private L2 caches, which are inclusive with 64 KB L1I and L1D caches. Our simulated cache hierarchy uses a directory-based write-back cache policy to keep the L2 caches coherent. Each L2 and its child L1 caches perform accesses for a single thread. We measured the sharing state of unique cache lines between all L2 caches over time, as well as how widely each of these cache lines was shared between L2 caches. We also measured the frequency with which each private cache shares data with each other private cache.

2.5   Evaluation of Inter-thread Communication

Producer-consumer communication may be analyzed by tracking reads and writes at a word granularity. This analysis would be hardware agnostic and may not reflect the communication that actually occurs between cores during execution. We choose to analyze communication *coherently* to qualify communication that manifests in inter-cache transactions. In this context, communicating reads are remote accesses to dirty cache lines, or lines that have been written to and not evicted from the writing core's private cache. This analysis will show actual movement of data from communicating accesses between private caches during execution, and will include the effects of *false communication* caused by *false sharing*. False communication refers to unnecessary communication between caches that are accessing different words in the same cache line. Our results show the frequency of coherent communication during execution and reveal patterns in this communication.

Write invalidations occur when a core writes to a cache line of which another copy exists in another core's cache. The writing thread must complete an invalidation of cache line copies in any other cache before the write may be completed. Writing to data that is widely shared will add latency for the write operation and increase traffic in the Network-on-Chip (NoC). We counted write invalidations during execution of the proxy applications to compute their frequency. We also observe any patterns between frequently writing threads and frequently invalidated threads.

3   Results and Discussion

3.1   Cache Line Sharing Analysis

Cache line sharing occurs when multiple threads read from a cache line within the same period of time, causing the copies of that cache line to exist in multiple private caches simultaneously. This analysis offers insight into how well data is isolated between threads and how often different threads are operating on the same or adjacent data.

Figure 1 shows the number of shared caches lines as a percentage of total L2 capacity. We sampled caches at equal intervals during the parallel phase of

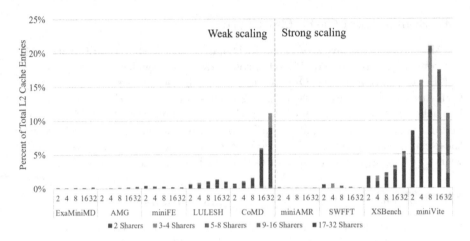

Fig. 1. Percent of L2 cache lines at various degrees of sharing

execution and averaged the shared cache line counts of these samples. These shared cache line state counts are grouped based on how many private caches hold cache lines at a time. OpenMP thread counts for each proxy application sweep from 2 to 32 threads in powers of two. We separated the proxy apps by scaling strategy and ordered them by average number of shared cache lines. For most proxy applications, very few cache lines have more than one copy in L2 caches. Only miniVite, CoMD, and XSBench show a significant number of cache lines in shared state. These cache line sharing rates demonstrate how well data is isolated between threads for these proxy applications. In order to correlate this cache line sharing to specific data and sections of code, we examined the program counters of load instructions that resulted in cache lines transitioning to shared state.

MiniVite shows the highest number of shared cache lines for various thread counts, and also shows the highest number of cache lines with high degrees of sharing. MiniVite is a graph analysis proxy app that examines connectivity of nodes in a graph to categorize these nodes into communities. Highly shared cache lines contain nodes in a graph that are connected to nodes in multiple communities. For this proxy application, the number of shared cache lines is high even for low thread counts, and some of the shared cache lines are widely distributed amongst L2 caches. Writes to highly distributed shared cache lines require multiple messages to invalidate copies, increasing the latency of the write operation and increasing traffic in the on-chip network.

We weak scaled the proxy apps for which we had a clear weak scaling option, keeping the amount of data per thread consistent. The proportion of shared cache lines remains similar as threads scaled up for all these weak scaled proxy apps except CoMD. CoMD shows significantly more cache line sharing when it is run with higher thread counts. This trend is an effect of the way we scaled the problem for CoMD. We kept the problem cubic and scaled each dimension by the cube root of 2 as thread counts doubled. Increasing the X and Y dimensions of this problem increases the surface area between thread data, which explains the increase in cache line sharing between 2 and 8 threads. At 16 threads and beyond, each thread processes less than two layers in the Z dimension. This causes atoms in some boxes to be read by both the previous and the following threads. Because of this, the proportion of shared cache lines greatly increases when the Z dimension is less than twice the number of threads. Maintaining the X and Y dimensions while increasing the Z dimension would control for these effects and eliminate cache line sharing. We confirmed that cache line sharing stayed consistent when we scaled CoMD in only the Z dimension.

XSBench also shows a higher number of shared cache lines as the number of threads increases. This cache line sharing primarily occurs during binary searches of nuclide lookup tables. When multiple threads perform binary look ups of energies from the same nuclide table, they share the first access to the halfway point in the table. These threads share more table accesses depending on how similar their search energies are. Increasing thread count increases the probability of other threads accessing the same parts of the nuclide tables. These nuclide tables are read-only during execution, so we don't expect this cache line sharing to translate to significant inter-cache communication.

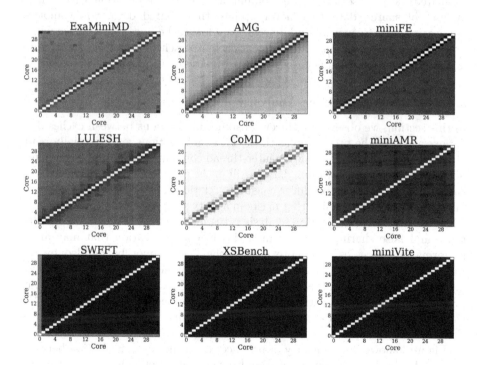

Fig. 2. Cache line sharing pairs with 32 cores

Figure 2 shows the frequency of each pair of cores holding the same cache line in their L2 caches. We collected this data for 32-core simulations. Darker regions of the maps indicate higher cache line sharing. These sharing heat maps offer a visualization of which cores share cache lines and show correlations in data accesses between thread IDs. Shading is normalized to the maximum value for each proxy app in order to show the behavior of these proxy apps, rather than to compare rates of cache line sharing between them. For most of these proxy applications, cache lines are typically shared between consecutive threads. Codes that demonstrate this pattern may benefit from a scheduler that maps consecutive threads to adjacent cores. In the cases of ExaMiniMD, AMG, miniFE, LULESH, and CoMD, each core shares more data with adjacent cores than any other cores. This suggests that mapping logically neighboring threads to adjacent cores will improve data locality and reduce communication delay between common sharers on a chip. This tendency to share with neighboring threads also shows that clustering adjacent cores may be beneficial for these proxy apps. Proxy apps with uniformly shaded maps, such as miniAMR, SWFFT, XSBench, and miniVite, display all-to-all sharing patterns.

While this cache line sharing analysis provides insight into how much data is being accessed by multiple threads, it does not demonstrate how often updates to shared data cause inter-cache communication. An application with a high amount of shared data may never update that shared data, while another application may frequently update relatively few cache lines. We analyze which proxy applications demonstrate frequent cache-to-cache interactions by measuring communication events caused by data updates.

3.2   Producer-Consumer Analysis

In this section, we observe producer-consumer interactions between caches during execution of the proxy applications. These interactions are essentially read-after-write operations. We analyze inter-thread communication from a coherence perspective, showing how often data is still in the producing core's cache when it is consumed. Coherence producer-consumer relationships occur when a consuming thread loads a cache line that exists in a dirty state in another private cache. This coherence communication analysis takes into account temporal access distance and false sharing, showing inter-thread communication that may affect performance. Accesses to remote dirty cache lines cannot be fulfilled by the LLC and require writeback by the private cache of the producing thread. This increases the latency of the consuming request. First, we measure the rate of producer-consumer transactions between caches for each of the proxy apps. We then analyze patterns in these accesses to understand how data moves between threads.

Figure 3 shows the frequency of producer-consumer communication between caches. We display this communication frequency per 1,000 instructions to compare rates between proxy apps and establish an estimate for the frequency of these transactions. Counting events per thousand instructions allows an estimation of the frequency of these occurrences while being agnostic towards the core

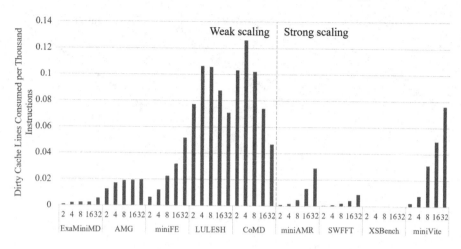

Fig. 3. Consumption rates of modified cache lines

design. Different core designs may execute instructions at different rates and different out-of-order execution capabilities to hide memory latency. Therefore, a simulated core model would be needed to determine the overhead of these communication operations. The normalization per 1,000 instructions is considering instructions executed by all threads, so the rates should be seen as rates per thread as long as the communication happens during parallel sections. If the number of communications grows sub-linear with the number of threads in the weak scaling cases, we would observe a decrease in the number of communication per 1,000 with a linear increase in total instructions. CoMD and LULESH are examples of this behavior, and they exhibit producer-consumer communication more than once per 10,000 instructions for some thread counts. For these two proxy apps, the consuming accesses rate does not increase linearly with thread count past four threads, while instruction counts increase proportionally to thread count due to weak scaling.

MiniAMR, miniFE, and miniVite show consistently increases in communication with higher thread counts. MiniAMR and miniVite are strong scaling cases and therefore see an increase on the total number of communications while the same work spreads across more threads. This trend is unexpected for miniFE, because this proxy app was weak scaled for these experiments. In this case, the number of producer-consumer interactions increases superlinearly with the number of threads.

Figure 4 shows the frequency of each pair of cores exhibiting producer-consumer cache transactions for a 32-core configuration. XSBench has negligible occurrences of producer-consumer relationships between cores with almost no writes to shared data, so its data has been omitted from this figure. To understand the code causing each of these communication patterns and what data is being communicated, we examined the program counters that caused communication between core pairs.

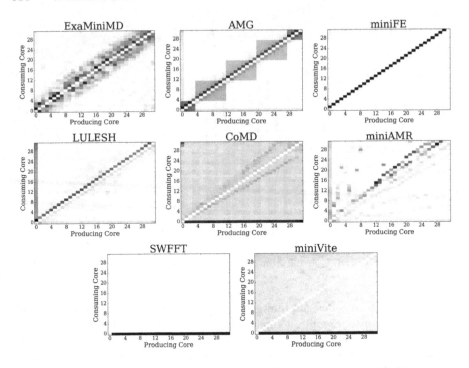

Fig. 4. Producer-Consumer coherence communication patterns with 32 cores

Multiple proxy applications show producer-consumer relationships between neighboring threads. This communication occurs in a single direction for AMG, LULESH, miniAMR, and miniFE, with threads producing data that is consumed primarily by threads with a higher ID. This one-sided communication could occur at the beginning of each iteration after neighboring threads updated their data. The final data updated by one thread would be the first data read by the following thread during a compute interval. Although both the previous and next thread would eventually read the updated data, the data would have been evicted by the producing thread's cache before the previous thread consumes that data at the end of its work iteration. A hardware agnostic evaluation of communication would observe this behavior as symmetric communication, but our coherent analysis reveals this communication may occur between caches asymmetrically and may be predictable, which would enable data to be pushed from producer to consumer in hardware or software.

ExaMiniMD shows symmetrical producer-consumer relationships, where threads produce data that is read by previous or following threads. This may be because ExaMiniMD uses dynamic scheduling, which makes thread interactions less predictable.

The four boxes of all-to-all communication for AMG occur during the *BuildIJLaplacian27pt* routine, when all threads are accumulating into the same array. While each thread accesses a different index of this array for their accumulations, false sharing causes 8 words of this array to map to the same cache line. Therefore, groups of 8 threads perform modifications to the same cache line, causing the cache line to migrate between that group of threads. The smaller boxes of communication between threads 0–3 and threads 28–31 suggest that the beginning of the shared array is offset within a cache line. This false communication could be avoided if the accumulation array is padded such that each thread index in the array maps to a different cache line. The compiler might also be able to avoid this situation by recognizing that threads accumulate to consecutive indices of the array and allocating one cache line for each index. It might also be beneficial if the code was written to utilize OpenMP's reduction capability instead of implementing its own reduction.

Significant communication to or from core 0, such as in the cases of LULESH, CoMD, SWFFT, and miniVite, are caused by serial sections of code. Serial sections may be problematic for scalability, and communication within these serial sections is on the critical path for the entire process, so this might introduce more overhead than communication within parallel sections.

The communication pattern of LULESH shows a one-to-all communication pattern, with significant consumption of data from thread 0 by all other threads. This communication occurs in the libgomp library when thread 0 broadcasts function pointers. LULESH has many consecutive short parallel regions, so this work distribution communication is frequent. This fine-grained parallel loop pattern is detrimental due to the work distribution (fork) and barrier (join) costs, and the serial sections in between loops limiting scaling. A coarser-grained parallelization strategy would mitigate these issues and reduce the amount of one-to-many communications like the ones exhibited by LULESH.

CoMD, SWFFT, and miniVite each show an all-to-one communication pattern, with thread 0 consuming a significant amount of data from all other threads. These consumption patterns occur due to code serialization, where there is a non-parallelized loop with thread 0 iterating over data produced by other threads. For CoMD, serialized reads occur when the atoms in boxes are being updated. This function is serialized per process, which limits scaling with OpenMP threads. For SWFFT, this behavior is the only occurrence of producer-consumer relationships. We observe this behavior when thread 0 distributes data between FFT steps. These serial phases substantially limit OpenMP scalability for SWFFT. For miniVite, serialization happens when thread 0 updates the ownership of graph elements for its process. The serialized loops reduce the parallel efficiency of OpenMP threads due to Amdahl's law. Avoiding serialization or finding a way to parallelize the loops would help scalability.

Preemptively moving data to caches of consuming threads might mitigate some of the overhead of these communications. This could be done in software by cache stashing, or in hardware via data movement prediction or prefetching.

3.3   Write Invalidation Analysis

Write operations to cache lines in shared state experience additional latency, because the write operation must wait for other copies of the cache line to

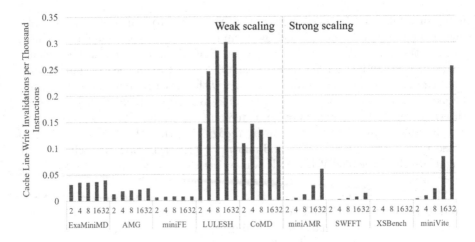

Fig. 5. Write invalidation rates

be invalidated. Write operations to cache lines with more sharers require more invalidation messages, which increases latency and network traffic. The latency might be covered up by an out-of-order core, but the additional network traffic might delay other memory operations. Invalidating cache lines from other caches can also induce future cache misses, which would be unnecessary in the case of false communication. We measured the frequency of write invalidations to understand how this communication occurs in the proxy apps.

Figure 5 shows write invalidations per 1,000 instructions. CoMD and LULESH experience on average at least one write-invalidation every 10k instructions even for low thread counts. MiniFE, miniVite, and SWFFT each show increases in write invalidation rates as thread counts increase.

Figure 6 shows how frequently the core on the x-axis invalidates cache lines from the core on the y-axis. XSBench has negligible occurrences of cache-to-cache write invalidations, so it has been omitted from this analysis. Similar to our previous analysis, we tracked program counters causing these invalidations to find out how this communication corresponds to the code.

For AMG, the invalidations to adjacent threads primarily occur during the relaxation routine. The invalidations between groups of neighbors, which appear as square boxes on the graph, are due to the same false sharing that we observed when analyzing AMG's producer-consumer communication patterns. Padding this array so that threads access disparate cache lines would reduce invalidation traffic as well as producer-consumer coherence traffic.

In CoMD, the invalidated cores are not always adjacent. The writes causing these invalidations occur primarily when threads are sorting atoms in each box after atoms are exchanged. The strange slope of the interactions occurs because the sorting loop is parallelized over the total boxes of the process including halo boxes, while force calculations are parallelized over only the local boxes. Cores 28-31 process halo boxes during this phase, while private caches at this time are

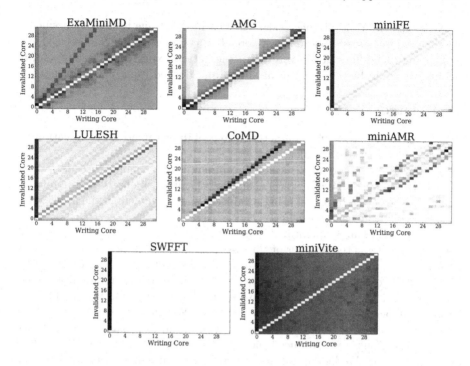

Fig. 6. Coherence invalidation patterns with 32 cores

filled with local box data. This communication may be reduced by splitting the loops that include halo boxes to iterate over local boxes before iterating over the halo boxes. Although this would decrease the write-invalidation traffic, this would introduce additional overhead from adding a separate parallel loop. Cores 30 and 31 invalidate data in core 0's cache because of the serialized updates preceding this operation.

For higher thread counts, miniVite shows a significant increase in write invalidations. Some of these write invalidations occur at the end of the Louvain iteration, when threads are overwriting the communities that nodes belong to. Write invalidations are also observed when information is updated for these communities after the Louvain iteration, overwriting data cached by threads during the iteration. The irregularity of graph accesses results in no discernible relationship between writing cores and invalidated cores.

Write invalidations caused by thread 0 of LULESH primarily occur in lib-gomp and are caused by the frequent serialization issue that we observed in the producer-consumer analysis.

In SWFFT, write invalidations increase with more threads. All invalidating writes come from core 0, exposing the same issue described in our analysis of producer-consumer patterns. These invalidations occur during the distribution phases, which are not parallelized with OpenMP.

Write invalidations are necessary when caches continue to hold data when it is written to by threads in a different core. This communication could be reduced by flushing cache lines in software when the data is expected to be updated, or the update could be predicted in hardware and flushed from private caches.

4   Related Work

Several publications include characterizations of inter-thread communication for specific multi-threaded workloads.

Barrow-Williams et al. [2] studied communication among threads for the SPLASH-2 [9] and PARSEC [3] benchmarks. Their work observed communication on a word granularity, showing producers and consumers in the application regardless of cache characteristics.

Hillenbrand et al. [6] quantified inter-thread communication for the PARSEC benchmark suite as the number of threads scaled up and measured this communication on a word granularity. Their approach abstracts out the hardware architecture, while our evaluation considers direct cache-to-cache communication.

In contrast to these two works, we examine data consumption and invalidation that occurs between caches at runtime. We include the effects of false sharing and disregard communication operations that do not result in cache-to-cache transactions, i.e., produced data that is evicted before being consumed by another cache. We believe our hardware-focused communication analysis is a better indicator of the impact communication has on performance.

Bienia et al. [3] introduced the PARSEC benchmark suite and characterized scalability as well as cache behavior. The authors measured and reported cache line sharing as the fraction of cache entries in shared state. We account for cache line sharing differently, by counting each unique shared state cache line once. Our approach to measuring cache line sharing shows how much data is shared between caches, without counting copies of the data. Bienia et al. also measured traffic from accesses to shared cache lines, but they did not differentiate by whether these accesses were communicating modified data.

Abadal et al. [1] measured the frequency of multicast operations in a Network-on-Chip during execution of SPLASH-2 and PARSEC benchmarks. They measured these multicasts for broadcast-based coherence as well as a directory-based coherence. The authors state that multicasts in a directory-based design are primarily due to write invalidations, which we measure in this paper.

Richards et al. [8] analyzed the performance of the ECP Proxy Apps with a focus on profiling, instruction mix, cache misses and memory bandwidth. The inter-thread cache-to-cache communication analysis in this paper complements their report with cache line sharing, producer-consumer interactions, and write invalidations in the context of OpenMP thread scaling.

5   Conclusion

In this work, we studied cache line sharing and cache-to-cache communication among OpenMP threads in HPC proxy applications. We identified CoMD,

XSbench, and miniVite as proxy apps that showed high cache line sharing. We then examined how often producer-consumer and write invalidation transactions occur. LULESH, CoMD, and miniVite showed the highest rates of communication among the proxy apps we studied.

Analysis of patterns in coherence traffic between cores running OpenMP threads provided insights into data movement between threads in these proxy applications. This analysis demonstrates to application developers how often communication in their code manifests as cache-to-cache communication at run time. In some cases, the patterns we observe reveal code serialization and false communication between threads. Application developers can use our methodology and results of our analysis to find where to parallelize serial sections of their code that cause considerable data movement, and where they can isolate data used by different threads to prevent false communication. When communication between threads is unavoidable, locality-aware thread placement and improvements in CMP architecture may reduce the overhead of this communication. Our characterization is useful for hardware designers considering data movement optimizations between caches or changes in the coherence protocol.

References

1. Abadal, S., Mestres, A., Martínez, R., Alarcín, E., Cabellos-Aparicio, A., Martínez, R.: Multicast on-chip traffic analysis targeting manycore NoC design. In: 2015 23rd Euromicro International Conference on Parallel, Distributed, and Network-Based Processing, pp. 370–378, March 2015. https://doi.org/10.1109/PDP.2015.26
2. Barrow-Williams, N., Fensch, C., Moore, S.: A communication characterisation of SPLASH-2 and PARSEC. In: 2009 IEEE International Symposium on Workload Characterization (IISWC), pp. 86–97, October 2009. https://doi.org/10.1109/IISWC.2009.5306792
3. Bienia, C., Kumar, S., Singh, J.P., Li, K.: The PARSEC benchmark suite: characterization and architectural implications. In: Proceedings of the 17th International Conference on Parallel Architectures and Compilation Techniques, pp. 72–81 (2008). https://doi.org/10.1145/1454115.1454128
4. DynamoRIO. https://www.dynamorio.org/
5. ECP Proxy Apps Suite. https://proxyapps.exascaleproject.org/
6. Hillenbrand, D., Tao, J., Balzer, M.: ALPS: a methodology for application-level communication characterization of Parsec 2.1. In: Proceedings of the International Conference on Computational Science, ICCS 2011. vol. 4, pp. 2086–2095 (2011). https://doi.org/10.1016/j.procs.2011.04.228
7. Livermore Unstructured Lagrangian Explicit Shock Hydrodynamics (LULESH). https://computation.llnl.gov/projects/co-design/lulesh
8. Richards, D., Aziz, O., Cook, J., Finkel, H., et al.: Quantitative performance assessment of proxy apps and parents. Technical report, Lawrence Livermore National Lab (LLNL), Livermore, CA (United States) (2018). https://proxyapps.exascaleproject.org/wp-content/uploads/2018/04/AD-CD-PA-1040PerfCompare.pdf
9. Woo, S.C., Ohara, M., Torrie, E., Singh, J.P., Gupta, A.: The SPLASH-2 programs: characterization and methodological considerations. ACM SIGARCH Comput. Archit. News **23**(2), 24–36 (1995). https://doi.org/10.1145/225830.223990

Making OpenMP Ready for C++ Executors

Thomas R. W. Scogland[1]([✉]), Dan Sunderland[2], Stephen L. Olivier[2],
David S. Hollman[2], Noah Evans[2], and Bronis R. de Supinski[1]

[1] Lawrence Livermore National Laboratory, Livermore, USA
{tscogland,bronis}@llnl.gov
[2] Center for Computing Research, Sandia National Laboratories, Albuquerque, USA
{dsunder,slolivi,dshollm,nevans}@sandia.gov

Abstract. For at least the last 20 years, many have tried to create a
general resource management system to support interoperability across
various concurrent libraries. The previous strategies all suffered from
additional toolchain requirements, and/or a usage of a shared programing
model that assumed it owned/controlled access to all resources available
to the program. None of these techniques have achieved wide spread
adoption. The ubiquity of OpenMP coupled with C++ developing a
standard way to describe many different concurrent paradigms (C++23
executors) would allow OpenMP to assume the role of a general resource
manager without requiring user code written directly in OpenMP. With
a few added features such as the ability to use otherwise idle threads to
execute tasks and to specify a task "width", many interesting concurrent
frameworks could be developed in native OpenMP and achieve high performance. Further, one could create concrete C++ OpenMP executors
that enable support for general C++ executor based codes, which would
allow Fortran, C, and C++ codes to use the same underlying concurrent
framework when expressed as native OpenMP or using language specific
features. Effectively, OpenMP would become the de facto solution for a
problem that has long plagued the HPC community.

Keywords: C++ executors · OpenMP tasks

1 Introduction

As high performance simulations reach extreme scales, the software engineering
and resource management challenges have become increasingly important. In
particular, managing machine-level parallelism, large numbers of threads, and
memory access patterns can be essential as individual machine nodes become
more capable and as the costs of data movement become prohibitive.

To manage the complexity of these systems, performance portability layers
(e.g. RAJA [13], Kokkos [7]) that support platform independent code written
in a higher-level abstraction are gaining wide adoption. In the broader computer science community, a similar approach of using higher-level work-runner

X. Fan et al. (Eds.): IWOMP 2019, LNCS 11718, pp. 320–332, 2019.
https://doi.org/10.1007/978-3-030-28596-8_22

abstractions has taken hold to allow algorithms to be expressed independently of the underlying execution system. These various efforts have spawned the current effort to define a fundamental executor concept and interface for C++, currently targeting C++23. This concept would support the use of user or vendor-defined executors with standard library algorithms to execute those algorithms in arbitrary contexts. Executors would generalize many aspects of RAJA and Kokkos, and would provide a common interface in which the next generation of platform-independent libraries could be written.

While these execution interfaces can make a component portable across different programming models or architectures, only code written using those interfaces gains those benefits. Simulations often consist of multiple components, libraries, and even languages. Composability between components in these complex systems can complicate their correct and effective use. The problem is often most severe when different components use different runtime systems, with each runtime system competing for resources. Attempts to solve the composability problem would provide application-level resource management [10] or a common substrates for resource management [8,15]. An especially promising approach uses OpenMP as a common thread pool and resource layer beneath other abstractions. Integrating a code written with OpenMP with a code using the RAJA or Kokkos OpenMP backend is no harder than integrating OpenMP codes, allowing modern C++ to interface (relatively) seamlessly with the occasional 30-year-old Fortran library that nobody admits to needing in their code but always seems to be there.

In a C++ executors world, this approach requires an implementation of the executor concept on top of OpenMP. This requirement is not, in itself, a problem. A parallel loop or a runner is straightforward to implement in OpenMP but executors and Kokkos and, to some extent, RAJA use a model that does not ideally match OpenMP. Some patterns cannot be expressed in OpenMP while adhering to their interfaces. Performance will suffer if these patterns are not enabled.

Our position paper proposes that two new developments, the executors proposal for the 2023 C++ standard and the increasing use of OpenMP as a resource manager, enable unique and synergistic solutions to these problems. The common timeframe for these standards provides a unique opportunity to codesign them. C++ is already the lingua franca for performance portability layers in HPC, and OpenMP is becoming the de facto runtime composition layer included in every major compiler implementation. Marrying the two in a way that provides best-in-class performance and composability for and between both models will open new possibilities for more performant, more maintainable, and more easily composed components and scientific applications.

This paper makes the following contributions:

- An analysis of the state of OpenMP tasking and offload from the perspective of abstraction layers and C++ executors;

– A proposal of two extensions to OpenMP to improve the composability of
  tasks, target regions, and parallel loops, as well as making asynchronous tasks
  more amenable to abstractions; and
– A discussion of the feasibility of implementing the extensions in both a
  research runtime and the OpenMP standard.

2 Background

For nearly a decade, the C++ standards committee (ISO/IEC JTC1/
SC22/WG21) has iterated on numerous designs of generic abstractions for execution, known as executors. Representing one of the most ambitious generic library
design efforts of its kind, the current proposal [11] aims to address the needs of
vastly different application domains, from embedded computing to high performance computing and everything in between. At least a subset of the features
proposed therein are likely to be merged into the C++ standard working draft
early in the C++23 cycle [18], with other portions expected to follow shortly
thereafter.

While the exact syntactic details of executors remain undecided, the various designs have fairly consistently focused several important axes in the design
space. The most prominent of these is the expression of cardinality of work, distinguished by the elaboration of separate interfaces for single and bulk execution,
somewhat akin to providing both a `parallel for` and `task` interface. Different
prominent stakeholders have tended to see either of these extremes as fundamental: GPGPU stakeholders, for instance, tend to consider bulk execution to
be fundamental. Networking stakeholders, on the other hand, tend to see single
execution as the fundamental operation. Designs that can incorporate both of
these world views have led to new paradigms in generic programming [12].

Another fundamental design axis that has appeared consistently across the
history of executors is the distinction between one-way execution ("fire-and-
forget" work) and two-way execution—that is, work that requires some means of
signaling completion, failure, and/or cancellation. Programming models based on
promises and futures, dating back to at least the late 1970s [4], are a traditional
example of the latter. Recently, the design of two-way executors has begun to
converge on push-style programming models [17] due to their ability to unify the
observer pattern [9] with future/promise semantics.

Across all of these dimensions, the basic interfaces of all proposals has had
one thing in common: Much like OpenMP's `tasks`, when in a parallel region,
they abstract over asynchrony. Work is allowed to be queued for later execution,
or run immediately, possibly singly or in bulk, and possibly with or without
a propagated value, but the basic expression of algorithms using any of these
interfaces is based upon the ability to asynchronously generate work. At present,
OpenMP can model single or bulk execution with or without signaling completion. Enabling asynchronous scheduling of these units of work however requires
that all the associated code can be wrapped in a `parallel` region, which is not
possible due to the interface itself as well as interference with the rest of the

program. There is also currently no way to model an asynchronous check for completion of a task. Though it can be modeled with atomics or similar, we leave exploration of this aspect for future work.

3 Requirements and Proposed Features

Since its introduction in version 3.0 of the specification, OpenMP support for task parallelism has evolved into an increasingly powerful tool to expose parallelism in application to be exploited by the OpenMP runtime system. Expressiveness has been expanded by allowing more sophisticated dependences and synchronizations between tasks, and the scope of task parallelism in OpenMP has expanded to encompass asynchronous offload to accelerators. However, the awkward relationship of task parallelism to thread parallelism has changed little from OpenMP 3.0 to 5.0. Otherwise promising use cases for task parallelism, of which C++ executors implementation is but one, are rendered difficult or impossible by the limitations of this relationship. We outline some of the issues below, along with a high-level view of some potential future changes to the specification to address them. The changes are comparatively light on new syntax, and the first is only semantic.

3.1 "Free-Agent" Threads

The first issue, and the one encountered even by programmers writing the simplest OpenMP program using tasks, is the requirement to create a team of threads even for a program comprised entirely of explicit tasks. In the absence of such a team of threads, the tasks would be executed only sequentially. This leads to the frequent idiom combining **parallel** and **single** or **master** to start a team of threads and then begin task creation on only one thread of the team, as shown in Fig. 1.

```
1   int main()
2   {
3       #pragma omp parallel
4       #pragma omp single
5       {
6           #pragma omp task
7               func1();
8           #pragma omp task
9               func2();
10      } // tasks join here
11  }
```

Fig. 1. Asynchronous tasking without free-agent threads

Related shared memory tasking frameworks like OmpSs [6], Cilk [14], Argobots [16], and Qthreads [19] simply make threads available for executing tasks immediately at program startup. While many OpenMP implementations already create threads upon initialization of the run time library, the current semantics of OpenMP forbid using those threads to execute tasks until one or more teams have been created. The constraint is more than an inconvenience, because the creation of teams segregates the available threads. Since neither threads nor tasks can be exchanged between two different teams of threads, the effect is to limit composability and load balancing.

The solution proposed for future OpenMP versions is to allow a pool of "free agent" threads maintained by the implementation to exist outside of a team and available to execute tasks. This new semantic would allow a program to execute tasks asynchronously on an implementation's thread pool without creating a parallel region, as shown in Fig. 2.

```
1   int main()
2   {
3       #pragma omp task
4           func1();  // executes on an available thread in the pool
5       #pragma omp task
6           func2();  // executes on another available thread in the pool
7       #pragma omp taskwait // tasks join here
8   }
```

Fig. 2. Asynchronous tasking with free-agent threads

The effect of the code, assuming that the implementation has a pool of threads ready to execute the tasks, is equivalent to Fig. 1. While the difference is just a few lines, it not only simplifies reasoning about how to use of tasks, a boon especially for new users, but also places fewer constraints on interleaving tasks with parallel regions or parallel loops.

3.2   Task Width

Another important issue is that OpenMP currently provides no way for the programmer to indicate when creating a task that the task includes further parallelism inside the task or to what degree. The implementation becomes aware of the nested parallelism only at the time the nested constructs within the task are encountered. If, however, the implementation had knowledge of the nested parallelism at task creation, it could plan to execute the task where and when adequate threads are available for the nested parallelism. The solution proposed for future OpenMP versions is to admit a clause on task-generating constructs to specify the degree of nested parallelism present in the task.

We propose to add a width clause to the task directive. The argument to the new clause would indicate the amount of nested parallelism created within the task, as shown in Fig. 3. A more restrictive way to accomplish the same effect would be to allow a nowait clause on the parallel construct, transforming its region into a task. The example in Fig. 4 shows the equivalent code using this alternate approach.

```
1    #pragma omp task
2        func1();  // no width specified, so assume 1 thread only
3    #pragma omp task width(5)
4    {
5        // width(5) indicates internal parallelism
6        #pragma omp parallel for num_threads(5)
7            for (int i = 0; i < MAX; ++i)
8                func2(i);
9    }
```

Fig. 3. Parallelism inside a task with a specified width

```
1    #pragma omp task
2        func1();  // no width specified, so assume 1 thread only
3    #pragma omp parallel for num_threads(5) nowait
4        for (int i = 0; i < MAX; ++i)
5            func2(i);
6    }
```

Fig. 4. Asynchronous parallel regions

A point in favor admitting the `nowait` clause on the `parallel` construct would be symmetry with the `target` construct, which already admits the clause. It would also be a convenient way to express asynchronous bulk parallelism. However, it does not support some use cases that are supported by task width for interoperability of OpenMP users' programs with libraries that use OpenMP internally. Consider the example shown in Fig. 5, in which the function call is made to a math library routine. Because the nested parallelism is hidden inside the library routine, the more restricted `parallel nowait` idiom does not support this use case.

An open question regarding semantics is whether the number of threads in the clause indicates maximum or minimum nested parallelism within the task. Additionally, should it reflect only first nesting level of parallelism, or all levels, if more than one level of parallelism is present within the task? This information may not be readily available even to the programmer if the nested parallelism is inside library calls. Even the basic indication that there exists nested parallelism with in the task, regardless of size gives the runtime system more information than it currently has for scheduling.

```
1   void user_func(...)
2   {
3       #pragma omp task width(5)
4       {
5           blas_library_call(...);    // allowed to use 5 threads internally
6       }
7   }
8
9   // (Inside the library)
10  void blas_library_call(...)
11  {
12      #pragma omp parallel for // gets up to "width" threads
13          for (int i = 0; i < MAX; ++i)
14              ...
15  }
```

Fig. 5. Task with a width calling library code

3.3 Broader Applicability

Progress on these issues is important not only for the success of OpenMP as an implementation platform for C++ executors, but also for other important use case scenarios. Among these use cases are real-time systems and GUI-based programs, in which an event loop runs continuously and spawns new work periodically or based on user input and sensors. Ever-increasing levels of hardware parallelism also motivate more flexible mechanisms to expose application parallelism and provide more information to inform run time task scheduling.

Increasingly, single-source programming models for portable utilization of heterogeneous compute resources, in which applications provide a single implementation that is generic over execution model and resources, are a popular approach to heterogeneous library design. Kokkos [7] is one such library that has had a significant impact on major portions of the ISO-C++ executor design process. Kokkos provides the concept of an ExecutionSpace that closely resembles an executor. Users write code that is generic over the specific ExecutionSpace type in order to express, with a single source, an algorithm that can run with multiple execution models.

The obvious concern in the design of the ExecutionSpace concept is restricting the programming model enough to provide low-overhead performance (relative to an execution-model-specific implementation) on all supported ExecutionSpace types. Specifically, Kokkos provides ExecutionSpace implementations for OpenMP, CUDA, thread-pool-based execution, and serial execution, among others. The restrictions on the ExecutionSpace design thus include abstractions that can map to a notional "intersection" of execution model restrictions for all of the supported backends. (ISO-C++ executor design is very similar in this respect.)

The extensions to the OpenMP programming model presented herein do not represent an expansion of that intersection, since (for instance) serial execution will always be a supported execution model. However, expanding the "intersection" of a subset of the supported execution models often enables an increase in the precision of the user's mental performance model for some generic code because programming model abstractions can be mapped to a smaller "outer product" of performance characteristics.

In this context the `nowait` clause on the `parallel` construct has a semantic much more similar to that of a CUDA kernel launch than the traditional use of the `parallel` construct. The restricted programming model that encompasses both the synchronous `parallel` construct's semantics and the asynchronous semantics of a CUDA kernel launch requires the user to assume that the *earliest* an algorithm's execution can begin is immediately upon invocation, and the *latest* the algorithm can finish execution is upon return from the next call to an explicit `Kokkos::fence()` on the `ExecutionSpace` used by the algorithm. They cannot rely on the encountering thread to block, or not to block. Presentation of a consistently asynchronous model, or at least a potentially asynchronous one, can help reduce the variability in behavior of the code across platforms.

4 Feature Interactions and Feasibility

The main challenge with this set of extensions is deciding how arrangements of asynchronous execution, tasks, parallel regions, and widths that were not previously possible can interact without harming backward compatibility or performance unduly. This section will discuss the various trade-offs and considerations necessary to integrate free-agent threads and task widths into OpenMP.

4.1 Task Joining

As discussed previously, OpenMP tasks either execute immediately in the encountering thread, in a serial context, or are joined at the end of their enclosing parallel region. As a result, there is currently no way for tasks to logically "run off" the end of a program. If however we allow tasks to run asynchronously at the top level of the program, we need to define what happens if tasks are still executing when `main` ends. For example, take the code in Fig. 2, if there were no `taskwait` at the end of `main` there would be no guarantee that either `func1` or `func2` would be done at the end of the program.

Given the way OpenMP is currently defined, there is logically a parallel region around the entire program comprising only the initial thread. If we extend this to make free agent threads accessible, we would assume that these tasks should join on return, and that may be what users would expect. This may result in deadlocks or unexpected issues however when a user calls 'exit()' or similar while tasks are outstanding. Given the considerations of implementations however, and the fact we want OpenMP to be usable when `main` is compiled without it, our recommendation is that tasks are allowed to be cancelled by the end of the program. Users always have the option to use either `taskwait` or `taskgroup` to join tasks if they want them joined, while it is harder to envision a way for them to opt in to cancellation.

4.2   Threads Available for `parallel`

Since threads may now be executing task work alongside the initial thread, it is possible to encounter a synchronous `parallel` region while some threads are busy. There are a number of options available to handle this situation:

1. Run the parallel region immediately with fewer threads.
2. Make `parallel` wait for the concurrent tasks to pause or finish before starting with all threads it would otherwise have been allotted.
3. Begin the parallel region with available threads and join others in as the tasks either finish or reach scheduling points.

Given the potential performance implications, the user will almost certainly want control over the choice of the options above. However the choice of default has implications both for performance and for backwards compatibility. When an OpenMP `parallel` region starts, it is provided with some number of threads. The actual number is always implementation-defined, and can be affected by a variety of environment variables through OpenMP's Internal Control Variables (ICVs). That said, when the *dyn-var* ICV[1] is set to false, the number of threads in each parallel region is fixed, and codes are allowed to rely on this property to access thread-local state and for various other reasons.

Given the requirements imposed by *dyn-var*, we propose that either option two or three is used when *dyn-var* is true, and allow only option one when it is false. The user can then control the general behavior they prefer with an existing ICV, get a more specific thread count with a task with a width or asynchronous parallel region, or use a taskwait to ensure tasks have joined before the `parallel` region starts.

4.3   Interactions Between Width and Num-Threads

The concept of the `width` clause for a task is simple on the surface–it tells the runtime that the task being created should be provided with a given level of parallelism, and that something in the dynamic scope of that task will make use of it. Unlike with `parallel nowait` there is no guarantee precisely *when* that parallelism will be used, so that many threads don't necessarily need to be immediately available. Given the way OpenMP is specified today, the simplest way to think about translating a task with a width of six would be to set the `nthreads-var` ICV to six inside a task as in Fig. 6.

This approach provides the desired behavior of controlling the number of threads used in a dynamic scope, and allows different values of width for tasks nested within one another while re-using a well established mechanism. It gets surprisingly close to the overall goal, even to providing the appropriate level of parallelism when calling into a library, although it does not provide the runtime or compiler with appropriate scheduling information. The downside is that if the number of threads is set this way it overrides the value from

---

[1] The value set by the `OMP_DYNAMIC` environment variable.

```
1   #pragma omp task // width(6)
2   {
3       omp_set_num_threads(6);
4   }
```

Fig. 6. A naive de-sugaring of a task with a width

`omp_get_max_threads()`, and it can be overridden relatively easily. It may be more appropriate to employ a mechanism like the thread limit on teams to resist called code expanding past the resources allotted, and to provide a method to interrogate the total number of threads available. While a parallel run in the tasks context could only have the number specified by the limit, an asynchronous task there could request more.

4.4 Feasibility

In order to explore the design space, we created an initial prototype runtime implementing the new semantics we describe for tasks outside of a parallel context. We considered implementation in the LLVM OpenMP runtime, GOMP, and BOLT [1] which is a user-level threaded version of the LLVM runtime implemented on top of argobots [16]. The LLVM and GOMP runtimes could both implement the pattern we have discussed, but currently rely on the scoping of parallel regions for memory management of their tasking runtimes. For example, while the task-running threads and per-thread contexts persist across parallel regions the task queues and attendant metadata do not. However, BOLT does not, instead relying on the argobots system to manage some of these details. As a result, a naive prototype is as simple as removing the checks for whether tasks should be allowed to be run asynchronously outside of a parallel context[2].

Given the structure of other runtimes we expect implementation of this feature to require a rework in the lifetime management of data structures, but relatively little change in implementation logic other than to take advantage of newly available information. We do not provide performance comparisons in this paper as none of the proposed features have a direct impact on performance in our implementation due to the underlying structure of BOLT. As such the prototype performs identically to a stock BOLT library, simply allowing expression of tasks in an alternative manner. We may explore performance impact on applications composed of multiple components and higher-level runtimes in the future.

Overall, free-agent threads, tasks with a width, and asynchronous parallel regions appear feasible from both a runtime and specification perspective. After further experimentation and performance testing with codes in the wild, some defaults and further mechanisms may become desirable. That said the base mechanisms show strong promise for being implementable and providing substantial

---

[2] In fact, the original naive prototype only required changing eight lines of code.

benefit to composability of OpenMP with itself as well as making it more practical as a substrate for libraries and systems with asynchronous or thread-pool-like interfaces such as C++ executors.

5   Related Work

The emergence of manycore and heterogeneous systems and increasing use of hybrid MPI-X programming models has led to a proliferation of frameworks to support performance portability, composition, interoperability, and resource management. Kokkos [7], and RAJA [13] provide performance portability frameworks, however they do so at the middleware level. By specifying memory and concurrency at the language standards level, performance portability policy support becomes a *compiler* rather than a middleware capability. This approach ensures support across platforms and provides vendor independent ways of implementing cross platform high performance simulation software.

OmpSs [5] is a task-based OpenMP-like programming model that has inspired many of the current features and behaviors of task parallelism in OpenMP. BOLT [1] provides an alternative implementation of the LLVM OpenMP runtime ABI on top of Argobots [16], which offers user-level threading to support overdecomposition and deeper nesting than is feasible with OS-level thread models. For hybrid MPI+X programming, OmpSs provides direct integration with MPI and BOLT provides integration with the MPICH implementation of MPI [2] using the Argobots [16] runtime framework. StarPU [3] provides integration of heterogeneous computing and software resources in a uniform manner via the runtime. It includes OpenMP 4 with a focus on task parallelism and extensions to support run time scheduling optimizations.

Lithe [15] provides a common runtime substrate to enable coscheduling of runtimes similar to CPU inheritance scheduling [8] while adding a hardware thread abstraction to ensure that multiple runtimes do not oversubscribe system resources. Modified versions of the runtimes (e.g., OpenMP and Threading Building Blocks) are required. The QUO [10] library provides an alternative approach to composing MPI and threading runtimes, managing heterogeneous thread and memory resources at the application level and manually quiescing and running thread groups via the pthreads system interface, thus manually avoid oversubscription of system resources in multiple interacting runtimes.

Our approach is based on the view that the upcoming incorporation of executors into the C++ language standard will make their use commonplace, and that leveraging the many high quality OpenMP implementations in open source and vendor compiler suites is a promising way both to support executors and to integrate C++ programs using them with native OpenMP code. Like other solutions to address the problems of composition and thread resource management, we seek to avoid unintended oversubscription of hardware execution resources. However, using OpenMP as the integration point provides the benefits of greater portability and high-level abstraction compared to ad-hoc and system-level frameworks.

6   Conclusions

Composing multiple frameworks and performance portability layers is an increasingly necessary for high performance computing at scale. However, standardizing on the portability layer has been difficult, leading to multiple implementations with no clear standard interface. In this paper we have argued that the ubiquity of OpenMP and the coming executors concept in the C++ standard provide a unique opportunity to ensure that both standards grow to a point where they can compose with one another to efficiently and effectively integrate components built with state-of-the-art techniques in C++ with the extensive performance-oriented ecosystem of OpenMP applications and libraries.

We analyzed the requirements for the extensions to tasking as well as the necessary extensions to the OpenMP standard to provide the necessary functionality. Specifically, we propose incorporating the concept of "free-agent" threads into OpenMP, allowing asynchronous execution of tasks and parallelism without a scoping restriction, and extending tasks with a width, allowing a task to represent a quantity of resources allocated to the code executed inside it. Finally we discussed an implementation of "free agent" threads in an OpenMP runtime along with some of the major design considerations for implementing these changes in the specification. While exploring this approach we found a few more potential future extension points, including a non-blocking mechanism for checking if tasks are complete and a mechanism for executing tasks in other teams, but we leave these for future work.

Acknowledgments. This work was performed under the auspices of the U.S. Department of Energy by Lawrence Livermore National Laboratory under Contract DE-AC52-07NA27344. Sandia National Laboratories is a multimission laboratory managed and operated by National Technology and Engineering Solutions of Sandia, LLC., a wholly owned subsidiary of Honeywell International, Inc., for the U.S. Department of Energy's National Nuclear Security Administration under contract DE-NA-0003525.

References

1. BOLT: A lightning-fast OpenMP implementation. https://bolt-omp.org/
2. Argonne National Laboratory: MPICH2: High performance and portable message passing. http://www.mcs.anl.gov/research/projects/mpich2
3. Augonnet, C., Thibault, S., Namyst, R.: StarPU: a runtime system for scheduling tasks over accelerator-based multicore machines. Technical report, RR-7240, Laboratoire Bordelais de Recherche en Informatique - LaBRI, RUNTIME - INRIA Bordeaux - Sud-Ouest, March 2010. http://hal.inria.fr/inria-00467677
4. Baker, H.C., Hewitt, C.: The incremental garbage collection of processes. ACM SIGPLAN Not. **12**(8), 55–59 (1977). https://doi.org/10.1145/872734.806932
5. Bueno, J., Duran, A., Martorell, X., Ayguadé, E., Badia, R.M., Labarta, J.: Poster: programming clusters of GPUs with OmpSs. In: International Conference for High Performance Computing, Networking, Storage and Analysis (SuperComputing). ACM, May 2011. https://doi.org/10.1145/1995896.1995961, http://portal.acm.org/citation.cfm?id=1995896.1995961&coll=DL&dl=GUIDE&CFID=61704752&CFTOKEN=92261478

6. Duran, A., et al.: OmpSs: a proposal for programming heterogeneous multi-core architectures. Parallel Process. Lett. **21**(2), 173–193 (2011). http://www.worldscinet.com/abstract?id=pii:S0129626411000151

7. Edwards, H.C., Trott, C.R., Sunderland, D.: Kokkos: enabling manycore performance portability through polymorphic memory access patterns. J. Parallel Distrib. Comput. **74**(12), 3202–3216 (2014). https://doi.org/10.1016/j.jpdc.2014.07.003. http://www.sciencedirect.com/science/article/pii/S0743731514001257. Domain-Specific Languages and High-Level Frameworks for High-Performance Computing

8. Ford, B., Susarla, S.: CPU inheritance scheduling. In: OSDI, vol. 96, pp. 91–105 (1996)

9. Gamma, E., Helm, R., Johnson, R., Vlissides, J.: Design Patterns: Elements of Reusable Object-Oriented Software. Addison-Wesley, Boston (1994)

10. Gutiérrez, S.K., et al.: Accommodating thread-level heterogeneity in coupled parallel applications. In: 2017 IEEE International Parallel & Distributed Processing Symposium (IPDPS), Orlando, Florida (2017)

11. Hoberock, J., Garland, M., Kohlhoff, C., Mysen, C., Edwards, C., Hollman, D.: P0443r10: a unified executors proposal for C++, January 2019. http://www.open-std.org/jtc1/sc22/wg21/docs/papers/2019/p0443r10.html

12. Hollman, D., Kohlhoff, C., Lelbach, B., Hoberock, J., Brown, G., Dominiak, M.: P1393r0: a general property customization mechanism, January 2019. http://www.open-std.org/jtc1/sc22/wg21/docs/papers/2019/p1393r0.html

13. Hornung, R., Keasler, J.: The RAJA portability layer: overview and status. Technical report, Lawrence Livermore National Laboratory (LLNL), Livermore, CA (2014)

14. Leiserson, C.E.: The Cilk++ concurrency platform. J. Supercomput. **51**(3), 244–257 (2010)

15. Pan, H., Hindman, B., Asanović, K.: Composing parallel software efficiently with lithe. ACM Sigplan Not. **45**(6), 376–387 (2010)

16. Seo, S., et al.: Argobots: a lightweight low-level threading and tasking framework. IEEE Trans. Parallel Distrib. Syst. **29**(3), 512–526 (2018)

17. Shoop, K., Niebler, E., Howes, L.: P1055r0: a modest executor proposal, April 2018. http://www.open-std.org/jtc1/sc22/wg21/docs/papers/2018/p1055r0.pdf

18. Sutter, H.: Trip report: winter ISO C++ standards meeting (Kona), February 2019. https://herbsutter.com/2019/02/23/trip-report-winter-iso-c-standards-meeting-kona/

19. Wheeler, K.B., Murphy, R.C., Thain, D.: Qthreads: an API for programming with millions of lightweight threads. In: IEEE International Symposium on Parallel and Distributed Processing, pp. 1–8. IEEE (2008)

Author Index

Printed in the United States
By Bookmasters